Adapting to Financial Globalisation

Adapting to the demands of financial globalisation is currently one of the most pressing preoccupations of bankers, financial institutions and financial authorities. Many aspects of this issue are addressed in this volume, based on a colloquium held in Vienna in April 2000 by the Société Universitaire Européene de Rechèrches Financière (SUERF) jointly with the Austrian National Bank.

Individual chapters, written by academics, central bankers and market professionals, focus on the strategic implications of global pressures which are tending to eradicate the previously clear boundaries of time, distance, legal frameworks, culture, languages and currencies. Topics covered include:

- Micro and macro economic perspectives.
- Financial risks, seen from both a systemic and a firm's point of view, and consolidation in the banking industry, including the various types of mergers and acquisitions.
- Market and credit risk, reasons for financial crises, and lessons from US financial history and the case for currency boards.
- Capital mobility, exchange rate volatility, and the participation of foreign and domestic banks in emerging markets.

Taken together, this book provides an excellent cross-section of current financial and economic theory.

Morten Balling has been President of the Aarhus School of Business, Aarhus, Denmark, since 1993. He has been a Council Member of the Société Universitaire Européenne de Rechèrches Financière since 1994. He holds many directorships of Danish companies and institutions and has written widely on monetary, banking and financial topics.

Eduard H. Hochreiter is General Secretary of SUERF and Senior Advisor and Head of the Economic Studies Division at Oesterreichische National Bank. He is a lecturer at the University of Economics, Vienna, and University of Vienna. He is the author of many articles in refereed journals.

Elizabeth Hennessy is a freelance writer and editor. Her publications include twelve corporate and institutional histories, including *The Domestic History of the Bank of England 1930–1960* (OUP 1992). She is currently writing a history of the London Stock Exchange, and is an editor of *Treasury Management International* magazine.

Routledge International Studies in Money and Banking

Adapting to Financial Globalisation

Edited by Morten Balling,
Eduard H. Hochreiter and
Elizabeth Hennessy

London and New York

First published 2001
by Routledge
11 New Fetter Lane, London EC4P 4EE

Simultaneously published in the USA and Canada
by Routledge
29 West 35th Street, New York, NY 10001

Routledge is an imprint of the Taylor & Francis Group

Typeset in Times by
M Rules
Printed and bound in Great Britain by
MPG Books Ltd, Bodmin

British Library Cataloguing in Publication Data
A catalogue record for this book is available from the British Library

Library of Congress Cataloging in Publication Data
Adapting to financial globalisation / edited by Morten Balling,
Eduard H. Hochreiter, and Elizabeth Hennessy.
    p. cm.
  Papers presented at a conference held in Vienna in April 2000 by
the Société universitaire européenne de recherches financières and
the Austrian National Bank.
  Includes bibliographical references and index.
  1. International finance – Congresses. 2. Monetary policy –
Congresses. 3. Banks and banking – Congresses. 4. Financial
services industry – Congresses. 5. Globalization – Economic
aspects – Congresses. I. Balling, Morten. II. Hochreiter,
Eduard. III. Hennessy, Elizabeth. IV. Société universitaire
européenne de recherches financières. V Oesterreichische
Nationalbank.
  HG205.A3 2001
  332′.042–dc21   00-066487

ISBN 0–415–25240–7

Contents

Figures

Tables

Contributors

Enrique Alberola-Ila
Economist, International Affairs Division, Banco de España, Spain

Josef Christl
Chief Economist, Creditanstalt AG, Austria

Andrew Crockett
General Manager, Bank for International Settlements, Chairman Financial Stability Forum, Switzerland

B. Gerard Dages
Assistant vice president, Federal Reserve Bank of New York, USA

E. Philip Davis
Professor of Economics and Finance, Brunel University, UK

Ignacio Fuentes Egusquiza
Senior Economist, Research Department, Banco de España, Spain

Hans Geiger
Professor, Swiss Banking Institute, University of Zurich, Switzerland

Linda Goldberg
Assistant vice president, Federal Reserve Bank of New York, USA

Barry Howcroft
Professor of Retail Banking and Director, Loughborough University Banking Centre, UK

Daniel Kinney
International officer, Federal Reserve Bank of New York, USA

Kenneth N. Kuttner
Senior Economist and Research Officer, Federal Reserve Bank of New York, USA

Karel Lannoo
Centre for European Policy Studies, Belgium

Jacques de Larosière
Advisor, BNP Paribas, France

Klaus Liebscher
Governor, Oesterreichische Nationalbank, Austria

Luis Molina Sanchez
Economist, International Affairs Division, Banco de España, Spain

Claes Norgren
Director General, The Swedish Financial Supervisory Authority, Sweden

Tommaso Padoa-Schioppa
Member of the Executive Board, European Central Bank, Germany

Adam S. Posen
Senior Fellow, Institute for International Economics, USA

Teresa Sastre de Miguel
Senior Economist, Research Department, Banco de España, Spain

Thomas Spanel
Economist, Creditanstalt AG, Austria

Peter Van Dijcke
Senior Economist, Artesia Banking Corporation, Belgium

Introduction

Morten Balling

The papers in this volume were all presented at a conference in Vienna at the end of April 2000. The common theme of the papers is financial globalisation and the ways in which banks, supervisory authorities and central banks should deal with it. Following the SUERF tradition, the colloquium was a combination of plenary sessions and commission discussions.

The first five papers in the book are contributions to plenary sessions. Papers 6 to 15 are contributions to the work in the commissions arranged in alphabetical order according to the author's surname.

Paper no. 1 by *Andrew Crockett*, General Manager of the BIS, deals with the links between financial and monetary (in)stability. One of the reasons why the financial sector is prone to instability is that fundamental value is extremely hard to assess. Return expectations are subject to powerful waves of optimism and pessimism, greed and fear. A second reason is that excess supply does not necessarily put immediate downward pressure on prices and profits. Lending booms can for a while sustain the development of imbalances. A third reason is that fragile balance sheet structures can intensify instability. Finally, safety nets designed for prudential reasons can weaken market discipline. Recently anti-inflation policies in Europe have in general been successful. The combination of a liberalised financial system and a fiat standard with monetary rules defined exclusively in terms of inflation is, however, not a sufficient condition for financial stability. Further research is needed in order to find appropriate anchors for financial and monetary stability. The Financial Stability Forum will be involved in research, which can increase the understanding of these crucial questions.

Paper no. 2 by Advisor *Jacques de Larosière*, Paribas, gives a survey of mergers and other strategic moves in the financial sectors of Europe, which have fundamentally changed the structure of the European banking sector. The author compares Europe with the US and observes that there are still many more banks in the US than in Europe, although the two zones are comparable in terms both of GDP and population. The average bank profitability is, however, much higher in the US than in the euro zone. Mergers in the European banking sector are classified as domestic transactions and cross-border transactions. In the 1990s one could observe relatively few very large domestic transactions and a larger amount of small cross-border transactions. Barriers to further restructurings still exist. The author mentions the absence of a European corporate law and takeover rules. The key to future success of European banks is adaptability. In this context, attention has to be paid to the development of the internet applications in financial activities and their impact on bank strategies.

Paper no. 3 by the Governor of the Austrian Central Bank, Dr *Klaus Liebscher,* focuses on central banking in the euro area, in particular in relation to safeguarding systemic stability. The author points out that the EMU intensifies competition in financial markets. While this has beneficial effects on productivity and efficiency, it may also have a risk-increasing effect. Contagion risk as well as the risk of eroding profit margins raise the vulnerability of financial institutions. It is the evaluation of the Governor that the principle of subsidiarity has worked well also in financial regulation and supervision. The ECB has, however, a consultative role in prudential supervision. The euro stands every chance of becoming a currency of global importance. In Central and Eastern Europe it is very likely that the euro will play a key role in the future.

The basis for paper no. 4 by *Claes Norgren*, Director General of the Swedish Financial Supervisory Authority, is the consultative 1999 document on a New Capital Adequacy Framework written by the Basel Committee on Banking Supervision. The new framework is supposed to replace the 1988 Basel Accord on measuring capital adequacy and the minimum standard to be achieved. Implementation of the new framework will represent a move from standardised risk weight calculations to a more differentiated approach. Information from external ratings and internal rating systems may be used to achieve a certain risk differentation.

In paper no. 5 by *Tommaso Padoa-Schioppa*, member of the board of the European Central Bank (ECB), the author attempts to describe plausible characteristics of the European banking landscape after the integrating effect of the euro has been effective for some years. The author points out that the speed of integration so far has been much higher in wholesale financial markets than in retail markets. National and cultural obstacles can be expected to slow down the integration in retail markets for some years to come.

Paper no. 6 deals with fiscal discipline and exchange rate regimes. The authors, *Enrique Alberola* and *Luis Molina,* show in their paper that a particular version of fixed exchange rate regimes, the currency boards, may effectively restrain fiscal policy by ruling out fiscal seignoriage. The authors apply comprehensive data from twenty-four emerging and transition countries. The attraction of currency boards is related to the perception in the market of the high commitment to the peg that the board provides.

Paper no. 7 by *Josef Christl* and *Thomas Spanel* gives an outline and evaluation of a model of transfer risk analysis which has been used by an international commercial bank for managing country risk. From a pragmatic point of view, the question is whether the symptoms of crisis can be detected sufficiently in advance to allow for pre-emptive measures to be adapted. A rating model is applied to the recent crisis in Thailand, Brazil and Russia. It turns out that the model captured the crisis in Thailand and Russia very well, while the exchange rate crisis of Brazil was not really perceptible.

In paper no. 8, *B. Gerard Dages, Linda Goldberg* and *Daniel Kinney* apply bank-specific data on lending by domestically- and foreign-owned banks in Argentina and Mexico in order to analyse differences in loan growth rates and volatility of lending. They find that bank health, and not ownership *per se*, is the critical element in the growth, volatility and cyclicality of bank credit. Diversity in ownership appears, however, to contribute to greater stability of credit in times of crisis and domestic financial system weakness.

US financial history provides a number of examples of financial crisis from which Europeans can learn. In paper no. 9 *E. Philip Davis* covers the 1929–33 stock market crash and banking crisis, the Continental Illinois case (1984), the US thrifts case (1979–89), the banking crisis in Texas (1985–89), the collapse of the junk bond market (1989) and the Russia/LTCM Crisis (1998). In the crises described too big to fail aspects, real estate lending booms and rising corporate leverage occurred in different combinations. In spite of all the institutional differences between US and Europe, there are lessons to be learned for people involved in designing an appropriate regulatory structure in Europe.

Paper no. 10 deals with the strategies developed by Spanish banks for adapting to financial globalisation. *Ignacio Fuentes* and *Teresa Sastre* compare by means of an empirical model bank interest rates of merged firms with those of non-merged ones. The analysis seems to indicate that mergers and takeovers do not *per se* give rise to generally differentiated forms of behaviour. An analysis in the paper of the effects of mergers on the profit-generating capacity and the level of efficiency does not provide clear answers. The remarkable growth of Spanish mutual funds has, however, significantly reduced the growth rate of traditional bank deposits. Spanish banks have expanded their activity abroad, in particular by investing in subsidiaries and branches in Latin America.

In paper no. 11 *Hans Geiger* focuses on payment intermediation in a global economy. The subject is important both for the economy as a whole and for the future of the banking industry. Different types of market transactions are connected with risks, which can be handled in different ways. Banks have over the years developed techniques which can protect the parties involved in international payment transactions. New technology is causing far-reaching changes in payment systems.

Deregulation and the emergence of technology have created highly competitive market conditions which have had a critical impact on consumer behaviour in relation to financial services. In paper no. 12, *Barry Howcroft* explains that banks have to respond strategically to these changes. The author applies a model in which the consumer behaviour is taken as being generally rational, and the choice environment is simplified by heuristics. Bank customers are classified according to their involvement and confidence. Knowledge of financial products varies considerably among the customers and banks must adapt their marketing and information to the ability of the customers to understand the characteristics of the products.

In paper no. 13 *Kenneth N. Kuttner* and *Adam S. Posen* analyse to what extent domestic inflation and interest rate surprises – fluctuations unexplained by past history and the systematic response of policy – contribute to short-run volatility in G3 exchange rates. They point out that the yen/dollar exchange rate has consistently shown significantly greater volatility than either of the other bilateral G3 exchange rates, and that the DM/dollar exchange rate volatility has gradually declined since the late 1970s. They relate the last observation to what they call increasing institutional transparency from the three successive US Federal Reserve chairmen: Burns, Volcker and Greenspan. The behaviour of the exchange rates in relation to the yen is considered to be consistent with decreasing transparency and increasingly unsystematic monetary policy responses of the Bank of Japan. Their investigations support the belief that monetary policy transparency matters for exchange rate volatility.

Financial supervision is organised in different ways in the EU countries. In some of the countries monetary policy and banking supervisory functions are combined; in other countries they are separated. In paper no. 14 *Karel Lannoo* discusses what kind of challenges these structural differences pose to the authorities. In the view of the author, the established systems for coordination and regular exchange of information among the national supervisors are insufficient given the degree of market integration. He recommends that a European Forum of Financial Supervisors should be established. Monitoring of financial stability should take place in an institution set up to observe systemic risk, and steps should be taken to create an EU Securities Committee.

The cost-to-income ratio and its dispersion is often used as an indicator of efficiency in the European banking industry. In paper no. 15, which was awarded the Marjolin Prize 2000 at the colloquium, *Peter Van Dijcke* analyses comprehensive bank account data from the EU countries in order to go deeper into the impact of globalisation on efficiency. The regression model applied tends to signal that changes in the composition of bank income and overhead has on average a small impact. The findings seem to confirm that changing scale and scope has a limited impact on the cost-to-income ratio. By using the available inputs efficiently in order to generate a given output level the direct impact on the ratio itself is much larger. The author warns against simple benchmarking according to the cost-to-income ratio because banks may produce different output mixes that have different costs of production. The bank consolidation process which has taken place in Europe in recent years has contributed to the reduction of the cost-to-income ratio but at a different pace across individual banks and across EU countries.

1 In search of anchors for financial and monetary stability*

Andrew Crockett

It was in the seemingly distant 1996 that Alan Greenspan coined the famous phrase, 'irrational exuberance'. He was not just making a passing remark. He was asking a question. His words encapsulated the dilemma of whether, and if so how, monetary policy should respond to asset prices. In fact, his public utterance *was* a response. The question has now become a familiar, if largely unanswered, one for central bankers.

Meanwhile, asset prices have moved higher and their volatility has increased. Far from discouraging investors, this seems merely to have increased the fascination of the equity market. TV stations devoted to the market, like CNBC, have enormously increased their viewership. The 'analysis' offered by their commentators resembles nothing so much as that of hyperactive sports announcers. Viewers are sports junkies with the added thrill of a bet on every twist in the action.

These large asset price swings are themselves a palpable manifestation of the increased financial instability experienced around the world since at least the 1980s. The issue of how to deal with instability has quickly forced its way to the top of the international policy agenda. Just as policy makers appeared to be emerging victorious from one exhausting battle, that against inflation, another equally challenging front was opening up. Lower inflation, it appeared, had not by itself yielded the peace dividend of a more stable financial environment.

Today, I will explore the conjecture that the link between these two developments is less coincidental than it might seem at first sight. In order to elaborate on this proposition, let me first briefly describe the anatomy of financial instability. I will then discuss the changes in the financial sphere that have led to the observed greater instability before moving on to examine the link with the monetary sphere in a historical perspective. I will finally raise some policy questions emerging from the analysis.

* Paper presented at 22nd SUERF Colloquium, Vienna, 27–29 April 2000.

The anatomy of financial instability

The term 'financial instability' is commonly used to refer to two types of phenomenon: large movements in asset prices and financial distress of institutions. The two are closely linked.

The movements in asset prices that raise concern are not so much those crystallised in short-term volatility. Unless extreme and a source of strains on markets or institutions, day-to-day volatility is part of the physiology of well-functioning markets. Rather, it is those medium-term swings that take prices far away from sustainable values; what economists term their 'fundamental' values. Such misalignments, when they finally reverse, typically do so suddenly and violently, in a 'crash'. In the process, they raise short-term volatility to pathological levels. This may result in some casualties. But the major casualties follow once the reversal continues, usually in a prolonged and painful phase.

Distress among financial institutions can occur without price misalignments. In this case, however, it tends to be localised and the result of firm-specific factors. Poor management is the most usual cause. The main policy concern is systemic, not individual, distress, when large portions of the financial system are affected. Systemic distress can arise from the spreading of difficulties from individual institutions or market segments. But more often than not it stems from exposures to a common factor. Asset price misalignments are probably the most typical example of such common factors.

We care about financial instability because it is wasteful. Asset price misalignments would not matter if economic agents saw through them and discounted them. But often they do not. The misalignments can profoundly affect consumption and expenditure decisions. They impinge on perceptions of wealth and investment returns as well as on external financing constraints. Higher equity and real estate prices, for instance, act as a magnet for capital, and make it easier for borrowers to access external funds. Misalignments result in misallocation of resources across sectors and over time. *Across sectors,* because capital is sucked away from those where prices are relatively more sluggish towards those where they are more buoyant. Just think, for example, of the equity buy-backs in the 'old economy' as IPOs surge in the 'new economy' or of the construction booms that accompany soaring property prices. *Over time,* because if sufficiently pervasive, the misalignments result in aggregate over-investment or over-consumption, well in excess of permanent income. Once they reverse, the backlash is inevitable. And it is all the more powerful if the ability of markets and institutions to intermediate funds and generate credit is severely impaired. Hence the broader financial crises that go hand in hand with the most severe economic recessions.

Recent history provides numerous examples of the processes just described. In some cases the damage has been contained, as with the stock market crash of 1987. In others it has been more pervasive, as with the banking crises in the Nordic countries and Japan in the late 1980s and early nineties, in Latin America in the eighties and nineties and in Asia in recent years.

Beyond specific characteristics, all of these episodes shared some stylised features. There is first an over-extension phase during which financial imbalances build up, accompanied by benign economic conditions. In this phase, asset prices are buoyant and their surge tends to feed, and be fed by, rapid credit expansion. Leverage, in overt or hidden forms, accumulates in balance sheets, masked in part by the favourable asset price developments. The trigger for the reversal is essentially unpredictable. It can reside either in the financial sphere (e.g. an asset price correction) or in the real economy (e.g. a spontaneous unwinding of an investment boom). The process then moves into reverse. *Ex post*, a financial cycle is evident.

Increased financial instability: the financial regime

Why is the financial sector so prone to instability? Certain characteristics inherent in all financial activity and in its institutional environment merit particular attention.

- First, *fundamental value is extremely hard to assess*. We can disaggregate it formally into expected returns, a discount rate and a risk premium. In fact, however, like beauty, fundamental value is largely in the eye of the beholder. A function of financial claims is to telescope into the present intrinsically uncertain cash flow streams. Past experience can be a flimsy anchor for these expectations. Consequently, they are subject to powerful waves of optimism and pessimism, greed and fear. We see what we want to see. Paradigms about how the world works colour our observations. We eagerly discount what is inconsistent with our theories or beat it into shape until it fits them.

  Such partial vision is true of individual agents taken in isolation. It is even stronger in the social behavioural patterns reflected in market prices. Price reactions to 'news' can go through phases in which, whatever the intrinsic information content, the news is interpreted as reinforcing the prevailing paradigm. We do not need to go as far as Keynes in explaining the inherent indeterminacy of asset prices in terms of beauty contests. I suspect that it is not so much a matter of consciously guessing the majority's view – most people are too risk averse for that – as of inadvertently falling victim of a shared vision.
- Second, in contrast to other industries, *in the financial sector excess supply does not necessarily put immediate downward pressure on prices and profits*. To the contrary, lending booms initially tend to sustain economic activity and boost asset prices, thereby improving for a while the financial condition of both borrowers and lenders. The mutually reinforcing process between perceived wealth and access to external funding

masks the extent of the underlying imbalance, until the process necessarily turns into reverse. Excess capacity and risk build up partly unnoticed.

- Third, generating *liquidity*, a key function of the financial sector, *can result in fragile balance sheet structures*, especially given its link with leverage. Fragile balance sheet structures can intensify instability. The sudden and sometimes indiscriminate retrenchment of suppliers of funds can cause institutions and markets to be starved of liquidity, exacerbating price declines and impairing the functioning of markets. If bank runs are the text book example, the market turbulence in 1998 has shown that markets are not immune to similar problems. Liquidity has a binary side to it; it is either on or off.

- Finally, *ill-designed safety nets can exacerbate instability*. The very forms of official protection historically put in place in response to financial instability can be counterproductive if they weaken market discipline without providing offsetting prudential incentives. This is the familiar moral hazard issue. The financial sector generally, and banking in particular, are characterised by an 'exit problem'. Institutions are allowed to remain in being when, in a more competitive environment without a safety net, they would have gone under much earlier. From this perspective, financial crises can be viewed as a kind of 'safety valve of last resort', a catalyst for needed structural adjustments.

While the above characteristics are inherent in financial activity and in the institutional safeguards put in place in the first half of the 20th century, a number of changes in the financial regime over the last twenty years have arguably increased the potential for financial instability. All of them can ultimately be traced back to the financial liberalisation and technological innovation that has gathered pace during this historical phase. The process have resulted in a broader range of services, at lower prices, and more accessible terms than ever before. But these great benefits have not come for free. Let me focus on four implications of the profound forces just mentioned.

- First, *competitive pressures have vastly increased and a wave of 'creative destruction' has affected both the real and financial spheres of the economy*. This has heightened uncertainty in the economic environment. Previously sheltered financial institutions have had to learn to measure and price risks. In some cases, they have had to compete with nimbler opponents, not saddled with burdensome cost structures inherited from the past. Net operating cushions have come under pressure, making it harder to earn a given return for the same amount of risk. Consequently, the incentives to take on added risk have increased. And for much the same reasons so has 'herd instinct', or the tendency to conform behaviour to the norm, for fear of being left behind and in the hope of limiting blame in case of failure.

- Second, *the new environment has structurally increased liquidity and the potential for leverage.* Think of liquidity as the ability to realise value, whether through the sale of an asset or external finance. Such external finance will only be supplied against some form of perceived value. Perceived value can be as transparently intangible as the future earning stream from a unit of capital or labour, or as deceptively tangible as a piece of property or financial asset. Think of leverage as the additional sensitivity of net worth to risk factors resulting from a liability *vis-à-vis* a third party. Leverage can be easily apparent, as in the case of a firm choosing to take out a loan rather than issue shares, or less obvious, as in the case of an uncovered option position or the extension of a contingent guarantee. It is then clear that the same kind of forces that have heightened competition have also provided the means and the incentives to increase the availability of liquidity and the potential for leverage. In other words, they have provided more fuel for the fire.
- Third, *the new environment has tended to raise the option value implicit in safety nets.* The reason is simple. *Ceteris paribus*, guarantees become more valuable as the environment becomes riskier.
- Finally, *financial globalisation has transformed geography*, with significant implications for the character of instability. Globalisation has heightened the significance of 'common factors' in the genesis and unfolding of financial distress. It has done so by extending and tightening financial linkages across institutions, markets and countries; by increasing the uniformity of the set of information available to economic agents; and by encouraging greater similarity in the assessment of that information.
- In addition, globalisation has heightened the significance of size asymmetries in the world, between the main industrial countries, on the one hand, and emerging market countries, on the other, that is, between core and periphery, to use a terminology commonly applied to the Gold Standard period. Freedom of capital movements has exposed the emerging market countries to the potential volatility of access to external funding. Portfolio adjustments that are comparatively minor for institutions in the countries originating capital flows are of first order significance for the recipients. This greatly increases the recipients' vulnerability to changes in sentiment, whether these are due to revised perceptions of economic conditions in the periphery or to developments in the core.

Some of the environmental changes just described are particularly acute during the transition from a sheltered to a liberalised environment. Others, I suspect, have a more permanent character. The bottom line is that market discipline alone may be insufficient to ensure the necessary degree of stability. Hence the issue of whether additional policy action is needed. But before I discuss this question, let me say something about the link between financial instability and the monetary regime.

Increased financial instability: the monetary regime

We have grown accustomed to believe that a monetary policy aimed at delivering price stability is the best protection against financial instability. There is undoubtedly a very large portion of truth in this statement. Realised inflation is a notoriously reliable leading indicator of financial instability. Just like asset price misalignments, inflation results in a misallocation of resources and masks the build-up of over-extension in balance sheets. Inflation can also provide fertile ground for price misalignments by encouraging excessive investment in inflation hedges or clouding the distinction between real and nominal magnitudes. Much of the financial instability observed in the seventies and early 1980s reflects these distortions.

Yet this conventional wisdom does not capture the whole story. There are numerous examples of countries following successful anti-inflation policies and yet unable to avoid financial crises. The Japanese and East Asian cases are the most obvious recent instances. And, paradoxically, success in taming inflation can provide an environment more vulnerable to those waves of excessive optimism that breed unsustainable asset price dynamics.

More fundamentally, I would conjecture that the combination of a liberalised financial system and a fiat standard with monetary rules defined *exclusively* in terms of inflation is not a sufficient condition for financial stability. I have already discussed the issues that pertain to the financial regime. The gist of the role of the monetary regime is straightforward. In a fiat money standard there is no exogenous constraint on the supply of credit except through the reaction function of the monetary authorities. If that reaction function is geared exclusively to controlling inflation, and low inflation is insufficient to deliver stability, then the monetary anchor cannot prevent the build-up of credit that accompanies the accumulation of financial imbalances. I will return to this later.

The search for a solution to this basic problem can be seen as a search for adequate anchors in the monetary and financial spheres. From this perspective, it may be instructive briefly to review the link between monetary and financial stability across regimes in the twentieth century.

In the Gold Standard, convertibility into gold acted as the single, common anchor for the monetary and financial regimes. The commitment to convertibility actually defined monetary stability, and gave way in cases of generalised financial crises. Few, if any, other constraints existed on balance sheets; the financial system was liberalised. The promise of convertibility was a rather brittle constraint on credit expansion and could not prevent waves of excessive expansion and instability. For this reason, among others, it was an unsatisfactory feature of monetary arrangements. Nevertheless, it represented a visible, exogenous constraint.

The progressive emergence of fiat standards in the interwar years obscured the link between the monetary and financial regimes. Monetary stability became progressively identified with price stability. The State's solvency, founded on the power to tax, became the sole basis for the acceptability of the currency. At the same time, the new regime loosened the constraint on credit expansion. This contributed further to the widespread financial instability during the period. The instability was the main motivation for the establishment of strict regulation of the commercial banking industry, including through a variety of liquidity, maturity matching and solvency requirements. A separate anchor in the financial sphere had been put in place.

During the Bretton Woods regime, the relationship between the monetary and financial anchors was somewhat ambiguous. A *de jure* gold convertibility clause for official transactions quickly developed into a *de facto* dollar (and hence fiat) standard. This coexisted with a complex web of regulations in the financial sphere, constraining both the balance sheets of institutions and international capital flows. Some of the controls were of a prudential nature (e.g. ceilings on deposit rates), others were rather targeted towards monetary control (e.g. ceilings on loans). But their end result was the same: they restrained the scope of financial cycles and their transmission across borders. For a while, the system delivered price and financial stability. But it did so at the expense of financial repression and increasing costs in terms of resource misallocation.

The environment that unfolded in the 1970s saw a relaxation of self-imposed and exogenous constraints. Greater willingness to use fiat money to finance deteriorating fiscal positions loosened further the constraints on the monetary regime. In the meantime, pressures had been building up to liberalise the financial environment. International financial markets came to play an increasingly important role in the generation and allocation of credit. Financial instability began to emerge again, coexisting with rapid inflation.

Financial liberalisation got into its stride in the 1980s and has continued to accelerate into the present day. The transformation from a government-led to a market-led system, to use Padoa-Schioppa and Saccomanni's famous term, was largely completed. In the monetary sphere, the adoption of a stricter stance against inflation finally began to bear fruit in the 1980s. In the nineties, monetary regimes with clear inflation objectives, buttressed by central bank independence, strengthened the credibility of the anti-inflation commitment. But still financial instability intensified, despite renewed efforts to improve prudential safeguards and to adjust them to the new environment.

Policy challenges: the search for anchors continues

This short review suggests that the economic history of the twentieth century can be seen as a quest to simultaneously secure the elusive twin goals of monetary and financial stability. Attaining this objective requires that the link between the monetary and financial regimes be understood, and that mutually reinforcing anchors be put in place in the two spheres. Let me start by considering the financial sphere.

There is little doubt that all of the work already done and put in train in order to strengthen prudential safeguards is in the right direction. Attention has been devoted to the three basic components of the financial system, namely infrastructures, markets and institutions. Much has been done to buttress payment and settlement systems and the weakest parts of the legal infrastructure. Several initiatives have addressed shortcomings in trading arrangements, particularly following the 1987 stock market crash. Above all, the prudential regulation and supervision of individual institutions has made enormous strides. Upgraded minimum capital requirements have been the cornerstone of this strategy; the Core Principles for Effective Banking Supervision provide a consistent, broader corpus of guidelines that has served as the model for regulatory and supervisory arrangements world-wide.

The Basel-based process has played a significant role in these endeavours. In fact, its three Standing Committees mirror the financial system's tripartite categorisation, with the Committee on Payment and Settlement Systems addressing one key element of the infrastructure, the Committee on the Global Financial System examining markets, and the Basel Committee on Banking Supervision looking after banking institutions. More recently, the establishment of the Financial Stability Forum, which I have the honour of chairing, has been playing a broader coordinating role, by bringing together representatives of the finance ministries, central banks, international regulatory bodies and the leading international financial institutions.

Whether the current efforts can, by themselves, be sufficient to guarantee financial stability is less clear. My previous analysis points to two potential weaknesses that still need to be adequately addressed.

The first relates to the *limitations of market discipline*. Undoubtedly, much can still be done to enlist market forces so as to strengthen financial discipline. In particular, there is ample room to improve disclosure standards, at the level of markets, institutions and countries. There cannot be discipline without information. Indeed, official efforts have wisely been stepped up in recent years to address possible gaps in this area. Likewise, more can be done about incentives. This implies limiting the explicit and implicit guarantees associated with safety nets, nationally and internationally. Even if information is there, perceptions of the existence of official protection may undermine the incentive to use it in the right way. Current efforts to involve the private sector more effectively in the resolution of international financial crises are an important step in the right direction.

Even so, I suspect that the problem runs deeper. It would be a mistake to believe that moral hazard is the only source of incentives for imprudent behaviour. As argued earlier, in a highly competitive environment there is no dearth of pressure to take on risks or to conform behaviour to the prevailing norms, regardless of their inherent validity. More prudent behaviour requires a heightened recognition that, in finance, an ultimate source of competitive advantage is the credit standing of an institution. This takes us to the issue of 'risk culture'.

Risk assessment technology has improved dramatically in recent years and has helped strengthen risk culture. But while economic agents and markets appear reasonably good at assessing the *relative* risk of instruments, debtors and counterparties, they seem to find it harder to evaluate the *absolute,* undiversifiable risk associated with the overall economic and financial environment. Indicators of risk tend to be at their lowest at or close to the peak of the financial cycle, that is, just at the point where, with hindsight, we can see that risk was greatest. Asset prices are buoyant, credit spreads are narrow and loan loss provisions are low. There is a sense in which risk *accumulates* during upswings, as financial imbalances build up, and *materialises* in recessions. The length of the horizon here is crucial. Yet, so far, the ability to anticipate, and hence prepare for, the rainy day has proved inadequate.

The second potential weakness relates to *the raw material on which the regulatory framework can draw*. It stands to reason that the regulatory apparatus should align its risk measures to those used by private participants. Such an approach reduces incentives to arbitrage the restrictions away ('game the system') and encourages improvements in risk management. From this perspective, the current proposals for the revision of the Capital Accord are a major step forward. This positive step, however, still leaves unresolved the problem posed by existing biases in the measures of risk, particularly the shortcomings in assessing the non-diversiable risk associated with the financial cycle. This is especially significant in the current environment. As other constraints on the balance sheets of institutions have been dismantled, prudential standards and agents' perceptions of risk have probably become a more important factor driving the credit cycle.

The bottom line is simple. If my conjectures are correct, there is a material risk that the current anchors in the financial sphere may, by themselves, be insufficient to deliver financial stability. In a sense, anchors are no better than the ground in which they are planted. And that ground could, at worst, turn out to be quicksand. Inadequate risk perceptions and inflated asset values can lead to serious distortions. What, then, would anchor the credit expansion process?

We have thus returned to the starting point of my remarks, to the basic dilemma that has begun to loom large in the policy choices of central bankers. Should monetary policy ever be directed to limiting the build-up of financial imbalances? In particular, should it respond to perceived asset price misalignments that, in the central bank's view, threaten financial stability?

The conventional view is that they should not. And for many good reasons. First, monetary policy should only respond to asset prices to the extent that they provide information about future inflation. Second, even if the central bank wished to prevent the imbalance from building up, by the time it could form a firm judgement about its existence, it would be too late. Pricking a bubble in its later stages risks precipitating the financial instability it is intended to avert. Third, the response of asset prices to monetary policy is highly unpredictable and dependent on market sentiment. A pre-emptive monetary tightening may even boost asset prices if it strengthens the market participants' sense that the central bank has inflation well under control. Fourth, who can say with confidence that an asset price movement is a bubble and not a reflection of fundamental values?

These arguments are powerful. But some doubts remain. Could there be circumstances in which the risks of inaction might exceed those of action? Allowing an imbalance to continue and grow is likely to exacerbate the severity of the eventual reversal. The worst of all possible worlds would be to react, or to give the impression of reacting, asymmetrically, only to price declines. This risks engendering an insidious form of moral hazard, in fact potentially more serious than others which have traditionally attracted greater attention.

Would a reaction function that implied responses to financial imbalances be inconsistent with strict inflation objectives? I do not think that this need *necessarily* be the case. At least at low inflation rates, financial instability is likely to raise the risk of price deflation. Avoiding imbalances that carry the potential for financial instability can thus can be reconciled with longer-term price stability objectives.

But even if this kind of reaction function were to be considered, a non-trivial political economy problem would remain. Communicating such a policy to the general public and justifying it would be harder in the absence of a clearer mandate. It would require serious educational efforts, not least since it could be interpreted as an unjustified intrusion into people's efforts to enrich themselves. Ironically, the largely abandoned reaction functions defined in terms of monetary and credit aggregates could provide a degree of in-built stabilisation and facilitate communication with the public.

To conclude, I am aware that my remarks have raised more questions than provided answers. I am convinced, however, that at this stage of our endeavours to secure financial and monetary stability it is worth standing back for a second and to ask such broader questions. It is only by doing so that we can gain the necessary sense of perspective to guide our efforts with renewed energy and conviction. To my mind, several issues require more attention than that received so far by academics, market participants and central bankers alike, the core SUERF constituency. Of these, I would stress two. We need to give more thought to ways of assessing and dealing with the systematic risks associated with the financial cycle. And we need to explore more fully, with a critical but open mind, the relationship between financial and monetary stability. If my conjectures turn out to be correct, these issues will inevitably gain further prominence in the years ahead. It is partly on finding adequate answers to them that the success of the elusive search of anchors for financial and monetary stability depends. As history demonstrates, this quest will no doubt continue; the stakes are high. The Basel process and the Financial Stability Forum will remain two focal places where it will be elaborated and pursued with vigour. But it is only through the pooling of everyone's efforts that the search can finally be successful.

2 Banking consolidation in Europe*

Jacques de Larosière and Eric Barthalon

According to the European Banking Federation, at the end of 1998, there were 2955 commercial banks in Western Europe (namely, members of the EU, plus Ireland, Norway, and Switzerland). These 2955 banks had total assets of 9144 billion euros, ran 99,456 branches and employed 1.84 million workers.

To this already large number of commercial banks should be added that of other deposit-taking institutions, like savings banks, mutual banks and cooperative banks. All in all, the Euro zone (i.e. the eleven members of the European Monetary Union) had more than 7000 deposit-taking institutions at the end of 1998.

It should therefore be no surprise that hardly a day passes without some mergers or other strategic moves being announced by European banking institutions. Last year was a bumper year with four large deals of a unit value in excess of US$10 billion, each of them creating entities with market capitalization between US$30 and 55 billion:

- In January 1999, the merger between Banco Santander and Banco Central Hispanoamericano created BSCH.
- After a six-month long battle against Société Générale which started in February, BNP is merging with Paribas, leading to the first bank in France and the second in the Euro zone in terms of market capitalization.
- In October, Banco Bilbao Vizcaya (BBV) and Argentaria announced their intention to form BBVA.
- At the same time, Bank of Scotland launched an unsolicited bid on Natwest, the outcome of which was finally overcome by the competitive offer of the Royal Bank of Scotland.
- In the meantime, Banca Intesa took over 70% of Comit.
- Hardly had BBVA been formed than a possible merger with Unicredito in 2002 is being envisaged.

* Paper presented at 22nd SUERF Colloquium, Vienna, 27–29 April 2000.

There is no sign that the consolidation process is abating. Just take a copy of the FT dated 19th January, 2000. You could read:

- that ABN Amro is about to close one in six of its branches in the Netherlands to redeploy resources to electronic banking. On the same page, you could also read that Citigroup is buying Schroders's investment bank activities;
- that the merger between two Portuguese banks – Banco Espirito Santo et Banco Portugues – was announced (a week earlier Banco Commercial Portugues and Banco Mello had decided to merge).

Then, early March 2000, came the announcement of the planned merger between Deutsche Bank and Dresdner. But on 5th April the €33 billion merger collaped.

And on 3rd April we learned that HSBC –the second bank in the world by market capitalization – was to acquire Crédit Commercial de France in an agreed bid.

After two hectic years, the year 2000 has thus already started on a very strong footing, which raises three questions:

- Why are we seeing so many restructuring operations in the European banking sector?
- Which are the different forms taken by these transactions and is there a predominant one?
- Why haven't we seen more cross-border operations?

I will briefly address these three questions, before trying to gauge what all that holds for the future.

I am afraid that in the course of what follows I will have to jump time and again from one definition of Europe – the euro zone (i.e. members of the EMU) – to another, which may or may not include other EU members – like Britain – or even non-EU members, like Switzerland. This will be for the sake of clarity and accuracy.

Why so many restructuring operations?

The rationale for m&a: too many large national banks, no big european bank

The European banking sector remains very fragmented: deposit-institutions, both large and small, are still numerous. Admittedly, the total number of deposit-taking institutions is still three times larger in the US (22,140) than in the euro zone (7040), although the two zones are comparable in terms of GDP and population. But, on the one hand, the legal framework in the US (McFadden Act) pushed in that direction for a long time by preventing multistate banking and, on the other hand, the speed of the consolidation has been faster there than in the euro zone: since 1980, the total number of deposit-taking institutions has fallen by 39% in the States, versus 25% here in Euroland. According to FITCH IBCA, there were thirteen 'major'[1] commercial banks in the USA, that is, a third of the forty-four 'major' commercial banks operating in the euro zone at the end of 1998. In short, it might be said that the US has many small banks – and particularly very small – but relatively few large banks, while Euroland is rich on both counts. Another way to express the differences between the two sides of the Atlantic is to note that the average headcount in US deposit-taking institutions was eighty-seven at year-end 1997 versus 290 in the Euro zone.

The European banking industry is increasingly exposed to global trends. One of them is the *increased competition from American banks*, who compare favourably in terms of revenues and costs.

Table 2.1 gives average indications over the years 1996 to 1998 concerning the 'major' banks in the US, the euro zone, France, Spain, and the UK.

Table 2.1 Average indications 1996–98 concerning 'major' banks in the US, the euro zone, France, Spain and the UK

	United States (%)	Euro zone (%)	France (%)	Spain (%)	UK (%)
(1) Net interest margin	3.22	1.68	0.93	2.66	2.19
(2) Non-interest income	2.65	1.19	0.89	1.36	1.75
(3) = (1)+(2) Total income	5.87	2.86	1.82	4.02	3.95
(4) Operating costs	3.80	1.98	1.26	2.67	2.59
(5) Loan loss provisions	0.39	0.31	0.24	0.39	0.22
(6) = (3)–(4)–(5) Pre-tax profits	1.67	0.57	0.32	0.97	1.13
(7) = (4)/(3) Cost/income ratio	64.8	69.2	69.1	66.4	65.6

Source: BIS quarterly report, 30/06/1999.

- Over the years 1996 to 1998, the average return (as measured by pre-tax profits) on total assets at 'major' banks in the euro zone (0.57%) has been on average a third of that achieved by US 'major' banks (1.67%). This poor showing stems basically from lower revenues.
- The net interest margin at 'major' banks in the euro zone (1.68%) has been on average half of that earned by US 'major' banks (3.22%). More interestingly, interest margins on both sides of the Atlantic have kept on diverging since the mid-eighties: rising in the US, falling in Europe.
- Furthermore, non-interest income at 'major' banks in the euro zone (1.19%), while rising rapidly in 1998, has been less than half of the US level (2.65%).
- All in all, total banking income (net of interests paid to customers) is on average 2.86% at 'major' banks in the euro zone, half of what they are at US 'major' banks (5.87%). But operating costs are significantly higher in

the US than in Europe. One can also remark that there are significant differences within Europe: for example, banking income in Spain is more than twice larger than in France.

- The existence of a large sector of non-commercial banks (like savings banks, mutual and cooperative banks), does not play a small role in accounting for the difficulties encountered by European commercial banks. It is often argued that the non-commercial banks distort competition by not having to pay for the cost of their capital. Furthermore, commercial banks are often forbidden to take over non-commercial banks while the opposite is allowed.

- Turning now to the cost to income side of the equation, it appears that the cost to income ratio at 'major' banks in the euro zone (69.2%) has been on average 4.4 percentage points above the US level (64.8%), even though a noticeable convergence has taken place towards the end of the period.

- The price for tougher competition and less efficiency is a less exuberant increase in market capitalization: while the capitalization of US banks has increased fourteenfold from its low of 1990 to 1999, that of euro banks has 'only' increased fivefold, despite an historic wave of privatizations (both measures are given in dollar terms). Obviously, the glass can been seen as half empty: if the recovered profitability of US banks is the benchmark, then there must be a lot of room for improvement in Europe.

Another reason for concentration is to be found in *deregulation, disintermediation and technological innovations* which tend to erode traditional distinctions between financial intermediaries. These very powerful trends open the door to non-bank players like insurance companies, e-brokers, large retailers (Tesco, Sainsbury). E-commerce tends to turn financial products into commodities, that is, low margin, high-volume products. The same forces also push traditional banks to broaden the scope of products and services they offer to their clients (electronic banking, complementary services to bank account management).

The introduction of the *Single Currency* only exacerbates further these forces. As a consequence of the euro, the domestic market becomes paneuropean. Actually, it had already largely done so for wholesale banking. The same can be expected in retail banking, even though there remain many national specificities (regulatory, tax, legal) that still fragment the market.

For various reasons, economic development argues in favor of an ever larger critical size (in terms of assets or market capitalization):

- Clients of banks (in wholesale banking) have changed in size, because they (corporate, insurance, other banks) have been merging for some time. The wave of mergers in the non-banking sector calls for – or can influence – mergers between banks.

- As long as the costs of managing larger and more complex organizations do not exceed the transaction costs[2] that would otherwise be incurred, size makes it possible to achieve economies of scale, through revenues synergies ('cross-selling' of products) and/or cost-cutting. Conventional wisdom has it that such cost-cutting efforts are required given the increasing costs of state-of-the-art technologies (information technology). It would pay to spread such costs over a larger base in capital-intensive areas like information collection and processing, back-office operations, telecommunications, custody. Yet, this point may be rather controversial as an essential feature of the IT revolution is the rapid fall in the costs of hardware and software. Some analysts contend that the IT revolution is actually lowering the cost of entry into the banking market.

- In a context where margins tend to fall due to excess capacity – the case of most European countries – volumes have to be increased.

These general statements need to be qualified. In some areas, a high degree of convergence and integration had been attained even before the introduction of the single currency: the market is already very much paneuropean. Most of the cost synergies are indeed concentrated in some activities like investment banking, asset management, custody, wholesale payment, credit cards. But it is not evident that commercial banks with no experience in investment banking and asset management can achieve substantial economies of scale when they extend the range of their activities to new lines of businesses.

Specific partnerships are often seen as an alternative to M&As: they presumably deliver the same technical benefits, while minimizing the traumatic side of mergers. Yet, it can also be argued that the more a bank is tied up in a web of partnerships in a rapidly changing environment, the more it risks to run into conflict of interests, the more it loses degrees of freedom. The jury is still out and will probably remain so for some time.

Be what it may, *most banks seem to favor a twofold M&A strategy*:

- Firstly, they are keen to defend their position in the domestic stronghold against potential foreign competitors, which leads them into mergers with national competitors.
- Secondly, in a more offensive way, they seek to establish bridgeheads in the paneuropean market by acquiring interests in foreign institutions. Such interests consist of at least large minority positions, but in some cases majority or even full-ownership is attained. The aim of such moves is to deter similar ones by competitors and to increase market shares.

Needless to say, the general fall in interest rates and the resultant overall rise in share prices have facilitated M&As in making shares of the bidders an attractive currency to the shareholders of the targets. As a matter of fact, most of the deals we have seen are all-share deals.

Which are the different forms taken by restructuring in the european banking industry? is there any dominant one?

Domestic mergers have been predominant

By and large, restructuring has taken place at a national level between European retail banks through 'friendly' deals. This is actually the only thing on which the different data sources we have consulted can agree: on average, they attribute at least two-thirds of the aggregate value of M&As to national deals. But this aggregate value is a matter of discussion: for 1998, it varies from 110 euro billion, according to Crédit Agricole to 182 US$ billion, according to WSJ Europe quoting Thomson Financial Securities. Be what it may, these are large figures. Over the last two to three years, M&As in the banking sector account for a very substantial slice of all M&As in Europe (almost 30% on average).

The aim of these national mergers has been presumably to strengthen domestic operators, to breed 'national champions' up to the point where they can successfully cope with European competition and cross-border mergers.

Table 2.2 shows deals with a unit value in excess of US$1 billion, as compiled by Thomson Financial Securities.

Table 2.2 Deals with unit value in excess of US$1 billion

Thomson Financial Securities Data	Total		European targets			Non-European targets	
	Number of deals	Value in US$ billion	Number of deals	Value in US$ billion	% of total	Number of deals	Value in US$ billion
1990	11	18.8	11	18.8	100.0	0	0.0
1991	9	23.3	7	19.2	82.4	2	4.1
1992	2	9.0	1	5.7	63.3	1	3.3
1993	3	5.2	3	5.2	100.0	0	0.0
1994	3	5.7	3	5.7	100.0	0	0.0
1995	14	40.7	14	40.7	100.0	0	0.0
1996	14	29.6	11	21.7	73.4	3	7.9
1997	25	77.9	20	66.5	85.4	5	11.4
1998	38	181.8	35	176.6	97.1	3	5.2
1999	21	143.0	21	143.3	100.0	0	0.0

Source: Thomson Financial Securities – *Wall Street Journal.*

Figures compiled by Crédit Agricole give an additional insight. Of all the deals announced or completed in 1998, only a third were domestic, but their aggregate value was 63% of the total. In short, what we are seeing is a combination of a few very large domestic operations on the one hand, together with numerous small cross-border operations, as if banks were testing the ground before embarking on larger cross-border deals.

Indeed, we have seen many cross-border acquisitions of minority interests in large institutions, or majority interest in minor institutions. The minority interests acquired in major institutions are sometimes very small, sometimes more substantial. The web of cross-holdings resulting from this process is becoming increasingly intricate. To name but a few of these links:

1 ING has taken a substantial stake in BHF.
2 San Paolo is controlling small banks in France: Banque Vernes, Banque française commerciale, Banque Morin-Pons.
3 ABN Amro has built up controlling stakes in Banque OBC, Banque Demachy-Worms, Banque NSM, Banca di Roma.
4 Deutsche Bank has a small stake in Caritro (Cassa di Risparmio Di Trento e Rovereto).
5 Crédit Agricole has a substantial interest in Banca Intesa.
6 BSCH has a web of relations with San Paolo IMI, Commerzbank, Banque Commerciale Portuguaise, Royal Bank of Scotland, Société Générale.
7 BNP-Paribas has a stake in the Cassa di Risparmio di Firenze.

These forays in foreign territories have encountered mixed results leading sometimes to retreat. Such was the case when:

• Comit sold its French network to Crédit du Nord.
• Dresdner Bank sold Banque Morin-Pons to Banco San Paolo.
• Citibank sold its French network to Banques Populaires and Banque Baecque-Beau.
• Midland sold its French network to Woolwich.
• While Natwest and Barclays basically stopped their operations in France.

Which certainly tells how lucrative is the banking market in France!

Leaving aside a small number of successful cases, like Dexia, Fortis and Meritanordbanken, full-scale cross-border mergers do not seem to have yet been great successes. In fact, they look more like small to medium size acquisitions than real mergers. Of course, the recently announced acquisition of the medium size and profitable Crédit Commercial de France by HSBC brings a new dimension to the issue.

Finally, we have also seen the establishment of new links between the insurance sector and banks. Given the complexity of the 'bancassurance issue', I will just mention it in passing. Insurance companies tend to have higher PEs than banks and they are eager to control distribution channels for their products. Rather than building up a new distribution network from scratch, it does make sense for them to gain access to retail banking networks.

If we try to combine a business line dimension with the geographic one, we can identify four types of moves:

1 Large players have acquired local and profitable niches.

- General Electric bought Crédit de l'Est and SOVAC.
- AXA acquired Banque Anversoise d'Epargne (ANHYP).

2   Networks that are domestic but diversified in terms of clients and/or products have been the targets of buyers seeking: (a) to build on geographic complementarity; (b) to increase market share; (c) to broaden their supply of products; (d) to achieve economies of scale by merging branch network or information systems.
- Lloyds took over TSB.
- Credito Italiano and Carimonte formed Unicredito.

3   International development has been the name of the game for very specialized banks or credit institutions like General Electric Services, Cetelem and Dexia
4   Geographic extension has also played a role in terms of diversification and growth for large universal banks with international ambitions:
- HSBC and ABN/Amro have sought to build on a strong local presence in foreign markets.
- By acquiring Bankers Trust, Deutsche Bank is showing its ambition to be a global investment bank.
- BBV and Banco Santander have focused on becoming dominant players in Latin America.
- But a few others, like Barclays, Natwest and Lloyds have streamlined their portfolio of activities and focused on their lucrative domestic market.

Why haven't we seen more cross-border deals?

Obstacles to cross-border deals

Throughout Europe, the banking industry continues to be seen as a strategic sector which remains under close surveillance of the national authorities. Regulation, supervision and lender of last resort operations remain indeed national responsibilities. Furthermore, since capital markets are still less developed in Europe than in the States, the banking sector plays a much greater role (in a ratio of at least 2 or 3 to 1) in the allocation of savings and credit.

On top of that, at a national level, and leaving Germany and Italy aside, the banking market is actually three to four times more concentrated in Europe than in the States. The top five deposit-taking institutions in each European country easily account for 40 to 55% of total banking assets, against 17% in the States. The top ten institutions share 60 to 80% of the market, versus 26% in the States.

In banks, like in other industries, top managements, staff and trade unions show some reluctance towards full-scale cross-border M&As, although, as we have seen recently, things are changing.

The problem is exacerbated by the absence of a European corporate law, which leaves no choice but to elect one of the national laws. Along the same vein, the EU lacks a directive on takeover rules, inspired, for instance, by the British model and addressing such issues as minority shareholders, trading in bidder's and target's shares, corporate control, timetable and so on. The lack of common rules definitely adds to the many uncertainties which surround M&As.

Large cash transactions are hardly feasible under current conditions. European banks currently trade at an average of 2.5 book value (3 to 4 in the USA). Even in the least profitable markets, banks trade above book value. If a bank trading at 2.5 book value were to be paid in cash, the acquiring institution would have to amortize the goodwill, the excess of the price over the book value, namely 60%, against its shareholder's equity. Few banks are financially strong enough to afford large cash transactions.

In cross-border deals, cost-cutting is more difficult to materialize for central functions as information systems, tax systems, products lines tend to remain national. In particular, Europe remains divided by its payment habits: some countries prefer checks while others favor giros. If the European consumer undoubtedly exists, European banking services remain largely to be invented. The main benefits of M&As are rather to be reaped in the form of asset size, increase in market shares, and diversification of revenues.

The web of cross-holdings which exist between European institutions may also be an obstacle to hostile bids. Until the proposals to change the capital gains taxation in Germany, there was another obstacle to the unbundling of that web of cross-holdings.

Finally, last but not least, the rapid development of internet and electronic banking may make cross-border deals less profitable to the extent that they involve traditional 'bricks and mortar' retail banking networks. It remains to be seen:

- whether traditional banks will add internet distribution to their panoply (i.e. brand, capital and customer base), potentially by-passing part of their traditional sales force;
- or whether internet-only providers will seize a very substantial share of the retail banking market (at the cost of adding physical channels and personal touch to their strategy);
- or whether some segmentation will take place.[3]

The answer will depend on cost and creativity (i.e. 'open finance', 'mutual-fund supermarkets, 'integrated personal financial management', 'total balance sheet approach', 'dynamic refinancing', 'mass customization', 'e-commerce portal').

The above-mentioned obstacles or issues are present in all European countries. Further difficulties exist or existed in some countries. In France, for example, the privatization process was not completed until recently: its importance superseded any other considerations for private sector operators. The profitability of private commercial banks is dented by the mutual sector, which is very large in France. And the implementations of synergies in the face of large restructuring is slowed down by the rigidity of labor markets and the sensitivity to layoffs.

Conclusion

At the end of 1999, Western Europe had almost fifty banks with a market capitalization in excess of €5 billion, not to mention a few additional large non-listed institutions. Half of those listed banks had a market capitalization in excess of €15 billion. Most of them, if not all of those institutions, would probably claim that Europe is or will be their domestic market. But it is also notable that no bank in the euro zone has a size, a width of services and a worldwide reach that makes it truly comparable to the greatest and very few 'global' financial institutions of the United States.

Therefore, the challenge for the European banks will be:

- to improve on their efficiency by rationalizing costs and trimming redundant networks;
- to expand growth internally and through partnerships and acquisitions;
- to strengthen their operations in high value added areas such as structured finance, corporate finance, cash and asset management and securitization.

The ambition is for the largest and best run of these banks to offer to their clients global services to cover the whole spectrum of banking requirements.

These goals cannot be achieved by applying automatic rules or doctrines. One reason is that changes are running too fast. As a prominent CEO in London said a few weeks ago: 'It is hard to be clear about strategy at a time of rapid change'. Fashions are also dangerous: they move from one idea to another without much research or evidence. For instance, a few months ago analysts were stressing the virtues of retail banking, but now they seem to have changed their minds . . .

The key to success is adaptability. In this respect, the question of M&A versus partnerships is still an open one and depends very much on circumstances.

There are obviously many positive feedback effects between M&A and share prices. Yet the risks of over-extension should not be underestimated, all the more so when cross-border deals are involved.[4] Successful M&A eventually depend very much on the ability of management to conceive well thought-through strategies, to develop synergies but also to combine cultures and to motivate teams.

Merging banks is in fact a very difficult art with more failures than successes. It requires extreme care, a clear methodology and a strong leadership from the highest levels of management.

Concerning the adaptability, great attention has to be paid to the development of the internet in financial activities and its impact on banks' strategies.

On-line banking, on-line brokerage are profoundly changing the present institutional setting. The internet is not only a user-friendly way to offer services to clients, it is also a powerful tool to increase efficiency and to reach new clients with less investment costs than those involved in expanding traditional branches.

The question is not: 'Will commercial banks *add* internet facilities to their existing panoply?' But: 'How to become, in all aspects, full financial internet players?' To stay on top, European banks must become themselves internet banks.

I believe European banks will develop a multi-pronged strategy:

- cross-border acquisitions where synergies can be realized by rationalizing networks and information systems in particular, but also where profitable markets can be reached (for instance, retail networks in those emerging countries where banking systems are still largely inefficient);
- partnerships where it is more efficient to use existing networks in order to market specific services in which one of the partners holds a competitive edge (cf. partnerships by special service companies like Cetelem or Locabail);
- internet activities (in this respect the recently announced alliance between BBVA and Telefonica and their launching of an on-line banking venture is of significance). I should also stress that e-Cortal and BNP.Net are leaders in their respective markets;
- eventually becoming truly global in terms of investment banking through internal and external growth (here the recruitment of very competent bankers is of the essence).

So, we have new and exciting challenges ahead of us on the way to European banking consolidation. Saving resources, keeping freedom of maneuver and reaching out towards profitable markets will, as always, remain the key principles of action.

Notes

1 The concept of 'major' bank is a judgemental concept based on a qualitative assessment, by FITCH IBCA, of a number of quantitative criteria the absolute value of which differs from one country to another.
2 'Transactions costs' refer to the real costs which have to be incurred to operate through the markets. Ronald Coase explained the existence of firms by reference to transactions costs: firms exist because they help to save transaction costs through a centralized decision-making process.
3 *Net.B@nk*, a virtual bank opened in 1996 in the USA, claims its operating expenses to be half those of comparable traditional banks.

4 According to a recent report by KPMG (*The Economist*, 4 December 1999), of more than a 100 large cross-border deals (banks and non-banks) around the world between 1996 and 1998, only 17% added value, the creation of value being measured by comparing movements in share prices with those of competitors in the first year after the merger.

3   Monetary policy and financial stability in a dynamic world*

Klaus Liebscher

Ladies and gentlemen,

The 22nd SUERF Colloquium deals with a highly interesting topic of mutual concern. Our success in adapting intellectually, politically, economically and financially to the 'global village' will determine our future welfare. I am delighted to address this distinguished audience and I would like to deal with the issue from the viewpoint of a central banker who shares the responsibility of securing a stable monetary framework for a dynamic and smooth development of the European economy within the Eurosystem.

But before doing so I would like to extend to all of you a very warm welcome to Vienna. I appreciate that the 22nd SUERF Colloquium takes place in Vienna as the OeNB has supported SUERF's activities for a long time and has jointly organized a number of seminars with SUERF in the past. We see SUERF as a unique organization that brings together the academic profession, central and commercial bankers alike and we have considerably benefited from its network and output over the years.

Our cooperation now reaches a new quality with the acceptance of our offer by the SUERF Management Board to house the SUERF General Secretariat in Vienna. In addition we supply one of our highly experienced staff members – Mr Hochreiter – as secretary general. The Bank and I personally are very much looking forward to this enhanced collaboration which, I am convinced, will also be of benefit to all of us including, but not limited to, the Austrian financial community.

Ladies and gentlemen,

The world economy enters the new millennium with very promising economic prospects. The positive prospects for a dynamic development are more broadly based in most if not all regions of the world.

Apart from the positive cyclical outlook it appears that trend growth

* Paper presented at 22nd SUERF Colloquium, Vienna, 27–29 April 2000.

should be higher and more sustainable than at any time during the last two decades. The good economic prospects in Europe and elsewhere for the longer term have much to do with continued market integration, ongoing deregulation, further liberalization measures and technological changes.

Although the direct growth effects of the introduction of the euro are still controversial in some circles, a recent empirical study by Andrew Rose (2000) suggests that the short-term growth effects could be considerable. If this is true we can expect a further substantial intensification of intra-European trade with an accompanying increase in growth rates.

Ladies and gentlemen,

More and more people argue that we have entered a New Economy. The proliferation of information technology, paired with a regulatory environment that is more conducive to entrepreneurship is said to have permanently raised the long-term trend of productivity and of real growth of our economies. While this important subject is beyond the scope of my address, I should nevertheless like to warn against too much optimism and to sound a note of caution. Still, it is true that new production and information technologies, combined with open markets intensify competition. This must at least have a temporary impact on productivity and thus on non-inflationary growth. Up to now perhaps more so in the US than in the EU, as the US is further advanced regarding a business friendly regulatory environment, the flexibility of markets and, of course, the internal integration of its economy. In my opinion, it is too early to tell if we witness the emergence of a New Economy. Even more so, because historical precedence – the economic euphoria of the 1920s when the proliferation of electricity and the telephone had a similar impact on productivity – underlines the wisdom of caution.[1]

But at the same time it is beyond doubt that deregulation of financial services, capital account liberalization and the possibilities to reorganize and redefine production processes offered by new technologies have put the world economy on a new footing. Clearly, we face new risks and these innovations open up major challenges for all of us. We have to re-examine the role of the national state *per se*, that of firms, employees and, of course, financial intermediaries and central banks.

Ladies and gentlemen,

One outgrowth for us central bankers is that in addition to our concern with price stability, our acknowledged home turf, we must increasingly also be concerned with the stability of the financial system both regionally and globally. Today we operate in an increasingly interdependent world where there is a growing divergence between the national political sphere and the global economic and financial sphere.

Ladies and gentlemen,

It has always been the duty of monetary authorities to secure both monetary and financial stability. Yet, issues of financial stability have moved up on the agenda, due to the growth of financial services, both in volume and in depth. Global capital flows have hugely increased over the last twenty years and these developments – as was shown, for example by Obstfeld (1998) – have restored a degree of international capital mobility that was not seen since the beginning of the last century. At the same time a plethora of new financial instruments has been created. Both developments offer great opportunities for market participants. The globalization of capital flows facilitates a more efficient allocation of world-wide resources. Since the seminal work of Arrow (1964) and Markowitz (1959), we understand better the beneficial role of financial instruments in providing opportunities of diversifying and sharing financial risks. New financial instruments increase and enhance these opportunities. But both developments represent challenges for monetary and supervisory authorities, as the increasing size and the increasing specialization of financial services and service providers at the same time create a new potential of risk.

Ladies and gentlemen,

The recent crises in Asia and elsewhere have directed attention towards the phenomenon of financial contagion both from the side of politicians as well as academics as emphasized in so-called third generation currency crisis models and various attempts to model systemic risk in the financial sector.[2] Through the global network of financial markets a crisis in one part of the world may quickly spread via a chain reaction to other places, with the potential to destabilize the global financial system. These crises have transformed the international agenda. At the global level plans for a new international financial architecture have abounded and the future role of institutions like the IMF and the World Bank has been widely and intensively debated. Prominent economists like Paul Krugman, Joseph Stiglitz, Stan Fischer, Barry Eichengreen and, of course, the Meltzer Commission, have formulated quite diverse and controversial proposals.[3]

Indeed, the reform of the IMF has also been on the agenda of the spring meeting of the Bretton Woods Institutions. I think we have made progress towards formulating a common European position around key issues like:

*   the universality of the Fund
*   the continuing need to provide both short- and medium-term financing consistent with its catalytic role and
*   systematic private sector involvement to promote crisis prevention.

Ladies and gentlemen,

The problems of systemic risk challenge all monetary, regulatory and supervisory authorities, from the international level down to the regional level.

Since there are other speakers who will deal with the role of global institutions, I will limit my remarks to two issues: First, I want to discuss some topics regarding the euro area; and second, I will cover the role of the national central banks in safeguarding systemic stability.

For more than a year, the Eurosystem, which includes the European Central Bank (ECB) and the eleven national central banks (NCBs) of the countries which have introduced the euro, has been in charge of the single monetary policy for the euro area.

The Treaty establishing the European Community clearly states that the primary objective of the single monetary policy shall be to maintain price stability. Furthermore, the Treaty stipulates that, without prejudice to the objective of price stability, the Eurosystem shall support the general economic policies in the European Community with a view to contributing to the objectives of the Community. The latter include, *inter alia*, sustainable and non-inflationary growth and a high level of employment.

The Treaty therefore establishes a clear sequence of objectives for the monetary policy of the Eurosystem, with price stability unambiguously being the *sine qua non*. Such an assignment of tasks to a central bank is nothing extraordinary. On the contrary, it reflects the consensus which has emerged over the last two decades to the effect that maintaining price stability is the best contribution monetary policy can make to sustainable and non-inflationary output growth and employment perspectives.

The belief that monetary policy should be geared towards price stability is firmly rooted in economic theory which demonstrates the costs of inflation, both in terms of allocative inefficiencies and arbitrary redistribution effects. At the same time, these arguments suggest that maintaining price stability in itself contributes to higher growth and employment. Several empirical studies have concluded that, across a large number of countries, it is on average those with lower inflation which appear to grow more rapidly.

While there is a widespread agreement on the benefits of price stability, it is less clear exactly what price stability means. In the context of its stability-oriented monetary policy strategy, the Governing Council of the ECB defined price stability as 'a year-on-year increase in the Harmonised Index of Consumer Prices (HIPC) for the euro area of below 2%'. According to this definition, price stability 'is to be maintained over the medium term'.

A forward-looking monetary policy requires a structured approach in order to interpret and synthesize all the information relevant for an assessment of the outlook for price developments; in other words, it requires a well-founded monetary policy strategy. The strategy of the Eurosystem is based on two pillars, the first assigning a prominent role for money and the second being a broadly based assessment of the outlook for price developments.

Of course, ladies and gentlemen, it is much too early to make a detailed assessment of the achievements of the single monetary policy. Nevertheless, the first sixteen months of the euro have been encouraging and there are good reasons to look to the future with optimism. Owing to very careful technical and conceptual preparations, both the monetary policy-making process and the implementation of monetary policy decisions have functioned efficiently from the very outset. At the same time, there can be no doubt that there is room for further improvement and that important challenges still lie ahead.

Ladies and gentlemen,

The successful introduction of the euro has created a large economic area and will lead to further integration of European goods and capital markets. In a way, the development in Europe can be expected to mirror global developments. The euro has already deepened and integrated financial markets and it will increasingly do so in the future. These developments have consequences for financial stability in several respects. I will mention just two of them.[4]

First, through EMU and the resulting increased integration of financial markets and institutions, new channels of contagion and systemic risk may emerge within the euro area. An example is the increasing importance of interbank market transactions, which often lead to large uncollateralized exposures, thereby creating contagion risks.

Second, EMU will intensify competition in financial markets. It will affect all market participants both within countries and across European national borders. Increasing competition brings benefits in the form of higher productivity and efficiency. However, increasing competition in the banking sector can also have a risk increasing effect. Shrinking profit margins due to more intense competition make it more difficult for banks to rebuild capital after a negative shock and increases incentives for (excessive) risk taking. Thus, fiercer competition also increases the probability of bank failures and systemic risk. Contagion risk as well as the risk of eroding profit margins raise the vulnerability of financial institutions.

Ladies and gentlemen,

This raises the question of whether current regulatory and supervisory arrangements are adequate. My clear answer is yes, but let me elaborate on that.

It is sometimes argued that this state of affairs requires more centralized regulatory and supervisory institutions at the international level. This view is often extended to the current European situation by claiming that the concentration of monetary policy in the hands of the European Central Bank should be followed by a concentration of supervisory and regulatory duties in a similarly centralized institution. Though centralization of some tasks might have its merits, I reject this option for the time being for the following reasons:

The first reason is a purely political one. The EU has been formed on the principles of subsidiarity, where power is shared among member states. Its aim has been to leave as many responsibilities as possible in the hands of the national authorities while transferring responsibilities to common institutions only when this was deemed both reasonable and feasible. Up to now the principle of subsidiarity, the cornerstone of European unification, has worked well, although it has been at times quite tedious. Taking into account both the positive experience with subsidiarity and the reluctance of national legislators to transfer responsibilities to centralized authorities, we have good reason not to rush to a centralization of regulatory and supervisory duties.[5] In addition, it is sometimes argued that regulatory variety and competition could minimize regulatory burden and regulatory capture.

The second reason for keeping regulatory and supervisory authorities decentralized relates to economic and institutional aspects. EMU comprises countries with different histories, cultures and behavioral traditions. Not only does this apply to the cultures in the true sense of the word, but also to the financial and regulatory practices. Due to their local knowledge national regulators have a comparative advantage in dealing with idiosyncratic national characteristics of their respective financial intermediaries. The upcoming unification and convergence of European financial markets will gradually remove these distinctions, but this cannot be expected to happen in the near future.

Ladies and gentlemen,

Considering these two reasons, I conclude – as said already before – that the existing supervisory and regulatory architecture provides a coherent and flexible basis for safeguarding financial stability in Europe. Still, it is clear, that keeping regulation and supervision decentralized requires a number of improvements at a practical level.

In this context I would like to mention the need for qualified staff, which ensures better risk assessment, the adaptation of European financial legislation, a convergence of supervisory practices and, last but not least, enhanced communication and cooperation. We need an enhancement of cooperation cross-sector and cross-country as well as between supervisors and central banks. With regard to the latter it seems to me that the necessary involvement of central banks in supervision is not fully understood sometimes.

This is important both for crisis prevention and crisis management. In my assessment progress has been made in both areas although it seems that crisis prevention is an even more difficult task than efficient crisis management. This is so because we cannot know in advance the nature, development and size of a potential crisis. Witness the problems encountered by those who try to develop early warning indicators.[6] Work in the IMF by Berg and Pattillo (1999) is not very reassuring for policy makers. None of the models they evaluate reliably predict the timing of crises. The positive message is that these models clearly forecast crises better than pure guesswork.

Ladies and gentlemen,

In the context of the Colloquium topic 'Adjusting to Financial Globalization' two tasks are important: First, supervision of financial institutions and second, safeguarding financial system stability.

Let me begin by examining the tasks assigned to the ESCB in the context of crisis prevention and crisis management. Art. 3 of Protocol No. 3 on the Statute of the ESCB and the ECB only states that 'the ESCB shall contribute to the smooth conduct of policies pursued by the competent authorities relating to the prudential supervision of credit institutions and the stability of the financial system'. In Art. 25 the consultative role of the ECB in prudential supervision is laid down. Thus, the regulatory and supervisory work is assigned to the national authorities. While the precise institutional responsibilities differ markedly across EMU, NCBs are involved in one way or another in all participating countries. The role of the Oesterreichische Nationalbank in supervising Austrian banks is a case in point. While the formal decision-making power rests with the Federal Minister of Finance, the OeNB is assigned important supervisory tasks: *Inter alia* we make on-site inspections, prepare expert opinions, report any significant findings and observations in the banking sector, collect and analyze supervisory statistics and participate in the so-called Expert Commission, comprising senior representatives of the Federal Ministry of Finance and the OeNB, to discuss issues of mutual supervisory concern. Thus, it is vital – just as is the case with some other central banks with a position similar to ours – that central banks be included in the relevant supervisory fora.

Ladies and gentlemen,

The decision by SUERF to relocate the secretariat to Vienna might also have been motivated by the fact that Vienna is quite near to Central and Eastern Europe. Indeed, Vienna is a very good place to be, if you want to build contacts to academics and bankers in the Accession Countries – and we are happy to support you in every way we can. Before concluding, let me therefore switch to a topic which is of great importance for Europe – the enlargement of the EU.

The EU enlargement to include Central and Eastern European countries is of paramount importance to Europe and especially to Austria both in political and economic terms. It should and can contribute to political stability and will enhance economic prosperity throughout Europe. Bearing these reasons in mind, the OeNB has been and will continue to be a fervent advocate of EU enlargement.

However, ladies and gentlemen, to keep the accession process manageable even now that the Union is negotiating with a comparatively large number of countries, it will be essential to key the pace of negotiations as objectively as possible to the further progress of the candidate countries toward fulfilling the conditions for EU membership. This involves two aspects: first, the speed of enlargement must not compromise its quality, and second, differences between the countries in the two former groups of candidates must be taken into consideration, if there is a factual reason to do so.

Against this background, let me briefly reflect on two connected issues that have to do with the approaching enlargement of the European Union, undoubtedly *the* crucial challenge to Europe in the course of the next years. The first issue is the role the euro plays in Central and Eastern Europe today, and will play in the future; the second issue is the nature of the link between EMU and enlargement.

Ladies and gentlemen,

As a result of the size and the economic clout of the single currency area in Europe, the stability-oriented institutional framework of EMU and the growing integration of the financial markets of the participant countries, the euro stands every chance of becoming a currency of global importance. The euro's chances are in fact best in Central and Eastern Europe, where the currencies the euro has replaced, above all the Deutsche-mark, traditionally played a key role. The euro has assumed this role since the beginning of last year, and in the words of Charles Wyplosz, the Central and Eastern European states – and considering the long term, also some of the CIS countries – may be seen as 'the euro's turf', above all if this area succeeds in posting sustained high growth rates, which we all hope will be the case.

A more detailed analysis shows that the single currency has become particularly important as a unit of account in international goods and service trade in the CEECs. Moreover, the euro is likely to play an ever larger role on the Central and Eastern European forex markets. The same is true of the euro as an investment and issuing currency for private users in the CEECs and, in the longer term, for pricing of goods and on the stock exchange.

For the monetary policies of Central and Eastern European countries, the euro is already a key currency today. In most of the monetary policy strategies of Central and Eastern Europe, exchange rates play a vital role and, wherever they are not a formal or informal intermediate target, they are at least a key monetary policy indicator. In nearly all cases it is the euro upon which the Central and Eastern European currencies are oriented, or to which they are formally linked. In the case of the managed float countries this is reflected by the fact that since the beginning of 1999 all these countries have been using the euro as a reference currency.

The countries which avail themselves of an exchange rate peg – be it a standard fixed peg, a crawling peg or an exchange rate managed by a currency board – mostly peg their currency to the euro only or to a basket in which the euro predominates.[7] Thus, the euro will obtain an even more central position as an anchor currency in Central and Eastern Europe than today. As a result, the euro will also gain in importance as an intervention and reserve currency in the region.

Ladies and gentlemen,

The Central and Eastern European countries which are involved in accession negotiations with the European Union are confronted with the basic question of how Economic and Monetary Union features in the overall context of enlargement.

As far as we can judge today, we see the economic and monetary policy integration of the candidate countries proceeding in three steps. In a first step, the candidates will accede to the European Union, then they will participate in the ERM II, the exchange rate mechanism of the Union, and finally, they will introduce the euro as their national currency.

In the period leading up to accession, the applicant countries will be confronted with two challenges, the first being to meet those EMU standards which are applicable to all EU member states. This means that they will have to create the legal preconditions for central bank independence, prohibit direct financing of budget deficits by the central bank and end public authorities' preferential access to financial institutions. A further prerequisite for EU membership is full liberalization of capital transactions.

The second challenge the accession candidates will need to tackle in the run-up to accession is that they will have to fulfill the economic conditions for membership in the European Union. These conditions consist in establishing a functioning market economy and attaining sufficient competitiveness to participate in the single market. Fulfillment of these conditions will allow the accession countries to integrate themselves successfully into the economic and monetary cooperation within the Union just as those incumbent EU member states which have not yet entered the euro area for the time being today.

Let me make very clear that fulfillment of the Maastricht convergence criteria is *not* a prerequisite for membership in the European Union. Still, a reasonable degree of macroeconomic prudence is essential in the run-up to EU accession, as stability-oriented policies facilitate structural change and foster the catching-up process in Central and Eastern Europe.

In this context, it is important to underline that there are no institutional constraints on exchange rate policies during the preaccession period. Any exchange rate regime is feasible during this stage, provided that it contributes to and is embedded in an overall set of policies that is sound and effectively geared toward stability. What really matters is not the exchange rate regime as such, but the consistency and soundness of the policy mix as a whole. Experience shows that stability-oriented policies underpinned by wide-ranging structural reforms contribute substantially to limiting exchange rate variability.

Ladies and gentlemen,

Not only institutional and legal aspects as well as the principle of equal treatment, but also economic considerations strongly suggest the step-by-step procedure. Adopting the euro too early could place severe strains on such countries' economies, and perhaps even trigger substantial and lasting disturbances. Such a course of action would be in the interest neither of the current euro area members, nor of future members of the euro area.

Therefore I would like to draw the conclusion that the key challenge facing the applicant countries in the next few years consists in strengthening their market economies and their competitiveness by firmly pushing ahead with structural reform and by subsequently adopting the Community acquis in the process. Only on this basis will the EU candidate countries from Central and Eastern Europe be able to attain durable and sustainable macroeconomic stability, and only by taking these steps will they ultimately be able to fulfill, in a lasting manner, the prerequisites for participation in the euro area.

Ladies and gentlemen,

In my remarks I focused on a number of issues central to the subject of your Colloquium. My intention was to signal the concern of central bankers towards systemic stability and crisis prevention, taking into consideration the role of NCBs in the ESCB in this context. In addition I wanted to stress the important factor of EU enlargement with the eyes of a central banker. In closing I would like to wish you much success in your deliberations and fine weather for your official excursion.

Thank you very much for your attention.

Notes

1 David, P. A. (1990), 'The Dynamo and the Computer: An Historical Perspective on the Modern Productivity Paradox', *American Economic Review Papers and Proceedings*, 355–61.
2 See Allen and Gale (2000), Hellwig (1997), Krugman (1997), Freixas, Parigi and Rochet (1999), Obstfeld (1996), Rochet and Tirole (1996).
3 'Jeffrey Sachs advocates the formation of an international bankruptcy court. Paul Krugman suggests that economists need to rethink their traditional antipathy towards controls on capital controls outflow, whereas Barry Eichengreen is among the many who advocate Chilean-style controls on capital inflows. Henry Kaufman recommends creating a single global super-regulator of financial markets and institutions, and Jeffrey Garten proposes a world central bank with responsibility for overseeing a new global currency. Stanley Fisher makes the case that, with a range of improvements in the system, a multilateral lender can effectively perform the main functions of a lender of last resort, even without being able to issue currency.' (See Rogoff, 1999, p. 21; for the detailed references to the articles mentioned in the quotation.)
4 Others are: macroeconomic risks (loss of instrument); mergers, acquisitions and transeuro banking.
5 In a recent report this was called 'economically sound, politically hopeless' (Favero et al. 2000).
6 Cf. Kaminsky, Lizondo and Reinhart (1997); Berg and Pattillo (1999).
7 Only two small Baltic Republics, Lithuania (which pegs its currency to the US dollar under a currency board arrangement) and Latvia (which pegs to the SDR) are exceptions. Both countries plan to switch to a euro peg, Lithuania in the second half of 2001 and Latvia once it joins the EU.

References

Allen, F., and D. Gale (2000), 'Financial Contagion', *Journal of Political Economy*, 108(1), 1–33.

Arrow, K. J. (1964), 'The Role of Securities in the Optimal Allocation of Risk Bearing', *Review of Economic Studies*, 31, 91–96.

Berg, A., and C. Pattillo (1999), 'Predicting Currency Crises: The Indicators Approach and an Alternative', *Journal of International Money and Finance*, 18(4), 561–86.

Cohen, S., J. Bradford De Long, and J. Zsyman (2000), 'Tools for Thought: What is New and Important About the "E-conomy"', *BRIE Working Paper No. 138*.

David, P. A. (1990), 'The Dynamo and the Computer: An Historical Perspective on the Modern Productivity Paradox', *American Economic Review Papers and Proceedings*, 355–61.

Favero C., Freixas, X., Perrson, T., and C. Wyplosz (2000), 'One Money, Many Countries. Monitoring the European Central Bank 2', London, CEPR.

Freixas, X., Parigi, B., and J.-C. Rochet (1999), 'Systemic Risk, Interbank Relations and Liquidity Provision by the Central Bank', *CEPR Discussion Paper* No. 2325.

Hellwig, M. (1997), 'Systemische Risiken im Finanzsektor', in: Duwendag, D. (ed.), 'Finanzmärkte im Spannungsfeld von Globalisierung, Regulierung und Geldpolitik', *Schriften des Vereins für Socialpolitik*, 123–51.

Kaminsky, G., S. Lizondo, and C. Reinhart (1997), 'Leading Indicators of Currency Crises', *International Monetary Fund Working Paper No. 97/79*.

Krugman, P. (1997), Currency Crises, Mimeo, MIT.

Markowitz, H. (1959), *Portfolio Selection: Efficient Diversification and Investments*, Cowles Foundation Monograph, 16, New Haven, Yale University Press.

Obstfeld, M. (1996), 'Models of Currency Crises with Self-Fulfilling Features', *European Economic Review*, 40(3–5), 1037–47.

Obstfeld, M. (1998), 'The Global Capital Market: Benefactor or Menace?', *Journal of Economic Perspectives*, 12(4), 9–30.

Oliner, S. D., and D. E. Sichel (2000), 'The Resurgence of Growth in the Late 1990s: Is Information Technology the Story?', Mimeo.

Rochet, J., and J. Tirole (1996), 'Interbank Lending and Systemic Risk', *Journal of Money, Credit and Banking*, 28, No. 4.

Rogoff, K. (1999), 'International Institutions for Reducing Global Financial Instability', *Journal of Economic Perspectives*, 13(4), 21–42.

Rose, A. (2000), 'One Money, One Market: Estimating the Effect of Common Currencies on Trade', *Economic Policy*, 15, 7–46.

Vives, X. (1999), 'Banking Supervision in the European Monetary Union', Mimeo.

4 A new capital adequacy framework for Europe*

Claes Norgren

The conjunction of the three themes that will be covered here at this conference is no coincidence. The globalisation of financial markets and the consolidation of financial firms are two of the main trends that drive the search for a new capital adequacy framework. The third trend is the rapid pace of financial innovation, creating ever-new financial instruments. Modern information technology is the great enabler, which makes all these trends possible.

Virtually instantaneous access to information and the power of real-time processing means that the separation of different countries and markets is rapidly disappearing. If a pricing anomaly is perceived to exist somewhere, it is almost always possible to structure and execute an arbitrage transaction to take advantage of it. This does not mean that those who do this always make money – oh, no, they lose money also. But the point is that the arbitrage can be executed, and that this creates links between different markets. There are no firewalls in the global financial system.

Again, it is modern information technology that makes it possible to hold large diversified financial firms together and to have a group-wide risk management structure. It is interesting to note that while the process of consolidation has been running rapidly in recent years – primarily in the national markets, but increasingly also involving the creation of cross-border groups – the economic merits of bank mergers have been widely disputed. As far as I am aware, most academic studies of actual cases have concluded that such mergers have been largely disappointing in terms of shareholder value. Notwithstanding, consolidation is happening in front of our eyes and we must assume that the trend towards the creation of very large financial organisations will continue. For the thinking of regulators and supervisors it is also important to take note of the fact that some of these groups can be of systemic importance in several countries. The stand-by organisation for crisis management too will have to acquire a cross-border capability.

* Paper presented at 22nd SUERF Colloquium, Vienna, 27–29 April 2000.

The Basel Committee

The heading for my remarks here today, 'A Capital Adequacy Framework', is the title of the consultative document sent out for comment in June of last year by the Basel Committee on Banking Supervision. Before continuing, it is worth looking for a moment at who exactly this group are and what their role is in the international system. The heading of my presentation also includes the word Europe so I will also discuss the EU-process in this area.

The Basel Committee was created in the 1970s. It comprises representatives from central banks and banking supervisory authorities in the G-10 countries and Luxembourg. It was this committee that, back in 1988, produced the so-called Basel Accord. This was a report that set out the details of an agreed framework for measuring capital adequacy and the minimum standard to be achieved, which the national supervisory authorities represented on the committee intended to implement in their respective countries. The Accord had finally also been endorsed by the G-10 central bank governors.

The Basel Accord is not a formal international treaty between states. In most, if not all of the countries the basic traits of the capital requirements for banks are fixed by law and neither banking supervisors nor central bankers can make promises concerning legislation.

I think that everybody agrees that the Basel Accord has been remarkably successful, despite – or perhaps because of – its rather informal character. Not only have the twelve countries directly involved implemented it with regard to their internationally active banks, so have a large number of other countries.

In the EU, where the relevant directives are closely modelled on the principles of the Accord, the decision was made to let this capital regime apply not just to the big internationally active banks, but also to domestic banks and all other regulated credit institutions. Given that the activities of banks and investment firms are to a large degree overlapping, the EU also decided to include investment firms.

This widespread adoption of the principles in the 1988 Basel Accord outside the G-10 group of countries creates a special responsibility for the current members of the Basel Committee. The plans that are now being drawn up must take into account the fact that a reformed capital regime is required worldwide. Committee members know that the eyes of the world are upon them, and that if they fail to deliver a regime that also answers the needs of countries outside their narrow group, their work will largely lose its relevance. Responsibility will then move to other fora.

As a member of the Basel Committee I am obviously prone to be biased here, but I sincerely feel that the fact that the Committee is not an international organisation like all others and that its agreements are not formal international treaties is helpful and gives a flexibility which would be difficult to have otherwise and a pity to lose. The Committee must now show that it is able to make just that flexibility pay off by delivering a new capital adequacy framework that can be used, with the necessary modifications, in the differing circumstances of the many countries of the financial world. Clearly, we do not work in isolation on this project. There is a permanent liaison committee for the contact with regulators from countries outside the G-10 group, and there are also many *ad hoc* meetings to discuss issues of particular concern to various groups of countries. The Basel Committee also invited regulators, banks and other interested parties from all over the world to submit their comments on the Committee's consultative paper. Many have taken that opportunity.

I should also here mention the largely parallel work on a new capital framework that goes on in the EU. Technically, the responsibility for that work lies with the Commission services, but with the constant involvement of the Banking Advisory Committee and that committee's technical subgroup, which discusses all proposals and also participates in the practical development effort. As eight EU member countries are represented in the Basel Committee there are very close contacts, and at the working level there is an extensive sharing of ideas and results, so as to avoid unnecessary duplication. In the end, of course, we expect that any new EU regulations will closely follow a new Basel Accord, but the influence in shaping this does not all go in one direction. The EU countries then have some additional issues to address, which follow from the decision to have the same capital regime for all banks, large and small, and also for other credit institutions and for investment firms.

Where are we now in the process of reform?

I have already mentioned that the Basel Committee has been conducting an extensive consultation process. In June 1999 we published a consultation document, which outlined the broad lines of the Committee's thinking about the components of a new capital adequacy framework. As many of you probably know, the consultation period ended only a few weeks ago on the 31st March and we are now in the process of compiling and evaluating the comments we have received. I must say that we had probably underestimated the interest that our work has created: the Basel secretariat has received well over 200 written responses. In parallel the EU consultation process has been taking place.

The Basel Committee has not been idle during the consultation period. As I said, the consultation document was really only an outline, where many important issues were only very lightly indicated. There has been a need to dig deeper and to investigate the difficult issues that hide under the principles. To this end a large group of people have been engaged in what can only be described as a massive R&D effort, which has been organised through a number of task forces, groups and subgroups. On some issues there have also been intensive contacts with industry groupings, to benefit directly from their ideas and development capacity.

We have learned a lot since last June, and we will now also take into account the comments we have received through the consultation process. The Committee's next aim is to bring out a second consultative document by the end of this year. I can assure you that this feels like a formidable task, given the amount of development work that we can see is still needed. The next document must in principle contain a complete package for the new Accord, with proposals or at least options indicated for all the major elements. In order to manage that, we shall in practice have to draw a line quite soon and say that no more new issues can be opened. We need to move purposefully towards the final round, remembering that some time is also needed after a new agreement is on the books before the new framework can become effective. We must not let the best become the enemy of the good.

Creating a framework

It is not by chance that the Basel Committee talks about its proposals in terms of a framework. The choice of words is intended to convey a point of view.

First, a capital regime that is intended to be used in many countries and apply to banks in widely different circumstances must be adaptable. While the broad principles and the structure are constant, technical rules must be capable of being varied with due regard to the complexity of the organisations to which they will apply and the resources of national supervisory systems. A new Accord must describe a framework into which individual countries can then fit their national regulations.

Second, while it is true that the devil is in the detail of many questions, all the technical detail just cannot be included in the Accord, or the text would collapse under its own weight. A text that tries to go into too much detail will also very soon be superseded. Financial innovation will create new instruments and market participants will agree on new procedures as their business develops. The Accord must concentrate on the broad principles for how capital requirements are to be determined, and leave the interpretation in individual cases to the national authorities. It is true that this may occasionally lead to situations where accusations fly that this or the other country (usually 'the other') has made an interpretation that is unacceptable, but leave that to be negotiated when it happens. You can never foresee where the difficulties will arise in this respect. For a new Accord to be of value, we must manage to explain and get acceptance for the spirit of what we want to achieve, not just the words that are there on paper.

Third, the new Accord aims at providing a framework also in the sense that it will include several alternative approaches for how the minimum regulatory capital requirement of a bank can be determined. While each of these approaches is valid in its own right, the Committee nevertheless expects that many banks – sooner or later – will want to move, and also should move, from the more standardised to the more individualised methods that will be described in the Accord. The incentive to do this will be that the more individualised methods will tie in better with banks' internal risk management procedures and also will allow regulatory minimum capital to be more closely adapted to banks' individual risk profiles than can be achieved by more standardised methods. At the same time, of course, banks will not be allowed to see a progression of this kind within the framework of the Accord as simply an easy way to get lower capital requirements. The permission to use the more individualised approaches will only be given to banks that have the appropriate risk management procedures and the technical skills to do this in a prudent manner. The stability of the individual institution and of the financial system should gain, not lose in the process.

Fourth, and finally, a framework for capital adequacy is more than a set of rules for computing a minimum regulatory capital requirement. '8%' is not the full answer. What the Basel Committee is saying is that there should be a comprehensive way of looking at capital adequacy which takes into account the bank's ability to identify, measure and control its various risks and the existence of an internal policy for capital allocation and the determination of an appropriate level of economic capital. Issues of transparency, for example the quality of the information that a bank gives to investors, depositors and other outsiders about its risk appetite and risk management procedures, are also relevant for this. Banks should be seen to fulfil sound capital adequacy requirements. That should not just be something between a bank and its supervisor.

To sum up: the new framework should be designed in a more comprehensive way. That is why the concept of the three pillars has been introduced. The minimum requirements which are the first pillar will be complemented by two other elements or pillars. Those are the supervisory review process and market discipline. The supervisory review process in combination with increased transparency is aiming at more broadly and effectively promoting financial stability.

Differentiation is key

On this occasion, where globalisation is on the agenda, it is useful to look a little bit closer at how the Committee envisages that the new capital regime can be made to answer the needs for the regulation of players all the way from the international super-league of financial institutions and down to local banks, which are active mainly in less sophisticated markets. Clearly, differentiation within the basic framework is the key word. Equally clearly, there lies a considerable challenge to regulators and supervisory bodies to get this differentiation right.

Giving sophisticated banks greater responsibility to determine their own required level of minimum capital requires a sophisticated supervisor, who is able to evaluate what the bank does and also has the authority to require corrective action if prudent standards are not met with. The overriding interests of financial stability remain firmly a responsibility of the supervisor/regulator.

Supervisory review process

In the June 1999 consultative paper, the Basel Committee laid great weight on one of the dimensions of differentiation, namely in the so-called second pillar of the proposed new Accord – the supervisory review process. While the concept as such was not new, the central position we wanted to give to it was new. The logic of this was the observation that no set of standard rules to calculate a minimum capital requirement could ever catch in an adequate way all the risks of the more complex banking organisations.

First, there are only so many factors that you can take into account in the explicit rules, and up to a point they can always be 'gamed', which is jargon for the observation that a bank can select its exposures in such a way as to minimise the required capital for the amount of true risk it is taking on. Second, an important part of the overall risk a banking organisation represents to the financial system is not really objective risks caused by its counterparties and positions. A central aspect of the risk profile lies in the quality of the bank's management and risk management procedures. A bank that is not able to properly identify and measure its various risks is considerably more dangerous than a bank with the same objective exposures but which has a best-practice risk management process. Similarly, a bank that lacks a developed policy for its risk appetite and for the level of economic capital its business plan requires is more likely to run into trouble than one where these policies are clear and where they are well known throughout the organisation.

In many cases, a discussion with a bank's management will be enough to bring about improvements. However, for the supervisory review to be a significant instrument to bring about increased stability, there must be some real authority behind. The supervisor must be in a position to demand that a risky banking organisation either reduces its risk exposures to a level more commensurate with its capital or else that it increase the capital base. In either case, the action has the effect of raising the regulatory minimum capital level for that particular bank. In some countries supervisors already have such explicit powers to raise the demands for minimum capital in individual cases, but in many jurisdictions this will be new. In view of the central role that this supervisory review has in the proposed new regime, it is important that countries explore how this can be fitted into their legal systems and institutional structures.

Close individual scrutiny in an active supervisory review of all banks is likely to be beyond the resources of most supervisory organisations. There is a need for the supervisor to develop appropriate screening methods to decide on where the highest priorities are. Focus must be primarily on the limited number of organisations that are really important in the functioning of the national financial system.

In most European countries the implementation of the supervisory review process will require important legal changes. Questions about the powers of supervisors and their accountability will surface.

Different approaches to risk weighting

A dimension of differentiation, which has come to occupy a much larger place in the thinking of the Basel Committee than was indicated in our earlier consultative paper, is the parallel existence of several approaches to the determination of the credit risk weights. Risk weighting is the technique used to achieve the basic differentiation of the regulatory capital requirement for counterparties or exposures of different types. For each exposure, you multiply by the appropriate risk weight and then you add up to get the total risk weighted amount for which capital cover is required.

In the current system those risk weights are fixed quantities, to be applied by all banks in the same manner. There is also almost no attempt to account for the varying credit quality of counterparties, beyond the division into three large categories: sovereigns, banks and others. In the consultative document we proposed that a certain amount of differentiation be brought in through the use of external ratings. Exposures to counterparties with such high rating could be given lower risk weights, and exposures where the counterparty has a poor rating a higher risk weight. I will not go into the detail of this proposal. Many of you will know that the proposal to rely in this way on external rating agencies has met with quite a bit of criticism. However, the basic proposal to seek more differentiated risk weightings has been seen as valid and no real alternatives to the external ratings have been identified.

The use of information from external ratings to achieve a certain differentiation of the risk weights will thus remain in the new standardised approach. However, we have made much more progress in developing alternatives than we thought likely in June of last year. In the consultative document we suggested that we were going to work hard to develop an alternative method of differentiation, based on the internal ratings systems employed by many banks. But while we believed that this concept was sound, we thought that it would be too optimistic to count upon this method being available from the outset to other than a limited group of sophisticated internationally active banks. What we proposed to do was in effect to certify the internal ratings processes of banks and to rely on them to come up with prudent numbers for the risk weighting of their exposures, both of high quality and of lower quality, and we did not believe that many banks were that far advanced.

On this point our thinking has developed, and also our appreciation of how much work banks have been devoting to overcome both theoretical and practical difficulties associated with the use of internal ratings to put numbers on the absolute requirements for economic capital. We thus now aim to include in our proposal not one internal ratings-based approach, but two. One, which is known as the foundation approach, we hope will be available to a fairly large number of banks to be used quite soon for at least part of their portfolios. In the other, more advanced approach, the bank will be expected to derive from its ratings model not just information about the probability of default – which is what external ratings basically do – but also about the severity of loss. In the foundation approach, assumptions about that parameter would probably have to be prescribed by the regulator in a fairly standardised way. While we don't expect this more advanced approach to be feasible from the outset for more than perhaps a small number of banks, it is important that this approach be there as a possibility for other banks to gain acknowledgement when they have improved their capabilities.

This dimension of differentiation has strong ties to the supervisory process. The supervisor must be in a position to evaluate the internal ratings work of banks that aim to use this to determine risk weightings. Not just the technical skills must be there, but also the organisation to support it. The internal ratings system must be an integral part of the bank's business and risk management process, not just exist as a clever mechanism to come up with lower capital charges. There is an obvious parallel here with the rules for the use of internal models for the determination capital charges for market risks – and then to note that credit risk is more important than market risks in most banking organisations.

The task ahead

Looking ahead, all those that are currently engaged in the work that the Basel Committee is orchestrating have a hectic period in front of them. There are many hard problems yet to resolve at the technical level. But such problems are for the Basel Committee to resolve. If we manage to do that, and if we can deliver by the end of the year a comprehensive document to be sent for a second round of comments, I feel that we will have come a long way. After some final adjustments we would then be able to hand a new Basel Accord over to the world at large. Make no mistake; there is still a fairly long process after that before the implementation is complete. But it is worth going through. A capital regime, which is based on sound principles and which includes a sufficient amount of flexibility to take care of the varying needs of banks in different circumstances, is a cornerstone for a safe adaptation to financial globalisation.

For Europe a new capital adequacy framework will have to be fitted in among the Banking Directives. This will be a process that will involve the political system and pass through the EU parliament. Clearly much work lies ahead, but if we can fit the new capital adequacy framework into the EU landscape, this will significantly improve financial stability in Europe.

Thank you.

5 Is a Euroland banking system already emerging?*

Tommaso Padoa-Schioppa

Introduction[1]

Is a Euroland banking system already emerging? The question I have chosen as a title for this Lecture highlights the fact that my remarks will not be policy-oriented and will not be primarily focused on the analysis of past developments. They will also tackle positive rather than normative issues.

The reasons for choosing this subject have to do with central banking as well as supervisory interests. I am of the view that even where banking supervision is entrusted to an agency which is separate from the central bank, central banks do have a vital interest in the banking industry. The banking industry is the key transmission channel for monetary policy; banks are the key operators in the payment system and they constitute the counterparty for the central bank operations. Just because supervision is entrusted to a separate agency, this does not mean that a central bank is uninterested in ensuring that banking supervision is conducted in such a way that problems of instability will not arise and threaten to jeopardise the conduct of monetary policy.

Speaking to an audience composed of academics, bankers and central bankers, I am mindful of the fact that this is an area in which problems of methodology and substance interact very deeply, as I will try to explain.

Let me just say before I enter into my theme that I feel honoured to deliver this Lecture because it is named after Robert Marjolin. I understand that the winner of the Marjolin prize will receive a copy of his memoirs. It is an exceptional book about an exceptional person. Let me quote just two extracts from Jean Monnet's memoirs referring to Marjolin: '*On savait déjà qu'il serait un des esprits les plus doués de sa génération*'.[2] That was in the early 1940s; later Monnet observed that: '*Marjolin avait acquis une grande liberté de pensée pendant la guerre. Il avait appris que l'intelligence sans l'action n'était pas satisfaisante*'.[3]

A most interesting passage in Marjolin's memoirs is about his adolescence. His real aspiration was to become a manual worker and he dropped out of

* Marjolin lecture delivered at 22nd SUERF Colloquium, Vienna, 27–29 April 2000.

school at the age of fourteen to begin work at a factory. He came from an extremely poor family and was living in an area of Paris so deprived that there was no running water. One might almost say that he came to lead the life of an intellectual essentially because he failed as a manual worker. Marjolin was so manually unskilled that at the age of fourteen – a few months after he started work at the factory – he was told that he would not make it and had better go back to school, which he did not do. He went to work as a clerk at the Paris Stock Exchange. At the age of twenty, he was at Yale University, and the rest is known.

Let me now move on to the substance of this Lecture, which I will organise under *five headings*. First, we will have to examine some problems of methodology. I will then try to answer the question by distinguishing between three major areas of banking business, namely wholesale, capital market and retail activities. Finally, I shall have a few words to say about the problems of cross-border mergers and ownership structure.

Methodological issues

There are indeed complex *methodological issues* to be addressed in attempting to establish whether a banking system is already emerging in Euroland. To start with, I shall mention two very popular, but – at least in my view – erroneous propositions, and then I shall state three other propositions, which may more profitably be considered.

The first error is to argue that all that really matters is the *single market, not the single currency*. Undoubtedly, the single market and the single currency are difficult to separate. It is also true that the effects of the single market have not yet developed in full, and had not developed in full by the time the euro came into existence. However, it is true – I think – that the multiplicity of currencies in the single market was a fundamental factor behind the preservation of the segmentation of the banking industry. The advent of the euro represented a major new event, which justifies raising the question of the emergence of a single banking industry with reference to Euroland, and not to the EU as a whole. As I will argue later on, it is indeed the existence of a single currency and a single central bank which very often unifies a banking system.

A second error is to argue that a single banking industry will only emerge when *cross-border mergers* occur. This idea is also very popular, and in a way it is an opposite statement to the first one, because if we were to make a similar statement for manufacturing, we would say that we do not yet have a single market. Only few cross-border mergers have taken place in key manufacturing industries in the forty years or more following the start of the common market. I think that this argument is erroneous because it focuses excessively on the ownership structure – an aspect to which I shall come later – which should not be used as the key criterion for assessing an industry's level of integration.

If we were guided by either of these propositions, answering the question would be rather simple. In the first case we would say that, yes, there is a single banking industry because the single market legislation has already created it. In the latter case we would say that there is not, because we do not yet have a 'critical mass' of cross-border mergers. If we reject these two propositions as incorrect – as I do – then we will need some other guidance, and in this regard I should like to propose *three other propositions*.

First, although banks are identifiable as a well-defined type of firm, banking is at the same time a *multi-product industry*: various banking products are exchanged in different markets, which are of different size and geographical coverage. This also explains why it is so difficult to find empirical evidence on the degree of integration of the banking market: data can be collected only with reference to the various markets for financial services in which banks are active players. This dual nature was one of the main difficulties experienced when the Second Banking Co-ordination Directive had to be drafted. The solution, which I still find very illuminating given the complexity of the Directive, was to combine a single definition with a list of permitted activities, and it is the combination of the two elements which really identifies banks.

The second and key proposition is that, while banks are a multi-product type of firm, they nonetheless form a *system*. The word 'system' is extremely important. We do not use this word for practically any other industry. There are many reasons why it is appropriate to talk of a banking system; these have to do precisely with the singleness of the currency and central bank, and, accordingly, of a common wholesale payment system and markets for liquid reserves, which are core aspects of a monetary system. First of all, a payment system is undoubtedly a system: participants are connected in a network, which also constitutes a channel for quick propagation of risks and instabilities. Second, liquidity – channelled through the banks – is a crucial component of the functioning of all financial markets. Third, confidence in the currency and the central bank influences all parties operating in the single currency area. The segmentation of financial markets may affect the way in which monetary policy impulses are channelled to different parts of the economy, but in the case where a liquidity need emerges in a specific segment of the financial system, it is always the central bank which bears the ultimate responsibility for it.

Hence, the existence of a common framework for accessing central bank liquidity is tying together euro area banks to a much larger extent than usually admitted, thus determining an integrated Euroland banking system. The US experience highlights the importance of this element. Following the liberalisation of geographical restrictions, no US bank is present in every state, and interstate banking is relatively limited, but the US financial system is commonly viewed as integrated. Nevertheless, even before the liberalisation, a common monetary policy and regulations implied that the structural trends and systemic disturbances in banking cut across state borders.

Hopefully, we will never face a situation of distress in the euro area. However, I take the view that the jurisdiction of the central bank *ipso facto* defines the borders of the banking system, meaning that I could even close my remarks here, with an affirmative answer to the question which I am addressing. However, I cannot refrain from providing additional corroborating evidence, which reinforces this conclusion even further. I will try to examine the degree of integration or segmentation of the markets for individual banking products – recognising the multi-product character of banking.

My last proposition is that the *law of one price*, which is the usual criterion for identifying the emergence of a unified market, provides only limited help in assessing the extent of integration in banking. This is the case not only for the widely accepted reason that there are transportation costs and other costs which explain price differences and impede equalisation of prices via arbitrage activity. More importantly, quality competition – as distinguished from price competition – is absolutely crucial in many of the products and services provided by the banking industry. Therefore, looking only at prices – even if comprehensive data were available – would be misleading.

With these certainly incomplete – but, in my view helpful – propositions in mind, we can proceed by breaking down the range of banking activities into three broad categories, which I will examine one by one. Within each of these broad categories a large number of individual products and services are provided by banks. The method, if it were applied in full, would imply going into each of these in detail, assessing whether the law of one price is applicable, or looking for other possible indicators of a single industry (in spite of price differences) when products are heterogeneous and quality competition is important.

Wholesale activity

The first group of products can be labelled under the heading *wholesale activity*. This is the market in which the two sides of the transaction are not the end-users – say, households or firms – but banks, or perhaps more broadly, financial institutions. In a way, the notion borrows terminology from the goods market, in which the wholesale market is the market which exists between the primary producer and the vendor servicing the final consumer.

The wholesale activity encompasses a wide range of activities conducted by banks. One way to see this is to note that whenever two parties in a transaction do not resort to the same bank as their service provider, the transaction in question will always require a wholesale transaction. Again, the classic example is from the payment system: whenever a bank customer has to make a payment to a counterparty having his/her accounts at a different bank, a wholesale transaction is initiated, namely an interbank transfer. A similar pattern occurs for many other types of financial transactions. The wholesale activity constitutes the inner core of the monetary and financial system – and of the banking industry – and also the part that comes closest to the central bank. It is the main channel for transmission of both monetary policy and potential financial instability.

In wholesale activity, product standardisation is high, and the law of one price can thus be applied in several respects when assessing market integration. To this end, I will briefly review three aspects, namely: *prices; cross-border flows*; and *infrastructure*.

Prices

The key component of the wholesale market is the transmission and diffusion of liquidity among banks. The largest part of this system of transactions takes place in the market for unsecured deposits, which amounts to more than 70% of the total interbank activity (according to the data collected by the ECB). In this market, the law of one price began to work within a few days of the launch of the euro, on 1 January 1999. At a very early stage, the spreads became virtually identical in all countries. The country-specific differences were quickly reduced to around two basis points, which is more or less the amount below which arbitrage would no longer be convenient. If there are differences, they are now often greater across individual banks within a country than across countries. Thus, we can say here that market segmentation disappeared almost immediately and we do have a single banking industry.

The process of market integration is somewhat less complete in the case of *secured repo transactions*, which are usually longer-term operations. The repo markets were established more recently and there are legal discrepancies which render the arbitrage mechanism less effective. As I have noted, however, the repo market is a minor component of the market for interbank transactions.

Cross-border flows

The statistics on cross-border flows reveal that market integration has indeed taken place and that there are increasing cross-border links between banks. Today the share of cross-border transactions is more than 50% of all unsecured and repo transactions (according to the data collected by the ECB). In large-value payments via TARGET, the share of cross-border flows was more than one-third in the first quarter of 1999 and rose to above 40% towards the end of the year. Most of the payments channelled via other major wholesale payment systems such as Euro I or EAF (Euro Access Frankfurt) represent cross-border transactions. Moreover, the amounts exchanged are extremely large. The average daily value of payments passing through TARGET is around 400 billion euro, and, through Euro I and EAF together, over 300 billion euro per day.

Market infrastructure

Here the key aspects relate to the wholesale payments infrastructure (TARGET, Euro I and EAF), which is already very strongly unified. This is not so much the case for another key component of the system, namely securities settlement, which is still fragmented to a significant extent. There were close to thirty systems operating in euro when it was launched. There is, however, a slow and – I would say – a tiring and energy-consuming process of consolidation towards a more limited number of systems under way. There are obstacles of various kinds which are slowing down a process of consolidation which – in theory – should be a natural one. I shall come back to questions relating to market infrastructure when discussing the other banking activities.

Capital market activity

The second set of products and services comes under the heading *capital market activity*. This field relates to the allocation of savings to the users of funds via marketable securities. It includes not only corporate finance services offered to firms which are in a position to tap capital markets, but also – in my view – that component of asset management which relates to managing asset portfolios, rather than to distributing the products and services to final investors.

Very highly specialised professional skills are required in both corporate finance and asset management activities, but not necessarily a very tightly woven distribution network. In this field, revenues are to a large extent earned in the form of fees and commissions, and quality competition is almost as strong as price competition. Finally, the activities in this category tend to be concentrated in a limited number of very large players. As a result of these features, the law of one price applies to a much more limited extent than in the case of the wholesale activity.

I shall focus on four aspects of capital market activity: *corporate finance services; asset management services; economies of scale;* and *market infrastructure*. However, it must be said that for the capital market activity the evidence is much more scattered than for the wholesale activity. With the sole exception of bond issuance, for which data are available, we can only rely on largely anecdotal and episodic evidence.

Corporate finance services

A frequently cited piece of evidence is that of the volume of euro-denominated bond issuance by private (i.e. non-governmental) entities, which has doubled during 1999. In addition, the spreads have narrowed significantly – demonstrating increased liquidity – and there has been a quick move on the part of the large and medium-sized European enterprises into the issuance of euro-denominated bonds as a regular source of finance. In doing so, firms can tap the savings of the whole euro area rather than only those of their original domestic market. In the first nine months of 1999 international issues targeted at non-domestic investors grew two and half times more than domestic issues, reflecting the fact that 'international bonds' can now be issued in the issuer's own currency – the euro. On the whole, data on both prices and flows show that the unification of the market has come about quickly.

It is more difficult to gather evidence in the field of *other corporate finance services*, which encompasses underwriting services, syndicated lending, structured finance for start-ups and the various advisory services relating to mergers and acquisitions and corporate restructuring. The relevant distinctions here are the degree of sophistication of the service in question and the size of the client. Insofar as these services are highly sophisticated and clients large, the euro area – if not global – market is already tending towards a high degree of integration.

Let me give a few examples. During the first half of 1999 the leading underwriters of bonds issued by European corporations were (according to 'Euromoney') the major European banks – often through their investment banking arm – together with the largest US investment banks. The 'league' in which these players compete is clearly not a domestic one. Similarly, the leading arrangers of international syndicated loans by European corporations include all the largest European banks together with major US institutions. Price differentials are widening, but this is a result of an apparently enhanced pricing of risk and not of remaining segmentation. Riskier operations, relating to takeover bids (Olivetti–Telecom Italia, Vodaphone–Mannesmann, Repsol–YPF and TotalFina–Elf Aquitaine, to quote the largest examples) entailed large fees, especially commitment fees, but the differentials in lending to very large corporations remain very thin.

Advisory services for mergers and acquisitions have developed fairly rapidly in the wake of the euro's introduction. Here, a large share of the market is held by US investment banks. In the field of provision of services to large corporations, it is very difficult to think of market segmentation: domestic banks cannot impose higher fees upon domestic corporations than their foreign competitors.

Asset management services

We can view asset management services as a complex set of activities which involves the actual business of managing the assets, the trading activity, and the distribution of services to individual savers or investors. Of these three activities, the first and the second, the actual management of assets and the trading activity, can be seen as part of what I am considering here under the heading of capital market activity. These two functions tend to be concentrated and subject to international diversification, as there are important economies of scale and benefits from spreading risks. Just to give a figure on the speed of change towards international diversification of the investment portfolios of final savers: from 1997 to 1999 the share of domestic stocks in European equity mutual funds fell from 49% to 33% (according to the statistics collected by the FEFSI). This shows how fast the process of moving away from purely domestic investments has been.

Economies of scale

Both in investment banking and asset management, economies of scale are extremely relevant, but could not be fully exploited before the euro owing to the segmentation of currencies. The advent of the euro has indeed triggered a significant movement towards consolidation within the banking industry. I will return to this issue later, but for now let me point out that more than twenty of the largest forty banks in the euro area have been involved in significant mergers in the period from 1998 to 2000. These mergers ensued only to a very limited extent on a cross-border basis, but they were largely triggered by developments in markets which are no longer domestic in any meaningful sense. In particular, the existence of large economies of scale in the capital market activities and the possibility to exploit these economies in a wider market have to be seen as major elements driving the recent wave of mergers.

The economies of scale are a result of many factors. In the euro area asset allocation is increasingly taking place on an industry rather than a country basis. Analysts are thus required to process industry-wide information, which means monitoring a large number of European companies. In addition, the provision of underwriting and other investment banking services to large players also requires a large scale on the part of banks. Finally, there are also benefits of size associated with selling financial products to large institutional investors.

Market infrastructure

While the payment infrastructure has been unified swiftly, the market infrastructure is still very segmented. The secured markets are, in a way, at the intersection of the payment capital and the market infrastructure, since the securities used as collateral need to be cleared and settled. Undoubtedly, a very significant consolidation of the infrastructure would, in principle, be called for. In practice, however, there appear to be relevant obstacles, and for the time being the number of genuinely successful moves towards consolidation have been limited relative to the number of announcements and the tension which has resulted. The main obstacles lie in ownership and managerial structures, technical impediments, legal or regulatory discrepancies, and what I would call national ambitions: namely, the desire to preserve a role for a country or a city as a domestically or internationally important financial centre.

As for the process of consolidation and integration, we have some systems moving on a fast, and some on a slow track. On the fast track, we find the derivatives markets (Eurex), the new equity markets (EURO.NM) and the government bond markets (Euro MTS). On the slow track, we find the traditional stock exchange markets. In my view it is not yet entirely clear what ultimate form this process of consolidation will take. The process is strongly promoted by the existence of the single currency and potential economies of scale, but somewhat impeded by the obstacles enforcing segmentation. One possibility of course – in my view a very theoretical one – is to have a single centre. A more likely possibility would be the achievement of a single network of a limited number of centres. This solution would make it possible to exploit the emerging opportunities as the importance of location gradually fades away.

Retail activity

The third set of products and services can be grouped under the heading *retail activity*. If one identifies activities in terms of the counterparty of banks, the predominant counterparty in the wholesale activity is another bank and in the capital market activity the corporate sector, or the issuers of securities, as I have mentioned. In retail activity, the counterparties are mainly households or small firms.

In the retail area *proximity to customers* counts most. Proximity is important precisely because these counterparties are scattered and have little mobility. Retail banking is perceived as the traditional business of banks, which the greater part of the public would identify as banking. A further characteristic of retail banking is high costs, especially staff costs. It is also the field in which the possibilities for exploiting contact with the customer for the provision of many other – not necessarily banking – services (such as, for instance, insurance services) seem greatest. This may explain why the consolidation process within the financial industry, when it has involved not only banks, has very often focused on retail services.

Here again, a number of detailed aspects are worth considering. Allow me to make some comments on the following: *loans and deposit-taking; other investment services to retail users; payment services;* and, once again, *infrastructure and technology.*

Loans and deposit-taking

In the case of loans and deposit-taking, all indicators point to the fact that proximity is indeed a fairly decisive factor. In the euro area, banks work with domestic customers in the case of more than 91% of their loans and close to 90% of their deposit base, according to the statistics collected by the ECB. Price discrepancies have diminished basically on account of macroeconomic factors, namely the convergence of interest rates, but those generated by microeconomic factors have persisted. In September 1997 lending rates to households in Italy and Portugal were higher than 10%, while they were below 6% in Belgium and Finland, according to the statistics collected by the ECB. Two years later, the highest cross-country difference within the euro area is slightly greater than 2 percentage points. Since we do not have risk-adjusted figures, it is very difficult to interpret this evidence.

High differentials in interest rates can be seen *within* euro area countries too. The range of lending and deposit rates in the German banking system, and the comparison of average country-wide figures with the rates prevailing in some German Länder, show that differences within countries are not very different from those between countries of the euro area. In Italy the dichotomy, in terms of interest rates, between the northern regions and the 'Mezzogiorno' is even more striking.

What is interesting, however, is that exactly the same phenomenon of market localisation can be seen in the United States. According to a survey conducted by the Federal Reserve, more than 90% of banks' clientele is located within a distance of less than twenty miles of the banks' premises. Proximity is thus an intrinsic characteristic of the retail market with or without the emergence of a currency embracing a wider area.

Other investment services to retail users

The same conclusion in respect of the importance of proximity may be drawn for other investment services to retail users, such as individual portfolio management, securities dealing and treasury management for small firms, etc. These products are quite closely related to ordinary bank deposits in terms of distribution, while usually requiring more customer advice.

Retail payment services

In the case of payment services we would have a single market if the cost and speed of payments were the same irrespective of whether the payment is cross-border or domestic. These conditions are not in place. The inquiries made by the European Commission and the Eurosystem indicate how great the differences in the service charges and quality of service are. Here, the product is of course quite standardised, meaning that the lack of compliance with the law of one price is very significant.

A study prepared by the Eurosystem in the spring of 1999 indicates that the fees charged to customers vary from EUR 3.5 to EUR 26 for small amounts, while they can reach from EUR 31 to EUR 400 for higher amounts. Some banks even have extra charges over and above these. A recent survey conducted by the European Commission in April 2000 showed that retail customers in the euro area countries are, on average, being charged a fee of EUR 17.10 for transferring EUR 100 between Member States. If these figures are compared with the results of the Commission studies undertaken in 1993 and 1994 (which indicated that the average transfer cost was EUR 24 for a transfer of EUR 100), it can be seen that the costs have come down, but not to a satisfactory level. The Commission also found that in 1993–94 the time needed to effect a cross-border credit transfer was 4.8 days on the average, but with substantial differences between countries. Furthermore, over 15% of the transactions took more than a week. In the survey of April 2000, the average duration was down to 3.4 days, with around 5% of the transfers taking more than a week. As the service provided in the case of cross-border payments is still poorer than that for domestic transfers, the higher price is not justified by better quality; in fact, in this area worse quality is combined with a significantly higher price, which makes these data all the more striking.

Retail infrastructure and technology

Technological developments are certainly a very important factor of change, which may profoundly alter current techniques for distributing financial services. A big question mark remains over the extent to which the advent and the spread of the use of new communication technology will remove and diminish the importance of the proximity factor in the case of retail services. However, if one imagines a society in which everyone is familiar with the Internet, it is hard to see any reason why one should continue to walk to the bank and, therefore, be sensitive to the proximity factor, when it is possible to communicate by other means. Anecdotal evidence from the United States shows that, for standardised products (e.g. the distribution of mutual funds), the diffusion of new distribution channels may affect the scope of local segmentation more than in the lending business.

The ownership structure

Turning now to the *ownership structure*, I maintain that an approach focusing on cross-border mergers as the key indicator of integration is a mistaken one. True, the economies of scale may be significant, and it is possible to exploit them to a larger extent in a single currency area; therefore, one should indeed recognise the existence of a concentration process, as is actually the case. However, should we consider the concentration process to be an indicator of the emergence of a single industry only to the extent to which it takes place across borders? The answer is, in my opinion, no.

Here again, we have useful examples from the United States. The removal of barriers to intra-state and interstate banking is a relatively recent development in that country; it is, incidentally, interesting that in Europe the single market for banking services was created not much later than in the United States. The result of liberalisation in the United States was that many banks did initially enter into mergers and acquisitions within states, but very few did so across states, usually with other banks in the vicinity, that is, in the neighbouring states. Only at a later stage did nation-wide operations become somewhat more frequent. This is to a large extent similar to what is happening in Europe today, with a large number of intra-state mergers and very few interstate cross-border mergers between banks in close proximity to one another (e.g. the Scandinavian and Benelux banks).

Let me say, however, that the analogy with the United States should not encourage too much optimism, as the impediments which still exist in Europe are much greater than those which exist in the United States. First, there are the very important linguistic factors, which I still see as the most significant. In addition, there are the attitudes of the public authorities, which may tend to consider intra-state mergers more favourably than cross-border mergers. There are also relevant differences in legislation. For instance, we do not yet have a Directive on takeover bids, nor legislation defining the statute of an EU company, as distinct from nationally-based undertakings. Thus, mergers across borders and mergers within borders are still two very different things.

Conclusion

Even though I have tried to exploit the available evidence I am aware that what has been said so far leaves the impression that we are dealing with a relevant, but unsettled issue. The subject will remain with us for several years and my intention was just to make a start on this issue and to give you some preliminary thoughts. In fact, I was unable to find any reliable attempt to deal with the subject in a comprehensive fashion; and I still have the impression that the present debate cannot, for the moment, rely on a sound and consistent set of information. Furthermore, the methodology for dealing with this issue will certainly have to be improved as we go along.

It is nonetheless possible – I think – to draw some conclusions even at this stage. First, in wholesale and capital market activities, the signs of the emergence of a single Euroland banking industry are rather strong, especially if we consider that only one and a half years have elapsed since the launch of the euro. In the case of retail activities and ownership structures, cross-border operations are largely lacking, but we should not expect the signs thereof to materialise very soon. After all, the two aspects – localised retail banking, which is the most visible area of banking for the public, and the lack of cross-border mergers – are present even in mature monetary and banking systems, such as the US system. We will probably continue, for some time to come, to observe these features in Euroland too.

Technology and infrastructure present a diversified picture and this is the area in which – in my view – the existing obstacles are least justified. Cost savings could be achieved through consolidation, and the competitiveness of the Euroland banking industry – *vis-à-vis*, say, the US banking industry – could be enhanced. On these issues there is an important role for policy to be played, including the competence of the European Commission in the field of competition. Furthermore, there are other fields in which public policies may help to foster the integration of the Euroland banking system. The focus of this Lecture was not, however, on policy issues, but rather on market developments.

Notes

1 I wish to acknowledge the assistance of Muriel Bouchet, Andrea Enria and Jukka Vesala in the preparation of this Lecture.
2 'It was already evident that he would be one of the most talented minds of his generation.'
3 'Marjolin had acquired a great freedom of thought during the war. He had learned that intelligence without action is not satisfactory.'

6 Fiscal discipline and exchange rate regimes

A case for currency boards?*[1]

Enrique Alberola-Ila and Luis Molina Sanchez

1. Introduction

Empirical evidence shows that fixed exchange rates do not provide more fiscal discipline than flexible regimes, despite the fact that, in principle, fixing the exchange rate imposes important restrictions on seignoriage revenues. A more detailed analysis of seignoriage allows to explain the channels whereby monetary financing is possible in the short and medium run even in an exchange rate peg. More precisely, it is argued that the traditional concept of monetary seignoriage is misguiding and that fiscal seignoriage, defined as the actual revenues accruing to government from the Central Bank, is a key variable to determine fiscal discipline. The paper shows that a peculiar version of fixed regimes, the currency boards, may effectively restrain fiscal policy by ruling out fiscal seignoriage. An indirect confirmation of these hypotheses is advanced by observing the empirical link between monetary seignoriage and fiscal seignoriage, and their relation with fiscal discipline.

During the nineties, the process of economic reform has gathered pace in Latin America, while a group of Eastern European countries has gone through a complete transformation to become market economies. The worldwide upsurge in the magnitude, scope and speed of financial movements has eased the implementation of the reform processes by providing the much needed inflows of capital, but, at the same time it has increased their vulnerability. Under these circumstances, macroeconomic stability has become the cornerstone for successful reform programs: in a context of financial globalization, countries which have been perceived by markets to have weak fundamentals, particularly in terms of inflation, public finance and/or current account, have suffered from swift reversals in the inflows of capital, which have put at stake the process of reform. While contagion or domino effects have also damaged countries with sound macroeconomic fundamentals, it is also true that their strains have been only transitory and that after some period of difficulty they have improved their position on a more solid basis.

* Paper presented at 22nd SUERF Colloquium, Vienna, 27–29 April 2000.

The quest for macroeconomic stability has traditionally had in the choice of exchange rate regime one of its central elements. Many countries have based their programs of economic stabilization on regimes of rigid or semi-rigid exchange rates. The rationale for this strategy is the following: Inflation is perceived as a structural problem, and fixing credibly the exchange rate allows them to tie down inflation expectations; this induces a more disciplined behavior in economic agents, facilitating overall economic reform. Price stabilization also contributes to discipline public accounts: in emerging market economies fiscal systems and, thus, the ability to obtain revenue are weak; as a consequence, the financing of the deficits is partially done through money creation by the Central Bank (seignoriage revenues). The fall in inflation should drastically reduce seignoriage revenues, promoting fiscal reform and fiscal discipline.

Nevertheless, the empirical evidence is at odds with this theoretical prior. In Figure 6.1 we observe that fixed exchange rate regimes have only attained a limited macroeconomic stability in emerging markets, compared to countries with flexible exchange rate regimes:[2] inflation performance is better but fiscal discipline does not improve: the total deficit is about the same, and the primary deficit (net of interest payments) is slightly higher. The weakness of the fiscal systems and the inability to finance them in an orthodox way tend to fuel inflation through monetization of deficits even when they are low, leading to the collapse of the peg in fixed regimes.

During the last years, in the above-mentioned context of economic globalization, the failure of some fixed regimes to provide sound macroeconomic basis to the economy has generated deep financial and economic crisis. The cases of Mexico and Brazil have made it clear that pegging the exchange rate is a risky strategy; as a consequence, fixed regimes as a way to promote economic discipline have fallen out of favour.

In contrast, a special type of exchange rate arrangement, the currency board, has shown its strength in this context of financial turmoil. At first sight, a currency board might just be considered a hardened version of a fixed regime, in which the exchange rate is predetermined by law and the growth in the monetary base is backed by foreign reserves. The aim of this article is to show that currency boards are intrinsically different from standard fixed exchange rate regimes because they deter monetary authorities from financing fiscal deficits. Moreover, we argue that this fiscal constraint is one of the main reasons for its current success to the extent that they can effectively deliver fiscal discipline.

The structure of the paper is as follows. In Section 2, we briefly develop the traditional view which links fiscal discipline to the process of money creation. In Section 3, it is shown how fixed exchange rates should be expected to generate fiscal discipline by reducing inflation and seignoriage, and empirically test this hypothesis. Section 4 develops the idea which is central to our discussion, namely, that the conventional concept of seignoriage is a bad indicator for fiscal discipline, and that a more restrictive concept, which we

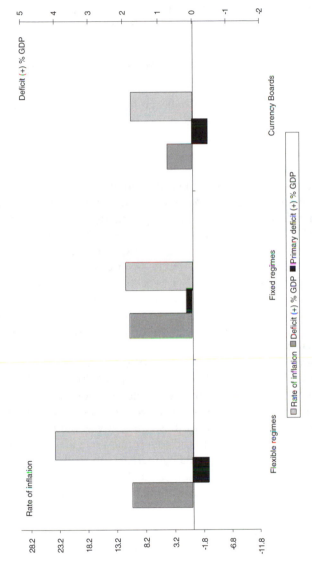

Figure 6.1 Economic performance of emerging market economies.

Note: Sample median for each variable. Exchange rate regimes are defined according to IMF 'strict' definition, that is, considering fixed exchange rate regimes as those labeled as 'pegged to a single currency' or 'pegged to a composite of currencies'.

denote as fiscal seignoriage, is more relevant to assess the disciplinary effects of the exchange rate regimes. In Section 5, we study how currency boards differ from standard fixed regimes in that they suppress fiscal seignoriage, by severely and effectively constraining the ability of the monetary authorities to finance public deficits. For this reason, they are expected to impose a much tighter constraint on fiscal policy and to induce a higher degree of fiscal discipline. Section 6 concludes.

2. Seignoriage as a source of deficit financing

The traditional approach to deficit monetization focuses on the following government budget constraint, which reflects the identity between the fiscal financing needs and sources, expressed in real terms:

$$d + (i - \pi)b = \dot{b} + \dot{m} \tag{1}$$

Financial requirements are given by the total deficit, which is the sum of the primary deficit (d) and the cost of the stock of debt in the hands of the private sector (b), measured by the real interest payments. The real interest rate is the difference between the nominal interest rate and inflation ($i-\pi$). The government can finance this deficit through two sources: in an orthodox way, by issuing debt in the capital markets, that is, by increasing the stock of debt in the hands of the private sector ($\dot{b}$),[3] or by asking the Central Bank to buy her debt and pay it with money created for this purpose. The revenue collected from this operation is known as seignoriage, which is commonly computed as the real increase in the monetary base, that is, the sum of banknotes and bank reserves ($\dot{m}$).

Industrialized countries usually follow an orthodox financing of the public expenditure, through taxes and, when deficits appear, through debt. On the contrary, emerging economies usually lack developed tax systems and capital markets. Under these circumstances, seignoriage becomes a relevant source of revenue: in principle, monetary authorities can increase the monetary base and transfer the resulting revenues to the government in a discretionary way; the excess real balances will be adjusted by increases in the level price.

Indeed, revenues from seignoriage have typically been considered as a special form of taxation. To see this, note that the increase in the monetary base can be decomposed into two components:

$$\dot{m} = \left[\frac{\dot{M}}{P} \right] = \frac{\Delta M}{M} \cdot \frac{M}{P} = \lambda m \tag{2}$$

where P is the price level and higher case letters refer to nominal variables. The first component is the rate of growth in the nominal monetary base (λ) and the second is the monetary base in real terms. In this expression, m is the tax base and λ is the tax rate.

Let us then consider the simplest form of money demand:

$$\theta \, \frac{M}{P} = k Y \tag{3}$$

in which real balances depend on the income level and k is a constant parameter. Note that the real money supply is the monetary base times the money multiplier (θ). Differentiating this expression, we obtain

$$\lambda = \pi + \frac{k}{\theta} \, \dot{y} \tag{4}$$

The rate of growth in income is usually of low order and the money multiplier usually takes values higher than unity. Thus, when inflation is moderate or high, the first term in the expression dominates and λ is expected to be closely associated with the inflation rate. Therefore, seignoriage is traditionally considered as an inflation tax.[4]

Seignoriage and inflation may thus play a central role in financing expenditures. Fischer (1982) computes seignoriage for developing countries and shows that it accounts in some cases for more than 20 percent of total revenues. Edwards and Tabellini (1991) observe that for Latin American countries the seignoriage in terms of GDP sometimes reached dramatic magnitudes. For the largest countries, it was around 20 percent in Argentina between 1973 and 1987, 8.24 percent Brazil (1983–87) and 4 percent in Mexico (1978–83). In our sample, the median of seignoriage is higher than 1.5 percent of GDP.

In this context, Sargent and Wallace (1981) suggested that inflation is a fiscal, rather than a monetary phenomenon because monetary policy is dominated by the financing needs of the government. Although this is probably a too radical view of the inflationary process, it well reflects the importance that fiscal aspects may have to explain inflation under certain circumstances.

An implicit assumption in these arguments is that the monetary base is discretionally managed by the Central Bank; or, in other words, that monetary seignoriage is supply driven. This assumption is, however, rather strong because the Central Bank is far from having a complete control on the base money. The monetary base consists of banknotes and commercial bank reserves. As our demand of money suggests real incomes is a central determinant of the monetary base, in particular, of banknotes. Compulsory bank reserves are determined by reserve regulations, while non-compulsory reserves depend on the nature and efficiency of the payment system, and usually display low interest elasticity. Therefore, the central bank may have difficulties in controlling the base money demand outside the compulsory reserves. Moreover, attempts to increase the monetary base beyond the desired holdings of banknotes and reserves may not be successful unless the Central

Bank is ready to accept the interest rate adjustments necessary for the private sector to increase the base money and make use of the expanded liquidity.

3. Exchange rate regimes and fiscal discipline

3(a) Fixed regimes as disciplinary devices

A credible fix of the nominal exchange rate (e) will anchor monetary policy to the reference currency and, admitting that some form of Purchasing Power Parity is expected to hold, it will also stabilize inflationary expectations and reduce the ability to collect seignoriage.

This is evident if we replicate expression (3) for the foreign country (denoted by an asterisk) assuming for simplicity that the parameters take the same value, and compare the values of λ and λ^*:

$$\lambda = \lambda^* + (\pi - \pi^*) + \frac{k}{\theta} \, (\dot{y} - \dot{y}^*) \tag{5}$$

The PPP theory, in terms of expectations, states that the expected depreciation of the exchange rate equals the inflation differences, $\dot{e}^e \approx \pi - \pi^*$. Therefore, if the exchange rate is credibly fixed, $\dot{e}^e = O$, and the seignoriage revenues of the anchor country are low, as expected, only a higher economic growth than the anchor country would provide higher seignoriage revenues.

Therefore, a fixed exchange rate does not only reduce inflation but it should also constrain seignoriage relative to a flexible regime, thus inducing more fiscal discipline. In principle then, fixing the exchange rate provides an attractive way to macroeconomic stabilization.

3(b) Data and econometric considerations

Before dealing with the empirical evidence of exchange rate regimes on fiscal seignoriage, it is important to make several considerations regarding the database and the variables and techniques to use, which will also be relevant for the rest of the analysis.

The first regards the choice of the sample. We take observations of twenty-four emerging and transition countries, of which fifteen belong to Latin America and nine are European states in transition. The sample for the former runs from 1972 to 1998, and for the latter it starts, in the majority of cases, in 1990. From this wide sample we have excluded the observations corresponding to currency boards schemes (seventeen additional observations), which will only be considered in the last section, and inflation and seignoriage outliers, leaving a sample of 373 observations. Countries must then be labeled according to their regime, which is not a straightforward task. As explained with more detail in the Annex, the International Monetary Fund (IMF) adopts a 'strict' definition which leaves out important stabilization efforts through semi-fixed exchange rate regimes, such as crawling pegs. Therefore, we consider two alternative samples: the IMF sample and a modified sample, in which, by examining more closely the nature of the exchange rate regimes, we expand the proportion of fixed exchange regimes from 49 percent to 60 percent. In estimation the different regimes are defined by a dummy variable which takes the value of one for fixed regimes and zero for the flexible cases; obviously, the distribution of the dummy will change depending on the sample it uses.

Secondly, focusing on the link between regimes and deficits, we have to consider which concept of deficit reflects more adequately fiscal discipline: overall deficits or primary deficits, v.g. deficits net of interest payments (d in expression (1)). It can be argued that the concept of deficit on which the fiscal authorities have some discretion is the primary deficit; furthermore, the bulk of interest payments may not be independent of the regime, since inflation is relevant to determine the real cost of debt (see note 4). Finally, very high inflations such as those eventually observed in our sample may completely distort the figures on interest payments, and therefore the magnitude of overall deficits. However, in all the contributions to this literature the results have always been presented either in terms of the overall deficits or both.[5] Thus, although the analysis of the primary deficit provides a better assessment of fiscal discipline, we will present the results for overall and primary deficits.

Another set of considerations is of econometric nature. The database allows the use of panel techniques in the analysis. In panel data estimation, individual effects are customarily included, but we consider that in some of our regressions this is inadequate. In particular, when regressing the variables against the regime dummies the results of the regression would be distorted; since introducing individual effects implies the subtraction of the cross-country averages from the variables in the regression, this would imply that what is regressed is the (cross-country) deviation of the dependent variable on the (deviation of) the regime dummy, therefore distorting the relevant relation to explore which is the *level* of deficit on the exchange rate regime.[6] In the rest of the cases (relation between deficits and seignoriage), we test on individual effects and introduce them when they turn out to be significant. Another problem which may arise in the data is heteroskedasticity, which leads to an important loss of efficiency in estimation, although the estimates are still unbiased and consistent. Since we are interested in the significance of the parameters rather than in their value, it is important to correct the estimations for heteroskedasticity. This is done by testing and in its case controlling for cross-country variances.

Finally, we must acknowledge the effect of economic activity on the deficit, which is expected to be countercyclical. Economic expansions have two consequences for public finances: first, the higher tax and tariff revenues associated with the expansion reduce the fiscal deficit; the second effect is evident from (4): expansion leads to a higher demand and an increase in seignoriage. However, the special characteristics in expenditure and revenue flows make the effect of the activity on the budget unclear. In particular, Gavin and Perotti (1997) show that under certain circumstances the deficit is procyclical. In any case, in the regressions below we control, when required, for the effect of the cycle, defined as deviations of growth from the sample average in each country.

3(c) Empirical evidence

Figure 6.1 in the introduction showed in a broad way that fixed regimes reduce inflation but they fail to improve the fiscal performance. In this section we formally explore the effect of fixed exchange rate regimes on fiscal discipline, which is proxied by the ratio of fiscal deficits to GDP, by using a large sample of data and panel regression techniques.

The effect of the fixed regime on the fiscal balance appears in Table 6.1. We have regressed the two measures of the deficit (as a proportion of GDP) against the regime dummy in both samples, and we have controlled by the lagged value of the deficit and the cyclical position of the economy and corrected for cross-sectional heteroskedasticity.[7] The value of the dummy is not significantly different from zero, regardless of the chosen fixed regime sample; in other words, fixing the exchange rate has no significant effect, neither on the overall nor on the primary deficit. For the IMF sample the sign is even positive, suggesting that the fixed regimes would be associated, albeit non-significantly, with higher deficits. Also note that the effect of the cycle on the overall deficit, which appears in the last row is negative and significant, implying that deficits are significantly countercyclical; this result is contrary to the results of Gavin and Perotti (1997).

Table 6.1 Fiscal deficits and the exchange rate regime

Sample	Overall deficit	Primary deficit
IMF		
Fixed regimes	0.04 (**)	0.26 (**)
(t ratio)	(0.20)	(1.14)
IMF modified (a)		
Fixed regimes	–0.07 (**)	–0.01 (**)
(t ratio)	(–0.39)	(–0.02)
Real business cycle (b)	(–)	(0)

Note: Estimation via weighted least squares, heteroskedaticity corrected by cross-sectional variance. An asterisk indicates that the variable is not significant at 90 percent level, and two asterisks mean that the variable is not significant at 95 percent level.

(a) Exchange rate regime is defined according to IMF 'strict' definition adding some episodes of exchange rate based stabilizations through not strictly fixed exchange rates.

(b) We show in brackets the sign of the effect of the real business cycle on the variables. A zero is shown when this effect is statistically not significant.

All in all, the effect of the fixed regime on fiscal discipline challenges the conventional wisdom: fixing the exchange rate *does not* generate disciplinary effects on fiscal policy.

3(d) Explanations

There have been some efforts in the literature to explain this apparent paradox. Although we will follow a different approach it is convenient to be familiar with them.

The first is based on the effects of exchange rate pegs on economic activity. The exchange-rate-based stabilization schemes (hereafter, ERBS) usually bring about rapid disinflation (due to the anchoring of external prices) and an economic expansion. Economic evidence is quite robust (see Kiguel and Leviatan, 1992; and references in Calvo and Vegh, 1998) and this result is confirmed in our sample, in which a regression of growth on the regime yields a highly significant positive sign.[8]

From a theoretical perspective, this initial expansion can be explained by inflationary inertia in the service sectors, which, in the aggregate, push down real interest rates (Rodríguez, 1982); or by the imperfect credibility of the new regime which incentives present relative to future consumption, inducing a consumption boom in the initial stages of the peg (Vegh, 1992). In both cases, the expansion is coupled with a growing current account deficit and the appreciation of the real exchange rate. In the medium run, demand exhausts its expansionary impulse and leads to recession and, most times, to the collapse of the fixed regime. This is the characteristic boom–bust cycle of ERBS.

Given the higher fiscal and monetary revenues accruing to the government in the expansionary phase, the government budget constraint is relaxed and this has perverse effects on fiscal discipline. From here, it follows that the end of the expansion is usually accompanied by a strong deterioration of the fiscal stance, which contributes to the abandonment of the peg, as Kaminsky et al. (1997) show. Moreover, regressing interest payments on the regime dummy indicates that fixing the exchange rate is associated with a lower cost of debt.[9] This may be due either to lower debt levels at the times of fixed regimes or, more probably, to a lower cost in debt financing. Both factors indicate that fixing the exchange rate eases the financial budget constraint of fiscal authorities which can borrow more freely and cheaply in international capital markets.

The second contribution, by Tornell and Velasco (1998) has a more analytical flavour and it is focused on the policy incentives induced by the peg, relative to other stabilization programs based on flexible exchange rates. It is evident that ERBS has very appealing macroeconomic implications in the short run for the policymaker, in terms of inflation, activity and public accounts. On the contrary, in monetary-based stabilizations (i.e. with flexible rates) the short-run trade-off is less attractive, since the decline in inflation is slow and activity initially recedes. As a consequence, exchange-rate-based stabilizations induce less fiscal discipline than monetary stabilization, since fiscal indiscipline does not have short-run inflationary effects in the first case. In contrast, fiscal profligacy within a flexible rate regime has immediate effects on inflation, and this exerts a deterrent effect on fiscal authorities.

4. Monetary versus fiscal seignoriage

The contributions outlined above provide valid arguments to explain the failure of fixed regimes in capping fiscal deficits, while they recognize their positive effects on inflation. Returning to our previous model, this suggests that monetary seignoriage is constrained under fixed regimes. Since the regression results show that even after controlling for the position in the cycle, that is, after taking into account the positive effects of the expansion, fixed regimes do not reduce the deficits, it is not obvious then how these deficits are financed by the government. One possibility is debt which, as suggested above, is easier to allocate in fixed rate regimes. The other possibility is that monetary seignoriage, which is the central link between inflation and fiscal deficits, is an inadequate proxy to assess the financing of deficits through the process of money creation. We explore this second hypothesis.

4(a) Fiscal seignoriage

Klein and Neumann (1991) first pointed at the misguiding use of the concept of seignoriage in the context of public finances. Seignoriage, understood as the rate of growth in money creation, is identified with an inflation tax, which, in strict terms, represents the opportunity cost of holding money. However, this private cost of holding money does not match the benefit accruing to the fiscal authorities. On the one hand, inflation generates a deadweight loss from which nobody benefits; on the other hand, and more importantly, the revenues from money creation do not necessarily flow to the fiscal authorities. It is evident that in the context of fiscal analysis, seignoriage should refer to the revenues effectively accruing to governments from the process of money creation. Indeed, stressing the difference between the first concept, to which we will refer as monetary seignoriage, and the second, denoted as fiscal seignoriage, turns out to be crucial in what follows.

Let us consider the balance sheet for flows of the Central Bank, expressed in domestic currency:

Changes in CB Balance Sheet

Reserves ($e\dot{r}^* + \dot{e}r$)	Monetary base ($\dot{m}$)
Private credit ($\dot{c}$)	Other net liabilities
Public debt ($\dot{f}$)	

Let us now recall the process of deficit monetization, as traditionally described: public debt holdings by the Central Bank increase and simultaneously money is printed out increasing the monetary base, v.g. $\dot{f} = \dot{m}$. This process reveals that the financing needs of the government are satisfied by the Central Bank through an increase in the holdings of public debt, $\dot{f}$, and that this variable is usually approximated by the changes in the monetary base. However, in view of the Central Bank balance sheet this description is extremely problematic.

First, note that the holdings of public debt are assets to the Central Bank, and that it may even obtain interest income from them; on the contrary, the traditional view assumes that public debt holdings just 'sink' into the Central Bank accounts and, of course, they generate no yield to the monetary authority. This is equivalent to saying that the Central Bank and the government can consolidate their balances, since debt holdings (and its yields) would disappear from this consolidated balance.[10] This is probably too strong an assumption for industrialized countries, but it is more realistic for the countries in our data set, at least for the first part of the sample. Thus, either if we accept such an extreme view or if we just recognize the privileged financing of deficits by Central Banks, we consider that the increase in government debt holdings by the Central Bank, $\dot{f}$, is a good proxy for the financing needs of government provided by the monetary authorities.[11]

Second, and more importantly, note that the Central Bank can keep on transferring resources to the government even if the monetary base is kept constant through adjustments in its balance sheet. Note that by reducing the level of reserves and the credit to the private sectors, the Central Bank can increase its holdings of public debt. More precisely, the holdings of government debt can be accommodated by changes in any other component in the Central Bank balance sheet, not just by increases in the monetary base:

$$\dot{f} = \dot{m} - (\dot{c} + \dot{e}r + e\dot{r}) \tag{6}$$

We will thus denote the increase in public debt holdings by the Central Bank, $\dot{f}$, as *fiscal seignoriage,* the actual revenues accruing to the government from the Central Bank to finance public deficit, in order to distinguish it from monetary seignoriage, $\dot{m}$, which just refers to the increase in the monetary base.

This distinction affects the budget constraint identity since the actual financing of the deficit by the monetary authorities is given by the fiscal seignoriage instead of the monetary seignoriage:

$$d + (i - \pi)b = \dot{b} + \dot{f} \tag{1'}$$

and therefore fiscal seignoriage is the relevant variable to analyze how government deficits are financed by the monetary authorities and how exchange regimes affect the ability to finance public deficits.

4(b) Empirical evidence

The discrepancy between fiscal and monetary seignoriage could a priori explain the protracted ability of fixed regimes to finance fiscal deficits, and therefore the lack of effects of fixing the exchange rates on fiscal discipline. To prove this hypothesis empirically we proceed in two steps: first, we test the link between deficits and the two alternative concepts of seignoriage and then how the exchange rate regime affects monetary and fiscal seignoriage.

The previous decomposition suggests that the relevant variable to explain how deficits are financed is the fiscal seignoriage and not the monetary seignoriage. Table 6.2 explores this hypothesis by regressing the fiscal deficit (overall and primary) on monetary and fiscal seignoriage, respectively, as a proportion of GDP. In all the cases, a lag of the dependent variable is included and the effects of the cycle are controlled for, when required. The results endorse our hypothesis: monetary seignoriage cannot explain fiscal deficits in any of the specifications, and the sign is even negative, albeit non-significant (implying that higher monetary seignoriage is, if anything, associated with lower deficits, which is contrary to the conventional hypothesis). On the contrary, fiscal seignoriage is significantly and positively correlated with fiscal deficits, both overall and, more clearly, primary deficits.[12]

Table 6.2 Fiscal deficits and seignoriages

Seignoriage	Overall deficit	Primary deficit
Monetary seignoriage	−0.02 (**)	−0.07 (**)
(t ratio)	(−0.63)	(−1.53)
Fiscal seignoriage	0.05 (*)	0.07 (**)
(t ratio)	(1.75)	(2.03)
Real business cycle (a)	(−)	(0)

Note: Estimation via weighted least squares, heteroskedaticity corrected by cross-sectional variance. An asterisk indicates that the variable is not significant at 90 percent level, and two asterisks mean that the variable is not significant at 95 percent level.
(a) We show in brackets the sign of the effect of the real business cycle on the variables. A zero is shown when this effect is statistically not significant.

Second, we consider the effects of fixing the exchange rate on fiscal and monetary seignoriage, with the corresponding lags and controls. Fixing the exchange rate should reduce monetary seignoriage through disinflation, but not necessarily fiscal seignoriage, which can be accommodated in the short and medium run by the Central Bank. Table 6.3 presents the results: the negative sign of the fixed regime dummy and its robust significance in every case confirms that fixed regimes reduce *monetary* seignoriage. On the contrary, the effects on fiscal seignoriage are non-significant, and the sign is even positive.

Table 6.3 Seignoriages and the exchange rate regime

Sample	Monetary seignoriage	Primary seignoriage
IMF		
Fixed regimes	−0.47	0.04 (**)
(t ratio)	(−2.55)	(0.16)
IMF modified (a)		
Fixed regimes	−0.65	−0.15 (**)
(t ratio)	(−3.57)	(0.60)
Real business cycle (b)	(0)	(−)

Note: Estimation via weighted least squares, heteroskedaticity corrected by cross-sectional variance. An asterisk indicates that the variable is not significant at 90 percent level, and two asterisks mean that the variable is not significant at 95 percent level.
(a) Exchange rate regime is defined according to IMF 'strict' definition adding some episodes of exchange rate based stabilizations through not strictly fixed exchange rates.
(b) We show in brackets the sign of the effect of the real business cycle on the variables. A zero is shown when this effect is statistically not significant.

These results suggest that the constraints imposed by the exchange rate regime on monetary seignoriage are overcome through adjustments in private credit and reserves in the balance sheet of the central bank. This allows to preserve fiscal seignoriage according to the financing needs of the fiscal authorities and regardless of the regime choice.

For our purposes, it is also interesting to consider the signs of the cycle effects. The effect is non-significant in the monetary seignoriage regression. On the contrary, the negative and significant sign of the cycle on fiscal seignoriage is more intriguing but we can advance the following interpretation: economic expansions reduce fiscal deficits and therefore the financing needs of governments. Since fiscal seignoriage can be discretionally managed, it is reasonable to think that it is lower in good times. This is an alternative route to stress that fiscal seignoriage is the relevant variable to study how deficits are financed.

The outcome of the statistical analysis can be summed up as follows: in Table 6.1 we have shown that, contrary to intuition, fixed exchange rate regimes have no effect whatsoever on fiscal deficits. This result can be explained by considering the distinction between monetary and fiscal seignoriage. Since fiscal deficits are financed by means of fiscal, not monetary seignoriage (Table 6.2) and fixed regimes tend to reduce monetary but not fiscal seignoriage (Table 6.3), it follows that pegging the exchange rate does not constrain deficit financing and therefore it will not provide fiscal discipline.

It could, then, be argued that for a fixed exchange regime to be sustainable, fiscal seignoriage should also be reduced. The reduction of foreign reserves and private credit to preserve fiscal seignoriage revenues can only be transitory because they are finite. But note that this is precisely the bottom line of first-generation models of speculative crises (Krugman, 1979): depletion of reserves eventually bring about the collapse of the regime. And this is what we actually observe in practice: fixed exchange rate regimes have been abandoned sooner or later in emerging countries amid speculative attacks which cannot be encountered.

From the approach followed in this analysis, it is clear that the key to fiscal discipline, and eventually also to exchange rate sustainability, is to design an exchange rate regime which effectively reduces fiscal seignoriage. Next, we show how the currency board regime may be up to this requirement.

5. The currency board as a disciplinary device

Around thirteen currency boards operate in the world when this paper is being written. Of these, only five can be considered as stabilization devices to stop deterioration of the macroeconomic environment. Argentina was the first big, relatively closed economy which adopted this scheme in 1991 when it was suffering hyperinflation, and it was followed by some European transition economies, like Estonia, Lithuania and Bulgaria and Bosnia.[13]

So far, none of these regimes has been abandoned. Although their experience is short, this is a remarkable record in a decade of big financial crises which have affected emerging countries and have led to the collapse of neighbour economies, like Russia, Mexico or Brazil. This positive outcome is probably related to the special characteristics of currency boards.

A currency board arrangement can be defined as

> a monetary regime based on an explicit legislative commitment to exchange domestic currency for a specific foreign currency at a fixed rate, combined with restrictions on the issuing authorities – the currency board – to ensure the fulfillment of its legal obligation. This structure implies that domestic currency be issued only against foreign exchange and that it remains fully backed by foreign assets.
>
> (IMF, 1997)

Therefore, the Currency Board replaces the Central Bank as issuing institution and the growth in the monetary base is determined by the evolution of foreign assets. This is the relevant feature of currency boards, because it implies that the authorities all but renounce the accommodation of the excess demand for liquidity. Moreover, currency boards are set by law, sometimes implying a constitutional amendment, like in Argentina. Thus, the explicit commitment for exchange rate management currency is higher than in standard fixed exchange regimes. Both factors tend to enhance the credibility of the currency board and they may contribute to explain its robustness. However, here we would like to stress the fiscal discipline aspects, which have been largely ignored in the analysis and which, in our view, are quite relevant to explain the success of currency board regimes.

By definition, in a currency board the increase in monetary base equals the increase in the value of foreign reserves:

$$\dot{m} = \dot{e}r + e\dot{r}$$

This implies that the credit to the private sector and, more remarkably, the claims to the government disappear from the Central Bank balance sheet. Thus, fiscal authorities cannot be financed by the monetary authority and fiscal seignoriage disappears. To be more precise, the only source of revenue for the government from the monetary institutions are the profits that the currency board may make, in particular, from the yields on foreign reserves.[14]

Returning to our previous discussion, the superiority of currency boards as disciplinary devices is now evident. Fiscal deficits are related to the ability to generate fiscal seignoriage, and the only exchange rate regime which rules out fiscal seignoriage is a currency board. Therefore, currency boards should discipline public finances.[15]

The adoption of currency boards has usually been implemented in a context of high macroeconomic instability, so that the persistence of previous instability may be evident in the first observations within the currency board regime. In spite of this, Figure 6.1 suggests that fiscal performance of currency boards is slightly better. Figure 6.2 displays with more detail the evolution of the main variables in the currency board regimes of Argentina, Estonia, Lithuania and Bulgaria, before and after the adoption of the arrangement. Some data are missing due to unavailability or to the short duration of the currency board. In any case, we observe that deficits tend to fall, sometimes with some lags, after the arrangement, even in Argentina, which went through a deep recession after the Mexican crisis. More remarkable is the comparison between monetary and fiscal seignoriage. Monetary seignoriage has been reduced due to inflation stabilization but it is still relatively large in some cases; on the contrary, fiscal seignoriage – as expected – has been drastically eliminated in contrast with the previous situation. Figure 6.3 summarizes this information of seignoriage after the adoption of the currency board and compares it with the performance of fixed and flexible regimes. While monetary seignoriage is similar in currency boards and fixed regimes, fiscal seignoriage is zero in currency boards.

For the sake of completeness, Table 6.4 presents the regression results of a currency board dummy on the relevant variables, comparing its performance with the rest of fixed exchange rate regimes (both IMF and modified-IMF samples). The dummy on both the overall and primary deficit is not significant, although it has the expected sign. On monetary and fiscal seignoriage, the currency board dummy is significant for all the cases. This more formal analysis can only be indicative due to the lack of observations (only seventeen) and the aforementioned inertia of fiscal variables at the initial

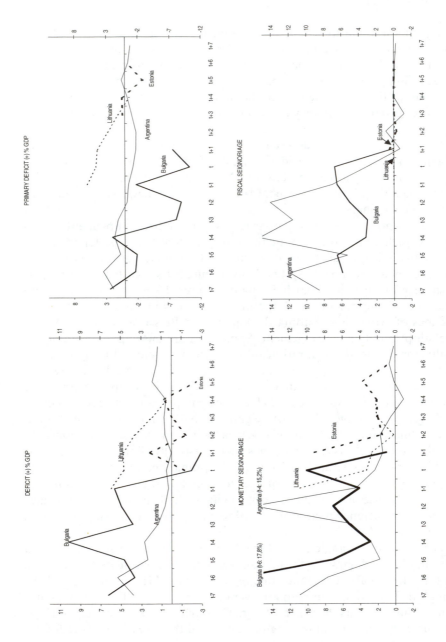

Figure 6.2 Economic performance of emerging market economies with currency board regimes.

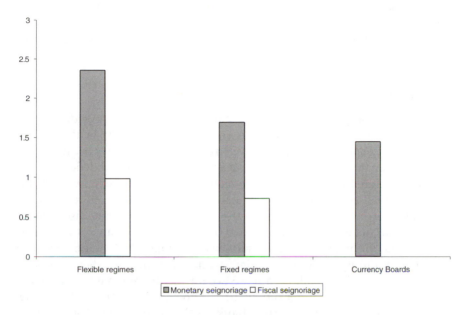

Figure 6.3 Economic performance of emerging market economies.

Note: Sample median for each variable. Exchange rate regimes are defined according to IMF 'strict' definition, that is, considering fixed exchange rate regimes as those labeled as 'pegged to a single currency' or 'pegged to a composite of currencies'.

Table 6.4 Fiscal variables and seignoriages in currency boards (CB) regimes

Sample	Overall deficit	Primary deficit	Monetary seignoriage	Fiscal seignoriage
IMF				
CB regimes	−0.39 (**)	−0.48 (**)	−0.82	−0.51
(t ratio)	(−1.06)	(−1.28)	(−2.63)	(−2.38)
IMF modified (a)				
CB regimes	−0.29	−0.33 (**)	−0.73	−0.56
(t ratio)	(−0.73)	(−0.80)	(−2.21)	(−2.74)
Real business cycle (b)	(−)	(0)	(+)	(0)

Note: Estimation via weighted least squares, heteroskedaticity corrected by cross-sectional variance. All regressions refer to a subsample including only fixed exchange rate regimes. An asterisk indicates that the variable is not significant at 95 percent level.
(a) Exchange rate regime is defined according to IMF 'strict' definition adding some episodes of exchange rate based stabilizations through not strictly fixed exchange rates.
(b) We show in brackets the sign of the effect of the real business cycle on the variables. A zero is shown when this effect is statistically not significant.

observations of the currency.[16] It is expected that the effects of the currency boards are only reflected in the medium run: given the short life of most currency boards this justifies the lack of empirical evidence arising from the statistical analysis.

6. Conclusions

This paper has analyzed the role of exchange rate regimes in providing fiscal discipline. The empirical analysis has shown that, despite their theoretical appeal, fixed regimes are unable to constrain fiscal authorities because they do not reduce the ability of the Central Bank to finance fiscal deficits.

The traditional view states that monetary seignoriage (the increase in the monetary base) allows the finance of fiscal deficit and that fixed regimes, by capping this source of revenue from the Central Bank generate fiscal discipline. This argument is refutable on two basis. On the one hand, it implicitly assumes that the management monetary base is completely discretional by the monetary authority in a flexible regime, while it depends on other structural factors; on the other hand, even if we accept the discretionality argument, monetary seignoriage turns out to be a bad indicator of the financing resources provided by the Central Bank to the government. The relevant variable has been shown to be fiscal seignoriage, that is, the revenues effectively accruing to the fiscal authorities from the Central Bank activity.

Thus, even if fixed regimes effectively constrain monetary seignoriage they have not limited fiscal seignoriage and therefore they have not induced fiscal discipline. Indeed, maintaining the flow of fiscal seignoriage in fixed regimes may require the depletion of foreign reserves. All in all, in a world of rapid shifts in capital flows, fixed regimes without strong macroeconomic discipline seem to be a perfect recipe for failure since they are taken as preferred targets for speculative attacks.

In this context, currency boards have become an attractive regime for stabilization. One reason is the perceived higher commitment to the peg, endorsed by legislation, that the currency board provides. The second reason, to which we have paid attention in this paper, is that they impose effective constraints on public finances by suppressing fiscal seignoriage and therefore they should act as strong disciplinary devices for fiscal policy. The fact that all the currency boards have survived the bouts of financial crises in recent years confirms the success of these arrangements.

Nevertheless, the choice of the exchange rate regime must be consistent with the economic, social and political circumstances to fulfill its goals. More precisely, the constraints on monetary and fiscal management imposed by currency boards require the very wide support of economic and social forces within the country. In this sense, currency boards can be identified with a deep institutional change, which transform the way economic policy operates. It is no wonder then that currency boards have been adopted either in countries anxious to avoid previous experiences with hyperinflation (like

Argentina) or with an overriding goal on which the whole population agrees, as it happens in East European countries with prospective EU adhesion. This important social consensus pushes ahead reforms and it is the actual basis for the sustainability of these regimes.

ANNEX: DATA SOURCES AND METHODOLOGIES

This section presents an overview of the data we have used in the empirical tests. We have selected twenty-four emerging and transition countries, of which fifteen are from Latin America, and the other nine are European transition countries.[17] The choice is made on the basis that for these countries the choice of exchange rate regime has played, and continues to play, a central position in policy strategies.

The data are taken from the IMF 'International Financial Statistics'. They include the official exchange rate, in units of local currency per US dollar (line ae), claims on governments of monetary authorities (line 12a, and, if they exist, lines 12b and 12c, which refer to local governments and public enterprises), reserve money (line 14), consumer prices (line 64), the government deficit or surplus (line 80), and nominal and real GDP (line 99). Data for interest payments on public debt from the IMF 'Government Finance Statistics' are used to construct series of primary deficit. In general, we have data from 1972 to 1998 for Latin American countries, and from 1990 to 1998 for European transition countries.

We define 'monetary seignoriage' as the annual change in reserve money scaled by nominal GDP, as in Fischer (1982), and 'fiscal seignoriage' as the annual change in monetary authorities' claims on government scaled by nominal GDP. It is immediately seen that these calculations are equivalent to the definitions appearing in the text. Consumer price indices are used to calculate the rate of inflation, and the cyclical position is computed as deviations from average growth. Finally, we have eliminated from the sample some data which could be considered as 'outliers' (see the main text). We have defined inflation outliers as those in the last decile of the sample, leaving observations whose inflation rate is less than 131 percent a year, and seignoriage outliers as those which fall beyond the 95th centile; this excludes observations whose monetary seignoriage is higher than 14 percent of GDP and whose fiscal seignoriage is higher than 18 percent of GDP. This leaves a maximum of 370 observations, although for some variables, most notably primary deficits, the availability of data is lower.

The more difficult issue we had to deal with was the definition of the exchange rate systems of each country in each year. Our main source of information had to be, in principle, IMF 'Exchange Rate Arrangements and Exchange Restrictions: Annual Report', in which the IMF classified exchange rate arrangements as 'pegged', 'limited flexibility' and 'more flexible arrangements'. So first of all we construct the 'IMF sample' of the main text taking fixed exchange rate regimes as those labeled as 'pegged' according to the IMF at the end of each year, as in Gavin and Perotti (1997).

But this definition poses many problems, as it does not include some ERBS instrumented via not strictly fixed exchange rates, like crawling pegs or crawling bands, which are labeled as 'more flexible arrangements' by the IMF. The IMF itself recognized this problem in a recent publication (IMF, 1999), and reclassified many countries' arrangements. Finally, the last available issue of IMF 'Exchange Rate Arrangements . . .', corresponding to 1999, labels the exchange rate regimes not as fixed or flexible like previously, but as currency boards, crawling pegs, target bands, etc., leaving the reader to decide which is a pegged exchange rate and which is not. One of the best examples of the possible inadequacy of IMF's previous definition is the Brazilian *Plano Real*, a 'genuine' ERBS dated in July 1994 which was instrumented within a crawling peg system from 1995, and which was labeled as 'managed floating' by the IMF.

Having this in mind, we have filtered the IMF sample and constructed an alternative to be used along with the former. We have added some episodes of semi-fixed exchange rate arrangements that countries implemented with a clear stabilization objective.[18] Finally, when a country changes its system we have changed its definition if the change occurs in the last six months of the year. In Table 6.A1 we show the differences between IMF stricter sample and our sample.

Table 6.A1 Differences between samples

Country	Date	IMF sample	Modified sample
Argentina	1979–1980	Flexible	Fixed (*Tablita*)
Argentina	1985–1986	Flexible	Fixed (*Plan Austral*)
Bolivia	1997–1998	Flexible	Fixed
Brazil	1986	Flexible	Fixed (*Cruzado*)
Brazil	1994–1998	Flexible	Fixed (*Plano Real*)
Chile	1978	Flexible	Fixed
Chile	1985–1997	Flexible	Fixed
Colombia	1992–1998	Flexible	Fixed
Ecuador	1995–1998	Flexible	Fixed
Honduras	1997–1998	Flexible	Fixed
Mexico	1988–1994	Flexible	Fixed
Uruguay	1978–1982	Flexible	Fixed (*Tablita*)
Uruguay	1992–1998	Flexible	Fixed
Venezela	1996–1998	Flexible	Fixed
Hungary	1995–1998	Flexible	Fixed
Latvia	1994–1996	Flexible	Fixed
Poland	1991–1998	Flexible	Fixed

Source: IMF (1999).

Finally, in Table 6.A2 we show the median of the main variables for the different exchange regimes, distinguishing between the two alternative regime samples.

Table 6.A2 Main features of the samples

	IMF sample	*Modified sample*
Number of observations		
Flexible regimes	218	152
Fixed regimes	155	221
Currency Boards	17	17
Flexible regimes		
Sample median		
Overall deficit	−1.73	−1.76
Primary deficit	0.48	0.18
Inflation	23.94	24.62
Monetary seignoriage	2.35	2.44
Fiscal seignoriage	0.98	1.19
Real GDP growth	3.75	3.44
Fixed regimes		
Sample median		
Overall deficit	−1.79	−1.59
Primary deficit	−0.17	0.31
Inflation	11.54	15.21
Monetary seignoriage	1.69	1.78
Fiscal seignoriage	0.73	0.73
Real GDP growth	4.71	4.61
Currency boards		
Sample median		
Overall deficit	−0.71	−0.71
Primary deficit	0.46	0.46
Inflation	10.60	10.60
Monetary seignoriage	1.44	1.44
Fiscal seignoriage	−0.00	−0.00
Real GDP growth	4.91	4.91

Source: Own calculations.

Notes

1 Comments by Ana Buisan, Pablo Hernández and Fernando Restoy, and those received at the Colloquium are gratefully acknowledged. The analyses, opinions and findings do not necessarily represent those of the Bank of Spain.
2 These data refer to emerging market economies in Latin America and East Europe. Details on the sample are given in the Annex.
3 A dot refers to rate of growth in the variables.
4 Inflation may have additional effects on the deficits. The first effect can be observed in expression (1): the interest payments term will be reduced by inflation as long as the nominal interest rate on debt does not properly reflect inflation expectations; this implies that only unexpected inflation can reduce the cost of debt service. The sign and magnitude of this effect depends on the inflation premium required for investing in domestic currency. Another effect, which is positive, is related to the fiscal drag; it refers to the higher taxes paid in progressive

systems when the price level rises and taxes are not adjusted for inflation. Finally, the so-called Olivera-Tanzi effect is negative, as it arises from the lags in the collection of taxes which may be relevant in situations of very high inflation.

5 Edwards and Tabellini (1991), Gavin and Perotti (1995), Tornell and Velasco (1998).

6 Note also that, if individual effects were considered, there would be no difference between countries with only one type of regime in the whole sample, since the resulting dummy value (which would be defined as deviation from the mean value of the regime) would be in both cases equal to zero.

7 Other controls include terms of trade or the real exchange rate, but they did not turn out to be significant when included in the deficit regressions.

8 The parameter and t-ratio (in brackets) of the fixed regime dummy is 1.13 (2.83).

9 The parameter is -0.15 (-2.33) for the IMF-modified sample. It is non-significant for the IMF sample.

10 See Klein and Neumann (1991). It is also important to note that this privileged financing affects the profit and loss accounts of the Central Bank. As a matter of fact, Central Banks in emerging countries usually display important losses because they are also used by the government as privileged source of financing for the public sector firms or to sustain dual exchange rate systems. Edwards (1997) computes the magnitude of Central Banks' losses, which in extreme cases amount to more than 4 percent of GDP. In our sample, it is not possible to compute these losses, which are conveyed in the deficit variable.

11 Privileged financing is expected to be highly correlated with the increase in f. It would also be useful to distinguish in the claims to governments between credits to the public sector and debt. The first item is more clearly associated with financing of deficits, while the second can be argued to be used for open market operations. Data do not allow for this distinction.

12 These results coincide with those of Sikken and De Haan (1998) which explore similar relations with alternative specifications in a univariate context.

13 The starting date and parity with the reference currency of these arrangements are: Argentina (April 1991, fixed parity 1:1 with the US dollar), Bulgaria (July 1997, fixed parity 1000:1 with the *Deutchmark*), Lithuania (April 1994, fixed parity 4:1 with the US dollar), Estonia (January 1992, fixed parity 8:1 with the *Deutchmark*) and Bosnia (August 1997, fixed parity 1:1 with the *Deutchmark*). The rest of currency boards correspond to colonies or are reminiscent of colonial times: Hong Kong, Djibouti, member countries of the Eastern Caribbean Central Bank, Cayman Islands, Falkland Islands, Gibraltar and Brunei. A detailed account of currency board operation and an evaluation of the regime can be found in IMF (1997) and references therein.

14 For example, in 1998 Argentina obtained 965 millions of pesos in interest payments for its foreign exchange reserves (around 2 percent of actual tax revenues). Central Bank's benefits accounts in 1998 around 863 millions of pesos, equivalent to 0.3 percent of GDP.

15 Note that currency boards do not necessarily require a strictly fixed exchange rate to operate. Although the management of currency boards has always been implemented within fixed exchange rates regimes, currency boards also would eliminate fiscal seigniorage if they were run in a managed float or in a crawling peg, that is, allowing for changes in the nominal exchange rate ($\dot{e} \neq O$). As the condition states, changes in $\dot{e}r$ could then be backed by equal changes in the monetary base. Also note that the effects of a currency board on fiscal discipline are very similar to those of the dollarization of the economy. In this second case, there is no need for the Central Bank or the currency board to operate, and the revenues from holding foreign reserves would disappear. On the positive side, the interest rate differentials between the currency board country and the reference should be

expected to dwindle too, as the peg of the exchange rate is perceived as irrevocable and the exchange rate premium disappears.
16 The results are also influenced by the poor fiscal performance of Lithuania, which still suffers from high overall and primary deficits. When Lithuania is excluded from the sample (leaving only thirteen currency boards observations), the currency board dummy is significant and displays the expected sign for the deficits.
17 Selected countries are Argentina, Bolivia, Brazil, Chile, Colombia, Costa Rica, Ecuador, Guatemala, Honduras, Mexico, Panama, Paraguay, Peru, Uruguay, Venezuela, Bulgaria, the Czech Republic, Estonia, Hungary, Latvia, Lithuania, Poland, Slovenia and Romania.
18 This could be the reason why we consider Brazil 1994 as a ERBS, although it was a crawling peg system, and a Money-Based Stabilization Bolivia 1986, a country which currency has been depreciating against the US dollar at a much slower pace than the Brazilian's one. However, in IMF (1999) Bolivia is considered again as a fixed exchange rate, as

> the deviations of the market exchange rate from the official exchange rate . . . are extremely tight . . . and that the regime is in practice a crawling peg aimed at maintaining the competitiveness of the economy.
>
> (IMF, 1999)

These considerations show that the definition of the regime is not an easy issue. To define these episodes we have consulted, among others, Kiguel and Liviatan (1992), Tornell and Velasco (1998), Hamann (1999) and IMF (1999).

References

Calvo, G. A. and Vegh, C. A. (1998) 'Inflation stabilization and BOP crises in developing countries', *Handbook of Macroeconomics* (forthcoming).

Edwards, S. (1997) *Crisis y reforma en America Latina*, Emece, Buenos Aires.

Edwards, S. and Tabellini, G. (1991) 'Explaining fiscal policies and inflation in developing countries', *Journal of International Money and Finance*, 10, S16–S48.

Eichengreen, B. and Masson, P. (1998) 'Exit strategies. Policy options for countries seeking greater exchange rate flexibility', *IMF Occasional Paper*, 168.

Fischer, S. (1982) 'Seignoriage and the case for a national money', *Journal of Political Economy*, 90, 295–313.

Gavin, M. and Perotti, R. (1997) 'Fiscal policy in Latin America', *NBER Macroeconomic Annual*, 11–71.

Gulde, A., Kähkönen, J., Keller, P. et al. (1999) 'Pros and cons of Currency Board arrangements in the lead-up to EU accession and participation in the Euro zone', paper presented at a Seminar on 'Currency boards in the context of accession to EU' organized by the European Commission in Brussels.

Hamann, A. J. (1999) 'Exchange-rate based stabilization: a critical look at the stylized facts', *IMF Working Paper* WP/99/132.

IMF (1997), 'Currency Board Arrangements. Issues and Experiences', *IMF Occasional Paper*, 151.

IMF (1999) 'Exchange rate arrangements and currency convertibility: developments and issues', *World Economic and Financial Surveys.*

IMF (various issues) 'Exchange Rate Arrangements and Exchange Restrictions: Annual Report'.

Kaminsky, G. L., Lizondo, S. and Reinhart, C. (1997) 'Leading indicators of currency crisis', *Board of Governors of the Federal Reserve System*, mimeo.

Kiguel, M. and Leviatan, N. (1992) 'The business cycle associated with exchange rate based stabilization', *The World Bank Economic Review*, 6, 279–305.

Klein, M. and Von Neumann, M. (1991) 'Seignoriage: what is it and who gets it?', *Weltwirschaftliches Archiv*, 206–21.

Krugman, P. (1979) 'A model of balance of payments crises', *Journal of Money, Credit and Banking*, 11, 315–25.

Masson, P. (1999) 'Monetary and exchange rate policy of transition economies of Central and Eastern Europe after the launch of EMU', *IMF Working Paper* PDP/99/5.

Rodríguez. A. (1982) 'The Argentine stabilization plan of December 20th ', *World Development*, 10, 801–11.

Sargent, T. and Wallace, N. (1981) 'Some unpleasant monetarist arithmetic', *Federal Reserve of Minneapolis Quarterly Review*, 5, 1–17.

Sikken, B. J. and De Haan, J. (1998) 'Budget deficits, monetization and central bank independence in developing countries', *Oxford Economic Papers*, 50, 493–511.

Tornell, A. and Velasco, A. (1998) 'Fiscal discipline and the choice of a nominal anchor in stabilization', *Journal of International Economics*, 46, 1–30.

Vegh, C. A. (1992) 'Stopping high inflation: an analytical overview', *IMF Staff Papers*, 39, 626–95.

7   Country risk analysis in the light of emerging market crises*

Josef Christl and Thomas Spanel

1. Introduction

Our paper outlines and evaluates a model of transfer risk analysis which has been used by an international commercial bank for managing the country risk of and allocating country limits to emerging markets over the last three years. The model is highly eclectic and pragmatic; despite this fact (or maybe even because of it) it proved to be a very useful instrument in the sense that it gave correct signals in advance for upcoming economic crises in several emerging market economies during the period from July 1997 (depreciation of the Thai baht) to January 1999 (devaluation of the Brazilian real).

Despite reported success in predicting crises in economic literature (e.g. Aylward/Thorne, 1998; Berg/Patillo, 1999; Kaminsky/Lizondo/Reinhart, 1998; Kaminsky, 1999), one may clearly challenge the view that it is possible to do this systematically. For example, from a theoretical perspective there may be doubt that sharp and predictable movements in the exchange rate are consistent with the actions of forward-looking speculators. From a more pragmatic and/or financial-market-oriented perspective, the question is whether the symptoms of crisis can be detected sufficiently in advance to allow for pre-emptive measures to be adopted. Of course, there is a clear need to develop a warning system that helps monitor a country's performance to see whether it may be slipping into crisis or not. Financial market participants are keen to have such a tool because they want to make money (or avoid losses), policymakers because they wish to avoid the crisis, and academics because they have a long history of fascination with financial crisis.

We believe that it is at least possible to see whether a country is in a zone of serious vulnerability – that is, whether its fundamentals are so weak that sudden shifts in expectations will trigger a crisis – and that the serious vulnerability will also adversely impact on its ability to service its foreign debt. If

* Paper presented at 22nd SUERF Colloquium, Vienna, 27–29 April 2000.

this is possible, the relative vulnerability of different countries might predict the relative probabilities of crisis happening in response to a shock such as a global downturn in confidence in emerging markets or global interest rate increases (see also Berg/Pattillo, 1999).

Our paper is organized as follows: Section 2 outlines the model used; Section 3 evaluates the signals and forecasts of the model for three case studies, namely Thailand, Brazil and Russia, and analyses the shortcomings of the country risk model in the light of the most recent experience. Section 3 also deals with those variables which turned out to be most sensitive in the diagnosis of a potential crisis. Section 4, finally, presents some conclusions.

2. The model

A basic premise of most empirical analyses of external debt repayment problems, country risk and creditworthiness is that a limited number of financial, macroeconomic, political and sociopolitical indicators can be identified as the main determinants of debt repayment behavior. Avramovic (1964), who carried out one of the first systematic studies, identified variables like the debt–GDP ratio, the debt–service ratio or import coverage by reserves as the most important factors in the analysis of international creditworthiness. His findings seem to have guided the selection of variables in many of the subsequent empirical analyses of external debt repayment behaviour. Even in studies where the independent variables selected are based on formal models of external loan demand and supply or utility maximization, they are often similar to those already identified by Avramovic.

The rating model we use starts with a differentiation between economic risk score (r_e) and political risk score (r_p). Both types of risk are characterized by one single score in the range of 0 (extremely risky) and 100 (no risk at all), that is, $100 \geq r_e$, $r_p \geq 0$. While the economic risk score is calculated with the help of the model presented further down, the political risk score stems from a questionnaire which is worked out by members of the International Branch of the banking group. This questionnaire deals with the social environment, internal and external security policy, relations with the neighbour countries and membership in international organizations.

The total risk score (r) of an emerging country is then calculated simply as the arithmetic mean of the economic and political rating:

$$r = 0.5 \cdot r_e + 0.5 \cdot r_p. \tag{1}$$

In its present form the economic model consists of thirteen variables which are connected by a linear weighting function (g_i). Every single variable of the model has its own valuation function, f, which assigns a score between 0 and 100 to a given value of a variable (v_i). These valuation functions are the same for all countries under consideration. Therefore:

$$r_e = \Sigma g_i . f(v_i) \quad \text{with } i = 1, \ldots, 13 \tag{2}$$

$$\text{and } \Sigma g_i = 1 \text{ and } 0 < f(v_i) < 100.$$

This economic ability and willingness of a country to service its foreign debt depends on several factors: on the wealth and strength of its economy, on its internal and external economic stability, on its vulnerability of export income, on the size and structure of the debt burden as well as on the liquidity available for debt service. Most of the variables used in the model (see Table 7.1) are probably self-explanatory and therefore need no extensive justification. The wealth and strength of an economy are characterized by GDP per capita in US\$ and real GDP growth, internal economic (not necessarily political) stability, the inflation rate as well as the ratio of budget deficit to GDP.

The external equilibrium of an emerging country is valued in the model by the state of the current account (as a fraction of GDP),[1] the vulnerability of its debt service capacity is measured by the export product concentration ratio. With respect to a country's burden of foreign debt, foreign debt as a fraction of exports as well as GDP has been used. Sometimes it is argued that because GDP is highly sensitive to exchange rate movements, exports should be used instead. Ades (1999), on the other hand, shows that a better solution might be to adjust GDP using an estimate of the long-run sustainable equilibrium exchange rate. The reason for using both variables in our model, however, is that small countries usually have relatively higher exports than larger countries and, therefore, a rating bias with respect to smaller countries would be introduced in the model if the variable 'foreign debt as a percentage of exports' only was used.[2]

The average interest rate on foreign debt is a measure which is intended to capture the development of the debt service capacity:[3] If exports – which in many countries are the most important and persistent source of earning currency reserves – grow at a faster speed than the given stock of foreign indebtedness (i.e. the average interest rate), the country's potential to service its foreign debt in future increases; if the opposite happens, its potential of servicing foreign debt decreases.

For each variable used the model offers a specific valuation function $f(v_i)$ (see Table 7.2). These functions stem partly from theoretical considerations, partly from definitional relationships of the balance of payments statistics or the systems of national accounts, and partly from purely empirical reasoning.[4] Most valuation functions are linear, those for GDP per capita are log-linear and the one for the inflation rate is exponential.

The model's weighting function for the different variables has been derived by a dynamic optimization process using a goal function which aimed to reconstruct a given ranking of the emerging market economies in our database, which was mainly determined by Moody's and Standard & Poor's ratings at the time when the model was built. It is therefore appropriate and necessary to test and adapt this weighting function from time to time. In our risk assessment procedure, we differentiate between four signals: 'positive',

Table 7.1 Variables and the weighting function

	Motive	Variable (v_i)	Weight (g_i)
Internal economy	Economic wealth	GDP per capita	0.10
	Economic strength	Real GDP growth	0.05
	Stability	Inflation rate	0.05
	Stability	Budget deficit in % of GDP	0.05
External economy	External equilibrium	Current account in % of GDP	0.10
	Vulnerability	Most important export good in % of total visible exports	0.05
	Size of debt burden	Foreign debt in % of total exports	0.07
	Size of debt burden	Foreign debt in % of GDP	0.08
	Structure of foreign debt	Short term debt in % of total foreign debt	0.10
	Ability to service debt burden	Debt service in % of exports	0.10
	Ability to service debt burden	Average interest rate on foreign debt divided by growth rate of total exports	0.05
	Liquidity	Foreign currency reserves in % of total imports (import cover)	0.10
	Liquidity	Foreign currency reserves in % of short-term indebtedness	0.10

Table 7.2 Valuation function of the model

Variable (v_i)	Weight (g_i)	Valuation		
		0 (= min)	50	100 (= max)
GDP per capita in USD	0.10	0	13,313	25,000
Real GDP growth, %	0.05	−3.0	2.0	7.0
Inflation rate, %	0.05	80.0	4.5	2.0
Budget deficit in % of GDP	0.05	−7.0	−4.0	−1.0
Current account in % of GDP	0.10	−6.0	−2.0	0.0
Most important export good in % of visible exports	0.05	72.5	41.25	10.0
Foreign debt in % of visible exports	0.07	200.0	120.0	40.0
Foreign debt in % of GDP	0.08	100.0	60.0	20.0
Short term debt in % of total foreign debt	0.10	30.0	20.0	10.0
Debt service in % of exports	0.10	30.0	20.0	10.0
Average interest rate on foreign debt divided by growth rate of total exports	0.05	2.0	1.25	0.5
Import cover in months	0.10	1	3	6
Foreign currency reserves in % of short-term indebtedness	0.10	50.0	100.0	200.0

'stable', 'negative' and 'early warning'. If the economic risk score ($r_{e, t}$) of a given country drops from period t to t+1 by more than 5 per cent, the outlook for period t+1 is characterized by 'negative', an increase by more than 5 per cent is labelled a 'positive' outlook, that is,

$$
\begin{aligned}
&\text{if } (r_{e, t+1}) \geq 1.05 \, (r_{e, t}) &&\Rightarrow \text{'positive'} \\
&\text{if } 0.9 \, (r_{e, t}) \leq (r_{e, t+1}) \leq 0.95 \, (r_{e, t}) &&\Rightarrow \text{'negative'} \\
&\text{if } (r_{e, t+1}) < 0.9 \, (r_{e, t}) &&\Rightarrow \text{'early warning'} \\
&\text{otherwise} &&\Rightarrow \text{'stable'}
\end{aligned}
\tag{3}
$$

(signal column header above the arrows)

The most serious risk signal in our model is 'early warning', which is defined as a drop in the economic risk score by more than 10 per cent within one period. The boundaries for different risk signals were developed by testing in ex-post analysis the behaviour of our model in several former crises, such as the Mexican crisis of 1994–95. Of course one also may question whether crises are sufficiently similar in various countries and over time to allow such kinds of generalizations from past experience.

3. Some case studies: Thailand, Brazil and Russia

The following empirical analysis uses in principle the data set and the forecasts of the International Institute of Finance (IIF) at a given point in time. The IIF covers at present about fifty emerging market economies and updates its forecasts usually twice a year.[5] The results produced by the model and consequently the risk perception – crucially depend on two factors:

- firstly, on the capability of the model to produce clear signals (given that the forecasts for the economic developments are correct); and
- secondly, on the quality of the forecasts for the periods ahead.

Even if a forecast had been completely correct, the model may not recognize a crisis. This can be learned from the description of the crises by the most recent data (ex-post analysis). On the other hand, if the forecasts for the present year and the year ahead are completely wrong, the model would clearly produce false signals.

3.1 Thailand

The devaluation of the Thai baht in mid-1997 was the headstart for the economic and financial crisis in Asia. The ex-post analysis with recent data shows that the country rating model gave a timely and good indication of Thailand's dramatically worsening creditworthiness. Already in the November 1995 analysis it signalled a 'negative' outlook for the year 1996 (see Table 7.3). In our analysis of August 1996, however, the outlook for 1997 was 'stable' as a result of an over-optimistic forecast. In February 1997 the model produced a clear signal of 'early warning' for 1997, with a deterioration of r_e by 11 per cent, and in September 1997 with a deterioration by more than 22 per cent. And again already in February 1997 we got a first strong 'positive' outlook for 1998, which indicated a rapid recovery of the Thai economy.

Table 7.3 The CA country rating indicator for Thailand: % change against previous year

Date of analysis	1991	1992	1993	1994	1995	1996	1997	1998	1999e	2000f
11/1999	2.3	3.5	0.7	−4.0	−6.4	−10.5	−16.8	13.0	38.2	0.6
12/1998	2.3	3.5	0.7	−4.0	−6.3	−10.5	−12.7	*11.5*	*9.8*	
06/1998	2.3	3.5	0.7	−4.0	−6.3	−9.9	−15.3	*21.5*	*36.7*	
09/1997	2.8	2.8	0.9	−3.6	−7.3	−9.2	**−22.4**	*20.4*		
02/1997	2.8	2.7	−0.5	−1.7	−7.9	−7.2	**−11.2**			
08/1996	2.8	2.7	−0.5	−2.3	−6.4	−0.9	−2.2			
11/1995	2.8	3.0	0.0	−4.3	−6.5	−5.4			Forecast	

Figure 7.1 tells the same story: the data and the forecasts available in November 1995 and August 1996 already gave a clear indication that the Thailand risk was increasing. Since February 1997 the slope of the curve changed dramatically and the anticipated extent of the deterioration was rather correct if one compares the older results with the November 1999 analysis. This shows that our 1995 and 1997 forecasts for the Thai economy were fairly accurate. The 1996 forecast had been a little bit too optimistic.

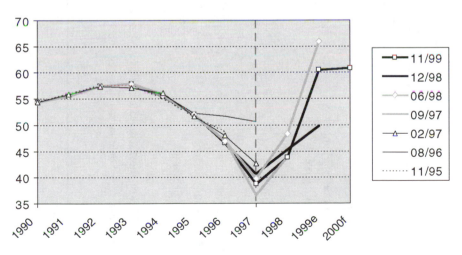

Figure 7.1 The CA country rating indicator for Thailand: historic rating results.

Table 7.4 Weighted rating points for Thailand

Date of analysis	1991	1992	1993	1994	1995	1996	1997	1998	1999e	2000f
GDP per capita	0.5	0.6	0.7	0.8	0.9	1.0	0.8	0.6	0.6	0.7
Real GDP, % change	5.0	5.0	5.0	5.0	5.0	4.3	0.9	0.0	3.3	3.5
Consumer prices, % change	2.0	2.7	3.2	2.2	2.0	2.0	2.0	1.5	5.0	4.2
Budget in % of GDP	5.0	5.0	5.0	5.0	5.0	5.0	4.0	1.0	0.0	0.0
Export concentration ratio	5.0	5.0	5.0	5.0	5.0	5.0	5.0	5.0	5.0	5.0
External debt in % of GDP	6.2	6.1	5.7	5.3	4.7	4.5	3.9	2.4	3.8	3.8
External debt in % of exports of goods & serv.	4.4	4.3	4.0	3.7	3.5	3.0	3.4	3.3	4.0	4.1
Debt service in % of exports of goods & serv.	9.4	10.0	10.0	9.4	9.2	8.8	3.5	2.4	5.8	5.6
Current account balance in % of GDP	0.0	0.4	1.2	0.5	0.0	0.0	5.0	10.0	10.0	10.0
Import cover in months	7.7	8.2	8.6	8.6	8.1	8.3	6.6	10.0	9.9	9.6
Interest rate on external debt / exports, in %	5.0	5.0	5.0	5.0	5.0	0.0	0.0	0.0	1.8	2.0
Reserves in % of short term external debt	5.4	5.1	4.5	5.0	3.7	4.8	3.7	6.2	8.4	8.9
Short-term external debt in % of total ext. debt	0.0	0.0	0.0	0.0	0.0	0.0	0.0	1.5	3.1	3.5
Total	55.5	57.5	57.9	55.6	52.0	46.6	38.8	43.8	60.5	60.9

We can ask the question which indicators made the largest contribution to the reduction of the economic risk score during the crisis. Listed according to their impact on r_e, which was reduced from 46.6 to 38.8 between 1996 and 1997, we identified the following critical variables (points of contribution are given in brackets):

- first of all, the debt service ratio (–5.3 points) which accounts for nearly two-thirds of the net decrease; by the way, Thailand's overall debt service in USD nearly doubled in 1997 to USD 17.5bn;
- furthermore, real GDP growth (–3.4 points): after strong growth in 1996 (5.5%) the Thai economy went into recession (–1.3%) in 1997;
- import coverage (–1.7 points); and finally
- reserves in per cent of short-term external debt (–1.1 points).

It is worthwhile to note that a strong positive impact stems from the current account deficit (+5.0 points), which was reduced mainly as a result of the recession the economy entered in 1997.

3.2 Brazil

The Brazilian crisis culminated in January 1999, when the National Bank abandoned the exchange rate regime and devalued the Brazilian real against the US dollar. Overall, the negative consequences of the Brazilian currency crisis of 1999 were heavily overestimated by many forecasters and analysts. Compared with the forecasts produced in early 1999, which anticipated a strong recession of –5 per cent and more for the Brazilian economy, the crisis was much smoother and shorter (in effect, most recent data show an increase of real GDP by 0.8% in 1999). The difficulties in the fundamentals forecast are also reflected in the results of our rating model.

Using the most recent data available, that is, February 2000 (see Table 7.5), the economic risk score shows the following pattern: r_e declined between 1997 and 1998 from 42.8 to 41.4 (–3.2%) and dropped further in 1999 to 39.1 (–5.4%). Our model produced a first 'negative' outlook in April 1997 for the corresponding year. In our analysis of October 1997 we got a 'negative' outlook for 1998, but in March 1998 we described the Brazilian situation as 'stable'. Six months later, in October 1998, we received a clear 'early warning' for 1998 and a strong 'positive' outlook for 1999.

In principle, all ratings for Brazil listed in Table 7.5 recognized the deterioration in 1998, but there was not such a clear signal for the crisis in 1999. In September 1998 the rating model produced the exact result for the year 1999 (as the ex-post analysis shows), but the 1998 rating was much too low, so that an improvement for 1999 was indicated instead of the opposite. Overall, the signals yielded by the model during the Brazilian crisis were rather mixed and not as unambiguous as in the Thai case. Thus, it was much more difficult to forecast the crisis in a timely and exact manner (although we expected – as many others did – an unavoidable devaluation of the real already in summer 1998 due to Brazil's high twin deficit and a dramatic capital flight).

Table 7.5 The CA country rating indicator for Brazil: % change against previous year

Date of analysis	1991	1992	1993	1994	1995	1996	1997	1998	1999e	2000f
02/2000	16.3	44.8	3.3	4.4	–9.3	–2.6	7.2	–3.2	–5.4	*15.8*
09/1999				4.2	–9.3	–2.0	7.8	–4.6	–2.2	4.7
03/1999				5.4	–9.1	–2.2	8.0	–7.6	**–10.3**	4.7
09/1998			–0.1	8.6	–7.9	2.7	1.9	**–14.4**	*10.0*	
03/1998		36.6	–0.9	9.6	–7.9	–0.5	–1.3	–3.3		
10/1997		36.6	–0.1	8.6	–7.9	–0.3	–1.4	–6.5		
04/1997		36.7	–0.3	8.1	–8.3	0.4	*–6.1*	–0.5		
12/1996	5.3	17.9	–1.1	–0.2	–11.8	–1.5	*10.2*			

Forecast

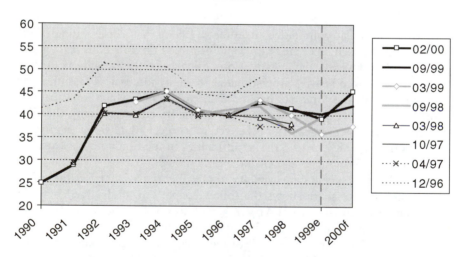

Figure 7.2 The CA country rating indicator for Brazil: historic rating results.

Table 7.6 Weighted rating points for Brazil

Date of analysis	1991	1992	1993	1994	1995	1996	1997	1998	1999e	2000f
GDP per capita	1.0	1.0	0.9	1.2	1.6	1.7	1.7	1.6	1.0	1.1
Real GDP, %-change	1.7	1.3	4.0	4.5	3.6	2.8	3.3	1.4	1.9	3.0
Consumer prices, %-change	0.0	0.0	0.0	0.0	0.0	0.8	1.9	2.9	2.3	1.6
Budget in % of GDP	0.0	0.0	0.0	0.0	0.0	0.9	0.7	0.0	0.0	0.0
Export concentration ratio	5.0	5.0	5.0	5.0	5.0	5.0	4.9	5.0	5.0	5.0
External debt in % of GDP	6.6	6.5	6.1	6.9	7.3	7.2	7.2	6.6	5.3	5.3
External debt in % of exports of goods & serv.	0.0	0.0	0.0	0.0	0.0	0.0	0.0	0.0	0.0	0.0
Debt service in % of exports of goods & serv.	0.0	0.0	0.0	0.0	0.0	0.0	0.0	0.0	0.0	0.0
Current account balance in % of GDP	9.2	10.0	9.8	9.3	4.3	3.6	2.3	2.0	1.7	2.2
Import cover in months	3.7	10.0	10.0	10.0	10.0	10.0	10.0	8.5	8.4	8.7
Interest rate on external debt / exports, in %	0.0	5.0	3.9	5.0	4.8	3.7	4.7	0.0	0.0	5.0
Reserves in % of short term external debt	0.0	0.7	1.8	2.4	3.8	4.1	3.8	5.6	5.4	5.6
Short-term external debt in % of total ext. debt	1.8	2.4	1.7	1.0	0.5	0.1	2.1	7.7	8.2	7.9
Total	28.9	41.9	43.2	45.1	41.0	39.9	42.8	41.4	39.1	45.3

3.3 Russia

The Russian crisis erupted with a spectacular devaluation of the Russian rouble against the US dollar; in August and September 1998. In mid-August, 6.3 roubles were paid for 1 US dollar, by 9 September the exchange rate had depreciated to 20 roubles. This sparked the Russian crisis, which resulted in a default on foreign debt and on domestic government debt, and devastated the Russian banking system nearly completely.

Our model reported an extraordinary decline in the economic risk score already three years before the crisis and indicated the permanently increasing vulnerability of the Russian economy. r_e worsened from 52 points in 1995 to 41.2 in 1996 and further, to 37.2 in 1997, and dropped by another remarkable 21.5% to 29.2 in 1998. The model produced two 'early warnings' in May 1997 and September 1997 and thus gave a very strong indication that Russia was about to default. And it is most likely that Russia would have defaulted before that if the IMF had stopped financial support for Russia some time earlier. It is also interesting that all our analyses issued between May 1997 and March 2000 show quite similar rating changes for the years 1996 and 1997 (not for 1998), although there were nearly three years in between the production of the first and the last analysis.

Table 7.7 The CA country rating indicator for Russia: % change against previous year

Date of analysis	1991	1992	1993	1994	1995	1996	1997	1998	1999e	2000f
03/2000	2.2	–48.0	155.1	0.5	11.4	–20.8	–9.7	–21.5	26.1	17.7
03/1999	2.2	–48.0	155.1	0.5	24.1	–24.1	–18.6	–34.9	–4.4	–4.4
01/1998	12.0	–51.0	170.6	–18.4	48.5	–19.1	–18.0	0.6		
09/1997	20.1	–56.0	170.6	–18.4	48.5	–19.4	**–13.4**	2.1		
05/1997	20.1	–56.0	150.6	0.7	25.8	–22.5	**–12.0**	5.1		Forecast

The dramatic development of the Russian Federation in 1997 and 1998 can also be learned from Figure 7.3. Starting in 1995, the rating indicator fell continuously. But apparently our forecasts prepared in late 1997 and early 1998 for the year 1998 were too optimistic (we expected 1998 to be the first year of slight economic growth after the tremendous adjustment recession). Moreover, we did not allow for a devaluation of the size that actually occurred. This was the main reason that our indicator for the year 1998 was flat or slightly upward moving. Only the analysis of March 2000, which includes the devaluation and the following economic crisis, shows an extremely steep downturn in the indicator.

The following variables had the strongest impact on Russia's declining rating score of 8.0 points, from 37.2 in 1997 to 29.2 in 1998, the year of crisis:

• First of all, the contribution of the debt service ratio to the rating score

Table 7.8 Weighted rating points for Russia

Date of analysis	1991	1992	1993	1994	1995	1996	1997	1998	1999e	2000f
GDP per capita	1.7	0.1	0.4	0.6	0.7	0.9	1.0	0.6	0.4	0.5
Real GDP, %-change	0.0	0.0	0.0	0.0	0.0	0.0	1.9	0.0	3.1	2.5
Consumer prices, %-change	0.0	0.0	0.0	0.0	0.0	0.1	0.8	0.4	0.0	0.4
Budget in % of GDP	0.0	0.0	0.4	0.0	1.3	0.0	0.0	1.7	4.3	3.6
Export concentration ratio	4.1	3.2	3.6	3.9	4.8	4.4	4.6	4.5	4.4	4.4
External debt in % of GDP	8.0	0.0	5.1	6.4	6.6	6.8	6.3	3.8	1.8	2.7
External debt in % of exports of goods & serv.	1.2	0.0	0.2	1.5	1.9	1.2	0.0	0.0	0.0	0.0
Debt service in % of exports of goods & serv.	0.0	6.5	8.9	9.3	8.3	7.9	6.9	1.2	0.9	1.6
Current account balance in % of GDP	10.0	0.0	10.0	10.0	10.0	10.0	10.0	8.0	10.0	10.0
Import cover in months	0.0	0.0	1.5	0.0	5.2	4.5	4.3	2.5	5.0	4.8
Interest rate on external debt / exports, in %	4.6	0.0	5.0	5.0	5.0	3.6	0.0	0.0	0.0	4.7
Reserves in % of short term external debt	0.0	0.0	1.4	0.0	2.9	0.0	0.0	0.0	0.0	1.0
Short-term external debt in % of total ext. debt	5.3	8.4	9.9	10.0	5.3	1.6	1.4	6.6	6.9	7.2
Total	35.0	18.2	46.4	46.7	52.0	41.2	37.2	29.2	36.8	43.3

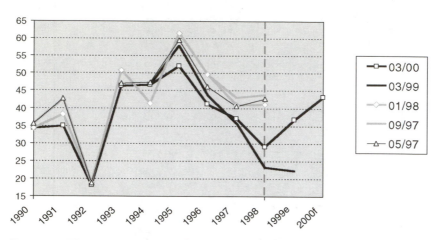

Figure 7.3 The CA country rating indicator for Russia: historic rating results.

sank by –5.7 points and explained nearly 70 per cent in the net reduction of the overall risk score. Russia's debt service increased by roughly 60 per cent in 1998. At the same time, nominal exports in US dollars fell markedly. Consequently the ratio exploded from 16 per cent in 1997 to 28 per cent in 1998.

*   Because of a shrinking nominal GDP in USD and an increasing gross external debt, external debt in per cent of GDP soared from 37 per cent (1997) to 62 per cent (1998). This resulted in another drop of r_e of 2.5 points.
*   The narrowing current account surplus in per cent of GDP added another two points to the declining economic risk score.

Besides, real GDP growth (–1.9 points) and a lower import coverage (–1.8 points) reduced the economic risk score. It is also interesting to note that, on the other hand, the improved debt structure (short-term debt in per cent of total external debt) for example due to additional IMF funding in July 1998 (US$5.8bn), added 5.2 points to the rating score.

Summing up, the model gave a clear early warning of the forthcoming Russian crisis in 1997. If we had forecasted a devaluation of the rouble in 1998, we would also have arrived at a further downturn of the indicator in 1998.

4. Conclusions

As our foregoing analysis has shown, the CA country risk assessment brought different results in the forecast of the crises in Thailand, Brazil and Russia. First of all, if we look at the model, it turns out that the model captured the crisis in Thailand and Russia very well, while the exchange rate crisis of Brazil was not really perceptible. Using the most recent data in Thailand the model produces the signals 'negative outlook' (1995), 'early warning' (1996) and 'early warning' (1997). The signals for the Russian crisis are 'early warning' (1996), 'negative outlook' (1997) and 'early warning' (1998). For Brazil, on the other hand, the model yielded 'positive outlook' (1997), 'stable outlook' (1998) and 'negative outlook' (1999), but no early warning at all. But compared to the severity of the crises in Thailand and Russia and their consequences on foreign indebtedness and the banking system, this reaction is probably even adequate.

With respect to the forecasts involved in the country risk assessment process, our forecasts for Thailand when the crisis came up were reasonably accurate and, therefore, we captured and managed the Thailand risk (as well as the whole Asian crisis) rather satisfactorily. Besides, our forecast for the Russian economy in 1997 was quite correct, but for 1998 turned out too optimistic. In Brazil, on the other hand, we took an overly gloomy view in our forecast. Tending towards the pessimistic side, however, is the superior strategy for a risk assessment process.

Appendix

Table 7.A1 Correlation matrix of variables used (V_i)

	V1	V2	V3	V4	V5	V6	V7	V8	V9	V10	V11	V12	V13
V1	–	0.12	0.02	0.01	0.00	0.05	0.00	0.03	0.17	0.07	0.01	0.01	0.03
V2	–	–	0.02	0.05	0.01	0.02	0.01	0.05	0.03	0.05	0.01	0.01	0.03
V3	–	–	–	0.41	0.06	0.25	0.41	0.28	0.05	0.16	0.03	0.07	0.43
V4	–	–	–	–	0.06	0.07	0.27	0.22	0.17	0.18	0.01	0.06	0.54
V5	–	–	–	–	–	0.00	0.08	0.07	0.00	0.02	0.02	0.00	0.07
V6	–	–	–	–	–	–	0.46	0.33	0.13	0.01	0.05	0.07	0.20
V7	–	–	–	–	–	–	–	0.75	0.09	0.02	0.09	0.10	0.38
V8	–	–	–	–	–	–	–	–	0.06	0.01	0.03	0.11	0.36
V9	–	–	–	–	–	–	–	–	–	0.07	0.01	0.04	0.02
V10	–	–	–	–	–	–	–	–	–	–	0.03	0.11	0.09
V11	–	–	–	–	–	–	–	–	–	–	–	0.02	0.01
V12	–	–	–	–	–	–	–	–	–	–	–	–	0.21

V1 = real GDP growth
V2 = inflation rate
V3 = export concentration ratio
V4 = GDP per capita
V5 = government deficit as a percentage of GDP
V6 = foreign debt as a percentage of GDP
V7 = foreign debt as a percentage of exports
V8 = debt service ratio
V9 = current account deficit as a percentage of GDP
V10 = import coverage
V11 = average interest rate on foreign debt divided by growth rate of total exports
V12 = foreign currency reserves in per cent of short-term indebtedness
V13 = short-term debt in per cent of total foreign debt

Notes

1 Given the findings of Kaminsiki/Lizondo/Reinhart (1998) a deviation of the real exchange rate from trend is one of the best single early warning indicators for an approaching currency crisis. We didn't introduce this variable because – first of all – reliable data on real effective exchange rates are for many countries not available and we apply the model for about 100 emerging market economies. Moreover, in our most recent estimations it turned out that – contrary to the results of Kaminski/Lizondo/Reinhart – the predictive power of the lagged real effective exchange rate with respect to default on foreign debt is comparatively low.
2 The correlation coefficient between the two ratios (foreign debt to total exports and foreign debt to total GDP) for a sample of 38 countriesis 0.46; moreover, high correlation can also be observed for GDP per capita and short-term debt in per cent of total debt as well as the debt service ratio and foreign debt as a percentage of exports. A correlation matrix of the model is given in the Appendix.
3 Let FD_t be the stock of foreign debt at time t and X_t exports in period t. Then it is obvious that leaving debt repayment and debt increase in period t aside, $i_t = FD_t/FD_{t-1}$ and $X_t = X_t/X_{t-1}$ and FD_t/X_t increases if $i_t > X_t$. See also Fink (1995).
4 For theoretical or empirical justification see e.g. Krugman (1979), Fink (1993) and (1995), Aylward/Thorne (1998), Kaminsky/Lizondo/Reinhart (1998) etc.
5 Sometimes, however, we changed the IIF forecasts in the light of new data or different views.

References

Ades, A. (1999) *Argentina: Don't Cry for Convertibility,* Global Economics Paper No. 16, Goldman Sachs.
Aylward, L. and Thorne, R. (1998) *Countries' Repayment Performance Vis-à-Vis the IMF, An empirical analysis,* IMF Staff Papers, Vol. 45, No. 4, 595–618.
Avramovic, D. (1964) *Economic Growth and External Debt*, Baltimore, Maryland: John Hopkins Press.
Berg, A. and Pattillo C. (1999) *Are Currency Crises Predictable? A Test,* IMF Staff Papers, Vol. 46, No. 2 (June 1999), 107–38.
Eichengreen, B., Rose, A.K. and Wyplosz, Ch. (1995) 'Exchange market mayhem: the antecedents and aftermath of speculative attacks', *Economic Policy*, Vol. 21, October, 251–311.
Fink, G. (1993) *Unternehmenswert der Banken und Länderrisiko,* Österreichisches BankArchiv 8/93, 599–613.
Fink, G. (1995) *Kreditrationierung mittels Länderrisikoanalyse,* Österreichisches BankArchiv 6/95, 455–64.
Kaminsky, L. (1999) *Currency and Banking Crises: The Early Warnings of Distress,* Washington: Mimeo (February 1999).
Kaminsky, L., Lizondo, S. and Reinhart, C. M. (1998) *Leading Indicators of Currency Crisis,* IMF Staff Papers, Vol. 45, No. 1, 1–48.
Krugman, P. (1979) 'A Model of Balance-of-Payments Crises', *Journal of Money, Credit and Banking*, Vol. 11, August, 311–25.
Ozkan, F. G. and Sutherland A. (1995) 'Policy Measures to Avoid a Currency Crisis', *Economic Journal*, Vol. 105, March, 510–19.
Sachs, J., Tornell, A. and Velasco, A. (1996) 'The collapse of the Mexican peso: what have we learned?', *Economic Policy*, Vol 22, April, 15–63.
Sachs, J. D. (1998) *Creditor Panics: Causes and Remedies*, Washington, DC: Cato Institute's 16th Annual Monetary Conference.
Soros, G. (1998) *The Crisis of Global Capitalism*, New York: Public Affairs.

8 Foreign and domestic bank participation in emerging markets

Lessons from Mexico and Argentina*

B. Gerard Dages, Linda Goldberg and Daniel Kinney

Over the past decade, numerous financial systems have opened up to direct foreign participation through the ownership of local financial institutions, frequently as a direct consequence of – and as a perceived solution to – financial crises. Significant increases in such foreign participation have characterized the transition experience of Eastern Europe and the post-Tequila Crisis period in Latin America. However, the crisis experience in Asia has been markedly different to date, and is more notable for the limited nature of majority investments by foreign banks, despite the need for large-scale recapitalization of the region's troubled financial systems.

Arguments supporting a policy of openness to foreign participation are far from universally accepted. The benefits to emerging markets of foreign participation in domestic financial systems are widely exposited and argued to be broad-based. These arguments are mirrored by a set of concerns over the potentially adverse effects of opening to foreign participation (or at least opening too quickly). There is a shortage of hard evidence to support either side.

This article contributes factually to the debate over the opening of emerging markets to foreign participation by exploring the experiences of Argentina and Mexico – two markets that exhibit a significant degree and duration of foreign bank activity.

We begin our analysis by presenting the opposing views on the role of foreign-owned banks in emerging markets.[1] Next, we argue that ownership *per se* is not a reason to expect differences in the lending patterns of domestic and foreign banks; instead, these would arise because lending objectives, funding patterns, market access, and balance-sheet health may vary. We then review liberalization efforts in Argentina and Mexico in the 1990s and examine local lending patterns by foreign-owned and domestically owned local banks, including state-owned banks. Our goal is to document these banks' relative stability in lending to different client bases and to examine the cyclical

* Paper presented at 22nd SUERF Colloquium, Vienna, 27–29 April 2000. Also first published in the September 2000 issue of the Federal Reserve Bank of New York *Economic Policy Review*, pp. 17–36.

properties of such lending. Throughout, we base our analysis on published quarterly loan data for individual banks in Mexico and in Argentina in the 1990s. We look at total lending, personal/consumer lending, mortgage lending, and the broad remaining group that includes commercial, government, and other lending.

Econometrically, we show that in these countries behavioral differences are apparent across certain types of banks. These are related to whether a bank is public or private, potentially reflecting the role of distinct lending motives across these institutions. In addition, bank behavior is significantly related to the asset quality of the bank portfolio. In response to some types of economic fluctuations, domestic privately owned banks with low levels of impaired loans can have more volatile lending than their foreign bank counterparts. We argue that these differences among foreign and domestic private banks are plausible and are to be expected, especially if the respective banks rely on alternative sources of funds.

Based on bank lending patterns from 1994 through mid–1999, overall we do not find any support for the view that foreign banks contribute to instability or are excessively volatile in their responses to market signals. In Argentina, extensive and rapid banking reforms have led to a system in which both foreign and domestic privately owned banks are responsive to market signals, but where behavior is now consistent with more diversified sources of loanable funds. In Mexico, despite reform efforts in the second half of the 1990s, many domestic banks continue to face significant asset quality problems. These banks have had shrinking loan portfolios in the post-Tequila Crisis period. Healthy foreign banks have emerged as an important engine for funding local investment and growth opportunities without raising lending volatility *vis-à-vis* their healthy local counterparts.

Foreign ownership of financial institutions in emerging markets

Arguments for foreign bank participation

There are three main arguments in favor of opening emerging market financial sectors to foreign ownership. First, consistent with traditional arguments in support of capital account liberalization, some contend that a foreign bank presence increases the amount of funding available to domestic projects by facilitating capital inflows. Such a presence may also increase the stability of available lending to the emerging market by diversifying the capital and funding bases supporting the overall supply of domestic credit. This type of argument is especially persuasive when applied to small and/or volatile economies.[2]

Second, some contend that foreign banks improve the quality, pricing, and availability of financial services, both directly as providers of such enhanced services and indirectly through competition with domestic financial institutions (Levine 1996). Third, foreign bank presence is said to improve financial system infrastructure – including accounting, transparency, and financial regulation – and stimulate the increased presence of supporting agents such as ratings agencies, auditors, and credit bureaus (Glaessner and Oks 1994). A foreign bank presence might enhance the ability of financial institutions to measure and manage risk effectively. Additionally, foreign banks might import financial system supervision and supervisory skills from home country regulators. While many of these goals ultimately may be achievable without foreign financial institutions, an increased foreign presence may meaningfully accelerate the process.

Although a sizable body of research has explored the potential benefits of financial liberalization broadly defined, few studies have focused on the potential benefits of increased foreign participation in banking and finance.[3] For the most part, these studies focus on bank efficiency spillovers but not on lending behavior. For example, a recent cross-country study shows that foreign bank presence is associated with reduced profitability and diminished overhead expenses for domestic banks, and hence with enhanced domestic bank efficiency (Claessens, Demirguc-Kunt, and Huizinga 1998).[4] Findings of increased domestic bank efficiency and heightened competition are also supported in the Argentine experience of the mid-1990s (Clarke, Cull, D'Amato, and Molinari 1999). Increased foreign competition in corporate loan markets reduced associated net margins and before-tax profits, and margins and profits remained higher in the consumer sector, which had not attracted comparable foreign entry.[5] Evidence on behavioral comparisons between foreign and domestically owned banks remains largely undocumented.

Arguments against foreign bank participation

Arguments against opening domestic financial systems to foreign ownership in part mirror the arguments presented above. One strand of concern contends that foreign-owned financial institutions will in fact decrease the stability of aggregate domestic bank credit by providing additional avenues for capital flight or by withdrawing more rapidly from local markets in the face of a crisis either in the host or home country. Others argue that foreign financial institutions 'cherry pick' the most lucrative domestic markets or customers, leaving the less competitive domestic institutions to serve other, riskier customers and increasing the risk borne by domestic institutions. Moreover, independent of the effect on aggregate credit generally or during a crisis, the distribution of credit may be affected, resulting in redistribution and potential crowding out of some segments of local borrowers.

These concerns blur into similar arguments centered on the principle that financial services represent a strategic industry best controlled by domestic interests, especially in the context of a state-directed development model in which domestic banks serve identified development interests. Such arguments are especially likely to be voiced by those domestic concerns that will be most negatively affected by financial sector opening, whereas any benefits are likely to accrue across broader segments of the economy.

Contrary to the argument that increased foreign ownership brings improved financial supervision, concerns are voiced over the multiple challenges to supervision raised by complex financial institutions active in a number of jurisdictions. These concerns are accentuated by asymmetries in information between home and host country supervisors.

Even many supporters of increased foreign ownership of banks argue that the sequencing of any such opening is critical, and that it should follow the consolidation and strengthening of the domestic financial system and/or the development of the necessary financial infrastructure, including supervision. Most of these concerns are generally unsupported by empirical evidence. However, recent research on the sources of financial crises has fueled an additional concern by establishing a pattern in which the crises tend to be preceded by financial liberalization (Kaminsky and Reinhart 1999; Rojas-Suarez 1998). Such studies, however, typically have not focused on or identified the role of foreign-owned financial institutions in contributing to or mitigating crises. The exception is Demirguc-Kunt, Levine, and Min (1998), who observe that over the 1988–95 period and for a large sample of countries, foreign bank entry generally was associated with a lower incidence of local banking crises.

The need for an understanding of the implications of an increased foreign bank presence is especially compelling in the wake of financial crises. In this context, foreign institutions may represent important sources of equity capital for domestic financial systems, particularly in postcrisis recapitalization efforts like those under way in Asia. In addition to helping to further the goal of an active and efficient private banking network, foreign institutions may bring important attributes that domestic financial institutions lack.

Conceptualizing the differences among banks in loan supply and volatility

The crux of some arguments for and against foreign bank participation could be better understood within the context of a conceptual framework of bank lending volatility and funding availability. Specifically, we expect that lending patterns will vary among state-owned, private domestically owned, and private foreign-owned banks to the extent that there are corresponding differences in bank motives or goals, in balance-sheet health, and in funding sources.[6] These differences would influence the interest rate sensitivity of the loan supply by any bank and the extent to which a bank expands or contracts lending in response to various market signals.

Some of the points raised in the aforementioned debate on credit volatility hinge on the idea that interest rate sensitivity of lending is likely to be greatest for banks with closer ties to international capital markets, and wider access to a range of profitable investment opportunities. In emerging markets, banks with foreign affiliates are likely to have such ties, potentially affirming the feature of having a more interest-rate-elastic loan supply than private domestically owned banks. Moreover, if profitability is more of a motive for private domestic banks than for state-owned banks, the state-owned banks would be expected to have the lowest interest rate sensitivity among this group.

However, despite such presumed differences across banks, it is inappropriate to conclude that foreign banks will necessarily have more volatile lending patterns. Loan supply and demand may differ across banks for numerous reasons. One such reason is that banks may be distinct from one another in terms of lending motives with respect to their clients. Through 'transaction-based' lending motives, improved economic conditions generate opportunities for expanding production and investment. Bank loans expand to accommodate part of this demand. Alternatively, through 'relationship' lending motives, bank lending helps established customers smooth over the effects of cyclical fluctuations or consumption. Under adverse economic conditions, lending expands to offset some of the revenue shortfall of clients; under good economic conditions, net lending by banks declines as borrowers pay back outstanding loans. Under these stylized conditions, relationship lending is countercyclical, while transaction-based lending is procyclical.

The *quality of bank balance sheets* can also influence bank responsiveness to market signals. Banks focused on balance-sheet repair will concentrate less on expanding loan availability when aggregate demand conditions improve, leaving profitable local investment opportunities underfunded. Thus, the poor health of banks could be associated with reduced loan variability, decreased sensitivity to market signals, and missed opportunities for profitable and efficient investment. An alternative and potentially more dangerous scenario arises when less healthy banks, instead of undertaking balance-sheet repair, focus on lending expansion in a gamble for redemption. Overall, if the local banking system's health is compromised, the presence of healthy foreign banks should reduce some of the negative current and future externalities attributable to unhealthy local lenders. In this scenario, foreign bank presence fills a domestic vacuum by providing finance for worthwhile local projects.

Lending sensitivity across banks will also depend on *the bank's sources of loanable funds*. If domestically owned banks rely more heavily on local demand deposits and cyclically sensitive sources of funds,[7] local aggregate demand shocks should generally lead to more volatile lending by private domestic banks than by their foreign-owned counterparts. In the same vein, smaller domestic banks with more narrow funding bases are likely to demonstrate the greatest degree of credit cyclicality, all else equal.[8]

Case studies: foreign versus domestic banks in Argentina and Mexico

As we turn to the specific experiences of Mexico and Argentina, our goal is to document some patterns in bank lending activity and provide factual evidence in response to two main questions. First, did foreign bank participation in local markets deepen or diversify local loan supply and improve the stability of bank lending? Second, did foreign bank participation increase the sensitivity of lending to market signals? Our conceptual discussion leads us to expect that healthy foreign banks will be more sensitive to market signals than unhealthy banks or state-owned banks with different lending goals. However, some types of aggregate fluctuations – such as those arising from local GDP cycles – may lead to more lending fluctuation by healthy local banks than by healthy foreign banks, especially if domestic banks have less internationally diversified funding bases.

Argentina and Mexico are both instructive case studies for examining the implications of broader foreign bank participation in domestic markets. Over the course of the last decade, both countries implemented reforms facilitating foreign bank entry and then experienced a substantive internationalization of domestic financial markets, with the pace of foreign entry sharply accelerating in the wake of severe financial crises. However, the Mexican and Argentine experiences have also contrasted markedly with regard to the pace, depth, and nature of foreign bank penetration. In Argentina, foreign banks now participate on an equal footing with domestic institutions and are active in all broad segments of the loan market. Until very recently, foreign banks in Mexico faced a competitive landscape dominated by large domestic banks. Furthermore, the financial sector as a whole remains fragile, with real loan growth yet to recover from the 1994 Tequila Crisis. We briefly outline the experiences of each country, focusing on financial sector reforms and the evolution of the foreign bank presence before turning to the data analysis.

Argentina: financial reforms and foreign entry

Introduction of the Convertibility Plan in 1991 marked a turning point in Argentine financial history. It heralded profound monetary and fiscal reform, broad deregulation of domestic markets, privatization of a majority of government-owned entities, trade liberalization, elimination of capital controls and, more generally, a macroeconomic environment conducive to foreign investment.

The Convertibility Plan succeeded in stemming hyperinflationary pressures and restoring economic growth relatively quickly. Within the financial sector, this contributed to enhanced intermediation: credit to the private sector almost doubled, reaching 19 percent of GDP by year-end 1994, up from close to 10 percent of GDP in 1990. Following the removal of restrictions on foreign direct investment and capital repatriation, the number of foreign banks operating in Argentina increased, but their assets remained below 20 percent of system assets through year-end 1994 (Table 8.1).

Beginning in early 1995, contagion from Mexico's Tequila Crisis severely tested the Argentine financial sector – sparking an outflow of almost 20

Table 8.1 Penetration of foreign banks into Argentine lending markets: foreign bank loans as a percentage of total outstanding loans in each category

Type of loan	1994	1997	1999
Personal	25.4	48.5	45.8
Mortgage	10.3	20.4	31.9
Commercial, government, and other	19.0	37.4	53.2
Total loans	*18.0*	*35.0*	*48.1*

Source: Authors' calculations, based on data from various issues of *Información de Entidades Financieras* (*formerly Estados Contables de las Entidades Financieras*), published by Banco Central de la República Argentina.

percent of system deposits. In the wake of the Tequila Crisis, the transformation of the Argentine financial sector accelerated. Efforts undertaken to reestablish confidence in the banking sector included the introduction of deposit insurance, a renewed commitment to privatizing inefficient public sector banks, the liquidation and/or consolidation of nonviable entities, and the dedication of substantial resources to strengthening supervisory oversight and the regulatory framework. Within this context, foreign banks were permitted to play an important role in recapitalizing the Argentine banking system.

Prior to the 1990s, very few foreign banks were present in Argentina, with US-based institutions – primarily Citibank and BankBoston – among the more active. Subsequent entry occurred mainly via the acquisition of existing operations, with foreign shareholders acquiring stakes in private institutions with a national or regional franchise – generally in better condition and with stronger distribution networks than privatized provincial and municipal banks. Such acquisitions accelerated dramatically beginning in 1996, with foreign banks acquiring controlling stakes in a majority of Argentina's largest private banks.[9] By 1999, roughly half of all banking sector assets were under foreign control, with foreign shareholders holding significant minority stakes in a number of other financial institutions.

The growing foreign bank presence dramatically altered the competitive landscape of Argentina's banking sector and catalyzed aggressive competition for market share, primarily via retail expansion. As shown in Table 8.1, foreign-controlled banks have been particularly successful in penetrating commercial, government, interbank, and personal loan markets. Although they still appear to lag behind their domestic counterparts in mortgage lending, this may change in the wake of the January 1999 privatization of a controlling stake in the national mortgage bank.

Overall, foreign and domestic banks in Argentina appear to compete aggressively in all segments of the local loan market. Details of foreign and domestic bank loan portfolios are provided in Table 8.2.[10] It is striking that foreign banks generally engage in the same types of broad lending activities as domestic banks, but are more heavily weighted toward relatively lower risk commercial, government, and other lending.[11] Overall, the recent growth in foreign bank presence and in commercial and government lending share implies that foreign banks are playing an increasingly important role in these segments of local financing. In addition, lending patterns by private domestic banks appear to be much more similar to those of foreign banks than to those of state-owned banks. Like foreign bank portfolios, Argentine private bank portfolios tend to have lower mortgage shares and higher shares of commercial, government, and other lending.

Table 8.2 Composition of bank loan portfolios by owner type: as a percentage of total bank loans

	Domestically owned banks						Foreign-owned banks		
	State-owned			Privately owned					
Type of loan	*1994*	*1997*	*1999*	*1994*	*1997*	*1999*	*1994*	*1997*	*1999*
Personal	5.2	5.8	5.9	13.2	10.4	6.1	14.1	13.3	5.5
Mortgage	32.1	32.2	35.1	9.4	13.2	15.0	11.0	11.7	14.7
Commercial, government, and other	62.7	62.0	59.0	77.4	76.4	78.9	74.8	75.0	79.8

Source: Authors' calculations, based on data from various issues of *Información de Entidades Financieras* (formerly *Estados Contables de las Entidades Financieras*), published by Banco Central de la República Argentina.

Foreign banks and loan supply patterns in Argentina

A key issue in the ongoing policy debate is whether patterns in loan issuance by banks have become more stable over time as foreign banks have become more entrenched. Using lending data from individual banks operating in Argentina, we compute weighted and unweighted averages of quarterly bank loan growth rates. We report the mean of these growth rates over time. We also compute the standard deviations of the loan growth rates, normalized by mean levels of loan growth. These normalized standard deviations are an indicator of average volatility per unit of loan growth. The unweighted numbers reflect averages across banks, regardless of the individual banks' importance in various lending markets. The weighted numbers reflect overall availability of loans by the respective classes of lenders (state-owned banks, domestic private banks, and foreign private banks).[12]

Among domestically owned banks, the state-owned banks exhibit relatively low average growth in loan portfolios.[13] The loan growth and volatility figures for these banks are quite striking in the crisis period, with average loan expansion close to zero and average normalized volatility at a very high level. In all periods, private foreign banks had both the highest quarterly loan growth and the lowest normalized variability of this growth. In the crisis and postcrisis periods, domestic private and foreign private banks had higher loan growth and lower normalized volatility than did domestic state-owned banks.

When lending volumes are weighted by bank size (Table 8.3, panel B), the crisis and postcrisis periods register generally higher loan growth for all types of banks. These findings, compared with those in panel A, imply that among all banks, the larger banks had more loan growth than the smaller banks. Larger foreign banks have greater average loan growth and equal or lower average volatility per unit of loan growth than their public and private domestic counterparts.

Table 8.3 Average bank loan growth: Argentina.
Quarterly percentage changes

Time period	All banks	State-owned banks	Private domestic banks	Private foreign banks
Panel A: Unweighted average across individual banks				
Precrisis	3.6	3.8	2.4	5.0
Crisis	2.0	0.3	2.1	3.0
	(0.7)	(14.3)	(1.9)	(1.1)
Postcrisis	3.2	1.5	3.2	4.3
	(0.9)	(2.4)	(1.0)	(0.8)
Panel B: Weighted average across individual banks				
Precrisis	2.2	1.4	1.4	5.9
Crisis	2.5	2.4	2.6	2.8
	(0.7)	(2.0)	(1.9)	(1.3)
Postcrisis	4.0	1.9	4.6	5.6
	(0.7)	(1.2)	(0.8)	(0.8)

Source: Authors' calculations, based on data from various issues of *Información de Entidades Financieras* (formerly *Estados Contables de las Entidades Financieras*), published by Banco Central de la República Argentina.

Notes: For single missing observations, we use data averaged across prior and subsequent periods. Calculations use real balances of outstanding loans of individual banks. The precrisis period for which data are available is second-quarter to third-quarter 1994, too short a period for standard deviations on the average loan growth rates. The Tequila Crisis period for Argentina is fourth-quarter 1994 to fourth-quarter 1995. The postcrisis period ends in second-quarter 1999. Normalized standard deviations are reported in parentheses.

As we noted earlier, another metric of lending stability controls for whether changes in loan volumes arise because of differing responses to market signals; alternatively, changing loan volumes can be more random and unrelated to macroeconomic fundamentals. Using time-series data from individual bank balance sheets, we perform pooled time-series regressions to test for differences across domestic, foreign, and state-owned banks in loan responsiveness with respect to real GDP and real interest rates.[14] This responsiveness is estimated using both unweighted and weighted regressions: unweighted regressions measure the responsiveness of an average bank, regardless of its size, while weighted regressions measure the responsiveness of total lending by a class of banks. The difference across these types of regressions can be interpreted as suggesting differences across larger versus smaller banks (or across total lending volumes versus average bank behavior) in the respective specific lending areas – that is, in total lending, mortgage lending, personal lending, and commercial and other lending. The results for second-quarter 1996 through second-quarter 1999 are summarized in Table 8.4.[15]

Table 8.4 Bank loan sensitivity to GDP: Argentina. Second-quarter 1996 to second-quarter 1999

	Total loans	Consumer loans	Mortgage loans	Commercial, Government and interbank loans
Panel A: Unweighted elasticities				
State-owned	0.37	−7.73***	−5.56	0.08
	(0.58)	(1.66)	(7.83)	(0.77)
Number of observations	90	73	73	73
Domestic privately owned	1.44**	−4.56***	−0.04	1.71**
	(0.61)	(1.53)	(7.17)	(0.70)
Number of observations	104	101	101	101
Foreign privately owned	0.90*	−6.28***	2.87	1.31**
	(0.46)	(1.32)	(5.52)	(0.54)
Number of observations	143	140	140	140
Domestic private equal to foreign private?	Yes	Yes	Yes	Yes
Panel B: Elasticities weighted by bank size				
State-owned	0.15	−8.25***	0.28	0.15
	(0.47)	(1.66)	(1.72)	(0.60)
Domestic privately owned	1.26*	−4.59***	1.06	1.12
	(0.66)	(1.75)	(3.64)	(0.74)
Foreign privately owned	1.00**	−7.44***	0.52	1.63***
	(0.46)	(1.44)	(2.73)	(0.52)
Domestic private equal to foreign private?	Yes	Yes	Yes	Yes

Notes: Standard errors are reported beneath the average elasticities drawn from ordinary least squares regressions over the percentage change in real loans against bank fixed effects, the percentage change in real GDP, and local real interest rate differentials *vis-à-vis* the United States. The equality test rows ask whether statistically the coefficients on private domestic and private foreign banks are equal to each other. Some outlier observations were omitted from the regression analysis.

* Statistically significant at the 10 percent level.
** Statistically significant at the 5 percent level.
*** Statistically significant at the 1 percent level.

In the post-Tequila Crisis period, total lending by Argentine state-owned banks was largely insensitive to GDP and interest rate fluctuations, a pattern that is attributable to a lack of sensitivity of both mortgage lending and commercial and related lending.[16] Personal lending, which accounts for only about 6 percent of the portfolio of state-owned banks, has been counter-cyclical. A 1 percent rise in GDP is associated with a 7.7 percent contraction in personal lending by the average state-owned bank, with a slightly higher contraction by larger banks.

In stark contrast to state-owned banks, private banks in Argentina – both domestically owned and foreign-owned – have been significantly more responsive to economic signals in the post-Tequila Crisis period. Total lending tends to be procyclical for both domestic and foreign banks, driven by the highly procyclical nature of lending to 'commercial, government, and other' clients. This type of lending is consistent with transaction-based, or arms-length, activity. The point estimate of the cyclical response by domestic private banks (at 1.44) is stronger than the response by foreign banks (at 0.90), as one would expect with domestic private banks more heavily reliant on local sources of funds. Yet, despite consistent patterns in the size of point estimates, statistically we cannot reject that both private domestic banks and private foreign banks have identical proportionate lending responses to cyclical forces in Argentina.

Both types of privately owned banks also have strong countercyclical patterns of personal lending. When GDP expands by 1.0 percent, personal lending contracts by 4.6 percent for the average domestic privately owned banks and by 6.3 percent for their average foreign-owned counterparts. Finally, a comparison of elasticities from the unweighted and weighted regressions suggests that smaller domestic banks have greater credit cyclicality than the larger domestic banks, which may lend additional support to the funding composition hypothesis.

Overall, the evidence on loan activity in Argentina supports a claim of differences in behavior across state-owned banks and private banks. However, domestic and foreign private banks exhibit comparable loan behavior, coexist in the distribution of larger and smaller banks within the top twenty-five banks nationally, and have loan portfolios of similar compositions. The banks respond similarly to market signals, including real GDP growth and real interest rates. Overall, foreign-owned banks appear to have provided greater loan growth than what was observed among domestic-owned banks, while reducing the volatility of loan growth for the financial system as a whole. Foreign banks also exhibited notable loan growth during the crisis period, suggesting that they may be important stabilizers of credit during such episodes. It is also noteworthy that state-owned banks had higher variability of lending as well as a smaller portion of this variability explained by macroeconomic fundamentals.

Mexico: financial reforms and foreign entry

In Mexico, recent efforts toward financial liberalization began in the early 1990s with the reprivatization of the financial sector, following a decade of nationalization and government-orchestrated bank consolidation.[17] After several years of rapid expansion by the newly privatized banks, however, Mexico's financial crisis – triggered by the 1994 peso devaluation – both revealed and exacerbated significant weaknesses in a large number of institutions. Since the crisis, authorities have responded with an array of support programs for financial institutions and their borrowers, intended to bolster the health of the financial sector; they have also opened the sector to foreign investment beyond the schedules originally negotiated under the North American Free Trade Agreement (NAFTA).[18] Pressures on bank condition, however, remain significant and widespread and continue to be an important driver of Mexican bank behavior.

In the early 1990s, only one foreign bank, Citibank, was permitted to conduct local banking operations, accounting for less than 1 percent of total loans. With the initiation of NAFTA in 1994, restrictions on foreign bank participation Mexico were gradually eased. Initial entrants generally established very small *de novo* subsidiaries engaged in wholesale, nonloan banking activities. On average, each of these foreign bank operations consisted of a single branch office with less than 100 employees and captured about 0.1 percent of loan market share. As Table 8.5 shows, foreign banks in 1995 cumulatively represented about 1 percent of the consumer and commercial, government, and interbank loans.

Table 8.5 Penetration of foreign banks into Mexican lending markets. Foreign bank loans as a percentage of current loans in each category

Type of lending activity	1992	1995	1998
Consumer	0.0	0.9	11.1
Mortgage	0.0	0.0	6.4
Commercial, government, and interbank	0.2	1.0	19.7
Total loans	*0.2*	*0.7*	*17.8*

Source: Authors' calculations, based on data from Comisión Nacional Bancaria y de Valores.

As in the Argentine experience, in the aftermath of the 1994–95 Tequila Crisis, foreign banks in Mexico began establishing a significant local retail presence (Table 8.A4). Despite a variety of support programs, twelve Mexican banks (accounting for roughly 20 percent of total loans) failed outright, prompting the authorities to intervene. The subsequent sale of these franchises (or portions thereof) provided an avenue for foreign bank entry into, and partial recapitalization of, the Mexican retail banking sector. As outlined in Table 8.A4, there were six foreign bank acquisitions of domestic retail operations through the end of 1998, with Spanish banks among the most active buyers. In addition, there have been six mergers of domestic banks with other domestic banks.

By 1998, foreign bank participation in the local loan market had grown from less than 1 percent prior to the crisis to 18 percent (Table 8.5). Foreign banks controlled two of the six largest banks (Santander Mexicano and BBV), held minority stakes in three more, and operated nineteen fully owned local subsidiaries (Table 8A.5). However, restrictions on foreign ownership remained in place until December 1998, prohibiting foreign control of Mexico's three largest banks (in aggregate, almost 60 percent of the loan market share). In the aftermath of this liberalization, two of the three largest Mexican banks have come under foreign control.[19]

As shown in Table 8.5, foreign bank lending has been concentrated in the commercial, government, and interbank sectors, with much lower penetration of the consumer and mortgage markets. This concentration may be a function less of strategic considerations than of pervasive weaknesses in Mexico's credit environment, which has been characterized by high real interest rates, a reduced pool of creditworthy borrowers, a breakdown in borrower discipline, and a legal environment that provides little creditor protection. This pattern is supported by a noticeable shift in domestic bank loan portfolios from consumer and mortgage lending over this same period – a shift that is due in part to the government acquisition of a large portion of these loans in the wake of the crisis.

Precrisis domestic lending to the consumer and mortgage sectors represented about 30 percent of the lending portfolios of banks, a ratio very similar to that observed in Argentina (Table 8.6).[20] However, by 1998, consumer and mortgage loans accounted for less than 18 percent of domestic bank loan portfolios and only 6 percent of foreign lending. Foreign bank activity remained concentrated (93.6 percent) in the consumer, government, and interbank market.

Table 8.6 Mexican bank loan portfolio composition: as a percentage of total current loans

Type of loan	Domestically owned banks			Foreign-owned banks		
	1992	*1995*	*1998*	*1992*	*1995*	*1998*
Consumer	12.0	5.6	3.3	0.3	6.9	1.9
Mortgage	16.0	22.4	14.3	2.0	0.3	4.5
Commercial, government, and interbank	72.0	72.0	82.4	97.7	92.8	93.6

Source: Authors' calculations, based on data from Comisión Nacional Bancaria y de Valores.

The condition of Mexico's banks over this period has also played a significant role in influencing loan behavior. Although objective measurement of Mexican bank condition is impeded by a lack of full transparency (for example, not all banks publicly release financial statements) and by changes in accounting standards over the sample period, a measure of impaired loans as a proportion of total loans can be used as a relative indicator of the depth of asset quality problems on bank balance sheets. Impaired loans are defined here as the sum of reported nonperforming loans, restructured loans, and the full amount of loans sold to the government.

The vast majority of domestic banks (88 percent), which represent the bulk of domestic bank lending in Mexico, had impaired loan ratios (ILRs) under 10 percent at the beginning of 1994 (Table 8.7). By 1998, in part because of improved accounting and reporting conditions, 41 percent of the banks (representing 93 percent of total lending by domestic banks) had ILRs exceeding 30 percent. While the bulk of foreign-owned banks (90 percent) remained relatively healthy, the larger foreign-owned retail franchises (accounting for 76 percent of foreign bank lending) also had ILRs in excess of 30 percent at year-end 1998, largely reflecting postcrisis acquisitions of troubled domestic banks by foreign banks.

Table 8.7 Impaired loan ratios (ILRs) of banks in Mexico

Nationality of Banks	Date	ILR: 0–10 percent		ILR: 10–30 percent		ILR: 30 percent or greater	
		% of Banks	% of Current Loans	% of Banks	% of Current Loans	% of Banks	% of Current Loans
Domestic	1994:1	86.4	94.4	13.6	5.5	0.0	0.0
	1998:4	58.8	7.2	0.0	0.0	41.2	92.8
Foreign	1994:1	100.0	100.0	0.0	0.0	0.0	0.0
	1998:4	90.0	24.1	0.0	0.0	10.0	75.9

Source: Authors' calculations, based on data from Comisión Nacional Bancaria y de Valores.

Note: Impaired loans are the sum of reported nonperforming loans, restructured loans, and the full amount of loans sold to the government.

The foreign bank effect on loan supply patterns in Mexico

The data presented thus far show that foreign banks operating in Mexico have focused their efforts mainly on commercial, government, and inter-bank lending. Given the condition of the Mexican banking sector, the potential for a broad and positive role for healthy foreign banks therefore seems substantial. Foreign banks could be an important absolute and diversified source of credit to firms, especially in an economy in which government-operated and domestic banks are heavily focused on balance-sheet repair instead of new lending. In this environment, funds provided by foreign banks can be a source of much needed capital for local profitable growth opportunities.

Our conceptualization of differences across banks that can lead to distinct lending behaviors emphasized bank health as a potentially important issue. Given the preponderance of impaired loans among Mexican banks in the second half of the 1990s, we consider the extent to which distinctions among banks in lending behavior are evident according to broad indicators of bank health. We use the previously defined ILR as an indicator of financial condition, whereby banks with an ILR in excess of 10 percent are considered to be in relatively poor financial health.

The loan growth and associated volatility of banks operating in Mexico appear in Table 8.8. By sorting banks in each period according to whether their ILR falls below or exceeds 10 percent, we observe significant differences in loan growth and in the volatility of this growth between healthier and less healthy banks. These differences pertain both to domestically owned and foreign-owned banks. In general, banks with higher impaired loan ratios had more volatile loan growth rates and lower (or negative) rates of loan portfolio expansion than banks with less problematic portfolios. In terms of average quarterly growth, both domestic and foreign banks with low ILRs continued to extend credit fairly steadily in the postcrisis period. In this healthier group, smaller foreign and domestic banks grew at a quicker pace than their larger counterparts, without increasing measured volatility per unit of loan growth.

Table 8.8 Average quarterly loan growth rates: Mexico: percent

Time period	All Banks	ILR less than 10 percent		ILR greater than 10 percent	
		Domestic	Foreign	Domestic	Foreign
Panel A: Unweighted average across banks					
Precrisis	9.6	9.5	26.9	1.3	–
	(0.5)	(0.6)	(1.8)	(8.7)	–
Crisis	16.0	20.1	15.5	1.7	–
	(1.1)	(0.8)	(0.3)	(9.9)	–
Postcrisis	9.6	11.7	18.2	–1.1	7.4
	(1.1)	(1.5)	(1.2)	(5.7)	(3.1)
Panel B: Weighted average across banks					
Precrisis	4.5	4.4	26.9	2.0	–
	(0.8)	(0.8)	(1.8)	(6.1)	–
Crisis	8.1	8.5	15.5	5.9	–
	(1.7)	(1.6)	(0.3)	(2.2)	–
Postcrisis	–0.3	9.1	12.6	–1.5	7.4
	(21.6)	(1.7)	(1.3)	(4.5)	(3.1)

Source: Authors' calculations, based on data from Comisión Nacional Bancaria y de Valores.

Notes: ILR is impaired loan ratio. For these calculations, we drop from our data sample the observations for individual new banks that represent their initial periods of entry and expansion. Inclusion of these initial data points would otherwise artificially show a sharp increase in the loan growth of foreign banks especially, along with higher variability of growth. Normalized standard deviations are reported in parentheses.

Lending by banks with low ILRs grew at high rates, leaving these banks to play an expanding role mainly in commercial finance, even as they remained a small part of the Mexican banking system (accounting for about 30 percent of the total current loans at the end of 1998). Although the full financial system continues to show small average contraction in the postcrisis period, it is evident that the extent of this loan contraction has been reduced by the presence of foreign banks, and by healthy banks in general. As we observed in Argentina, the more extensive role played by foreign banks in Mexico does not appear to have come at the expense of greater lending volatility.

Next, we consider these lending fluctuations in the context of Mexican real demand growth and real interest rate differentials *vis-à-vis* the United States.[21] Since a small number of very large banks have dominated lending activity in Mexico, we anticipate large distinctions between our results presented as averages across individual banks and averages across all lending, even when bank condition is considered. In general, however, the domestic banks with sounder reported asset-quality ratios are smaller banks engaged in limited retail lending.

For the post-Tequila Crisis period for which we have data – second-quarter 1995 through fourth-quarter 1998 – our sorting of banks according to domestic versus foreign ownership and according to ILRs is highly revealing (Table 8.9).[22] In Mexico, on an unweighted basis, the banks most responsive to cyclical fluctuations were the domestically owned ones with low nonperforming loan shares (particularly smaller banks). Indeed, behavior by these banks is strikingly similar to the behavior reported for the private banks in Argentina. Lending to commercial and other clients is strongly procyclical, consistent with transaction-based, or arms-length, lending, as was observed in Argentina. Lending to consumer and mortgage clients is in general statistically insignificantly correlated with real GDP growth in Mexico. Our conceptual framework presented earlier anticipated the finding here that the banks with lower impaired loan ratios are more responsive to fluctuations and market signals than are banks with more problematic loan portfolios.

Regarding the foreign banks operating in Mexico, there appears to be a strong behavioral distinction among banks with lower ILRs versus the few banks observed with higher ILRs. The foreign banks with low ILRs appear to behave similarly to domestically owned banks with low ILRs. As anticipated, and as observed in the Argentine case, the point estimates on responses are higher for the domestic banks in this group with low impaired loan ratios. Their larger response elasticities to GDP stimuli are consistent with domestic banks having heavier reliance on domestic sources of funds. Still, as we observed in the case of Argentine private banks, we cannot reject similar behavior by these banks with low ILRs but different nationalities of owners. The foreign banks with high ILRs behave differently from all other categories of banks in our sample, with procyclical consumer lending and countercyclical commercial and other lending.

Several findings stand out in this empirical analysis. First, bank health appears to be a key factor distinguishing the responsiveness to market signals

Table 8.9 Bank loan sensitivity to GDP: Mexico.
Second-quarter 1995 to fourth-quarter 1998

	Total loans	Consumer loans	Mortgage loans	Commercial, Government and interbank loans
Panel A: Unweighted elasticities				
Banks with impaired loan ratios under 10 percent				
Domestic banks	1.67***	−0.62	−2.02**	1.67***
	(0.56)	(0.69)	(0.97)	(0.57)
Number of observations	153	78	50	153
Foreign banks	0.93*	−0.04	0.29	1.02**
	(0.51)	(1.11)	(1.40)	(0.53)
Number of observations	190	28	20	182
Domestic private equal to foreign private?	Yes	Yes	Yes	Yes
Banks with impaired loan ratios above 10 percent				
Domestic banks	0.85*	0.09	0.26	1.35***
	(0.49)	(0.44)	(0.48)	(0.50)
Number of observations	178	165	159	178
Foreign banks	−1.51	2.94*	−0.08	−1.58
	(1.81)	(1.55)	(1.72)	(1.85)
Number of observations	16	16	15	16
Panel B: Elasticities weighted by bank size				
Banks with impaired loan ratios under 10 percent				
Domestic banks	1.55***	−0.43	−1.11	1.52**
	(0.49)	(4.14)	(2.26)	(0.65)
Number of observations	153	72	46	152
Foreign banks	0.92	0.40	0.31	0.93
	(0.71)	(1.42)	(17.7)	(0.94)
Number of observations	190	26	20	181
Domestic private equal to foreign private?	Yes	Yes	Yes	Yes
Banks with impaired loan ratios above 10 percent				
Domestic banks	0.97***	0.15	−0.73***	1.76***
	(0.10)	(0.22)	(0.23)	(0.15)
Number of observations	178	165	158	178
Foreign banks	−1.26***	2.81	0.26	−1.37**
	(0.44)	(1.73)	(1.67)	(0.59)
Number of observations	16	16	15	16

Notes: Standard errors are reported beneath the average elasticities drawn from ordinary least squares regressions over the percentage change in real loans against bank fixed effects, the percentage change in real GDP, and local real interest rate differentials *vis-à-vis* the United States. The equality test rows ask whether statistically the coefficients on private domestic and private foreign banks are equal to each other. For these calculations, we drop from our data sample the observations for individual new banks that represent their initial periods of entry and expansion.

* Statistically significant at the 10 percent level.
** Statistically significant at the 5 percent level.
*** Statistically significant at the 1 percent level.

among both domestically owned and foreign-owned banks in Mexico. Second, point estimates show more volatile lending with respect to GDP by domestically owned banks, a finding consistent with our earlier conceptualization. Specifically, if healthy domestically owned banks (all else equal) rely more heavily on domestic sources of funding (particularly smaller banks), lending by these banks will be more sensitive to local cyclical conditions than lending by their foreign-owned counterparts. In Mexico, we observe that foreign banks with low ILRs facilitated more overall responsiveness of the financial system to market forces and were important providers of credit during the crisis period and in the subsequent period of financial system weakness. These results appear to confirm that foreign banks thus far have had a stabilizing impact on domestic financial system credit in Mexico and Argentina.

Conclusion

The Asian crisis amply demonstrated a range of deficiencies in local financial systems and precipitated calls for reform in accounting and disclosure practices, bank corporate governance, and home country supervision and regulation. It is often argued that opening domestic financial sectors to increased foreign ownership can meaningfully accelerate improvements in all three areas, and that it should be (and historically has been) a key element of reform efforts in the aftermath of a financial crisis. At the same time, various arguments emphasize the potential adverse effects of foreign ownership. To date, the postcrisis financial landscape in Asia has been characterized only by limited examples of majority foreign ownership of domestic financial institutions.

This article has sought to contribute to the debate on financial sector openness in emerging markets by reviewing the experiences of Mexico and Argentina with regard to foreign bank local lending. We conclude that in both countries, foreign banks exhibited stronger loan growth than all domestically owned banks and had lower associated volatility, contributing to greater stability in overall financial system credit. Additionally, in both countries, foreign banks showed notable credit growth during recent crisis periods and thereafter. In Argentina, there are striking similarities in the portfolio composition of lending and the volatility of lending by private foreign and private domestic banks. In Mexico, there are behavioral similarities in terms of cyclical fluctuations and loan portfolios among banks with comparable, low impaired loan ratios but different ownership. We found that domestically owned and foreign-owned banks with low problem loan ratios behave similarly, and we found no evidence that the foreign banks were more volatile lenders than their domestic counterparts. The ranking of banks according to their responses to cyclical fluctuations is consistent with an outcome that arises when foreign banks bring to the emerging market a broader, more diversified supply of funds.

Overall, these findings suggest that bank health, and not ownership *per se*, has been the critical element in the growth, volatility, and cyclicality of bank credit. Diversity in ownership has contributed to greater stability of credit in recent periods of crisis and financial system weakness. The positive Argentine and Mexican experiences could be broadly instructive for other emerging markets as they contemplate more extensive foreign bank participation in their local economies.

Notes

1 We define foreign-owned as reflecting majority control; this definition does not necessarily imply majority share ownership.
2 Some of these arguments parallel those supporting the repeal in the United States of the McFadden Act, which restricted interstate bank branching and limited diversification of US bank loan portfolios. Meltzer (1998), for example, emphasizes the importance of risk diversification as an argument for removing legal and regulatory obstacles to bank branching internationally.
3 Other research considers the postliberalization dynamics of deposit taking and its responsiveness to bank riskiness in Mexico, Argentina, Chile, and Canada (Martinez Peria, Soledad, and Schmukler 1999; Gruben 1999).
4 Demirguc-Kunt, Levine, and Min (1998) present similar results.
5 Burdisso, D'Amato, and Molinari (1998) also show that bank privatization increased Argentine bank efficiency, and that the consolidation of retail banking led to scale-efficiency gains. Privatization led to reduced portfolio risk and more efficient allocation of credit.
6 This section closely follows Goldberg (2000). In a domestic banking system, arguments about lending sensitivity to fluctuations follow the tradition of Peek and Rosengren (1997, 2000) and Hancock and Wilcox (1998).
7 As argued by Peek and Rosengren (1997) and Hancock and Wilcox (1998), local demand deposits are positively correlated with the local business cycle.
8 Of course, increased use of foreign sources of funds can also make lending in emerging markets more sensitive to foreign cyclical fluctrations.
9 This distribution is documented in Table 8.A1; the timing of acquisitions of domestic banks is documented in Table 8.A2.
10 Our sample of Argentine bank data was constructed by identifying and including all data for all banks that were among the twenty-five largest in any sample year. This resulted in a total sample of thirty-seven institutions, with as few as twenty-five and as many as thirty-two in any given quarter. All loan data discussed are measured in real terms, constructed using consumer price index (CPI) deflators. Loan data are from various issues of *Información de Entidades Financieras* (formerly *Estados Contables de las Entidades Financieras*), a publication of Banco Central de la República Argentina. In addition, Argentine real GDP data are from the Board of Governors of the Federal Reserve System (in thousands of 1986 pesos); the real interest rate was calculated using the nominal interest rate (period average); the CPI series is from *International Financial Statistics*.
11 These findings are consistent with the observations of Burdisso, D'Amato, and Molinari (1998).
12 To compute the reported statistics, we first calculate the percentage change in current loan volumes for each individual bank within each period. Unweighted and weighted averages of these loan growth rates are then constructed by period. The mean and normalized standard deviations of these series over respective periods of time and for respective samples of banks are reported in Table 8.3 for Argentina and in Table 8.8 for Mexico.
13 State-owned banks include Banco de la Provincia de Buenos Aires, Banco de la Nación Argentina, Banco Hipotecario, Banco de la Ciudad de Buenos Aires, Banco de las Provincia de Córdoba, Banco de la Pampa, Bice, Caja Ahorro, and Banco Social de Córdoba.

14 Specifically, we perform ordinary least squares regressions over the time-series panels of individual bank data. The percentage change in real loans (nominal loans deflated by the CPI) is regressed against the percentage change in real GDP, levels of real interest differentials *vis-à-vis* the United States, and bank-specific fixed effects. Regressions test for differences in estimated responses across banks in relation to public, private domestic, or foreign ownership. 'Gaps' in loan series – defined as missing observations with nonmissing observations for the time periods immediately before and after them – are filled in by taking the mean of the surrounding observations.

We also have generated results (available from the authors) based on an alternative methodology, using clustering of errors by quarter across all banks. This approach specifies that the observations are independent over time (clusters) but are not necessarily independent within a period. The error-correction algorithm affects the estimated standard errors and variance-covariance matrix of the estimators, but not the estimated coefficients. In general, as implemented, this approach provides a more conservative view of the statistical significance of the estimated elasticities with respect to GDP and other time-series variables. The terms that are marginally significant at the 10 percent level sometimes lose statistical significance at this level.

15 In the regression results presented for Argentina and Mexico, we do not report coefficients on interest rate terms. In all regressions, the estimated coefficients are small, so a 1 percentage point increase in the interest rate differential is associated with a 0.01 to 0.03 percent change in loan volumes. These estimated effects often are not statistically significant. Generally, we cannot reject equality of interest rate coefficients on lending by domestic and foreign banks.

16 This general insensitivity to market signals also characterized the loan volumes of public banks in the precrisis and crisis periods for which we have data: second-quarter 1994 to first-quarter 1996 (Table 8.A3, panels A and B).

17 During the nationalization of the Mexican banking system, only two banks remained independent: Citibank, which had been active in Mexico since 1929, and domestically owned Banco Obrero.

18 See Graf (1999), among others, for an extensive discussion of these reforms.

19 These foreign acquisitions are not reflected in the available data, which ended with 1998.

20 Our sample of Mexican banks includes all banks active in Mexico each year, where data are provided by the Comisión Nacional Bancaria y de Valores. This sample comprises a universe of fifty-nine banks over the 1990s, although the number of banks active in any given quarter varies because of bank closures, mergers, and acquisitions, as well as the establishment of *de novo* operations. The number of banks included in the analysis ranges from a low of twenty in 1991 and 1992 to a high of fifty-three in 1996; there were thirty-seven at year-end 1998.

21 Raw Mexican loan data exhibit many extreme observations related to new bank entry, government intervention, mergers, and acquisitions. We eliminate extreme single-quarter changes from our sample.

22 We present results using ILRs above 10 percent. Broadly similar results also arose using higher ratios (20, 30, 50 percent). The main difference is that the higher the ILRs of domestic banks, the lower their estimated responsiveness to cyclical fluctuations. Our regression results for domestic unhealthy banks are potentially biased by the fact that once a bank is intervened by the Mexican government, data for that bank generally become unavailable. We have a total of seventeen intervened banks in our sample; if we had data for all intervened banks through the end of the sample period, we would have an additional 100 observations of unhealthy banks to use in the regressions. If we assume that intervened banks would on average be less responsive to market signals than nonintervened banks, then we would expect to see less responsiveness for this bank class as a whole if we had access to a more complete data set for Mexico.

Appendix

Table 8.A1 Argentine financial system: total lending by the top twenty-five institutions: December 1998

Ranking	Institution	Total loans (US$m)	Market share (%)	Foreign owner, foreign voting share (%)/date
1	Banco de la Nación Argentina[a]	10,113	12	
2	Banco de la Provincia de Buenos Aires[a,b]	8,932	11	
3	Banco de Galicia y Buenos Aires	6,744	8	
4	Banco Río de la Plata	5,530	7	O'Higgins Central Hispanoamericano 10.0/1998:4
5	BankBoston National Association	5,259	6	Banco Santander Central Hispano 64.3/1997:2
6	Banco Francés	5,151	6	BankBoston 100.0/Before 1994:2
7	Citibank	4,524	5	Banco Bilbao Vizcaya 58.8/1996:4
8	Banco Hipotecario[a]	4,122	5	Citibank 100.0/Before 1994:2
9	HSBC Banco Roberts	2,706	3	HSBC 100.0/1998:1
10	Banca Nazionale del Lavoro	2,326	3	Banca Nazionale del Lavoro 100.0/Before 1994:2
11	Banco Bansud	2,077	3	Banamex 60.0/1995:4
12	Banco Quilmes	1,506	2	Bank of Nova Scotia 70.0/1995:1
13	Banco de la Ciudad de Buenos Aires[a]	1,470	2	
14	Banco Credicoop Cooperativo Limitado	1,264	2	
15	Banco del Suquía	1,122	1	
16	Banco de la Provincia de Córdoba[a]	948	1	
17	Banco Bisel	842	1	Caisse Nationale de Crédito Agricole 30.0/1996:1
18	Banco Tornquist	794	1	O'Higgins Central Hispanoamericano 100.0/1995:4
19	Banco Sudameris Argentina	757	1	Banque Sudameris 99.9/Before 1994:2
20	Banco de la Pampa[a]	700	1	
21	ABN Amro Bank	674	1	ABN Amro 100.0/1995:2
22	Lloyds Bank	666	1	Lloyds Bank 100.0/Before 1994:2
23	Banco de Inversión y Comercio Exterior	649	1	
24	Banco Mercantil Argentino	636	1	
25	Banco Supervielle Société Générale	616	1	Société Générale 75.4/Before 1994:2
	Loan subtotal of top twenty-five institutions	70,128	85	Foreign share of top twenty-five institutions 46.4
	Total system loans	82,544	100	

Source: Estados Contables de las Entidades Financieras, Banco Central de la República Argentina.

[a] Indicates a state-owned bank through the end of 1998.
[b] Data are as of November 1998.

Table 8.A2 Summary of Argentine bank mergers:
December 1998

Acquired bank	Acquiring bank	Date of acquisition
Foreign banks acquiring domestic banks		
Banesto Shaw	Banamex, via Bansud	1995:4
Del Sud	Banamex, via Bansud	1995:4
Crédito Argentino	Bilbao Vizcaya	1997:3
Quilmes[a]	Bank of Nova Scotia	1997:4
Roberts	HSBC	1998:1
Río de la Plata	Santander	1997:2
Francés	Bilbao Vizcaya	1996:4
Foreign banks acquiring foreign banks		
Crédit Lyonnais[b]	O'Higgins Central Hispanoamericano	1996:1
Deutsche Bank	BankBoston	1997:1

[a] Quilmes was effectively controlled by Bank of Nova Scotia by first-quarter 1995, although a majority stake was not acquired until third-quarter 1997.
[b] Formerly Tornquist.

Table 8.A3 Bank loan sensitivity to GDP: Argentina:
Second-quarter 1994 to first-quarter 1996

	Total loans	Consumer loans	Mortgage loans	Commercial, Government and interbank loans
Panel A: Unweighted elasticities				
State-owned	0.10	1.30	2.17	−0.19
	(0.53)	(1.63)	(3.23)	(0.58)
Number of observations	52	45	45	45
Domestic privately owned	0.00	−2.50**	−3.41	0.52
	(0.38)	(1.08)*	(2.14)	(0.39)
Number of observations	99	99	98	99
Foreign privately owned	0.37	0.74	0.57	0.33
	(0.46)	(1.30)	(2.74)	(0.47)
Number of observations	65	65	59	65
Domestic private equal to foreign private?	Yes	No*	Yes	Yes
Panel B: Elasticities weighted by bank size				
State–owned	0.06	0.87	0.39	−0.24
	(0.30)	(1.78)	(0.32)	(0.37)
Domestic privately owned	0.16	−2.90***	−0.28	0.31
	(0.30)	(1.09)	(0.59)	(0.32)
Foreign privately owned	0.56	0.63	0.79	0.49
	(0.40)	(1.32)	(0.76)	(0.44)
Domestic private equal to foreign private on GDP?	Yes	No**	Yes	Yes

Notes: Standard errors are reported beneath the average elasticities. These results are drawn from ordinary least squares regressions over the percentage change in real loans against individual bank fixed effects, the percentage change in real GDP, and local real interest rate differentials

Table 8.A4 Summary of Mexican bank mergers: December 1998

Acquired bank	Acquiring bank	Date of intervention	Date of acquisition
Foreign banks acquiring domestic banks			
Merprob	Bilbao Vizcaya	–	1996:1
Oriente	Bilbao Vizcaya	1995:1	1996:3
Cremi	Bilbao Vizcaya	1994:3	1996:3
Mexicano	Santander Mexicano	–	1997:2
Confía	Citibank	1997:3	1998:3
Alianza	GE Capital	–	1997:4
Domestic banks acquiring domestic banks			
Unión	Bancomer	1994:3	1995:2
Obrero	Afirme	1995:2	1997:1
Sureste	Internacional (BITAL)	1996:2	1998:1
Atlántico	Internacional (BITAL)	1997:4	1998:1
Centro	Mercantil del Norte	1995:3	1997:2
Banpaís	Mercantil del Norte	1995:1	1997:3
Foreign banks acquiring foreign banks			
Chemical	Chase	–	1996:2
Santander de Negocios	Santander Mexicano	–	1997:4

Source: Effective dates of acquisitions, mergers, and interventions were compiled by the authors from press reports and data provided by Comisión Nacional Bancaria y de Valores.

Notes to Table 8.A3 – *continued*

vis–à-vis the United States. The equality test rows ask whether statistically the coefficients on private domestic and private foreign banks are equal to each other. Some outlier observations were omitted from the regression analysis.

* Statistically significant at the 10 percent level.
** Statistically significant at the 5 percent level.
*** Statistically significant at the 1 percent level.

Table 8. A5 Mexican financial system – total lending by institution: December 1998

Mexican institution	Total loans (pesos m)	Share (%)	Foreign ownership/ country stake (%)/ Entry date
Banamex	186,245	21.3	None
Bancomer	191,407	21.9	Bank of Montreal/Canada 17/March 1996
Serfin	115,680	13.3	HSBC, J.P. Morgan/United States 29/December 1997
Bital	56,897	6.5	Santander, BCP/Spain 16/September 1993
Santander Mexicano	49,618	5.7	Santander/Spain 52/September 1997[a]
Bilbao Vizcaya	52,899	6.1	BBV/Spain 67/March 1996[a]
Centro	21,305	2.4	None
Mercantil del Norte	25,003	2.9	None
Banpaís	27,132	3.1	None
Citibank	16,900	1.9	Citibank/United States 100/December 1991[a]
Interacciones	3,145	0.4	None
Inbursa	21,999	2.5	None
Mifel	2,202	0.3	None
Invex	1,702	0.2	None
Banregio	1,358	0.2	None
Del Bajío	2,912	0.3	Sabadell/Spain 10/December 1998
Quadrum	1,411	0.2	None
Ixe	2,482	0.3	None
J. P. Morgan	1,327	0.2	J. P. Morgan/United States 100/September 1996[a]
Chase Manhattan	9	0.0	Chase Manhattan/United States 100/June 1996[a]
Afirme	4,991	0.6	None
Fuji Bank	831	0.1	Fuji Bank/Japan 100/June 1995[a]
Bank of Tokyo-Mitsubishi	907	0.1	Bank of Tokyo-Mitsubishi/Japan 100/March 1995[a]
Bank of America	989	0.1	Bank of America/United States 100/June 1995[a]
ABN Amro Bank	537	0.1	ABN Amro Bank/Netherlands 100/September 1995[a]
Republic National Bank	605	0.1	Republic National/United States 100/September 1995[a]
Banco de Boston	518	0.1	Bank of Boston/United States 100/December 1995[a]
B. N. P.	1,002	0.1	B. N. P./France 100/December 1995[a]
Bansí	663	0.1	None
Dresdner Bank	2,414	0.3	Dresdner/Germany 100/March 1996[a]
Société Générale	445	0.1	Société Générale/France 100/March 1996[a]
I.N.G. Bank	1,460	0.2	I.N.G. Bank/Netherlands 100/June 1996[a]
First Chicago	66	0.0	First Chicago/United States 100/September 1996[a]
GE Capital (Alianza)	1,005	0.1	GE Capital/United States 100/December 1997[a]
American Express	391	0.0	American Express/United States 100/June 1996[a]
Nations Bank	64	0.0	Nations Bank/United States 100/December 1996[a]
Comerica Bank	2,410	0.3	Comerica Bank/United States 100/September 1997[a]
Total	872,485	100.0	

Source: *Boletín Estadístico de Banco Multiple*, Comisión Nacional Bancaria y de Valores.
[a] Foreign controlled.

References

Burdisso, Tamaro, Laura D'Amato, and Andrea Molinari. 1998. 'The Bank Privatization Process in Argentina: Toward a More Efficient Banking System?' Unpublished paper, Banco Central de la República Argentina, October.

Claessens, Stijn, Asli Demirguc-Kunt, and Harry Huizinga. 1998. 'How Does Foreign Entry Affect the Domestic Banking Market?' World Bank Policy Research Working Paper no. 1918, June.

Clarke, George, Robert Cull, Laura D'Amato, and Andrea Molinari. 1999. 'On the Kindness of Strangers? The Impact of Foreign Entry on Domestic Banks in Argentina.' Unpublished paper, World Bank, August.

Demirguc-Kunt, Asli, Ross Levine, and Hong-Ghi Min. 1998. 'Opening to Foreign Banks: Issues of Stability, Efficiency, and Growth.' In Seongtae Lee, ed., *The Implications of Globalization of World Financial Markets*. Seoul: Bank of Korea.

Glaessner, T., and D. Oks. 1994. 'NAFTA, Capital Mobility, and Mexico's Financial System.' Unpublished paper, World Bank, July.

Goldberg, Linda. 2000. 'When Is Foreign Bank Lending to Emerging Markets Volatile?' Unpublished paper, Federal Reserve Bank of New York, July.

Graf, Pablo. 1999. 'Policy Responses to the Banking Crisis in Mexico.' *Bank Restructuring in Practice*. BIS Policy Papers, no. 6, August.

Gruben, William, Jahyeong Koo, and Robert Moore. 1999. 'When Does Financial Liberalization Make Banks Risky? An Empirical Examination of Argentina, Canada, and Mexico.' Federal Reserve Bank of Dallas Center for Latin American Economics Working Paper no. 0399, July.

Hancock, Diana, and James Wilcox. 1998. 'The Credit Crunch and the Availability of Credit to Small Business.' *Journal of Banking and Finance* 22 (August): 983–1014.

Kaminsky, Graciela, and Carmen Reinhart. 1999. 'The Twin Crises: The Causes of Banking and Balance-of-Payments Problems.' *American Economic Review* 89, no. 3 (June): 473–500.

Levine, Ross. 1996. 'Foreign Banks, Financial Development, and Economic Growth.' In Claude E. Barfield, ed., *International Financial Markets: Harmonization versus Competition*. Washington, DC: AEI Press.

Martinez Peria, Maria Soledad, and Sergio Schmukler. 1999. 'Do Depositors Punish Banks for "Bad" Behavior? Market Discipline in Argentina, Chile, and Mexico.' World Bank Policy Research Working Paper no. 2058, February.

Meltzer, Alan. 1998. 'Financial Structure, Saving, and Growth: Safety Nets, Regulation, and Risk Reduction in Global Financial Markets.' In Seongtae Lee, ed., *The Implications of Globalization of World Financial Markets*. Seoul: Bank of Korea.

Peek, Joe, and Eric Rosengren. 1997. 'The International Transmission of Financial Shocks: The Case of Japan.' *American Economic Review* 87, no. 4 (September): 495–505.

———. 2000. 'Collateral Damage: Effects of the Japanese Bank Crisis on Real Activity in the United States.' *American Economic Review* 90, no. 1 (March): 30–45.

Rojas-Suarez, Liliana. 1998. 'Early Warning Indicators of Banking Crises: What Works for Emerging Markets? With Applications to Latin America.' Deutsche Bank Securities working paper.

Author information

B. Gerard Dages and Linda Goldberg are assistant vice presidents and Daniel Kinney an international officer at the Federal Reserve Bank of New York.

Acknowledgements

The authors thank Kevin Caves for careful and dedicated research assistance and Jennifer Crystal for excellent general assistance. They also acknowledge the useful comments of Giovanni Dell'Arricia, Jane Little, and two anonymous referees, as well as those of participants at the February 2000 IMF/World Bank/IADB Conference on Financial Contagion, members of the April 2000 Federal Reserve System Committee on International Economics, and participants at the April 2000 SUERF Colloquium on Adapting to Financial Globalization.

9 Financial stability in the euro area

Some lessons from US financial history*[1]

E. Philip Davis

Introduction

There are important structural parallels between the new euro area and the US. Both are large monetary areas – in which developments can have repercussions for global financial stability – and are rather closed in the sense that external trade is a small proportion of GDP. There are subsidiary fiscal areas within the overall monetary area; and banking sectors are fragmented and are not generally diversified. Meanwhile, in the wake of EMU, convergence of the euro area financial system with those of the US is widely expected to accelerate (Davis 1999a, 1999b). This will probably result in a more securitised financial system, with bank credit accounting for a smaller proportion of financial claims.

Viewed both in the light of the structural parallels and likely behavioural convergence, we suggest that a close examination of US financial history will be highly instructive of potential issues for the euro area in terms of financial stability, both in the transition to a securitised system and in the future steady state. Accordingly, the paper examines the stylised facts underlying selected periods of systemic risk in US financial history, to see what lessons there are to be learnt for the euro area. Naturally, features of particular episodes of financial instability are unlikely to recur in detail, so we concentrate on generic aspects. Particular focus is put on two aspects, following the points made above. First, we assess the link of crises to structural features of a large monetary area with segmented banking systems and regional economic specialisation. Second, we consider how disintermediation, growth of securities markets and enhanced competition may link to financial instability.

We define financial instability (also referred to as financial disorder or systemic risk) as a sequence of events entailing heightened risk of a financial crisis, where a financial crisis is seen in turn as 'a major and contagious collapse of the financial system, entailing inability to provide payments services

* Paper presented at 22nd SUERF Colloquium, Vienna, 27–29 April 2000.

or to allocate funds for investment'.[2] Note that instability of institutions and markets tends to be a necessary but not sufficient condition for a financial crisis in this sense.

It should be noted at the outset that the article does not seek in any way to comment upon the current structures of supervision and monetary policy in the euro area.[3] Nor does it seek to make any specific predictions regarding systemic risk. Also, it is not suggested that EMU will lead to an increase in the absolute level of risk, although its nature and locus may change.[4] Generally, our aim is to map out some of the challenges that may face both authorities and market participants in the euro area in the light of the likely evolving structure and behaviour of its financial markets.

The events covered are the 1929–33 stock market crash and banking crisis, the 1970 Penn Central crisis, Continental Illinois (1984), the US thrifts (1979–89), the regional banking crises in Texas (1985–89), the stock market crash of 1987, the collapse of the junk bond market in 1989 and the Russia/LTCM crisis of 1998. The paper is structured so as to present stylised features of the euro area and US and a brief overview of theories of financial instability, followed by account of each event, in each case drawing out some of the lessons and warning signs. We conclude with broader lessons for macroprudential surveillance.

1 Background items

(a) The US and EMU – similarities and contrasts

The parallels in terms of overall economic structure between the Euro area and the US are illustrated in Table 9.1. The two areas have similar shares of world GDP and world trade, which far exceed the next-largest area, Japan (8 per cent of GDP and 10 per cent of exports). The areas are also fairly 'closed' in that exports are less than 10 per cent of GDP, a marked contrast to EU countries themselves to date. Another feature – common in this case to all OECD countries – is the dominance of services in GDP, and the insignificance of agriculture. There are also sovereign (euro countries) or semi-sovereign (US states) fiscal areas within the overall monetary area, although note that the Federal level of taxation and expenditure is much more important in the US than in the EU.

As regards financial structure, banking sectors in the US and EU are both fragmented (Table 9.2). There are 23,000 banks in the US and over 7,000 in the euro area.[5] Concentration is even lower in the euro area (12 per cent of bank assets is accounted for by the top five firms) than in the US (16 per cent).[6] The high branch/population ratio in the euro area is one indicator of potential excess capacity relative to the US. Note also that banks are generally not diversified across the monetary area in the EU (due to the existence till recently of independent monetary areas) or the US (owing to the ban on interstate banking and branching that was lifted only recently).

Table 9.1 European Union and US, economic indicators, 1997

	Population	GDP (% of global)	Exports (% of GDP)	Exports (% of world trade)	Agriculture (% of GDP)	Industry (% of GDP)	Services (% of GDP)
EU-15	374	25	9	–	2	30	68
EU-11	290	19	12	20	2	31	67
US	268	20	8	15	2	26	72

Source: EMI (1998).

Table 9.2 European Union and US, banking sector indicators, 1996 (*1995)

	Number of banks	5-firm concentration ratio	Population per branch	Interest margins
EU-15*	8165	10	2255	2.1
EU-11*	7361	12	1950	2
US	22846	16	3778	3.4

Source: Davis (1999b).

Table 9.3 European Union and US, financial structure indicators, end-1996, $ billions (% of GDP)

	Equities	Govt bonds	Private bonds	Bank assets	Total	Institutional assets (1995)
EU-15	4518 (55)	4617 (56)	2945 (36)	18066 (207)	30146 (345)	6214 (74)
EU-11	2447 (35)	3818 (55)	2391 (34)	14321 (206)	22976 (331)	4041 (59)
US	8458 (117)	6965 (96)	4327 (60)	5580 (73)	25330 (331)	10501 (145)

Source: Davis (1999b).

Turning to flow of funds data, whereas total financial claims relative to GDP are similar in the US and Europe (around three times GDP), at present there are sharp contrasts between the US and Europe in terms of the size of securities markets relative to banking (Table 9.3). Banking assets are over 200 per cent of GDP in the euro area (and the EU-15), while US banking assets are only 73 per cent of GDP. On the other hand, US equity markets are three times larger than those in the euro area, and public and private bond markets are also considerably larger. Correspondingly, institutional investors are much less important in the euro area than in the US. The fact that the total of financial assets is comparable suggests securitisation in the US involved a substitution for banking and not merely a growth in the overall financial superstructure.

There are strong arguments that EMU is unleashing forces leading to convergence, with the euro area developing a more securitised financial system, and bank credit accounting for a smaller proportion of financial claims. Indeed, already there has been massive growth of private bond issuance in euros and of euro area mutual funds. EMU will 'leverage' existing forces pushing European finance in this direction, such as technological development; deregulation and liberalisation (i.e. the regulatory environment); increased and transformed wealth of individuals; and globalisation. Without going into detail, we highlight some of the main points.

Securities market integration in EMU is assisted by a number of factors. Tendencies to equalisation of risks and returns on financial assets are generated by aspects of monetary integration (elimination of exchange rate uncertainty; in some countries, reductions of inflation uncertainty; and tendencies to a common business cycle driven by a single monetary policy) and by fiscal integration (fiscal consolidation and a focus on credit risk-based arbitrage in the context of the no-bailout clause) (Davis 1999a). Further key factors are freedom of institutional investors to diversify holdings of government bonds, corporate bonds and equities within the expanded 'domestic' zone and enhanced contestability of markets for underwriting in euro countries. In an integrated and unified securities market, with a euro-wide issuer and investor base, there may plausibly be a greater concentration of trading among firms. Liquidity of bond markets should be enhanced owing to the wider and more diverse range of investors accessing the euro markets (i.e. there are forms of economies of scale to market size).[7] Transactions costs should fall owing to competition between traders and markets and further scale economies. Integration, liquidity and lower transactions costs would in turn make the markets attractive to issuers, relative to bank loans.[8] Factors such as social security reform in the context of the ageing of the population simultaneously boost the growth of institutional investors, again accelerating securities market growth and disintermediation (Davis 1999b).[9] There is also increased openness of the Eurozone countries to cross-border competition in banking, with EMU 'leveraging' the deregulation of the Single Market programme.

Finally, euro companies may wish to issue more equity and less debt for structural reasons. First, monetary integration will leave euro area national economies – and hence their corporate sectors – more vulnerable to asymmetric shocks. Second, increased banking competition – and securitisation – may undermine exclusive banking relationships (Petersen and Rajan 1993), owing to competition between lenders, and as a corollary, lenders will be less willing to rescue firms in financial distress, as they could not charge higher interest rates to finance such 'implicit insurance'.[10] An offsetting factor may be shareholder pressure to lever up to increase returns on equity. In any case, investors will probably demand responsiveness on the part of the management to 'shareholder value' concerns (such as transparency, protection of minority shareholders and greater profit orientation) before providing equity.

These elements are likely to entail a relative shrinkage of banking relative to securities, and may in the process put banks' profitability under pressure, not least because banking sectors already show signs of excess capacity (Davis and Salo 1998).[11,12] Precise convergence of financial systems is unlikely. The US banking system was historically more strictly regulated in terms of products and geographical location than the European. Equally, there are various structural factors that would limit balance-sheet convergence with the US and within Europe, such as the possibly differing liquidity preferences of the household sector, fiscal differences and residual regulatory differences. Nevertheless, the tendency is clear.

An important supplementary question is whether the fragmentation and localisation of the euro area banking sector is a durable feature or is likely to be removed. The period since EMU has so far been characterised by mergers mainly within national borders and not across borders, as would be needed to diversify risk. Legal, regulatory and political barriers may underlie this. Also there are large public and mutual banking sectors in most euro countries, which are relatively resistant to consolidation. These factors suggest that the emergence of a euro-wide banking sector will be a protracted process, and the legacy of fragmented national banking systems will persist for some time. The slow erosion of within-state banking in the US since the abolition of the regulation restricting interstate banking may indicate a comparable ceiling to likely progress in the euro area.

(b) Elements of a theoretical framework for financial stability analysis

Besides illustrating the similarities and outlining convergence mechanisms, it is also useful as a preliminary to analysis of periods of systemic risk to set out some elements of a framework for analysing and seeking to predict periods of financial instability. This is set out in detail in Davis (1999c), drawing on Davis (1995a). There, it is suggested that many of the strands of the theory of financial instability have a contribution to make to our understanding of financial crises, but that the explanations are in most cases partial. In our view, a selective synthesis drawing on the evidence of actual crises set out in the second lecture is the correct approach to adopt. It is suggested that these are helpful in the present context in interpreting some of the events detailed below. The theories are those of:

- 'debt and financial fragility', which suggests that over-indebtedness and banking crises are a normal feature of the cycle (Fisher 1933; Kindleberger 1978; Minsky (1977);
- 'monetarist' that bank failures impact on the economy via a reduction in the supply of money (Friedman and Schwartz 1963);
- 'uncertainty' as opposed to risk as a key feature of financial instability, linked closely to confidence, and helps explain the at times

disproportionate responses of financial markets in times of stress (Shafer 1986);
- 'disaster myopia' that competitive, incentive-based and psychological mechanisms lead financial institutions and regulators to underestimate the risk of financial instability (Guttentag and Herring 1984);
- 'asymmetric information and agency costs' that these well-known market failures of the debt contract help to explain the nature of financial instability, e.g. credit tightening as interest rates rise and asset prices fall (Mishkin 1991).

And complementing these:

- 'bank runs' that panic runs on banks (which may follow the various stimuli identified by the above theories) link to the maturity transformation they undertake, and the relatively lesser liquidity of their assets (Diamond and Dybvig 1983);[13] such theory can also be applied to securities market liquidity (Davis 1994, 1999d);
- 'herding' among institutional investors as a potential cause for price volatility in asset markets, driven for example by peer-group performance comparisons, that may affect banks and other leveraged institutions (Scharfstein and Stein 1990; Davis 1995c);
- 'industrial' that effects of changes in entry conditions in financial markets (Davis 1995a) can both encompass and provide a supplementary set of underlying factors and transmission mechanism to those noted above.

With these elements of a framework in mind, we now go on to examine some specific experiences of the US, and the lessons in each case for the euro area. *Those already familiar with the events may move directly to the latter (italicised)*.

2 The stock-market crash and the Great Depression (1929–33)

The 1920s saw a rapid economic expansion, which in combination with financial innovations such as investment trusts led to marked rises in equity values, which is often characterised as a speculative bubble. Stock market speculation was financed by rapid increases in borrowing. There was a large and broad-based expansion of private debt in the 1920s; outstanding corporate bonds rose from $26 bn in 1920 to $47 bn in 1928 (over 50 per cent of GNP). Small businesses and households increased indebtedness sharply; outstanding mortgages rose from $11 bn in 1920 to $27 bn in 1929. Indeed, as noted by Taggart (1985), business debt was proportionately higher in the 1920s than the 1980s (and 1990s). Monetary policy was tightened from mid-1928 onwards, to seek to curb the stock market boom. Initially, higher nominal interest rates had little effect, as stock market lending remained profitable, though general prices began to fall and demand began to weaken. The stock market collapse coincided with minor events such as the Hatry crisis in London; but it appeared more to be the deflation of a speculative bubble, where prices had departed from fundamentals. (See Galbraith 1954 for a highly readable account.)

The crash led to a sharp tightening of credit, which was initially counteracted by the Fed as lender of last resort. Industrial production began to fall sharply in 1929–30. The fall in stock prices spread to commodities, which led to widespread default on international and domestic bank loans and depression in commodity exporting countries. Beginning in 1930 there was a flight to quality in the bond market – cutting off a source of credit – and an increasing number of bank failures. The number of US banks halved over 1929–33. As well as deteriorating loan quality owing to the recession, crash and commodity price falls, banks suffered from cash withdrawals and from outflows of gold from the US, the nominal money supply contracted over 1931–33 while high-powered money increased, reflecting the flight to cash. Prices fell sharply, increasing pressure on debtors holding debt contracts written in nominal terms, with the debt service/GNP ratio rising from 9 per cent in 1929 to 20 per cent in 1933.

Among debtors, insolvency rates were very high for small businesses, farmers, mortgage borrowers, and state and local government, which given asymmetric information had no alternative sources of credit to banks. (Bernanke 1983 cogently argues that the severe macroeconomic effects of the Depression links to the loss of information following bank failures.) Only large corporations were relatively immune, given their stronger internal cash flows. The wave of bank failures came to a climax in March 1933, resulting in a panic and closure of all banks. The Fed did not respond as lender of last resort,[14] nor did the banks act as a 'club' to suspend cash payments to depositors, as they often had in the nineteenth century when the Central Bank did not exist (they now considered maintenance of stability to be the Fed's responsibility).[15] US GDP remained depressed in the wake of the banking crisis throughout the 1930s. Summers (1991) notes that all of the effects of the financial crisis were aggravated by an absence of automatic stabilisers (i.e. increase in government expenditure relative to taxation in a recession). Before the Second World War, a 1 per cent decline in GNP generated a 0.95 per cent fall in disposable income, whereas since 1945 it has only generated a 0.39 per cent fall.

The Depression was, of course, a global rather than purely US phenomenon. A feature that worsened the global crisis was a trade war, prompted by the US Smoot-Hawley tariff increase. Developing countries that had borrowed heavily in the 1920s, and/or were dependent on commodity exports, together with advanced countries that sought to maintain fixed exchange rates (such as France and Germany), were hardest hit by the overall crisis.[16] A major feature in Continental Europe was failure of major universal banks such as the Austrian Kreditanstalt, partly owing to collapses in the value of their equity holdings. In addition, countries such as the US, with a structure of small and poorly diversified banks, suffered more runs and panics than those with nation-wide branch systems, such as Canada and the UK, and as a consequence suffered more adverse macroeconomic consequences (Haubrich 1990). (Although it is argued by Kryzanowski and Roberts 1989 that there was also 100 per cent implicit deposit insurance in Canada.)

The US regulatory response was to tighten regulation of banks and thrifts. Entry controls were imposed, asset and liability composition restricted, capital requirements imposed, self-dealing restrictions tightened, and deposit insurance was introduced. Besides seeking stability, some of these regulations sought to reallocate credit to 'socially desirable' purposes such as housing. Some analysts such as Kane (1985) attribute to these restrictions the difficulties US institutions underwent in the 1970s and 1980s in the context of high inflation and innovation (compare the discussion of the thrifts crisis below).

The international transmission of shocks from a large monetary area, which fed back onto the economic situation in the US, is a relevant consideration for an equally large area such as the euro zone, particularly for countries, for example in Eastern Europe, that may seek to maintain fixed exchange rates with the euro zone.

The Federal Reserve system was relatively new in the 1920s and 1930s, and had not yet developed a consistent approach to financial instability – although the bank club arrangement that had existed prior to the emergence of the Fed was in abeyance. Uncertainty about reactions was hence a major problem. The new arrangements in the euro area also suggest a need for vigilance. In this context, 'clubs' of banks, which have been an important bulwark against financial instability may be harder to maintain in the broader euro area.

Rising corporate leverage is – as in other cases – a danger sign. As noted, the warranted level of leverage in the euro area could decline after EMU, implying a need for downward adjustment by the corporate sector.

The relative stability of nation-wide banking in Canada compared to local or regional banking in the US illustrates the benefits of diversification across the monetary area – which banks in the euro area have not yet achieved (note that besides area-wide branching it could be achieved via securitisation, as was later the case via FNMA in the US). Note, however, that the recession was not an 'asymmetric shock' in the sense that the appropriate monetary policy for the monetary area was inappropriate for certain localities.

Finally, the lack of automatic stabilisers in the US pre-war highlights the need for such shock absorbers to be maintained in Europe, to complement monetary policy in the case of symmetric shocks, and to make up for the lack of monetary response if shocks are asymmetric.

3 The US thrifts crises (1979–89)

US savings and loans institutions (or thrifts) are a long-established form of mutual bank, which in the 1980s were subject to two linked crises, a 'maturity mismatch' crisis at the beginning of the decade and a 'loan quality' crisis in the mid to late 1980s. However, it is suggested that the genesis of these events lies several decades further back. As noted, in the tightening of regulation and compartmentalisation of the US financial system which ensued after the crises of 1929–33, thrifts were assigned responsibility for provision of residential mortgages (usually long term, at fixed rate) while interest-rate ceilings were imposed on bank deposits. Such a system sought to provide stability and protection for the institutions.

But problems arose as the regulatory structure came to conflict with economic conditions. Already in the 1950s and 1960s interest rates were occasionally high enough to result in disintermediation of deposits to market instruments such as Treasury bills, but in practice rates soon fell, and the high denomination of bills limited depositor interest. Imposition of ceilings on thrifts' own rates – at their own request – in 1966, prevented their liability rates exceeding asset yields. In the 1970s the problems became more serious as, first, under pressure from inflation, interest rates rose for long periods above the deposit ceilings (typically around 5 per cent depending on maturity) and, second, the development of money-market mutual funds enabled small depositors to shift to money-market instruments. Thrifts thus suffered increasingly from liquidity problems. To prevent such disintermediation, interest-rate ceilings were progressively raised, while the institutions switched heavily into wholesale funding (after being permitted to issue unregulated Money Market Certificates, with a denomination of $10,000 in 1978). This, however, exposed a serious problem of interest-rate risk owing to the mismatch between the existing stock of fixed-rate long-term mortgage assets (often at low interest rates) and high-interest short-term floating-rate liabilities. This effect was particularly severe after US monetary policy was tightened in 1979 (while the recession also increased bad debts). Net worth, earnings, and capitalisation declined and failures increased.

Rather than seeking orderly closure of the whole industry while net worth remained positive, the authorities sought to enable them to continue in business, in the hope that eventually profitability could be re-established, as new mortgages at higher interest rates replaced old unprofitable ones. The problem was deferrable because confidence was retained and insolvent institutions were allowed to continue operating. In acts of deregulation dated 1980 and 1982, thrifts were allowed to diversify assets away from long-term home mortgages in the hope of speeding the return to profitability, and capital standards were relaxed. The level of deposit-insurance coverage was increased in 1980. Finally, as regards interest-rate controls, they were further eased as permission was granted for issue of high-interest/low-denomination, money-market deposit accounts in 1982, and interest-rate ceilings were finally abolished in 1986. Heightened risk-taking was the response, as many thrifts tried to grow out of their problems by rapid expansion, diversifying into high-yield and high-risk assets such as land, development, construction and commercial real estate as well as 'junk bonds' although there was also considerable expansion in traditional fields of mortgage lending (and some fraud). Risk was often concentrated in narrow types of business as well as geographically. Real estate was particularly favoured due to generous depreciation provisions in the tax code at the time. Growth tendencies were particularly marked in the South-West, which experienced an oil-related boom over 1983–85.

Depositors were content to finance such ventures, given the generosity of US deposit insurance, which covered 100 per cent up to $100,000 per bank – hence individuals and even pension funds could hold $100,000 deposits with many banks in total safety, despite increased credit and interest-rate risk. With low capital standards and limited liability, equity holders had little to lose, particularly for thrifts that were technically insolvent (438 in 1984). Managers, who had often entered the industry *de novo* or taken over faltering institutions, had little reputational or monetary capital at risk. And reductions in supervisory budgets, as well as disruptive reorganisations, over this period meant monitoring of these trends was highly imperfect. After declines in commodity prices in 1985–86, as well as overbuilding and tightening of tax laws, the office real estate market collapsed, and many of the other speculative loans proved non-performing (see also Section 5). In combination with low capital ratios, resulting insolvency was widespread – thrifts were unable to sell remaining mortgages on secondary markets to pay off depositors. There was also evidence of insider abuse, fraud, mismanagement and unsound banking practices, such as inadequate credit appraisal, at many of the insolvent institutions, although pursuit of higher yields via acceptance of high risk was probably the overriding factor. Such problems were compounded by the fact that the deposit insurer (FSLIC) lacked the resources to wind down all the insolvent thrifts, which were thus left to operate while taking ever-increasing risks. Pauley (1989) recorded that at the end of 1988, 360 thrifts were insolvent according to 'generally accepted accounting principles' (GAAP) and another 150 had negative GAAP capital after deducting goodwill. A further 292 had GAAP net worth of under 3 per cent of assets. In combination with those already closed or merged, assets of these institutions amounted to $540 bn. The second thrifts crisis occurred without runs, except in Ohio and Maryland in 1985 when a panic took place among depositors with privately insured thrifts (see Davis 1995a).

The policy response was to guarantee deposit-insurance liabilities (the danger of not doing this could have been loss of faith in insurance of banks, and hence widespread runs and failures) and set up a corporation (Resolution Trust) to acquire ailing thrifts, closing them or selling them to other institutions. Meanwhile, under the FIRREA (Financial Institutions Regulatory Reform and Enforcement Act) of 1989 remaining thrifts were subjected to tighter capital standards and limits on types of investment. Reserves were required against risk of future defaults on higher risk assets – which in turn reduced ability to meet the new capital standards. As a consequence, the industry shrank and by the mid-1990s less than half of the institutions present in 1980s still existed, while assets fell around 20 per cent from 1989 to 1995 (Eisenbeis et al. 1999).

The role of high inflation in the run-up to the thrifts crisis reduces its relevance to current circumstances. Nonetheless, the thrifts crises offer a number of key lessons (Barth and Litan 1999). Institutions that may be viable under a certain form of regulation and set of market circumstances may become unviable in another – implying a need to examine closely the evolution of different sectors in EMU. In effect, excess capacity may emerge and needs to be removed in a non-disruptive and low-cost manner. Restrictions on activities can play an important role in generating instability. Moreover, disintermediation – in this case via money market funds – presents a particular challenge in this context. Real estate lending has been shown, in this and many other cases, to be a source of pitfalls for banking sectors (Herring and Wachter 1999). Detection of such problems at an early stage requires close supervision and early recognition of non-performing loans. Forbearance in the case that institutions have zero net worth, combined with generous and mispriced deposit insurance is a recipe for moral hazard and thus risk-taking and major credit losses to the insurer, especially if it is linked to ill-judged financial liberalisation. Whereas the dangers of forbearance are well understood, as seen in the Nordic banking crises where swift action was taken, in some EU countries deposit insurance is even more generous than in the US.

4 The Continental Illinois Bank failure (1984)

The Continental Illinois bank, at the time one of the largest US banks, suffered from non-performing loans arising from the LDC debt crisis and the weakness of commodity prices, after a rapid and concentrated increase in lending both to LDCs and the energy sector in the early 1980s. Partly due to the US regulations against interstate banking, it was also forced to rely heavily on wholesale deposits, 40 per cent of which were from the international markets, and 16 per cent domestic interbank deposits. In 1984, after a period when the bank had to pay a higher price for its wholesale deposits, large depositors began to withdraw funds, as concern about the quality of its loan portfolio grew. The Penn Square failure of 1982 was important background to the crisis, as uninsured depositors suffered losses. The run started in the international interbank market, as Japanese, European, and Asian banks began to cut credit lines and withdraw overnight funding. Only later did US non-banks begin to follow. Such withdrawals reached $8 bn per day, outstripping liquidity and capital. The run continued despite an announcement by the Federal Deposit Insurance Corporation (FDIC) that all of the bank's liabilities were guaranteed.

The authorities feared systemic risk if the bank failed – adverse rumours had already caused difficulties at Manufacturers' Hanover bank, and ex-post calculations by the FDIC suggested that 2,299 banks had deposits and of these 179 might fail if Continental failed. Accordingly, the authorities instituted a major rescue operation. This entailed a $5.5 bn line of credit arranged by twenty-eight banks, $2 bn of new capital infused by the FDIC and a group of commercial banks, and discount window funds from the Fed (with

$4.5 bn in discounts being done in the week beginning 16 May). Partly as a result of this, there was no contagion to other institutions or markets. While the bank was not explicitly nationalised, the government placed a representative on the executive board of the bank.

The issue of whether a bank may be too-big-to-fail can arise in a large monetary area as well as within the much smaller confines of, for example, individual EU countries. In other words, there may be institutions whose failure can pose a systemic threat across the whole monetary area and not just within a region. This occurred despite the size of Continental Illinois being quite small relative to US GDP, and linked rather to it being at the core of the money market. Naturally, moral hazard considerations suggest that associated rescue operations be avoided whenever possible. In this context, the danger of banks relying too heavily on wholesale funding – as was indeed partly a product of the US interstate banking restrictions – were underlined. Such heavy reliance is not at present typical of the euro-zone as a whole, although there are tendencies for some national banking sectors to become heavily dependent on foreign interbank lending,[17] and most cross-border interbank lending in the euro area is unsecured (ECB 2000a). Continental's assets were very undiversified, unlike typical universal banks in Europe.

5 The Texas banking crises (1985–89)

The Texas financial sector suffered a major reversal in the mid-1980s, with no less than 400 banks becoming insolvent over 1985–89 (Gunther et al. 1995), and Texas accounted for 50 per cent of US bank failures over this period. Also nine of the ten Texan bank holding companies were provided with new ownership under federal assistance or were purchased by out-of-state institutions. These banking difficulties came on top of the thrifts crisis, as outlined in Section 3.

This pattern mainly reflected the impact of the weakening of oil prices on the region's economies. The rises in oil prices in the 1970s had led to a boom in the regional economy, which spawned a great deal of speculative real estate expenditures, all of which was highly dependent on the energy business. Even when oil prices began to ease in 1982, banks were unwilling to accept lower growth from lesser demand for loans from the energy industry, but rather continued to grow by shifting loan growth to real estate (perhaps an illustration of what Guttentag and Herring (1984) entitle 'disaster myopia'). At a national level, real estate development was also encouraged by the Economic Recovery Act of 1981, which encouraged investors to finance real estate purely for the tax benefits. And furthermore, as outlined above, the thrifts were inadequately supervised and insolvent thrifts were allowed to continue operating in negative net worth, thus financing real estate that would not otherwise have been built and contributing to oversupply. In Texas, thrifts tended to be state chartered and had yet more liberal asset powers than federally chartered institutions – loan-to-value ratios could be up to 100 per cent.

When oil prices weakened after 1980, and finally collapsed in 1986, they inflicted a sharp adverse shock on Texas. In the context of overbuilding, as outlined above, such effects were magnified. Since US banks were obliged to operate in one state at a time,[18] they were highly vulnerable to region specific economic downturns, being unable to diversify their activities across diverse regional economies. Note that the Federal Reserve could not appropriately respond to such a shock by reducing interest rates, since the rest of the US economy was actually boosted by the fall in oil prices. Accompanying the oil price counter shock was fiscal action (the Tax Reform Act of 1986) to reduce the tax incentives for real estate investment, which reduced demand for new real estate investment and reduced the market value of projects under construction and already built.

The Texan real estate banks were particularly vulnerable to such a shock because they were heavily invested in construction and development loans as well as loans to commercial property – to a greater extent than similar banks elsewhere in the US. Indeed in 1983–86, banks in Texas had construction loans three times larger as a proportion of assets than banks elsewhere in the US. On top of the region-specific shock, this was an important reason for poor performance relative to other banks across the US (Eisenbeis et al 1999) – banks in effect aggravated their own problems of vulnerability to asymmetric shocks. It was reflected in average losses for real estate banks of no less than 11 per cent of assets over the period 1986–90, and over 2 per cent a year from 1987 to 1989. Texan banks also had lower capital adequacy ratios when entering the crisis period than banks elsewhere in the US (although they were not obviously undercapitalised till much later), as well as higher operating expenses. Accordingly, over 100 banks per year failed during 1988–90, several years after the initial shock to oil prices.

The banking crisis was accompanied by a significant shift from correspondent banking links to use of the Federal Reserve payments system, as this protected against counterparty risk. Banks were particularly sensitive to this in the wake of the Continental Illinois crisis, and the risk that their own counterparty would not be considered as too-big-to-fail (Clair et al. 1995). This facility helped to minimise spillovers from banking problems to the payments system.

Research into the causes and consequences of the Texan crisis (Gunther et al. 1995) suggest that the regional economic downturn was indeed a key feature underlying the bank failures, but there was not a strong knock-on effect in terms of a local restriction on credit supply leading to further repercussions on the macroeconomy. Possible reasons for this were that banks and financial intermediaries from outside the area may have provided necessary lending, while businesses were able to make use of commercial paper and other types of securities market financing.

Texas was of course not unique in having banking difficulties in the 1980s and early 1990s. Another regional crisis occurred somewhat later in New England (Randall 1993; Jordan 1998), amid a slowdown in the region's economy and real estate market.

Europe has seen a number of real-estate-based banking crises, such as those in the Netherlands, in 1979, and the Nordic countries in 1989–93. However, the regional banking crises in the US illustrate the additional point that locally or regionally specialised banks may be vulnerable to asymmetric shocks which affect the local industry but are not area-wide and thus which it would be appropriate for monetary policy to counteract. The additional importance of assessing vulnerability to such shocks, and the need for vigilant supervision of risky activities, is underlined. The role of asset prices and commodity prices as causes of financial instability in the absence of general inflation in the mid-1980s is noteworthy (it was also a marked feature of the Japanese real estate and banking crisis). Furthermore, the crises underline the need for detailed data to be maintained at a 'regional level' on lending and economic activity within a large monetary area.

As noted in Section 1, full diversification of banks in the euro area has not yet been achieved, although the risk of asymmetric shocks is rather less than in the US at present, since euro countries have relatively diversified industrial bases.[19] Research into the effects of the Texas crisis on regional economic activity may, however, underestimate potential effects in the euro area – at least until pan-euro securities markets are fully developed – given the importance of banking to corporate and household sector financing. It may be less easy for borrowers to switch to CP for example. In addition, the scope for cross-border financing may be less in the euro area than in the US states, given differing legal and accounting features as well as barriers to information flows and lesser development of rating agencies.

Finally, it is worth noting that whereas US households are (and were) typically diversified across the nation via direct and indirect equity holdings, even if their banks were local, European households generally have all of their savings still within national borders, making them more directly vulnerable to asymmetric shocks.

6 US equity markets in 1987

Whereas popular accounts tend to focus on the events of October 19–20, focus on the crash itself abstracts from the need for an explanation why the market rose so much prior to the crash. Davis (1995a), summarising available accounts, suggests that there was a deviation between fundamentals and prices – a form of speculative bubble – which was reflected in historically unprecedented yield ratios between bonds and equities. Such a situation leads to a suspicion that forms of herding or trend-chasing, led by institutions fearing to perform worse than their peers, was involved. But clearly many other factors may have played a role in generating buoyant investor expectations, such as the merger wave in many countries, falling interest rates over 1987, buoyant economic prospects, rapid money and credit growth and lower transactions costs, which fostered an impression of high liquidity and led investors into the illusion that they could exit before prices fell sharply.

As regards the immediate causes of the collapse, since a bubble relies on continuously rising prices, it can be burst by any form of adverse news; in practice, factors underlying the crisis itself may have included current account imbalances between the US, Germany and Japan, which led to fears of a falling dollar and caused rises in long-term US interest rates in the week prior to the crash. Also, tensions in the policy co-ordination process between the G-3 countries (following the Plaza and Louvre accords on exchange rates) may have played a role in triggering the crisis. Evidence supportive of the bubble hypothesis is that none of these items could in themselves justify a price adjustment of the magnitude observed (Fortune 1993).

Some commentators in the United States also blamed the interaction between pension fund managers' portfolio insurance and index arbitrage strategies for causing volatility at the time of crash itself.[20] Basically, it was considered that computer-driven sell orders for futures, which are a normal feature of portfolio insurance (or 'dynamic hedging') strategies when prices fall helped drive the market down much faster than would otherwise have been the case. The initial wave of selling of futures is thought to have driven futures to a discount to the market itself (known as backwardation) as well as reducing stock prices themselves and triggering further portfolio insurance-related sales of futures. The backwardation, seen as a market failure in the futures markets, encouraged index arbitrageurs to sell stocks and buy futures, thus, according to Brady (1989), leading to a so-called cascade effect or accelerating declines in prices.

Note also that *if* US pension funds were relying on portfolio insurance strategies to protect them against market falls, such strategies could be held partly responsible for provoking the bubble. Only in the US was portfolio insurance used to a significant extent, whereas markets collapsed worldwide.[21] The view of the crash itself as dominated by portfolio insurance is also disputed (for a survey see Fortune 1993).[22] What is less disputed is that institutions were heavily involved in the selling wave that accompanied the crash, with a particular tendency to dispose of cross-border holdings. Such sales helped to generate the contagion across markets, which was such a feature of October 1987.

The crash posed major issues for monetary policy makers in both the short and medium term. In the short term the major concern was to avoid potential systemic risk arising from failure of investment banks, which was combated by an easing of liquidity and moral suasion on banks to lend. Such an easing was continued, however, owing to fears that there would be a major recession in the wake of the crash. In fact the latter fears seem not to have been justified, and the easing of monetary conditions sowed the seeds of inflation in a number of countries.

The crash showed a need for a broad awareness on the part of monetary policy makers of the broader risks to systemic stability in a securitised financial system – in this case from the risk of failure of brokers and dealers following the share price collapse. Detailed aspects of market mechanisms may have a crucial

role to play. The need for such awareness increases with the relative impor-
tance of securities markets. Second, as in the Great Depression, the crash
showed how financial instability in a large monetary area can spread world-
wide – although unlike the Depression, transmission in this case was limited to
equity prices themselves. Third, in a securitised financial system, even trading
strategies of institutional investors and aspects of securities-market structure
may become crucial aspects of systemic instability at times of stress.

7 The failure of the high yield (junk) bond market (1989)[23]

US corporate finance in the 1980s was marked by a rapid growth in leverage,
much of which was associated with issuance of high yield bonds. Whereas
there had always been low rated or speculative bonds on the market – often
a result of loss of credit rating by firms ('fallen angels') – in the late 1970s and
early 1980s the investment bank Drexel Burnham Lambert set out to create a
market for bonds that would have low credit ratings at issue. An additional
stimulus was the decline in the private placement market, as life insurers
sought greater liquidity (Crabbe et al. 1990). Initially, the market was largely
a source of finance for small emerging companies which could not easily
find credit from other lenders, while offering equity-like risks and rewards to
investors seeking high yields. But the market also attracted take-over and
LBO activity, often enabling corporate raiders to take over large companies
from a small asset base. Issuance grew rapidly. Drexel undertook to make
markets in the securities, aided by certain savings and loans and insurance
companies having close relationships with the firm.

Initially other US investment banks sought to distance themselves from the
market, but were eventually attracted by the high profitability of primary
issuance activity. Investors, such as Savings and Loans institutions and insurance companies were keen investors, given the market offered equity returns
together with guarantees and security associated with bonds. Also they were
partly forbidden by regulation from investing directly in equities. Bush and
Kaletsky (1990) suggest that junk bonds enabled such companies to offer
higher yields to retail investors and gain market share at the expense of more
prudent competitors, thus increasing the onus on them to hold junk bonds
too. It is a matter of controversy whether risk was underpriced in the market;
while the yields seemed generous enough to compensate for realised defaults,
these occurred in the context of a period of prolonged economic expansion.[24] High leverage, the high prices paid for companies (whose security
thus depended on inflated asset values) and accounts and prospectuses based
on an indefinite continuation of expansion gave grounds for caution. It can
be suggested, in effect, that junk bonds dispensed with the credit analysis usually performed by banks, leaving investors to rely on liquidity and
diversification to protect themselves.[25] As discussed below, the former proved
an illusion in changed circumstances; the latter also (given higher defaults
than anticipated) to some degree.

By 1989 the market had reached a value of $200 bn and issues were still proceeding briskly. These included part of the financing of the $25 bn RJR/Nabisco take-over, the largest yet. But the market was weakened by a number of factors which increased uncertainty arising particularly from a default at Campeau, a Canadian conglomerate that had financed purchases of US retailers by junk bonds as well as sharply increasing supply and declining liquidity. Fundamentals worsened sharply when the government's Savings and Loans bail-out bill ordered thrifts to dispose of all junk bonds, although it is not clear this was sufficient to account for all of the subsequent decline. As a consequence, prices fell rapidly, liquidity collapsed and new issues dried up.[26] In the wake of this came the failure of Drexel Burnham Lambert, the main market-maker in February 1990,[27] as the declining value and liquidity of its holdings of junk bonds – in effect, they turned into loans – led to a downgrade of its own debt by the rating agencies and consequent inability either to rollover its commercial paper or to obtain substitute bank finance. It is notable that the market failure occurred without a tightening of monetary policy or a recession, though the later slowdown in the US weakened the market further. No intervention was felt necessary to rescue[28] Drexel – whose failure was felt to pose no systemic threat – nor the market itself. Issuance was near zero through 1990, though a tentative recovery was apparent by the end of 1991.

Reliance of companies on bond markets rather than banks for finance raises the issue of the stability of such markets. Elsewhere (Davis 1994) we have suggested that securities market liquidity resembles in some ways[29] that of banks, in that both provide forms of 'liquidity insurance' to investors that can be disrupted by 'runs' from the instrument, be it deposits or the bonds traded. Market makers play a crucial role in securities market liquidity, and liquidity failure can harm them (as in the case of Drexel) as well as investors and borrowers. On the other hand, it is a nice judgement whether a given securities market crisis gives a need for monetary intervention. There is always a risk of generating moral hazard in such cases – in the junk bond case the market was not felt worth saving. (In contrast, there was policy action when the CP market failed in 1970 during the Penn Central crisis.)

8 Russia/LTCM and US securities markets

In considering the events of 1998, it is important to note that the crisis followed a long bull period, where equity prices had risen sharply and credit quality spreads on bonds had contracted. Issuance even of low grade bonds was very high. The Asian crisis had had little effect on this pattern, although bid-offer widening was apparent in the mortgage backed securities market – where LTCM was active – in April 1998. The trigger for serious turbulence was the moratorium on sovereign debt and effective devaluation of the rouble by Russia in August. It led to a sharp fall in equity prices, a *rise* in core government bond prices (in the context of a 'flight to quality') and a rise in spreads, most markedly on low grade corporate bonds (although the rise in yields was cushioned by an overall fall in bond yields). Issuance collapsed for the US high yield market (to $2 bn in October compared with $15 bn per month in the second quarter), and was sharply reduced for all private debt instruments. Crucially, it was apparent at the time that not all of the widening in spreads was linked to credit risk perceptions, but to an extreme liquidity preference and a general unwillingness to deal in corporate bonds. In the words of McDonough (1998), there was an 'abrupt and simultaneous widening of credit spreads globally, for both corporate and emerging market sovereign debt, [which] was an extraordinary event beyond the expectations of investors and financial intermediaries'.

Underlying these patterns, a wide variety of institutions had taken long positions in Russia and other emerging markets. The spillover to the US and other mature markets was linked to the financing of these positions in a leveraged manner in those markets. Rapid attempted liquidation by a large number of investors in the context of high leveraging led to sharp price changes. The overall widening of spreads in turn inflicted heavy losses on the significant number of large investors which had purchased other higher-risk and/or lower-liquidity assets (e.g. junk bonds or mortgage backed securities – and off-the-run[30] Treasuries) while going short in high-quality debt on the assumption that the existing widening that had occurred after the initial Asian crisis would be unwound (i.e. spreads would 'mean revert'). Such losses led to further margin calls, liquidation and hedging, putting further demands on liquidity.

LTCM was one such investor, a hedge fund with large and (50:1) leveraged positions across what were thought to be a diversified range of financial markets. US and European banks had major credit exposures to it. Simultaneous price shifts in previously uncorrelated markets in the wake of Russia wiped out its capital and threatened insolvency. A rescue was undertaken by private-sector banks to preserve orderly market conditions (McDonough 1998). Notably, there was concern if LTCM had suddenly been put into default, its 75 counterparties would have rushed to 'close out' hundreds of billions of dollars of positions, causing massive illiquidity and price shifts, harming both the counterparties and other market participants. Such a move might generate further uncertainty in a vicious circle, which would ultimately impact sharply on the cost of capital.[31]

Despite the rescue, LTCM heightened uncertainty by leading to fear of the unknown regarding unwinding of its positions and similar hedge fund[32] or bank failures which would entail the unloading of assets into illiquid markets at distressed prices. There was a sharp increase in price volatility and departures from normal pricing relationships (spreads between long-term on-the-run and off-the-run Treasuries widened from a norm of under 10 bp to 35 bp, despite similar duration and the same credit risk) implying a major premium was placed on liquidity. Further widenings were seen in the yield spreads on eurodollar bonds and on private sector instruments over US

Treasury bills, as well as on swaps of fixed for floating rates, showing also heightened concern about counterparty risk. Even in currency markets such as the dollar-yen, there was a sharp rise in bid-offer spreads – and, separately, a one-day move of 15 yen as the so-called yen carry trade was rapidly unwound. There was concern about a possible credit crunch – as issuance of corporate debt and commercial paper fell, but a rise in bank lending tended to substitute – apparently US non-financial firms were able to switch between markets and backup lines of credit with banks, on tighter terms.

Much larger institutions than LTCM had similar if not greater positions with comparable leverage, that is, the markets lacked 'macro portfolio diversification'. LTCM had $80 bn in US Treasury arbitrage positions while commercial banks had $3,000 bn. Direct creditors and counterparties of LTCM were hence not the only ones likely to be hit by losses from an enforced unwinding of LTCM's positions. In such circumstances, market makers were naturally reluctant to take the opposite side of the market.[33] According to the *Wall Street Journal*, they 'cut back on the size of trades, quoted wider bid-offer spreads or did not quote at all'. Consequently, liquidity plunged and market prices moved to levels which were at times wholly unjustified by fundamentals. Markets that were traditionally uncorrelated became highly correlated, and VaR models were interpreted as prompting further sales. There was paralysis among long-term investors who could have corrected pricing anomalies, due to risk aversion and/or lack of credit. Trading techniques such as dynamic hedging and portfolio insurance apparently worsened such tendencies, and exacerbated market price movements once they began. The result was intensified focus on paper that could be liquidated quickly, regardless of its quality in other respects.

Securitised financial systems bring risks with them that are wholly absent in bank dominated systems that have characterised Europe till recently. The risk that a hedge fund could need a (private sector) rescue is evidence of this. Emphasis is also placed on the scope of 'macro portfolio diversification', that is, whether a range of institutions is effectively adopting similar positions. Meanwhile even 'core' and generally highly liquid markets such as US government bonds can become illiquid at times of severe stress, thus posing difficulties to issuers and investors. On the other hand, banks proved able to offer substitute finance for markets.

9 Some broader lessons for macroprudential surveillance

We now go on to examine some of the broader generic lessons of US financial turbulence, which is useful for the euro area as well as other OECD countries and emerging market economies. We would suggest that US historical experience as outlined above (Table 9.4), in common with experience elsewhere in the world (Table 9.5), suggests financial instability manifests itself in three main ways (Davis 1999c), although within these broad groups there are many sub-categories and further distinctions to be made.

Table 9.4 US financial instability

Date	Event	Main feature
1929–33	Stock market crash and banking crisis	Price volatility after shift in expectations and bank failures following loan losses
1979–89	US thrifts	Bank failures following loan losses
1984	Continental Illinois (US)	Bank failure following loan losses
1985–89	Texas banking crisis	Bank failures following loan losses
1987	Stock market crash	Price volatility after shift in expectations
1989	Collapse of US junk bonds	Collapse of market liquidity and issuance
1998	Russian default and LTCM	Collapse of market liquidity and issuance

For detailed accounts see Davis (1994, 1995b, 1995c).

Table 9.5 Further episodes of financial instability

Date	Event	Main feature
1970	US Penn Central Bankruptcy	Collapse of market liquidity and issuance
1973	UK secondary banking	Bank failures following loan losses
1974	Herstatt (Germany)	Bank failure following trading losses
1982	LDC debt crisis	Bank failures following loan losses
1985	Canadian Regional Banks	Bank failures following loan losses
1986	FRN market	Collapse of market liquidity and issuance
1989	Australian banking problems	Bank failures following loan losses
1990	Swedish commercial paper	Collapse of market liquidity and issuance
1990–91	Norwegian banking crisis	Bank failures following loan losses
1991–92	Finnish banking crisis	Bank failures following loan losses
1991–92	Swedish banking crisis	Bank failures following loan losses
1992–96	Japanese banking crisis	Bank failures following loan losses
1992	ECU bond market collapse	Collapse of market liquidity and issuance
1992–93	ERM crisis	Price volatility after shift in expectations
1994	Bond market reversal	Price volatility after shift in expectations
1995	Mexican crisis	Price volatility after shift in expectations
1997	Asian crisis	Price volatility following shift in expectations and bank failures following loan losses.

For detailed accounts see Davis (1994, 1995b, 1995c).

One generic type of crisis is bank failures following loan or trading losses. Examples include the Texas banking crisis and the US thrifts crisis (as well as the LDC debt crisis, the banking crises in Japan, the Nordic countries and Australia and the Asian crisis). Many developing countries have suffered such crises in recent decades. Within those banking crises one may distinguish those that were confined to the domestic financial system as opposed to those that were also linked to cross-border bank lending and indebtedness in foreign currencies (LDC debt, Asia).

A second type involves extreme market price volatility after a shift in expectations. Such crises are distinctive in that they tend to involve institutional investors as principals, and are focused mainly on the consequences for financial institutions of sharp price changes which result from institutional 'herding' as groups of such institutions imitate one another's strategies. Whereas violent price movements may in themselves not have systemic implications,[34] these may emerge when such movements threaten, for example, institutions that have taken leveraged positions on the current levels of asset prices. Examples are the stock market crash of 1987, the ERM crisis, the 1994 bond market reversal and the Mexican crisis. There were also elements of this in the Asian crisis.

A third type, which is linked to the second, involves protracted collapse of market liquidity and issuance.[35] Again often involving institutional herding, the distinction with the second type is often largely one of whether markets are sufficiently resilient, and whether market maker structures are suitably robust. Also such crises tend to characterise debt markets rather than equity or foreign exchange. The risks are acute not only for those holding positions in the market but for those relying on the market for debt finance or liquidity – which increasingly include banks. Examples in the past have tended typically to be rather specific and idiosyncratic markets, which by nature relied on a narrow investor base, market maker structure and/or issuer base (junk bonds, floating rate notes, Swedish commercial paper, ECU bonds). However, the events described in Section 8 following the Russian default and the rescue of the hedge fund LTCM were much more serious, as liquidity failure was threatened in markets such as the US securities repurchase (repo), swaps, commercial paper (CP), corporate and Treasury bond market (see IMF 1998; Davis 1999d). The main historical precedent was the Penn Central bankruptcy and its effect on the US commercial paper market. In these cases liquidity was threatened in core markets, thus leading the US authorities to take decisive action.

An immediate point to make is that most periods of financial instability in Europe have linked to the first type of crisis (i.e. banking crises), with market crises occurring in, or largely originating in the US (although US banks have made far greater losses from credit risk than market risk). The likely securitisation of euro area markets may pose similar challenges there. Given that securities market problems are likely to generalise across the monetary area while banking crises can remain local, the former would be more likely to provide a challenge directly to the ECB.

On the other hand, the presence of both banks and securities markets as a source of financing in a monetary area is beneficial in offering a form of diversification for the financial system – and indeed, banks have often offered substitute finance (e.g. after LTCM[36]) when securities markets are closed while securities markets substituted for banks in the Texan banking crisis. European financial systems would thus become less vulnerable to economic repercussions of banking crises as securities markets develop.

Generic features of the crises may also be helpful in pinpointing potential danger signs in the euro area. Table 9.6 provides a summary of the features of

Table 9.6 Features of selected episodes of US financial instability

	Great Depression (1933)	Continental Illinois (1984)	Thrift crisis (1979–89)	Texas banking crisis (1985–9)	Stock market crash (1987)	Junk bond market (1989)	Russia and LTCM (1998)
Debt accumulation	●	●	●	●	●	●	●
Asset price boom	●		●	●	●	●	●
Concentration of risk	●	●	●	●	●		●
Regime shift	●		●	●	●		●
New entry of intermediaries	●		●	●	●		●
Innovation	●				●	●	
Monetary tightening	●					●	
Declining capital adequacy of financial institutions	●	●	●	●	●	●	●
Credit rationing/liquidity failure/bank runs	●	●		●	●	●	●
Contagion between markets	●				●		●
International transmission	●				●		●
Action by the authorities	●	●	●				●
Severe macroeconomic impact	●						
Dysfunction of financial system/economic collapse	●						

Source: Davis (1995a).

the US financial crises outlined above, which was developed also in the light of the theories listed in Section 2. We consider these to be the most basic dataset that is suggested by US experience as being common to crises.[37] As shown in Davis (1999d), a wider range of crises reflect similar features.

Notably, in advance of crises, the stress is laid on:

- Debt accumulation (economy wide, by individual sectors or in individual markets).
- Asset price booms (be it property or equity prices).
- Concentration of risk on the part of financial institutions (implying excessive optimism in respect of potential 'correlations').
- Unanticipated regime shifts towards laxity on the part of monetary, fiscal or regulatory authorities (including 'financial liberalisation').
- Easing of conditions for new entry of intermediaries to the relevant market.
- Financial innovation (and rapid growth of the markets concerned).
- Declining capital adequacy of financial institutions.
- Monetary tightening or unanticipated regime shifts towards rigour on the part of monetary, fiscal and regulatory authorities.

Of course, many of these features have occurred separately without entailing a crisis, and indeed are part of the normal functioning of a market economy. It is their combination and acuteness that is crucial. There are conceptual distinctions between these features: monetary or other forms of policy tightening is a *triggering mechanism* which may indeed be warranted by the other elements, while most of the other elements are *propagation mechanisms* arising from an *initial shock* (such as changes in regulation or technology in the real economy or financial markets). Moreover not all of these features were present in all cases. Nevertheless, we suggest that they constitute a useful checklist derived from actual experience – and that the experiences themselves warrant considerable attention.

Conclusions

We would suggest that the episodes that have been specified are of interest in the light both of structural similarities of the euro area to the US and of the likely evolution of the euro area towards the US model. Such evolution is widely predicted in terms of the importance of capital markets, institutional investment and publicly available information regarding issuers and borrowers (as opposed to the European tradition of banking intermediation based on private information and close banking relationships).

Table 9.7 seeks to summarise the key lessons of each crisis according to the division set out at the outset between those elements relating to securitisation and those linked to structural elements, as well as some elements common to the generality of financial crises. US history shows in particular in a large and

Table 9.7 Summary of lessons from US financial instability

Date	Event	Structural elements	Securitisation elements	General features
1929–33	Stock market crash and banking crisis	International transmission; new monetary arrangements; lack of bank diversification on asset and liabilities side; importance of automatic stabilisers		Corporate leverage; equity prices and financial stability
1979–89	US thrifts	Lack of bank diversification on asset side	Disintermediation, excess capacity, and the viability of banking sectors	Real estate lending risks; forbearance; deposit insurance
1984	Continental Illinois (US)	Lack of bank diversification on asset and liability side		Too-big-to-fail
1985–89	Texas banking crisis	Lack of bank diversification on asset side		Real estate lending risks
1987	Stock market crash	International transmission	Importance of institutional investors' trading strategies; systemic role of non-banks	Equity prices and financial stability
1989	Collapse of US junk bonds		Importance of securities market liquidity	
1998	Russian default and LTCM		Systemic role of non-banks; importance of securities market liquidity	

diverse monetary area with segmented local banking markets, that regional crises can pose a major challenge to policy makers, while the existence of a large monetary area in a global sense means that there will inevitably be international transmission of shocks generated within it. There is also a need for special care in the case of new monetary arrangements that have not yet experienced major financial instability.

Meanwhile money and securities market liquidity become of great systemic importance in a securitised financial system; equity prices too may become of major importance for financial stability; disintermediation becomes a major factor with which banks must contend and adjust as best they can; that non-banks such as investment banks and even hedge funds may become of systemic importance; and that even institutional investors' strategies can cause major asset price shifts which threaten systemic stability. More generally, whereas European financial instability has traditionally been of a pattern of bank failures following loan and trading losses, the likely securitisation of euro area markets may pose challenges arising from the occurrence of crises of a type more characteristic of the US, linked to price volatility in asset markets following shifts in expectations (which may threaten leveraged institutions that hold positions in these assets) or the collapse of market liquidity and issuance, which threatens institutions needing to transact or issue in such markets. On the other hand, the presence of both banks and securities markets is beneficial in offering a form of diversification for the financial system – and indeed, we have cited cases where banks have provided substitute finance when securities markets are closed, and vice versa.

US experience shows that issues such as too-big-to-fail can arise in a large monetary zone in the same way as a small state with a concentrated banking sector; the thrift crisis underlined for all time the dangers of forbearance in respect of banks with zero or negative net worth, and deposit insurance guarantees. Finally, real estate lending booms and rising corporate leverage are shown in the US, as in Europe, to be major warning signs for financial instability.

It may be added that we have by no means exhausted the material that recent US financial history provides, as for example:

- the Penn Central bankruptcy of 1970 showed that liquidity of money markets, even one as established as US CP, is not necessarily robust, and liquidity failure may prompt policy action. Accordingly, the growth of money market financing of non-financial corporations – itself likely to accompany the integration of financial markets in the EU – may broaden the locus of systemic financial instability beyond banks;
- the LDC debt crisis shows *inter alia* the risks of cross-border lending to emerging markets – that also came to the fore for Asia for EU banks – partly driven by disintermediation of banks from domestic corporate lending and intense competition;

- the capital crunch of 1990–1 showed again the dangers of high corporate leverage and real estate lending (again related to concentration of bank lending on high risk borrowers following securitisation), see Davis (1995c), as well as the role constraints on bank lending can play at a macroeconomic level;
- and the Mexican crisis showed the growing influence of mutual funds on cross-border flows.

Having set out the various ways in which the euro area may learn from lessons of history in the US, it remains to note some of the recognised challenges in respect of financial stability in the euro area. The ECB (1999) provide a number of suggestions. They note that EMU will reinforce prevailing trends in EU banking sectors, notably *reduction of existing excess capacity, pressure on banks' profitability, growth of internationalisation*, spread of mergers and higher conglomeration (author's italics). Among pressures on banks' profitability were the reduction in forex activities, securitisation and disintermediation and the decrease in correspondent banking owing to centralisation of treasury functions by large firms. In this context, EMU 'will also affect the features and magnitude of banking risks', whereby in the context of the development of deep and liquid markets, which can facilitate direct access for the best borrowers and the 'resultant *concentration of risky borrowers among banks could increase credit risk*'. Maturity transformation risk and country risk from increased involvement in non-euro markets were also highlighted. More recently, the ECB has noted the rapid growth of the euro interbank market, with a high proportion of unsecured activity,[38] as well as growing concentration of such lending (ECB 2000a). The patterns of real estate prices in some countries is seen as a potential source of risk at the time of writing (ECB 2000b).

Notes

1   The author is Professor of Economics and Finance at Brunel University and also an Associate Member of the Financial Markets Group at LSE, Associate Fellow of the Royal Institute of International Affairs and Research Fellow of the Pensions Institute at Birkbeck College, London (e-mail: e_philip_davis@msn.com). The descriptions of historical events in Sections 2–8 are based in part on material from the author's book *Debt, financial fragility and systemic risk* (Davis 1995a), the publishing rights in which are held by Oxford University Press. Davis (1995a). The author thanks Dick Brealey, Peter Brierley, Richard Bronk, Glenn Hoggarth, Arild Lund, Geoffrey Wood and participants in seminars at the Bank of England, the Royal Institute for International Affairs, the Instituto Superior de Economia e Gestão, Lisbon as well as at SUERF for helpful comments. Views expressed are those of the author and not necessarily those of the institutions to which he is affiliated.

2   An issue arises as to whether the definition should include the mispricing of financial assets. We suggest that while this may accompany a financial crisis, the failure of payments and of credit allocation of funds are the defining features. Arguably, mispricing of financial assets is quite common (e.g. in asset bubbles, exchange rate

misalignments and mispricing of credit risk) without entailing a financial crisis, or even systemic risk, whereas failure of payments and of credit allocation are only seen in a crisis. Mispricing may nonetheless, we suggest later, be part of the overall pattern which builds towards a crisis.

3   See Aglietta (1999), Bruni and De Boissieu (1999) and Prati and Schinasi (1999) for recent contributions. One aspect of interest for financial stability may be the contrasting methods of providing liquidity in the US and euro area.

4   For example, a decline of relationship banking and growth of securities markets could lead to a decline in credit risk and a risk in market risk.

5   Note that a number of these are not separate institutions.

6   On the other hand, given the larger size of the euro area banking system, the value of financial assets accounted for by the top five banks is larger.

7   Note however that peripheral government bond markets are tending to suffer loss of liquidity to those with benchmark status.

8   Governments might for example increase the proportion of their debt issued in the form of securities from the current 44 per cent, while companies would be encouraged to issue corporate debt or equity instead of borrowing from banks.

9   Social security reform is nevertheless partially linked to EMU, as it may be driven by fiscal integration (the constraints of the stability pact in particular).

10   There will still be reputational costs to 'walking away' from a banking link, even in a transactions based banking system.

11   In the longer term, the remaining banks may be highly profitable if they can profit from non-interest activities (and cut costs) like their US counterparts.

12   Besides the above-mentioned branch density, the indicators of excess capacity used by Davis and Salo include the proportion of banks earning less than the real money market rate on their equity and the proportion of banks with provisions in excess of 50 per cent and 100 per cent of their net interest income.

13   Note that such 'runs' lead to a contraction in the money supply, in line with the monetarist view, if the depositors seek cash, but not if they 'run' to 'safer' banks.

14   This failure was linked to a conflict between Washington and New York in the wake of the death of Benjamin Strong.

15   See Gorton (1988).

16   Bernanke and James (1991) offer an international comparison of links from finance to the real economy in the Depression, focusing on the exchange rate regime, deflation and financial crisis. They suggest that banking crises significantly aggravated the downturns.

17   The risk in such patterns is that the availability of non-domestic interbank funds might not be reliable, as the banking sector becomes exposed to institutions that have no stake in the stability of the domestic financial system. Domestic banks could face a cut-off of credit at times of stress, especially when they are seen to face a common shock (see Section 5).

18   A more recent reform has facilitated cross-state banking, and at the time of writing banks are becoming more widely diversified across the country.

19   Asymmetries in asset price and credit growth are marked at the time of writing, however (ECB 2000b).

20   Index arbitrage involved buying and selling simultaneously a stock index futures contract and the underlying stocks, so as to profit from any discrepancy (known as spread or basis) between them.

21   Indeed, in the UK the crash was largely irrelevant to pension funds, since at the time their funding status relied on estimates of future dividend growth, that were unaffected by the crash, rather than market values.

22   On the one hand, any form of strategy which aimed to lock in current values, such as stop-loss selling of equities (that is, selling when the price had fallen to a pre-specified level), would equally have induced a rush of sales when the market fell;

and this was probably the more prevalent strategy. Also Fortune (1993) suggests that the discounts between stock index and futures prices were in fact illusory, resulting from such phenomena as delays in reporting of individual share prices, late openings or trading halts for individual stocks, but their appearance led traders to panic; in other words, the problem was in the cash market and not the futures markets. Moreover Grossman (1988), examining US daily transactions data for 1987 as a whole, found no link from stock market volatility to programme trading.

23 See Bush and Kaletsky (1991).
24 The 1990–91 slowdown exacted a heavy toll of bonds, with default rates of 8.8 per cent in 1990 (Moody's 1991).
25 Although in principle the lead manager should offer credit assessment, balance may have been affected by the attraction of the front-end fee.
26 Whereas trading was $400 mn a day before Campeau, it was $150 mn in December.
27 It accounted for 50 per cent of trading.
28 However, the authorities were careful to ensure an orderly rundown of its affairs.
29 The similarities should not be exaggerated – markets cannot become 'insolvent' like banks, and an investor who 'sits tight' till liquidity is restored need not make a loss.
30 On-the-run Treasury securities are the most recently issued stocks and heavily traded; off-the-run are earlier issues of the same maturity which lack liquidity, being largely in the hands of long-term investors. As both are obligations of the US Treasury, there is no distinction in credit risk, and the spread is one of the 'cleanest' indicators of liquidity risk.
31 The US investor Warren Buffett reportedly sought to resolve the situation, but his help was refused.
32 One of the key issues raised by the crisis was the lack of transparency of hedge funds, despite which banks appeared willing to offer financing. See Basle Committee (1999).
33 The institutions making markets had themselves been financially weakened in the crisis.
34 They may, however, lead to resource misallocation.
35 It is not denied that all sharp price changes will tend to affect market liquidity to a greater or lesser degree.
36 Penn Central in 1970 was another example (Davis 1994).
37 See also Demirguc-Kunt and Detragiache (1998a and b).
38 In mitigation, the maturity of the unsecured activity is typically short. Growth of interbank repo transactions is limited by the lack of integration of securities settlements systems across the eurozone.

References

Aglietta M (1999), 'A lender of last resort for Europe', paper presented at the LSE Financial Markets Group conference on the Lender of Last Resort, LSE, July 13 1999.

Barth J R and Litan R E (1999), 'Lessons from bank failures in the United States'. In ed. G Caprio et al. *Preventing bank crises; lessons from recent global failures*, World Bank and Federal Reserve Bank of Chicago.

Basle Committee on Banking Supervision (1999), 'Banks' interactions with highly leveraged institutions (The Brockmeijer Report)', BIS, Basle.

Bernanke B S (1983), 'Non monetary effects of the financial crisis in the propagation of the Great Depression', *American Economic Review*, 73, 257–76.

Bernanke B S and James C (1991), 'The Gold Standard, deflation and financial crisis in the Great Depression; an international comparison', in ed. Hubbard R G, *Financial markets and financial crises*, NBER, University of Chicago Press.

Brady N (1989), *Report of the presidential task force on market mechanisms*, US Government Printing Office, Washington DC.

Bruni F and De Boissieu C (1999), 'Lending of last resort and systemic stability in the euro zone', paper presented at the LSE Financial Markets Group conference on the Lender of Last Resort, LSE, July 13 1999.

Bush J and Kaletsky A (1990), 'When the Junk Pile Topples', *Financial Times*, 14/2/90.

Clair R T, Kolson J O and Robinson K J (1995), 'The Texas banking crisis and the payments system', *Federal Reserve Bank of Dallas Economic Review*, First Quarter, 13–21.

Crabbe L E, Pickering M H and Prowse S D (1990), 'Recent Developments in Corporate Finance', *Federal Reserve Bulletin*, August, 76, 593–603.

Davis E P (1994), 'Market liquidity risk', in eds Fair D and Raymond R, *The Competitiveness of Financial Institutions and Centres in Europe*, Kluwer Academic Publishers.

Davis E P (1995a), *Debt, financial fragility and systemic risk*, revised and extended version, Oxford University Press.

Davis E P (1995b), 'Financial Fragility in the Early 1990s, What can be Learnt from International Experience?', LSE Financial Markets Group Special Paper No. 76.

Davis E P (1995c), 'Institutional investors, unstable financial markets and monetary policy', in eds F Bruni, D Fair and R O'Brien, *Risk management in volatile financial markets*, Kluwer, Amsterdam (also Special Paper No. 75, LSE Financial Markets Group).

Davis E P (1999a), 'EMU and financial structure', *Financial Market Trends*, OECD Paris.

Davis E P (1999b), 'Institutionalisation and EMU; implications for European financial markets', *International Finance*, 2, 33–61.

Davis E P (1999c), 'Financial data needs for macroprudential surveillance – what are the key indicators of risk to domestic financial stability?', Handbooks in Central Banking – Lecture Series No 2, Centre for Central Banking Studies, Bank of England. (www.bankofengland.co.uk/ccbs/lshb02.pdf).

Davis E P (1999d), 'Russia/LTCM and market liquidity risk', The Financial Regulator, 4/2, 23–8.

Davis E P and Salo S (1998), 'Excess capacity in EU and US banking sectors – conceptual, measurement and policy issues', LSE Financial Markets Group Special Paper No. 105.

Demirguc-Kunt A and Detragiache E (1998a), 'The determinants of banking crises in developing and developed countries', *IMF Staff Papers*, 45, 81–109.

Demirguc-Kunt A and Detragiache E (1998b), 'Financial liberalisation and financial fragility', IMF Working Paper No WP/98/83.

Diamond D and Dybvig P (1983), 'Bank Runs, Deposit Insurance and Liquidity', *Journal of Political Economy*, 91, 401–19.

Eisenbeis R A, Horvitz P M and Cole R A (1999), 'Commercial banks and real estate lending; the Texas experience', *Journal of Regulatory Economics*, forthcoming.

European Monetary Institute (1998), 'Annual Report 1997', EMI, Frankfurt.

European Central Bank (1999), 'Annual Report 1998', ECB, Frankfurt.

European Central Bank (2000a), 'EMU and banking supervision', ECB Monthly Bulletin, April 2000, 49–64 (www.ecb.int/pub/pdf/mb200004en.pdf).

European Central Bank (2000b), 'Asset prices and banking stability', ECB, Frankfurt (www.ecb.int/pub/pdf/assetprices.pdf).

Fisher I (1933), 'The Debt Deflation Theory of Great Depressions' *Econometrica*, 1: 337–57.

Fortune P (1993), 'Stock market crashes; what have we learned from October 1987?', *New England Economic Review*, March/April, 3–24.

Friedman M and Schwartz A J (1963), 'A monetary history of the US 1867–1960', NBER, New York.

Galbraith J K (1954), *The Great Crash*, Houghton Mifflin, Boston, Mass.

Gorton G (1988), 'Banking panics and business cycles', *Oxford Economic Papers*, 40, 751–81.

Grossman S (1988), 'Program trading and market volatility; a report on interday relationships', *Financial Analysts Journal*, July–August, 18–28.

Gunther J W, Lown C and Robinson K J (1995), 'Bank credit and economic activity; evidence from the Texas banking decline', *Journal of Financial Services Research*, 9, 31–48.

Guttentag J M and Herring R J (1984), 'Credit Rationing and Financial Disorder' *Journal of Finance*, 39: 1359–82.

Hardy D C and Pazarbasioglu C (1998), 'Leading indicators of banking crises; was Asia different?', IMF Working Paper No. WP/98/91.

Haubrich J G (1990), 'Nonmonetary effects of financial crises; lessons from the Great Depression in Canada', Journal of Monetary Economics, 25, 225–52.

Herring J and Wachter S (1999) 'Real estate booms and banking busts: an international perspective', Working Paper No 99–27. Financial Institutions Center, The Wharton School, University of Pennsylvania.

IMF (1998), 'World Economic Outlook and International Capital Markets, Interim Assessment December 1998 – Financial Turbulence and the World Economy', IMF, Washington DC.

Jordan J S (1998), 'Resolving a banking crisis; what worked in New England', *New England Economic Review*, September/October, 49–62.

Kaminsky L G and Reinhart C M (1996), 'The twin crises; the causes of banking and balance-of-payments problems', International Finance Discussion Paper No. 544, Board of Governors of the Federal Reserve.

Kane E (1985), *The gathering crisis in Federal deposit insurance*, MIT Press, Cambridge, Mass.

Keeley M C (1990), 'Deposit Insurance, Risk and Market Power in Banking', *American Economic Review*, 80: 1138–99.

Kindleberger C P (1978), *Manias, Panics and Crashes, A History of Financial Crises*, Basic Books, New York.

Knight F H (1921), 'Risk, uncertainty and profit', Boston; No. 16 in a series of rare texts in economics republished by the LSE.

Krugman P (1991), 'Financial Crises in the International Economy', in ed. M Feldstein, *The Risk of Economic Crisis*, Univ. of Chicago Press.

Kryzanowski L and Roberts G S (1989), 'The performance of the Canadian banking sector, 1920–40', in *Proceedings of the 25th annual conference on bank structure and competition*, Federal Reserve Bank of Chicago.

McDonough W J (1998), 'Statement to the House of Representatives Committee on Banking and Financial Services, October 1 1998', Federal Reserve Bank of New York.

Minsky H P (1977), 'A Theory of Systemic Fragility' in eds E I Altman and A W Sametz, *Financial Crises*, Wiley, New York.

Mishkin F S (1991), 'Asymmetric Information and Financial Crises: A Historical Perspective', in ed. R G Hubbard, *Financial Markets and Financial Crises*, University of Chicago Press, Chicago.

Moody's (1991), 'Corporate Bond Defaults and Default Rates 1970–90', Moody's Special Report, Moody's Investors Service, New York.

Pauley B (1989), 'The thrift reform programme, summary and implications', Salomon Brothers, New York.

Petersen M A and Rajan R G (1993), 'The effect of credit market competition on firm-creditor relationships', paper presented at CEPR/ESF workshop in financial regulation, Toulouse, June 1993.

Prati A and Schinasi G (1999), 'Financial stability in European Economic and Monetary Union', forthcoming in 'Princeton Studies in International Finance', Princeton University Press.

Randall R E (1993), 'Lessons from New England banking failures', *New England Economic Review*, May/June, 13–38.

Scharfstein D S and Stein J C (1990), 'Herd behaviour and investment', *American Economic Review*, 80, 465–79.

Shafer J R (1986), 'Managing Crises in the Emerging Financial Landscape', OECD Economic Studies, 8: 56–77.

Summers L H (1991), 'Planning for the next financial crisis', in ed. M Feldstein, *The risk of economic crises*, University of Chicago Press.

Taggart R A (1985), 'Secular patterns in the financing of US corporations', in ed. B M Friedman, 'Corporate capital structures in the US', University of Chicago Press.

Timlen T M (1977), 'Commercial Paper – Penn Central and Others', in eds E I Altman and A W Sametz, *Financial Crises*, John Wiley, New York.

Wojnilower A M (1980), 'The Central Role of Credit Crunches in Recent Financial History', Brookings Papers on Economic Activity, 1975:2, 277–326.

10 Strategies developed by Spanish banks for adapting to financial globalisation

Mergers, acquisitions and other strategies*

Ignacio Fuentes Egusquiza and
Teresa Sastre de Miguel

Since the late eighties, Spanish bank markets have been undergoing major changes that have affected both their structure and the nature of strategic interaction among Spanish banks. These major changes have been a natural outcome of the heightening competitive pressure exerted on all countries' banks by processes such as deregulation, globalisation of financial and economic activities, the development of new technology and the prospect of greater integration of European financial markets.

Globalisation of financial and economic activities, by increasing the degree of interdependence all over the world, has favoured the development of more internationally integrated markets. This process has also been accompanied by a world-wide trend towards convergence in consumer preferences and fast widespread technological advances. As a result, markets of a larger dimension have emerged and previous competitive advantages of market participants have changed.

Against this transformed financial landscape banks have started to develop different strategies to tackle the demands of this new environment. In the case of Spanish banks, two main strategies have been developed: domestic mergers and acquisitions, and business diversification. These have been the main responses of a banking system where competitive pressures have remarkably increased and margins have narrowed progressively.

A third type of strategy has also been adopted by some institutions: business alliances without full integration into a single firm. Very different kinds of alliances have been developed – some of the latest with non-financial firms – although some common features can be observed in many of them. They have usually been intended to develop and share technological advances or new products and sometimes to access new markets. In most cases they have been established between Spanish banks and banking firms of other countries, generally of European ones. The fact that cross-country mergers

* Paper presented at 22nd SUERF Colloquium, Vienna, 27–29 April 2000.

have shown to be rather difficult to undertake in Europe, except for some few cases, may have influenced the decision of establishing business alliances. These can be seen either as a subsidiary mechanism or as a step previous to further integration into a single firm.

1 Introduction

As a result of the consolidation process via mergers and acquisitions, the level of concentration in the Spanish banking industry has increased and the share in the system's total assets of the ten biggest banking groups grew from almost 50% in 1992 to nearly 70% in 1999 (see Table 10.1) .The structure of the savings bank and credit co-operative sectors has also changed with a significant reduction in the number of institutions – the number of savings banks fell from around 80 in the eighties to 51 in 1998 and the number of credit co-operatives from 150 to 97 in the same period.

Table 10.1 Spanish banking system concentration (total assets)

	1992		1999	
	pta	%	*pta*	%
Deposit money institutions	94.337	100.0	168.057	100.0
Four big banks (a)	28.153	29.8	90.569	53.9
Big ten	46.361	49.1	114.720	68.3

Source: Banco de España (BE).

(a) Merger between BBV and Argentaria is considered as completed in 1999 data.

However, this process of concentration has not prevented a growing degree of competition in almost all the relevant segments of the Spanish banking markets. Mergers and the opportunities for reorganisation involved may either provide gains in efficiency that bear on marginal costs or give rise to increased market power, or both together. Faced with this set of possible repercussions, it may well be asked whether the increase in price competition between Spanish banks since the start of the nineties has been checked, to some extent, by the increase in concentration and the potential rise in merged banks' market power. It is also worth evaluating whether merged banks have actually obtained gains in efficiency and, should this be so, whether these have translated into improved profitability and higher levels of soundness.

Simultaneously, Spanish banking institutions have also reconsidered strategies related to product-mix and business structure. In general terms, they have sought to attain an increased diversification of their business, sometimes by going into a merging process. Spanish banks have offered new products such as investment and pension funds, derivative instruments and, more recently, they have launched securitisation programmes. They have also sought business diversification by increasing their international activity in two different ways: on one hand, directly increasing their activity in foreign currencies or with foreign residents and, on the other, expanding into foreign markets through the acquisition of financial companies in other countries, mainly in Latin America.

Co-operative alliances with banks of other European countries have been adopted as an alternative competitive strategy in a global market. This strategy allows firms to join their resources in a less structured way than mergers, maintaining a greater degree of independence.[1] This formula seems fairly adequate to attain specific purposes – many related to technological improvements – and to limit the risks involved in the development of new products. It also seems very attractive as a way to access new markets and share the acquired knowledge of each bank participating in the alliance. However, several issues may make this kind of agreement unstable. Firstly, a procedure for revenue and cost sharing needs to be established which might become unsatisfactory for some partner if unforeseen permanent shocks happen. Second, merging or combining business cultures may be extremely hard in a loose institutional set-up with diffused management responsibilities.

The main purpose of this paper is to provide some empirical evidence on the effects of concentration strategies on interest rates set by banks and on the efficiency, profitability and soundness levels of banking institutions. It also analyses the impact of diversification strategies on business structure, profit generation and risk profile by focusing on changes observed in the structure of financial statements. The third strategy above-mentioned can hardly be analysed yet since this is a fairly recent trend and the information provided by financial statements does not seem to be very adequate to figure out the impact of these agreements on the performance of financial institutions.

The paper is organised as follows. Section 2 analyses the effects of concentration strategies on bank interest rates and the transmission mechanism and also assesses the impact of merger processes on the levels of efficiency, profitability and solvency of merged institutions. Section 3 analyses diversification strategies adopted by Spanish banks and their effects on the financial statement structure. Section 4 concludes.

2 Mergers and acquisitions

Mergers and other forms of consolidation may influence bank interest rates insofar as the increase in size and the opportunities for reorganisation involved may either provide gains in efficiency that bear on marginal costs or give rise to increases in market power, or both together. Gains in efficiency would be obtained on moving onto a greater scale of activity (if there are economies of scale)[2] and/or owing to the possible reduction of X-inefficiencies, derived from inadequate management and organisation of resources that might have placed a bank above its cost curve.

Mergers and acquisitions may give banks the opportunity to redirect their activity towards business areas that involve an increase in income greater than that in costs, thereby achieving an increase in profitability. Some authors have also pointed to a potential effect on banks' capital adequacy insofar as mergers and acquisitions may allow for a greater diversification of risk with the same capital base.[3]

Thus, it may well be asked whether the increased price competition among Spanish banks has been checked, to some extent, by the increase in concentration and the potential rise in merged banks' market power. It is also worth assessing whether merged banks have actually obtained gains in efficiency and, should this be so, whether these have translated into improved profitability and higher levels of soundness.

To analyse these issues two types of methodology will be used. The first, of an econometric nature, is used to seek the influence of the above-mentioned phenomena on the determination of bank interest rates and is based on the estimation of interest rate equations with panel data. On one hand, this allows prices of merged firms to be compared with those of non-merged ones. On the other, the effect of competition on banks' interest rates can be analysed by using an indicator of their course over time. Although the most widely used variable for this purpose is concentration, this does not seem appropriate according to recent developments in the Spanish banking system. Instead, the cross-section dispersion of bank interest rates is the indicator used in this paper.

The second methodology, used to assess the impact of mergers on efficiency, profitability and soundness of merged institutions, consists of a case-by-case analysis of most of the mergers and take-overs that have taken place in Spain in the period 1988–98.

Influence on the determination of bank interest rates

Theoretical setting

The estimation of equations that determine bank interest rates is based on the first-order conditions of a Klein-Monti type model,[4] in which intermediaries maximise profits in the current period and have the capacity to set the price in both the credit and the deposit markets. There is a third, competitive market in which they are not able to influence the price (the interbank or government debt market) and to which they resort to seek a return on surplus liquidity or borrow funds. Consequently the latter market is one of adjustment between the market for credit and that for deposits. Under these assumptions, the interest rates on credit and on deposits are determined separately and independently. In addition, if it is assumed that there is product differentiation and strategic interaction between bank intermediaries, banks' decisions on prices will depend on the actions of rivals or competitors, so that the elasticity perceived by each bank will be the outcome of: the price elasticity of the consumers whose demand it satisfies and the degree of rivalry among market participants.

One of the features inherent to the credit market is the risk arising from the uncertainty about collecting loan principal and interest. So as to take this aspect into account, the probability of incurring past-due loans which, along with interest rates, determines the expected return on the loan portfolio, has been introduced into the above-mentioned model.

The overall consideration of all these aspects in a current profit maximisation model gives rise to two first-order conditions.[5]

$$r_L^i = \left[p^i + \frac{p^i}{\eta_L^i + \eta_L^M} \right]^{-1} (r + c_L^i) \tag{1}$$

$$r_D^i = \left[1 + \frac{p^i}{\eta_D^i + \eta_D^M} \right]^{-1} [r + c_D^i] \tag{2}$$

where:

r_L^i : lending interest rate extended by bank i.

r_D^i : deposit interest rate offered by i.

r : marginal financial cost – usually some type of representative market rate.

c_L^i : marginal operational cost of credit extended by i.

c_D^i : marginal operational cost of deposits raised by i.

p^i : probability of the typical client of bank i paying for the credit in due time = 1 – average probability of recording past-due loans.

η_L^i : elasticity of the demand for credit received by i if competitors do not react (related to consumer characteristics).

η_D^i : elasticity of the supply of deposits raised by i if competitors do no react

η_L^M : degree of rivalry of firms in the credit market:

η_D^M : degree of rivalry of firms in the deposit market.

One of the features of this model is that the credit market and the deposit market are independent, that is, loan rates and deposit rates are determined separately.

By making appropriate assumptions, expressions (1) and (2) can be embedded in the following empirical equations.[6]

$$r_L^i = \beta_0 + \beta_1 r + \beta_2 c_L^i + \beta_3 p^i + \beta_4 \eta_L^i + \beta_5 \eta_L^M + \varepsilon_L^i \tag{3}$$

$$r_D^i = \gamma_0 + \gamma_1 r + \gamma_2 c_D^i + \gamma_3 \eta_D^i + \gamma_4 \eta_D^M + \varepsilon_D^i \tag{4}$$

According to these equations, interest rates set by banks depend on: (1) marginal financial cost, usually represented by a market rate such as inter-bank or government debt rates; (2) marginal cost, approximated by operational costs per asset unit in the current analysis; (3) degree of rivalry of firms, as reflected in the cross-section dispersion of bank interest rates; (4) cyclical movements in price-elasticity, approximated by GDP rate of growth; and (5) the probability of recording past-due loans – which has been approximated by the ratio of non-performing loans to total credit extended.

The idea underlying the use of dispersion in interest rates as an indicator of changes in the degree of competition among bank intermediaries is as follows: as the competitive pressure in a market with a certain degree of product differentiation heightens, the companies participating in said market will have less ability to set prices differentiated from those set by the rest of the competitors, whereby price set by each company will tend to converge. Nonetheless, this reduction in dispersion could likewise be the outcome of a wide range of circumstances. Hence, this variable cannot be univocally interpreted as a competition indicator. However, if the non-sample information relative to events in the Spanish banking sector is taken into account, the declining tendency of dispersion should be interpreted as evidence of greater competitive pressure.[7]

The estimation of equations (3) and (4) has been made with a panel of Spanish banking institutions, banks and savings banks. This allows to control for a series of characteristics proper to each bank which give rise to non-observable heterogeneity and which are included in the individual effects of both equations (ε_L^i, ε_D^i). Thus, included in these effects there would be a series of aspects which define the management and organisational framework proper to each intermediary and which basically determine the degree of X-inefficiencies. A decrease in the magnitude of these X-inefficiencies in a bank would clearly reduce its marginal cost, even though it were not necessarily reflected in its accounting costs. As long as marginal cost is affected, the model predicts an impact on bank lending and deposit rates. However, this channel is not accounted for by any of the variables included in equations (3) and (4), except for the individual effects ε_L^i and ε_D^i

A dummy variable (FUS) has been added to capture the possible differential effect of merger processes on the interest rates of the entities resulting from such processes. This dummy takes a value equal to one in these entities during the three years following the merger or take-over date[8] and a value equal to zero in the remaining observations. This dummy has been introduced into the equations in two different ways: either directly, so that it affects the individual effects, or interacting it with the indicator of market competition. In the first case it would reflect the impact on interest rates of organisational changes that could have a bearing on the level of X-inefficiencies; while in the second instance it would reflect an effect of consolidation processes on the competitive response of intermediaries.

The analysis has not included all the mergers that have taken place in the period under consideration, since a series of prior conditions was established which had to be met by the merger for its inclusion in the analysis. Firstly, mergers where the main motivation was the reorganisation of financial groups were excluded, since they do not fit into the pattern of mergers between independent institutions. A size criterion has also been established so as to consider a merger operation, excluding from the analysis all those mergers where the entity merged or taken over does not exceed 15% of the total assets of the larger-sized entity. This is to avoid the inclusion of operations in which it is highly likely that major changes will not be detected in view of the small size of one entity in relation to the other.

Applying these criteria, eighteen merger operations were included in the analysis. Of these, two involve large private banks, two medium-sized subsidiaries and the remaining fourteen various savings banks. Three of the mergers are between more than two entities, the rest being between two institutions.

All the data are annual average values obtained from the information on interest rates provided monthly to the Banco de España by banks and savings banks and from the accounting information included in confidential statements. The sample of intermediaries included in the panel data corresponds to those which have reported interest rates on an ongoing basis. The information covers the period from 1988 to 1998.

Results of the estimations

Table 10.2 offers the results of the estimations. These should be interpreted with some caution in view of the scant number of mergers and take-overs in the sample. The key aspects of these results are as follows:

(a) In general, the competitive response of Spanish intermediaries resulting from consolidation processes is not lower, on average, than that shown by other entities. There are even signs that this response may have intensified in the mortgage market if regard is paid to the sign and the t-ratio value of the coefficient of the variable resulting from interacting the competition indicator with the merger dummy variable.
(b) The potential organisational changes related to X-inefficiencies – and not reflected in accounting costs following consolidation processes – do not appear to have affected the level of either mortgage loan interest rates or deposit interest rates.
(c) The variable used to approximate to the changes in the degree of average competition in bank markets has a high explanatory power in the two interest rate equations, indicating the relevance this factor has had in determining Spanish bank rates in the nineties.

Table 10.2 Bank and savings bank interest rates (1)

Variables	Deposits maturing 1–2 years		Mortgage loans		
	Differences	Differences	Differences	Differences	Differences
FUS (2)	—	0.21 (0.7)	—	-0.20 (0.9)	—
GDP growth	-0.27 (19.9)	-0.26 (19.2)	—	—	—
[Government debt rate] (-1)	0.79 (35.5)	0.79 (34.6)	—	—	—
Operating expenses per asset unit	-0.20 (2.6)	-0.21 (2.8)	0.27 (3.2)	0.27 (3.3)	0.27 (3.1)
3-month interbank rate	—	—	0.95 (54.2)	0.95 (54.4)	0.95 (54.1)
Spread (debt – interbank)	—	—	0.15 (5.5)	0.15 (5.4)	0.15 (5.4)
[Deposit rate dispersion] (-1)	-2.19 (22.5)	-2.20 (22.1)	1.97 (30.5)	1.97 (30.5)	1.96 (30.3)
[(Deposit rate dispersion)* FUS] (-1)	—	0.11 (0.9)	—	—	0.09 (1.6)
Variable transformation	Differences	Differences	Differences	Differences	Differences
Number of firms	128	128	128	128	128
Number of observations	758	758	758	758	758
Longest time period	1990–1997	1990–1997	1990–1997	1990–1997	1990–1997

(1) The t-ratios are in brackets. Standard errors are robust to heteroskedasticity and serial correlation. A more detailed explanation of estimation and testing can be found in Fuentes and Sastre (1999).
(2) FUS: dummy with value equal to one for merged institutions during the three years following the merger and value zero in the remaining observations.

The results obtained appear to confirm those from other, more qualitative, studies in which significant differences are scarcely detected in the firms resulting from mergers compared with certain control groups or with the remaining market participants. This may be interpreted in the sense that mergers and take-overs *per se* do not give rise to generally differentiated forms of behaviour, and that there are other types of factors which determine whether potential effects of a merger arise or not. Therefore, it is appropriate to supplement these results based in the use of statistical inference by using a case-by-case methodology. This analysis is accomplished in the following section where the effects of each merger on profitability and efficiency are analysed.

Effects of mergers on financial ratios in the period 1988–98

To study these effects a case-by-case analysis[9] of mergers is made by comparing changes in the values of certain financial ratios of the institution resulting from the merger process with the same ratios calculated for a comparable group the selection of which will depend, in each case, on the characteristics of the entities that have merged.

Table 10.3 Financial ratios

Group 1: Profit-generating capacity (a) (b)
- Total income: interest income + commissions + result on financial operations
- Interest expenses
- Gross income: total income – interest expenses
- Operating expenses
- Net income: total income – interest expenses – operating expenses

Group 2: Efficiency and productivity
- Operating expenses / average total assets
- Operating expenses / total income
- Operating expenses / gross income
- Productivity per employee: average total assets / number of employees
- Productivity per office: average total assets / number of branches
- Number of employees and branches following merger

Group 3: Indicators of market share and total assets growth
- Growth rate of total assets
- Market share (in terms of total assets).

Group 4: Indicators of business structure
- Lending-deposit activity in pesetas (as a percentage of total assets)

Group 5: Indicators of capital adequacy
- Capital / total assets

(a) All of these indicators are expressed as a percentage of average total assets (ATA).
(b) Although ROE is widely used as a profit-generating capacity ratio, it has not been used in this analysis because of the erratic behaviour of some items – mainly net provisions and profit and losses from securities and real estate sales – that are included in the calculation of final profit.

Methodology and ratios used in the analysis

To analyse the impact of mergers on banks, several indicators have been selected which seek to measure the effects of the merger on various aspects of bank activity. Five groups of indicators are specified (see Table 10.3): (1) profit-generating capacity; (2) efficiency and productivity; (3) market share and asset growth; (4) business structure; and (5) capital adequacy.

In each merger these indicators have been calculated annually for the four years prior to the operation and the four years after, or for those years for which data were available if the subsequent period ran past 1998.

The indicators have been obtained from the information in the financial statements of the merged institution during the period subsequent to the merger and by aggregating the corresponding items in the financial statements of the institutions intervening in the merger process for the previous period. The values of these indicators are compared in each case, with those that would be obtained from a specific control group for each type of entity.[10]

The control groups considered in this study are the following ones: the group of four major banks, in the case of mergers between large banks; the group of subsidiary banks of domestic banks for mergers of this type; and the total sum of savings banks for mergers between these institutions.

The comparison is established between the average of the four years prior to the merger with the average of the four years after. The values obtained for each year are also analysed. The analysis attempts to locate potential improvements in the values of these indicators for each entity *vis-à-vis* the values of the control group. The results are presented as the change observed in the difference between the average values of the entity analysed and the control group before and after the merger. A significant improvement in the compared values of a high number of indicators in a specific section would be indicative of the fact that the merger has proven positive for the entity in that area of activity. A 'significant improvement' in an indicator is taken to be a positive change in its average value higher than one standard deviation of the difference *vis-à-vis* the control group.[11] A 'significant worsening' would be a negative change higher than one standard deviation, while relatively insignificant changes would be those in the range of ±1 standard deviation.

In Figures 10.1 to 10.3 the main results of this analysis are summarised while Tables 10.A1 to 10.A3 in the Appendix draw together the whole results of the analysis conducted. Generally, changes in relation to the control group are expressed in basis points, except in the case of market indicators (where a distinction is made only between a positive and a negative change) and in the case of the number of employees and offices (where only an increase or a decrease in this number is indicated). Moreover, information is given on the initial situation of the entities taking part in the merger, showing whether these had higher or lower efficiency ratios than the control group considered.

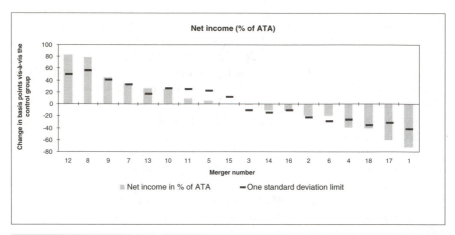

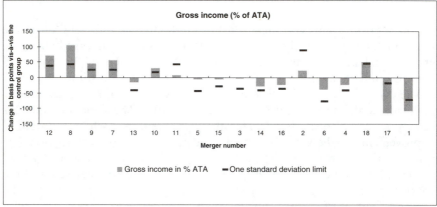

Figure 10.1 Profit-generating capacity.

Source: BE.

Note: There is a significant improvement when the length of the bar exceeds the segment.

Summary of results

The results of the analysis carried out do not differ too much from those of other studies carried out on the effects of mergers in the Spanish banking system. As an examination of Figures 10.1 to 10.3 shows, the effects of the mergers analysed on the profit-generating capacity and the level of efficiency of the institutions are not very clear. In some cases signs of improvement are detected in comparison with the control group, while in other mergers these effects are not so clear and deteriorations are even observed after the merger.

However, it may be cautiously ventured that the mergers analysed had a certain favourable effect on financial expenses (see Table 10.A1). This might be related to the increase in market power of some of the analysed

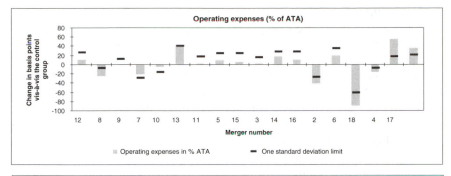

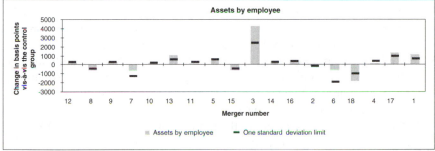

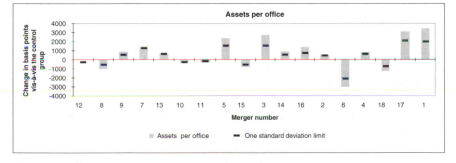

Figure 10.2 Efficiency and productivity.

Source: BE.

Note: There is a significant improvement when the length of the bar exceeds the segment.

institutions following the merger, owing to their market share having risen in their regional area of operation, but to confirm this supposition, it would be necessary to have more in-depth analysis. This effect is counteracted by the negative evolution observed in total revenues, due to the change observed in the balance sheet structure with a higher proportion of operations with narrower margins (see Table 10A.3), so that the final effect on gross income and net income is uncertain (see Figure 10.1).

In most of the cases analysed there does seem to be a slight improvement in the ratio of operating costs to average total assets (see Figure 10.2).

However, the changes seen are, in many cases, barely significant and if the analysis is limited to those mergers in which significant changes are observed, the results are much more ambiguous.

Significant increases in productivity per office and productivity per employee have been detected in most of the cases analysed (Figure 10.2) due to the combined effect of balance-sheet growth and the reduction in the number of offices.

Nonetheless, these increases in productivity have not been clearly reflected in the efficiency ratio (operating costs/average balance sheet) due to the downward rigidity of staff costs and, to a lesser extent, of overheads. In the case of staff costs this rigidity is explained by the costs associated with making staff cutbacks, since the compensation paid or the costs arising from early-retirement plans curb the reduction in staff costs. In the case of overheads the reason could have been an increase in some costs associated with the process of internal reorganisation. When analysing the other efficiency ratios used, which relate operating costs to gross and total income, the results are less clear because, in certain cases, productivity gains have had a negative impact on the level of income generation if they occurred as a consequence of a growth in business areas with lower margins.

When comparing the changes in the number of employees and offices with the growth of total assets after the merger (see Tables 10.A2 and 10.A3), it is clear that in most cases in which after the merger there is an increase in market share, neither the number of employees nor the number of offices decreases. Conversely, in all those cases in which there is a reduction in the number of employees and offices, except in one, in which the result is uncertain, there is also a slowdown in the growth of total assets and losses of market share. This suggests the existence of two types of mergers, those in which business expansion criteria predominate and others in which criteria of cost cutting and productivity increases predominate. However, the differences between these two groups are not clear, since as commented above, the reductions in staff and offices are not always reflected in changes in operating costs, so that the differences between the two groups are not very evident when comparing their efficiency ratios.

The clearest effect in the mergers analysed, as can be seen in Figure 10.3, is the increase in the capital-adequacy ratio of the merged institutions, due largely to the disclosure in books of reserves upon the revaluation of assets recorded at cost price during merger processes. Although this effect is a purely accounting phenomenon, it is of economic relevance for some institutions, particularly savings banks, since it allows them to increase their available capital[12] and thereby have a larger margin for making new investments. It also contributes to improving their financial ratios, which could be reflected in a smaller risk premium, reducing their financing costs, and thus improving their profit generating capacity.

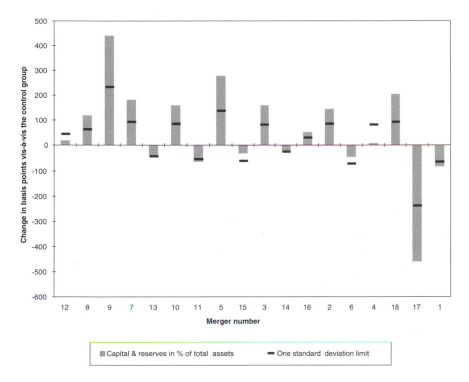

Figure 10.3 Capital and reserves.

Source: BE.

Note: There is a significant improvement when the length of the bar exceeds the segment.

3 Other strategies

In addition to concentration via mergers, Spanish banking institutions have adopted other alternative strategies to adapt their business structure to the demands of the new operating environment. This environment is characterised by heightening competition that pushes operating margins down, by the emergence of new business opportunities linked to technological development and by the growing globalisation of financial business, making it possible to expand to new markets.

Given these new prospects, Spanish banking institutions have sought to reshape their business in two main ways. First, by product diversification, offering new financial products to customers in an attempt to maximise the productivity of the distribution network. And second, by internationalisation of the business, through entry into other countries' markets via the direct provision of financial services, the opening of new branches or the acquisition of institutions operating in these countries.

In both cases the adoption of these strategies has been reflected in the structure of the banks' financial statements, introducing changes in the composition of the business, in the generation of profits and costs and in the general risk profile.

Product diversification strategies

In Spain's case, one of the most important developments in recent years has been the growth observed in mutual and pension funds and in derivatives business.

By means of these product diversification strategies, banks fulfil at least two objectives. First, they avoid the loss of share in the markets for capturing savings and the loss of revenue derived from the reduction in lending-deposit intermediation activity. And second, these strategies help enhance the effectiveness of the distribution network through harnessing existing means to market new products.

In both cases, an attempt has been made to widen the financial products offer in order to avoid losing customers and to optimise the existing distribution network. The effect on financial statements has been a shift in business off banks' balance sheets and a shift in revenue from the net interest income towards the gross income. Another strategy discussed in this section is the securitisation of banking assets, although this has only acquired some importance in the final months of the period analysed.

Mutual funds and pension funds

The growth of these types of institutions in recent years has been most significant. An example of this is the change in the value of shares in mutual and pension funds, expressed as a percentage of total customers' funds managed by deposit institutions, which has risen from 13.5% in 1995 to 29.5% in 1998. This shift in savings has triggered a significant heightening of competition in the market for bank liabilities, and has prompted a decline in the growth rate of traditional bank deposits. Spanish banks have reacted to this structural change, pursuing a highly active policy of marketing mutual and pension funds via their banking group subsidiaries. By means of this strategy they have been able to maintain their share in the market for savings, as well as minimising the revenue they would have forgone if these funds had been managed by financial groups not belonging to the banking sector.

This strategy of marketing financial instruments alternative to traditional vehicles has had a significant impact on the structure of banks' financial statements. This can be seen in the upper part of Figure 10.4, which plots the growth of the net asset value of mutual funds managed by banking group subsidiaries as a percentage of the total assets managed by these groups. In the period from 1995 to the first half of 1999, this percentage rose from 8.5% to almost 20% for all banks and savings banks, with the increase in funds managed by banks somewhat greater than that of savings banks. This line of business has been developed to a greater extent in large banking groups,[13] as can be observed in the figure; the percentage of mutual and pension fund assets managed by subsidiaries of the four major Spanish banking groups accounts for almost 30% of the total assets of these banking groups.

The substitution of shares in funds for bank deposits, even though the former remain within the banking groups, causes a change in the structure of these groups' profit and loss accounts. This is because revenue obtained through the traditional lending-deposit activity, which was included in the net interest income, is replaced by revenue arising on various commissions charged in relation to the marketing and management of these funds, which will be included in the gross income.

This shift is reflected in the trend of the variables shown in the lower part of Figure 10.4. The first two variables seek to approximate the revenue obtained in business with funds,[14] as information for the entire period is not available on commission charged exclusively in connection with services associated with mutual and pension funds for the whole group of banks. The first variable plots the course of commission revenue in the banking groups' consolidated financial statements – as a percentage of net interest income – and, though including commission revenue not associated with this business, which has also posted significant increases during the period analysed,[15] its clearly rising trend would appear to reflect the growing significance of revenue obtained from this business in banking groups. As can be seen in the figure, during the period under analysis, total commission revenue rose from a share of 33% of net interest income in 1995, to 46%, in the first half of 1999. The second variable shows the difference between net commissions in the consolidated balance sheets and the individual balance sheets, expressed as a percentage of average total assets. A significant portion of this variable relates to commission revenue associated with the management of the funds of the subsidiary managers. Although some caution is required given that this is only an approximation to the variable it is actually wished to analyse, the changes recorded appear to confirm the growing contribution of mutual and pension fund business to profit generation at banking groups.[16] The third variable analysed does capture precisely the revenue obtained from mutual and pension fund-related business, albeit only for the four major banking groups.[17] As can be seen, revenue arising from this business rose from 7.4% of net interest income in 1995 to 16.7% in 1998, rising to close to 20% in the banking group with the largest volume of business in these markets. Lastly, another estimation of the significance of revenue obtained from the management of these funds is obtained from the percentage accounted for by net income attributable to the management companies that are subsidiaries of banking groups in relation to their total consolidated net income,[18] which has fluctuated around 30% over the last three years.

As can be deduced from the figures set out, Spanish banking groups'

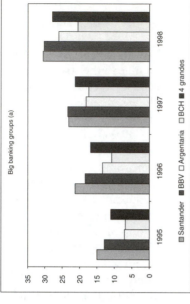

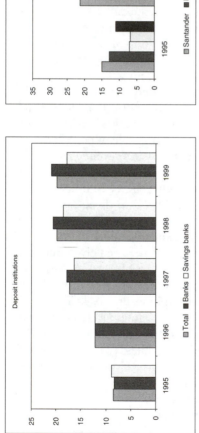

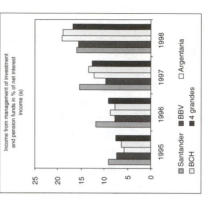

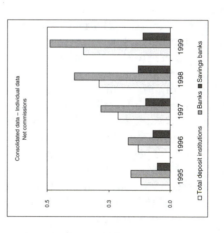

Figure 10.4 Investment funds managed by subsidiaries of banking groups in % of total balance of banking groups.

Source: BE and banks' public annual reports.
(a) Data from banks' public annual reports.

business in managing and marketing mutual and pension funds represents a considerable portion of the group's total business, yielding a significant revenue that has been growing in recent years. This switch from traditional banking business (lending-deposit intermediation) to this new form of intermediation through funds has been more intense at large banking groups, which generally have greater resources when it comes to designing and offering more sophisticated financial products to their customers. Nonetheless, the other deposit money institutions have not lingered behind; savings banks and other smaller entities have harnessed their resources to offer products of this nature. Undoubtedly, the depth and width of banks' distribution network has played a key role in enabling them to concentrate a good portion of their activity in the management of mutual and pension funds.

Derivative business

Other markets that have grown considerably in recent years are those for financial derivatives, including here both organised and over-the-counter markets. The emergence of more sophisticated financial products and the growing activity in securities markets has triggered the growth of these products, used both for hedging and for speculation.

Spanish banks have likewise been involved in this process and have increasingly used these products in recent years. The top half of Figure 10.5, which shows certain activities recorded in off-balance sheet accounts, reflects the evolution of derivatives operations recorded in the memorandum accounts of banks' individual balance sheets, expressed as a percentage of average total assets (ATA). As can be seen, these operations underwent a continuous increase during the period analysed, and the foregoing percentage for the aggregate of banks and savings banks climbed from 64% in 1995 to 105% in the first half of 1999. The figure also shows that the use of financial derivatives is much greater at banks than at savings banks, although use at the latter has been on a constant accelerating trend, while there appears to have been a slowdown at banks in the final years of the period.

As regards the structure of the products used (see middle part of Figure 10.5), interest-rate derivatives are by far those most used by Spanish banks. That said, there is a growing tendency to use securities derivatives owing to the strong growth of securities markets in recent years and to the growing use of stock exchange index references for remunerating liabilities-side banking products.

Loan securitisation

The securitisation of loans from banks' credit portfolios is another form of product diversification. This offers further advantages. It allows the volume of the credit portfolio to be lessened, with the subsequent reduction in own resources for capital requirement compliance purposes. Likewise, it provides

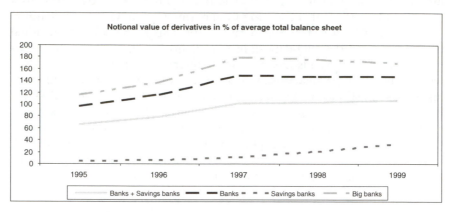

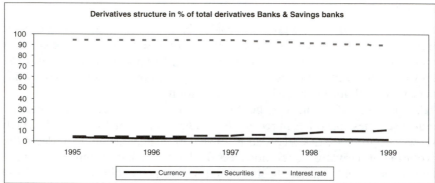

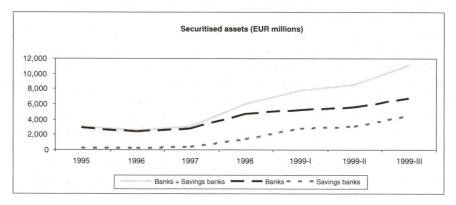

Figure 10.5 Off-balance sheet activity.

Source: BE and banks' public annual reports.

for securities that may be used as collateral in operations with the ESCB, thereby alleviating Spanish banks' collateral shortage problem.

The use of this mechanism by Spanish banks has been very limited owing to the scant flexibility of the legislation in force. However, the new regulation promulgated in 1998 has greatly facilitated the use of securitisation mechanisms and, in recent months, these operations have been growing significantly for all banking groups, as can be seen in the lower part of Figure 10.5. Nonetheless, the volume of loan securitisation is still relatively insignificant, as a proportion of banks' balance sheets, standing at slightly over 1%. Consequently, it would be reasonable to believe that it will continue growing significantly in the coming years, attaining a weight similar to that which these instruments have in other countries. Moreover, the large volume of mortgage loans on Spanish banks' books will be conducive to this growth, since these assets are particularly appropriate for securitisation programmes.

International expansion strategies

In addition to product diversification, Spanish banks, following the general trend towards the globalisation of financial activity, have undertaken the internationalisation of their activity. They have done this by means of entry into the financial markets of other countries with which close links were maintained, namely Latin America, and by increasing their business in the major international financial and offshore centres. European Monetary Union (EMU) has also contributed to increasing the degree of internationalisation of banking business, although its most evident effects to date have been confined to business areas more related to money and capital markets. The impact so far on the retail business segment has been very limited.

These developments have prompted an increase in the weight of business with non-residents on banks' balance sheets. They have also led to a change in the structure of profit generation and a restructuring of the risk profile associated with banking business.

Table 10.4 shows business with non-residents on the individual balance sheets of Spanish banks (excluding subsidiaries' business), along with the percentage of foreign assets and liabilities (including subsidiaries).

As can be seen in block 1, which presents the data without subsidiaries' business, Spanish banking institutions' business with non-residents during the period under analysis has risen slightly both at banks and at savings banks. However, the increase in this latter group has been smaller, being the level of business with non-residents in relation to total business[19] far lower than at banks. It is the large banks that have recorded the biggest increase and whose level of activity with non-residents has reached the highest level, accounting for almost 30% of their total business in the first half of 1999.

The greatest degree of internationalisation has taken place in those segments most closely related to wholesale markets, such as treasury management or securities operations. Of considerable significance has been the strong increase in the internationalisation of securities-related business in the final years of the period analysed. The driving force here has no doubt been EMU, which has contributed to setting in place a European securities market by eliminating foreign exchange risk. This same factor has also favoured the strong increase in the international business of savings banks in the treasury area in the last two periods analysed, by smoothing their access to the new European money market and opening up the possibility for them of trading with other countries' banking institutions. In the case of banks, such business had already acquired great relevance: first, because large Spanish banks and the branches and subsidiaries of major foreign banks were already routing a sizeable volume of operations via international money markets; and second, because a detailed knowledge of the counterpart is not needed, given that Spanish banks were mainly acting as borrowers. Operations involving the placement of resources predominated at savings banks, meaning greater risk. Here the creation of the European money market has helped drive this business by reducing operational risk – TARGET has had a bearing on this – and transaction costs (exchange rate risk associated with lending to EMU banking institutions has been removed and liquidation through TARGET is less expensive).

Despite the increase in business with non-residents, the main activity of Spanish banks, loan-deposit intermediation, is still predominantly domestic, particularly in the case of savings banks, whose main activity is concentrated in the retail segment. At large banks, which conduct more wholesale lending, the weight of international activity is somewhat greater, albeit well below those of other areas of business.

However, to appreciate the real significance of foreign business in the balance sheets of Spanish banks, the business carried out through their subsidiaries, particularly those located abroad, must also be considered. Consolidated balance sheet data broken down by country are not available for all banking groups for the whole period analysed. Nevertheless, block II of Table 10.4 includes an approximation of the total foreign activity of Spanish banking groups. As can be seen, the weight of such business, when the business carried out through subsidiaries is included, is much greater in the case of banks, particularly large banks, where it reached levels of almost 50% of total business in the second half of 1999. In the case of savings banks, business conducted through subsidiaries is very limited and remained practically unchanged throughout the period analysed.

These developments have been determined largely by the expansion of the major Spanish banking groups into Latin American financial markets through the acquisition of majority shareholdings in their domestic financial institutions. The increase in the presence of Spanish banks in this region is part of a strategy to consolidate long-term investment. It is sought to obtain a significant degree of penetration in the financial markets of these countries in order to benefit from the growth potential of markets that are less

Table 10.4 International activity of Spanish banking system (in % of total operations)

	1995	1996	1997	1998	1999
(1) Individual statements					
Operations with foreign residents					
Total classified (a)					
Banks	23.6	25.6	26.6	26.6	27.9
Savings banks	5.7	5.4	5.2	6.8	7.7
Big banks	24.9	27.0	27.9	28.0	29.4
Credit/deposit activity					
Banks	11.6	12.3	13.3	13.5	15.1
Savings banks	1.8	1.9	2.0	2.4	2.7
Big banks	13.2	13.6	14.7	15.2	17.3
Operations with credit institutions					
Banks	39.6	43.5	44.3	45.1	46.2
Savings banks	21.7	20.3	18.6	21.9	27.7
Big banks	41.9	47.1	47.3	47.6	47.6
Securities portfolio					
Banks	12.7	13.1	14.6	18.1	24.8
Savings banks	1.3	1.8	4.8	9.2	10.8
Big banks	14.9	15.4	16.5	21.5	28.6
(II) Consolidated statements					
Operations with foreign residents					
Assets					
Banks	27.6	29.6	36.7	37.5	38.4
of which subsidiaries	4.0	6.2	14.1	15.6	18.4
Savings banks	9.3	8.2	7.5	8.7	9.2
of which subsidiaries	2.0	1.9	1.9	1.7	1.7
Big banks	22.5	25.0	35.4	35.6	47.2
of which subsidiaries	5.6	8.8	20.1	22.2	25.5
Liabilities					
Banks	22.0	27.3	33.9	35.6	41.4
of which subsidiaries	3.0	4.1	8.0	8.2	10.7
Savings banks	4.5	4.2	4.9	6.4	7.6
of which subsidiaries	1.8	0.9	1.0	1.0	1.2
Big banks	24.5	30.9	38.4	40.5	46.9
of which subsidiaries	4.2	5.9	11.4	11.7	14.9

Source: BE.

Note: Calculated adding all the concepts which are classified by residence of the client.

developed than those in Europe. It is for this reason that much of the investment has taken the form of majority shareholdings, which enable control to
be exerted over the management of the acquired institutions.

This strategy is now being reflected in the financial statements of Spanish
banking groups. International expansion is changing the geographical structure of the revenue and the risk profile of the institutions that have chosen
this course.

Figures 10.6 and 10.7 try to capture these changes. Figure 10.6 compares
the developments in the individual balance sheets of the institutions (which
do not include the activity of their subsidiaries in Latin America) with those
in their consolidated ones (which do).[20] Figure 10.7 examines the changes in
the geographical distribution of the total revenue of the four largest Spanish
banking groups.[21]

As can be seen in the upper two charts of Figures 10.6 and 10.7, the contribution to the revenue of large Spanish banking groups generated by the
activity of their subsidiaries in Latin America is becoming increasingly
important. This is shown by the difference between the consolidated statements and the individual ones when considering financial revenue and costs.
At the beginning of the period, these items were more favourable in the individual statements, as a consequence of the inclusion in the consolidated
balance sheet of the activities of subsidiaries with lower margins than in
commercial banking. However, in recent years the opposite has been the case,
with the difference reaching almost half a percentage point for all deposit-
money institutions and 1.2 percentage points for the group of large banks.
The main factor explaining this behaviour is the inclusion in the consolidated balance sheets of the accounts of the subsidiaries acquired in Latin
America which have higher operating margins. This incorporation has taken
place in recent years, as shown by the change in the percentage of institutions
located abroad that are consolidated under the global integration method,
which rose from 29% in 1996 to almost 40% in 1998.

Figure 10.7, which includes data from the annual reports of large banking
groups, shows that the percentage of these groups' total revenue (from interest, fees and commissions and financial operations) obtained from business in
Latin America rose from 10% in 1995 to almost 41% in 1998. Indeed, this was
the only geographical area for which the percentage rose. In the case of the
banking groups with most activity in the area (BBV and Santander), the percentage was 50% or more.

Data for the whole period on the importance of international activity in the
consolidated balance sheets of the various groups of banks are not available.
Nor are they available on the distribution of activity by country. The only balance sheet data available relate to the division between business in Spain and
abroad according to the consolidated balance sheets for the second half of
1999. For all banks, the percentage of foreign business was around 20% of the
total balance sheet. However, this percentage varied greatly across groups.
While it exceeded 37% for large banks, for savings banks and the other

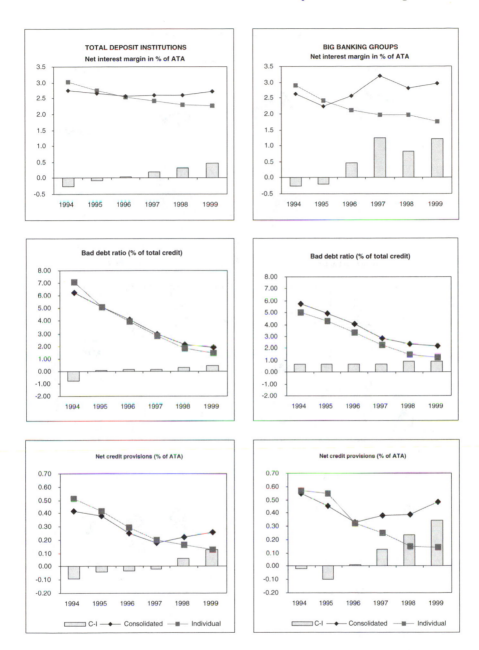

Figure 10.6 Consolidated versus individual financial statements.

Source: BE and banks' public annual reports.

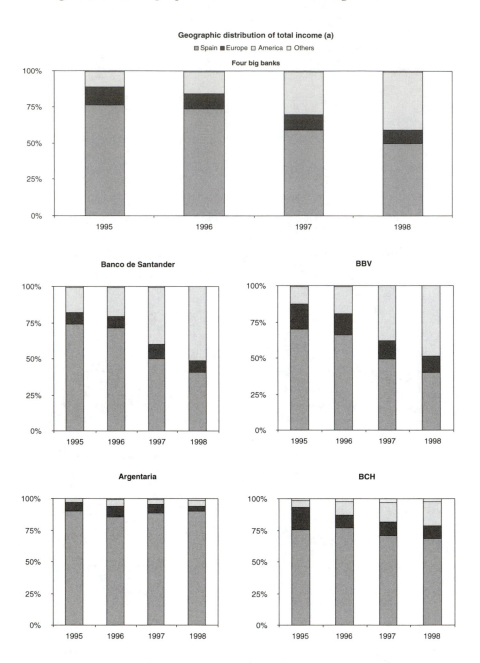

Figure 10.7 Geographic distribution of total income.

Source: Banks' public annual reports.

Note: (a) Total income includes interest income, commissions and net profit of financial operations.

banking groups it hardly reached 4%. The distribution by area of business is more homogeneous than in the case of the individual balance sheets. The areas with the highest degree of internationalisation were treasury management, deposit taking and bond issuing, with percentages of foreign business of around 25%. The area with the lowest level of internationalisation, at around 15%, was lending.

This expansion of business in developing financial markets has a positive impact on the generation of revenue. However, it also affects banks' risk structures. The middle and lower sections of Figure 10.6 compare the paths of two variables related to the level of credit risk in the consolidated and individual balance sheets. They show that the larger weight of activity in Latin America has increased bad debt ratios and net credit provisions in the consolidated balance sheets with respect to the individual ones.[22] These developments reflect the risk involved in the expansion in developing countries where there are better growth prospects but, at the same time, higher risks due to the lower stability of their economies and the lower degree of development of their financial markets.

However, as mentioned above, the strategy of Spanish banks in the region is one of long-term investment trying to obtain a significant degree of penetration in their markets in order to benefit from their higher growth potential. As a result, very strict criteria are being applied when making provisions for the possible risks arising from such activity. Evidence of this is the accelerated amortisation of goodwill and the policy for provisioning for credit risk. Much larger provisions in the consolidated balance sheets achieve a very high degree of cover for doubtful assets. Additionally, international expansion allows to diversify macroeconomic risk as it makes it easier to spread lending and deposit base across regions subject to different economic cycles.

International expansion by Spanish banks can be expected to continue in the future, in the case of both large groups and in that of smaller banks which currently have low levels of internationalisation. It is likely that there will also be greater geographical diversification, with a slowdown in the growth of business in Latin America as targets are achieved, and an acceleration in the growth of business in other euro-area countries as the single market is consolidated in Europe. Also, foreign banks are likely to capture a growing share of domestic retail markets. One of the key factors in future developments will be the outcome of the various processes of co-operation and merging with banks of neighbouring countries (France, Portugal, Italy) that have been announced by several Spanish banks.

4 Conclusions

The consolidation of the banking industry does not appear to have lessened the growing degree of competition which has been seen in the sector in recent years. A bigger size offers, in principle, greater capacity to set prices out of line with the market, but in an environment characterised by a fierce competition, it is probably very costly – in terms of market share – to take advantage of this fact.

The basic effect of any merger or takeover is to widen the range of strategic alternatives available to a bank, by enabling it to attain a size which, in the absence of this process, it could probably not have achieved and by requiring a reassessment of existing organisational arrangements. It seems that in the case of mergers and takeovers in Spain one can speak of two types: those which have sought to expand business and those which have opted for increases in productivity and improvements in the level of efficiency. The ambiguity of the results obtained in terms of profitability per unit of assets would suggest that it is practically impossible to achieve both things at the same time; that is, the growth in the gross income of certain merged institutions as a result of a strategy of business expansion is usually accompanied by an increase in operating costs which tend to compensate the higher income. On the other hand, those institutions which opt for a significant reorganisation, with elimination of duplications in their office networks, seem to suffer a loss of income-generating capacity, so that the productivity and efficiency gains are not transformed into improvements in profitability, at least within a four-year period.

Overall it may be said that although the mergers analysed in this study give no clear results as regards improvements in the profit-generating capacity or efficiency levels of the merged institutions, from the viewpoint of the banking sector they can be mostly considered satisfactory, since they have been an instrument for achieving some positive objectives: a) certain reductions in costs, although these have been small; b) implementation of rationalisation plans which, although they have not been immediately reflected in banks' profit and loss accounts due to the difficulties and high costs of staff cutbacks in Spain, have certainly served to improve the competitiveness of some institutions; and c) improvements in capital-adequacy ratios, which have helped to facilitate investment growth. These effects observed in the mergers analysed, have most likely helped put the merged institutions in a better position to confront the growing competition in the financial sector, specially in those cases where merged institutions were of a relatively small size and competitors in the same regional market.

The effects of other strategies have also helped banking institutions to confront growing competition. Strategies based on product diversification like the development of investment and pension funds, derivative products and securitisation, take advantage of the delivery system of banking institutions and allows them to compete in other market segments while minimising the loss of business and income. Moreover, by widening the range of products offered, Spanish banks have rationalised the use of their branch networks and increased their efficiency levels. Finally, these strategies, as they reduce the size of the balance sheet, allow banking institutions to expand their level of activity with fewer problems of capital resources.

While keeping in mind that investments in countries where macroeconomic stability has not been fully achieved tend to increase business risk, thus requiring a good deal of caution by banking institutions and also by supervisory authorities, strategies based on business internationalisation adopted by Spanish banks have also increased profitability and reinforced their competitive position in domestic and European markets. On the one hand, the high margins obtained in these new markets have increased revenues, while helping to diversify macroecomic risk associated with a bank's portfolio of loans and deposits.[23] On the other hand, investments in Latin-American financial companies have placed Spanish banking institutions in a privileged position on those financial markets, characterised by a great growth potential. That fact may be a very attractive feature in the near future when the process of restructuring European banking markets actually starts.

Notes

1 Moreover, some agreements – mainly those that involve reciprocal shareholding – seem to have been established for a defensive reason, as a way to resist future take-overs.
2 According to some empirical studies on the Spanish banking system (Fanjul and Maravall 1985, Delgado 1989, and Raymond and Repilado 1991), economies of scale have been observed at branch level, but not at firm level.
3 See Reboredo (1997).
4 See Klein (1971) and Monti (1973).
5 See Fuentes and Sastre (1999) for a more detailed presentation of the model.
6 See Fuentes and Sastre (1999).
7 An example of a similar framework used to analyse price dispersion can be found in Abbott (1994).
8 There are grounds for believing that some of the possible effects of a merger on interest rates may be of a more permanent nature. However, merger effects would be hardly disentangled from those caused by other factors in the simple framework considered in this paper. Furthermore, a majority of studies consider that most of the effects brought about by mergers cease to be felt after three or four years. See, for instance, Peristiani (1996) and Vander Vennet (1996).
9 In Rhoades (1998) this same methodology is applied.
10 The control groups considered also include the merged institutions.
11 Standard deviations have been calculated from the differences over the eight-year period analysed.
12 The use of accountancy methods based on the principle of historic cost are the origin of these hidden reserves which appear when the asset is valued at current prices.
13 Data on large banking groups have been obtained from each institution's public annual report.
14 These approximations have been used as no information is available on the actual amount of revenue obtained from business with mutual and pension funds in the consolidated financial statements for the entire period analysed and for all the banking groups.
15 According to the data for 1998 and 1999, which do give a breakdown of commission associated with mutual and pension funds, such commission accounts for around 47% of the total at banks and around 45% at savings banks.

16 The bigger differences recorded at the group of banks, although due in part to the greater weight that fund-related business has at these entities, are also justified by a greater weight of revenue components unrelated to fund business.
17 See note 13.
18 The net income attributable to management companies that are subsidiaries of banking groups is calculated by applying the percentage represented by the net asset value of the funds managed by this group of management companies to the net income of all the management companies.
19 Total business only includes balance sheet items for which the breakdown into domestic or foreign counterpart is available.
20 It should be noted that the consolidated balance sheets also include the activity of subsidiaries of other countries and of other subsidiaries. The differences identified are therefore not only due to the subsidiaries in Latin America, but they can be used as an indicator since there are no separate data for consolidated revenue by country and the weight of these subsidiaries in total business is significant.
21 Data on large banking groups have been obtained from each institution's public annual report.
22 These differences do not arise in the case of savings banks, whose investments in Latin America are practically nil.
23 Cross-border diversification allows the lending and deposit base to be spread across regions subject to imperfectly correlated macroeconomic shocks.

Appendix

Table 10.A1 Pre- to post-merger change in performance relative to control group (a)

Basis points

Merger number	Bank or Savings bank	Acquiring firm more efficient	Profit generating capacity				
			Total revenues in % ATA	Interest expenses in % ATA	Gross income in % ATA	Operating expenses in % ATA	Net income in % ATA
12	SB	No	93	−21	72	11	83
8	SB	No	−3	109	105	−26	79
9	SB	Yes(e)	−9	54	45	0	45
7	SB	Yes	−63	120	56	−22	34
13	SB	No	1	−17	−16	42	26
10	SB	No(d)	−26	57	31	−6	25
11	SB	Yes	9	−1	8	2	10
5 (b)	SB	Yes	−49	46	−4	9	5
15	SB	No	46	−51	−5	5	0
3	SB	Yes	−43	40	−3	2	−1
14 (b)	SB	No	8	−35	−27	18	−10
16	SB	Not clear	35	−58	−23	11	−12
2	B	No	66	−43	23	−42	−19
6	SB	Not clear	−4	−35	−39	19	−20
4 (b) (c)	SB	Yes (d)	−43	19	−23	−16	−39

Table 10.A1 cont.   Basis points

| | | | Profit generating capacity | | | | |
Merger number	Bank or Savings bank	Acquiring firm more efficient	Total revenues in % ATA	Interest expenses in % ATA	Gross income in % ATA	Operating expenses in % ATA	Net income in % ATA
18	B	No	29	21	51	-90	-40
17	B	Yes	-102	-13	-115	55	-60
1	B	Yes	-135	27	-107	36	-72
Summary			8 better (4 SC) 10 worst (6 SC)	9 better (6 SC) 9 worst (4 SC)	8 better (4 SC) 10 worst (5 SC)	11 better (5 SC) 6 worst (4 SC) 1 no change	8 better (5 SC) 9 worst (5 SC) 1 no change

Source: BE.

ATA: Average total assets SC: Significant change.

Notes:
(a) The average value for the four years preceding the merger are compared with the average value for the four years after the merger in such a way that a positive sign indicates an improvement and a negative sign indicates a worsening.
(b) Mergers between more than two firms.
(c) In the post-merger period only three years were analysed due to data problems.
(d) Refers to the biggest firm involved in the merger operation.
(e) Slightly above efficiency ratios values of the control group.

Table 10.A2 Pre-to-post merger change in performance relative to control group (a)

Basis points

						Efficiency and productivity ratios			
Merger number	Bank or Savings bank	Acquiring firm more efficient	Operating expenses in % ATA	Operating expenses in % TR	Operating expenses in % GI	Assets per employee	Assets per branch	Employees reduction	Branches reduction
12	SB	No	11	360	1137	206	-37	No	No
8	SB	No	-26	-226	778	-606	-1039	No(f)	No
9	SB	Yes(e)	0	-9	602	323	902	No	Yes
7	SB	Yes	-22	-367	276	-744	1486	Yes (g)	Yes
13	SB	No	42	331	588	1009	593	Yes	Yes
10	SB	No(d)	-6	-174	283	199	-357	No	Yes
11	SB	Yes	2	54	192	96	-305	No	No
5 (b)	SB	Yes	9	-36	216	699	2384	Yes	Yes
15	SB	No	5	-49	-56	-594	-798	Yes(h)	No
3	SB	Yes	2	-82	53	4264	2739	Yes	Yes
14 (b)	SB	No	18	97	-120	417	923	No(i)	Yes
16	SB	Not clear	11	156	-42	518	1394	No	No
2	B	No	-42	-244	-812	-130	587	Yes	Yes

Table 10.A2 cont.

Basis points

Merger number	Bank or Savings bank	Acquiring firm more efficient	Efficiency and productivity ratios					Employees reduction	Branches reduction
			Operating expenses in % ATA	Operating expenses in % TR	Operating expenses in % GI	Assets per employee	Assets per branch		
6	SB	Not clear	19	162	−508	−626	−2959	No	No
4 (b)(c)	SB	Yes(d)	−16	−242	−588	153	842	No	Yes
18	B	No	−90	−971	−1216	−1780	−1302	Yes	Yes
17	B	Yes	55	230	−334	1359	3083	No	No
1	B	Yes	36	15	−521	1166	3461	Yes	Yes
Summary			11 better (5 SC) 6 worse (4 SC) 1 no change	8 better (6 SC) 10 worse (6 SC)	9 better (4 SC) 9 worse (5 SC)	12 better (8 SC) 6 worse (3 SC)	11 better (10 SC) 7 worse (6 SC)	9 yes 9 no	11 yes 7 no

Source: BE

ATA: Average total assets TR: Total revenues GI: Gross income SC: Significant change.

Notes:
(a) The average value for the four years preceding the merger are compared with the average value for the four years after the merger in such a way that a positive sign indicates an improvement and a negative sign indicates a worsening.
(b) Mergers between more than two firms.
(c) In the post-merger period only three years were analysed due to data problems.
(d) Refers to the biggest firm involved in the merger operation.
(e) Slightly above efficiency ratios values of the control group.
(f) There is an increase in the first year after the merger and a reduction afterwards.
(g) After the merger the number of employees decreased but it increased in the following years.
(h) It increased in the last years of the post-merger period.
(i) In the first year of the post-merger period there was a reduction in the number of employees.

Table 10.A3 Pre- to post-merger change in performance relative to control group (a)

Basis points

Merger number	Bank or Savings bank	Acquiring firm more efficient	Total assets growth rate	Market share	Loans and deposits in % of total assets (j)	Capital and reserves in % of total assets (k)
				Other indicators		
12	SB	No	Better	Better	−5	21
8	SB	No	Not clear	Worst(f)	1851	121
9	SB	Yes(e)	Better	Better	−784	440
7	SB	Yes	Worst	Worst	−196	182
13	SB	No	Not clear	Worst(g)	−181	−44
10	SB	No(d)	Worst	Worst	−197	161
11	SB	Yes	Better	Better	−667	−63
5 (b)	SB	Yes	Worst	Worst	−1162	277
15	SB	No	Worst	Worst	204	−32
3	SB	Yes	Worst	Worst (h)	−1658	160
14 (b)	SB	No	Worst	Better(i)	772	−21
16	SB	Not clear	Not clear	Better	−513	54
2	B	No	Worst	Worst	525	147
6	SB	Not clear	Worst	Worst	642	−46
4(b)(c)	SB	Yes(d)	Better	Better	142	9
18	B	No	Worst	Worst	−1224	203
17	B	Yes	Not clear	Better	−1574	−460
1	B	Yes	Not clear	Not clear	−819	−83
Summary			9 worse	10 worse	6 increase	11 increase
			9 better	7 better	(3 SC)	(9 SC)
			5 NC	1 NC	12 decrease	7 decrease
					(8 SC)	(9 SC)

Source: BE.

NC: No change SC: Significant change.

Notes:
(a) The average value for the four years preceding the merger are compared with the average value for the four years after the merger in such a way that a positive sign indicates an improvement and a negative sign indicates a worsening
(b) Mergers between more than two firms.
(c) In the post-merger period only three periods were analysed due to data problems.
(d) Refers to the biggest firm involved in the merger operation.
(e) Slightly above efficiency ratios values of the control group.
(f) The average value falls after the merger due to the evolution in the pre-merger period.
(g) The drop was just after the merger; in the following years it recovers part of the lost share.
(h) There is an improvement just after the merger but in the following years declines to levels below the pre-merger period.
(i) There is an increase just after the merger which is lost in the following years.
(j) Loans plus deposits in pesetas divided by total assets.
(k) Capital, reserves and non-distributed profits divided by total assets.

References

Abbott, T.A. (1994) 'Observed price dispersion: product heterogeneity, regional markets, or local market power?'. *Journal of Economics and Business* 46, 21–37.

Delgado, F. (1989) 'Economías de escala en el sistema bancario español'. Tesis doctoral, Facultad de CC Economicas, Madrid.

Fanjul, O. and Maravall, F. (1985) 'La eficiencia del sistema bancario español'. Alianza Editorial, Madrid.

Fuentes, I. and Sastre, T. (1999) 'Mergers and acquisitions in the Spanish banking industry: some empirical evidence'. Banco de España, Documento de Trabajo 9924.

Klein, M.A. (1971) 'A theory of the banking firm'. *Journal of Money*, Credit and Banking, May, 205–18.

Monti, M. (1973) 'A theoretical model of bank behaviour and its implications for monetary policy', Societé Universitaire Européenne de Recherches Financières, reprint of L'Industria, no 2, 1971.

Peristiani, S. (1996) 'Do mergers improve the X-efficiency and scale efficiency of US banks'. Research Paper 9623. Federal Reserve, New York.

Raymond, J.L. and Repilado, A. (1991) 'Analisis de las economías de escala en el sector de Cajas de Ahorros'. *Papeles de Economía Española*, 46, 87–107.

Reboredo, J.C. (1997) 'Incentives to merge and bank soundness. The case of Spanish savings banks'. Universitat Autonoma de Barcelona, Working Paper 371.97.

Rhoades, S.A. (1998) 'The efficiency effects of bank mergers: an overview of case studies of nine mergers'. OCDE.

Vander Vennet, R. (1996) 'The effect of merger and acquisitions on the efficiency and profitability of EC credit institutions'. *Journal of Banking and Finance*.

11 Globalisation and payment intermediation*

Hans Geiger

1 Introduction

1.1 Payment intermediation

The term 'financial intermediation' is generally used to describe the financial service industry's role as a middleman between the ultimate saver and the ultimate investor (financial intermediation I). The impact of globalisation on this first type of intermediation and vice versa has been widely and controversially discussed among bankers, supervisors, politicians, and academics. Without commenting further on this issue, it is sufficient to say that globalisation of financial intermediation and markets can reduce the cost of capital in different ways and thus contribute to the economic wealth of the world (Stulz 1999).

In addition to this 'financial intermediation I' there does exist a second sphere of financial intermediation which can be described as payment intermediation or financial intermediation II (McAndrews and Roberds 1999: 1). It stands for the financial function of the middleman between the payer and the payee in a market transaction. According to Merton and Bodie 'clearing and settling payments' is one of the six core functions performed by a financial system (Merton and Bodie 1995: 5). Although payment intermediation is a less popular subject than financial intermediation I it has equally important economic and strategic aspects in the context of globalisation.

It is the goal of this paper:

- to make a contribution to understanding the economic relevance of payment intermediation in the context of globalisation;
- to illustrate the opportunities and threats facing the banks in their role as payment intermediaries in our globalising economy.

---

* Paper presented at 22nd SUERF Colloquium, Vienna, 27–29 April 2000.

1.2 Globalisation and the forces of change in banking

'Globalization . . . reflects the progressive integration of the world economies' (World Bank 2000: 2). It can be described in the following words: 'The need of a constantly expanding market for its products chases the global enterprise over the entire surface of the globe. It must nestle everywhere, settle everywhere, establish connections everywhere. The global enterprise has, through its exploitation of the world market, given a cosmopolitan character to production and consumption in every country.' If we replace the expression 'global enterprise' by the word 'bourgeoisie', this quotation is the original wording of the Communist Manifesto of Marx and Engels, written in 1848 (Marx and Engels 1848: 3). In fact globalisation is by no means a new phenomenon, it has been around for many centuries, mostly in times of peace. Pax Augusta and Pax Britannica were famous eras of intensive border-crossing relations and activities.

Geographical distance is an important, but not the only border whose crossing is a constituent element of globalisation. Other boundaries that traditionally separate economic markets and activities are time, political territories, legal frameworks, cultures, languages, and currencies. These boundaries determine the relative costs of market transactions.

In this article the word 'local' stands as the opposite term for 'global', thus including both 'national' and 'regional' aspects.

If globalisation is no new phenomenon, what are the reasons which attract the attention of academics, bankers, and SUERF today? From a historic perspective there are only three really new aspects, namely:

*   The enormous progress in *information and communication technology* which leads to a collapse of space and time, two decisive physical boundaries between markets.
*   The creation of a common *European currency area*. Euroland is emerging as a border-less market that until recently was strongly segmented by currency borders.
*   Today's globalisation is not a stand-alone development, but rather one manifestation of *six fundamental forces of change* (White 1998). These are, besides technology and Euroland, liberalisation, value orientation, new demographic trends, and progress in the theory of finance. Two further manifestations of these forces are the phenomenal rate of innovation in financial products and processes, and the emergence of new competitors (Figure 11.1). Many of today's strategic challenges of banks do not primarily or exclusively stem from globalisation, they are often also relevant in a local context. Both from a practical and a theoretical standpoint we cannot isolate globalisation from the six forces of change and its further manifestations, because all these forces work in combination.

Underlying Forces   *Consequences*

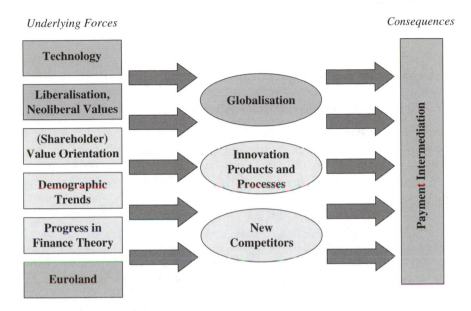

Figure 11.1 The forces of change in banking.
Source: Modified from White (1998).

With respect to the role and strategy of banks in the payment business for global market transactions, several new aspects come into play:

- Not only goods, persons, and capital, but also *services and knowledge* in the form of information can be transported across borders. 'The growing importance of services and information in the world economy means that an increasing proportion of economic value is weightless – that is, it can be transmitted over fiber-optic cable rather than transported in a container ship' (World Bank 2000: 4).
- The geographical and organisational *deconstruction of the value-chain* leads to a further cross-border division of labour. 'Foreign trade has grown more quickly than the world economy in recent years, a trend that is likely to continue' (World Bank 2000: 5). This global deconstruction of the value-chain is promoted by reduced transaction costs of physical and digital market transactions crossing any type of borders.[1]
- '*Financial flows* across national borders have risen far more quickly than trade in recent years' (World Bank 2000: 6).
- The geographical deconstruction of the value-chain is in some spheres compensated by the growing impact of *multinational companies* in the global economy; 30 per cent of world trade takes place within multinational companies (Neue Zürcher Zeitung 1999: 20).

• The Internet, global brands, *electronic commerce*, and global connectivity all lead to networks of worldwide and border-crossing relations and dependencies.

2 A concept for payment intermediation

2.1 The importance of payment intermediation

Payment intermediation is of highest importance for the economic wealth of the world. Without the use of money and other payment mechanisms, today's division of labour through market transactions would be impossible, the world would remain stuck in a prehistoric, self-sufficient economy. The lower the costs of payments and thus of market transactions, the more advantageous the division of labour, the more intensive the competition, the higher the wealth of an economy.

The history of market transactions is the history of decreasing transaction costs and increasing efficiency of payment methods: from self-sufficiency to barter to commodity money to paper money to bank money. Due to the partial and increasing replacement of cash (coins, banknotes) by 'bank money' or book payments, the banks have moved into their present intermediary role, substituting the counterparty both for the seller and the buyer (McAndrews and Roberds 1999: 10). The future development of an emerging new type of money, digital or electronic money, may result in a further reduction of the transaction costs. Such a development would cause a partial replacement of book-entry payments by digital money and could challenge the very role of banks as intermediaries in the exchange economy.

Payment intermediation is not only important for the economy as a whole, but also for the future of banks, both in a global and a local context. Payment services are one area where banks still enjoy significant advantages over other competitors. Since banks are challenged at many fronts in financial intermediation between the saver and the investor, their role in payment systems might become a decisive factor for future success or failure. But it would be dangerous to assume that the past advantages of banks in payment services will survive naturally and will remain unchallenged (Llewellyn 1999: 19–20). Banks, both as individual firms and as an industry group, must therefore clarify and possibly redefine their role and strategy in the area of payment intermediation.

2.2 Classification of market transactions

There are many different ways to structure the field of payment intermediation. Classification by the types of underlying market transactions of the banks' customers makes sense in our context. Such a classification leads to three general categories, which are described in Figure 11.2.

1   *Commercial Transactions*
    1.1   B2B Business to Business
       •   Domestic or International
       •   Physical or Digital
    1.2   B2C Business to Consumer
       •   Domestic or International
       •   Physical or Digital

2   *Financial Transactions*
    2.1 β2B, β2C Bank to Business or Consumer
    2.2 β2β Bank to Bank

3   *Street Side Transactions*

Figure 11.2 Classification of market transactions.

1 Commercial transactions

1.1 B2B   Business to business: This is an area of rather complex transactions, because both sides have specific needs for administrative and financial services within their business processes. The values of the payments are often quite large. Operating and financial costs (interest, risks) are equally important. In the area of operating cost, it is not only the cost of the payment that matters, but the cost of the whole market transaction (see Section 2.3).

1.2 B2C   Business to consumer: These are typically mass transactions with high volumes and normally low amounts. The services required by the two parties can be highly standardised. Low operating costs are more important than the financial costs.

Both B2B- and B2C-transactions can be split up further into:

* Domestic and international/border-crossing transactions.
* Transactions of physical goods and services, and digital goods and services.

The latter can be offered and delivered via telecom networks. This sub-category is made in view of the growing importance of electronic commerce. Digital goods sold and delivered over electronic networks have produced a growing and urgent need for micro-payments, where the actual costs of payment are often larger than the potential values of the goods sold (Crameri 2000: 2).

2 Financial transactions

2.1   β2B, β2C   Bank to business and bank to consumer transactions: The underlying transaction is a financial product or service delivered by a bank to its customers (e.g. securities or forex transactions and asset management). The transaction value is often high. The financial costs are more important for high amounts, whereas the operating costs do matter more for small amounts. Financial transactions may be provided nationally and internationally with slight differences. They are typically digital and can be offered, delivered, and paid over electronic networks. Linking delivery and payment through electronic mechanisms can result in the elimination of counterparty risk and thus of a significant cost factor.

2.2   β2β Bank to bank transactions are normally of high or very high value, hence the financial costs are extremely important. The benefits of 'delivery versus payment' (DVP) mechanisms are even higher than in the case of β2B-and β2C-transactions. They are conducted nationally and internationally, often traded over electronic exchanges, and delivered and paid over dedicated networks.

3 'Street side' transactions

Interbank β2β   This category does not fit naturally into the classification. Street side transactions are not original market transactions of the bank's customers, but rather derived or secondary transactions. All non-cash payments for those primary transactions, where the buyer and the seller do not have their accounts in the same bank, trigger such secondary (clearing and settlement) transactions between the banks and banking systems involved. As both small and large primary transactions require such street side solutions, both operational and financial costs are highly relevant. The street side payment systems have traditionally been organised by country (and currency), thus making cross-border transactions expensive and inefficient.

For financial (β2β and β2C) and digital commercial transactions the street side systems have not only the potential to settle the payment, but also the delivery side of 'digital goods', such as securities or news. DVP-mechanisms are of highest relevance.

2.3 Some characteristics of payment transactions

The following characteristics of payments and payment systems are important in a global context:

* In the view of both buyers and sellers payments are not independent financial services, but rather derived services and thus an *integral part of a primary market transaction*. Such a market transaction consists of four

phases: Information, agreement, settlement, and enforcement or adaptation (Schmid and Lindemann 1997: 14 and Geiger 1999: 7). Payment is one element within phase three (Figure 11.3). The sales agreement between the seller and the buyer (phase two) is an agreement to deliver and pay the product or service immediately or later.[2]

• There are three different modes for the *timing of payments*: Payment before, simultaneous, and after delivery of the product or service. The aspect of timing has considerable consequences for risk management of all parties involved.

• As shown earlier, the large number of different payment products can be grouped in *three* broad *categories*: Cash (notes and coins), book-entry transfers (electronic or paper based), and digital or electronic money. 'Electronic money refers to "stored value" or prepaid mechanism for executing payments via point of sale terminal, direct transfer between two devices, or over open computer networks such as the Internet. . . . [They] include "hardware" or "card-based" mechanisms (also called "electronic purse") and "software" or "network-based" mechanisms (also called "digital cash")' (Bank for International Settlements 1998: 3–4). European bank supervisors and central banks decided to authorise only banks and similarly supervised intermediaries to issue such digital money. This supervisory policy seems to protect banks from competitors from other industries in the field of electronic money. However, it might be dangerous for the banks to rely on such a regulatory concept. There exist several different strategies for new competitors who could escape this problem. One example is 'digital money' based on credit, that is, a 'pay later' product, which is not covered by the above definition of the Bank for International Settlements (BIS) (Weber 1999: 91).

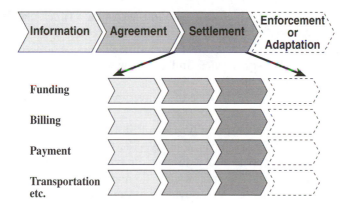

Figure 11.3 The four phases of market transactions.

Source: Modified from Schmid and Lindmann (1997).

- There are important differences between *domestic and international* payments. Nearly 99 per cent of the quantity and 90 per cent of the value of all non-cash payments are still domestic, but cross-border payments are growing much faster than the domestic ones (The Boston Consulting Group 1999: 1–4).
- *Effectiveness and efficiency* of payments can be measured in terms of cost, quality, productivity, and risk. The ultimate goal for the payee and payer is not the isolated efficiency of a payment transaction, but rather the cost and the quality of the whole business process. In general, domestic payment services in the developed world are quite effective and efficient, whereas international payments are expensive, time consuming, and often neither user-friendly nor reliable.[3]
- The weaknesses and *deficiencies* of the *international retail payment system* were demonstrated in a survey initiated by the European Commission in 1994. The study encompassed 1,058 trans-border payments between 34 endpoints in twelve countries, each to the amount of 100 ECU. The payee was supposed not to bear any cost, that is, he should receive the full 100 ECU. The result was extremely disappointing. The average cost of one payment was 25.40 ECU, the average total time elapsed from the payment instruction by the payer to the availability for the payee was 4.8 working days, and in 36 per cent of the cases the payee did not receive the full amount (Retail Banking Research Ltd 1994: 16–17). These inefficiencies are so grave that they inhibit the development of global (or in this case even European) B2C-business. Although some improvements have been achieved since 1994, prices for international retail transfers still remain intolerably high and no substantial progress has been made regarding the timeliness of the payments (European Central Bank 1999: 7).
- Payments are not just technical operations, but financial transactions subject to three *financial risks,* well-known from other banking activities (Hitachi Research Institute 1993: 49):
  - The *market risk*, which can arise in the case of a time delay between agreement, delivery, and payment of a market transaction.
  - The *credit risk*, which results from a time difference between delivery of the product or service and the payment (in the cases of 'pay before' and 'pay later').
  - The *liquidity risk* in the case of delayed payment or delivery.

These financial risks are especially relevant in the case of high-value payments. They can arise for the payer, the payee, or the intermediary. They are managed reasonably well in most domestic payment systems, whereas in international transactions they are often little understood and not well controlled. In the case of large-value payment systems, especially for financial transactions, supervisors worry about the potentially contagious effects of the current payment systems. This can result in a systemic risk.[4]

- Payments are not only geographical transfers of money; in bridging time they often incorporate implicit or explicit *funding* of the transaction by the payee, the payer, or the intermediary.
- Information and communication *technologies* are decisive design factors of payment services and systems. The striking progress in these technologies and the digitalisation of the underlying market transactions ('E-commerce') leads and will continue to lead, to fundamental changes in the payment intermediation function of financial and other service providers. The international trade and payment transactions, typically not well supported by today's payment systems, will be particularly affected. A special development, whose potential and consequences have not yet clearly emerged, is the development of digital money.
- The act of payment is a major element of the transaction both for the payee and the payer. Payment services can therefore play a crucial role for the satisfaction and *retention* of both payee and payer as *customers* for the bank. In addition, the provision of payment services gives the bank a privileged access to transaction-based information about their customers, no doubt valuable in other transactions.

2.4 The street side infrastructure of payment intermediation (β2β)

All non-cash payments for transactions, where the buyer and the seller do not have their accounts with the same bank, trigger clearing and settlement transactions between the banks and the banking systems involved. As both small and large transactions require such secondary or street side transactions, this is a formidable task, necessitating among other complex things the mastering of both operational and financial costs within the worldwide banking community. These street side systems are the very heart of an effective and efficient payment system. The systems have traditionally been organised by each individual country. Sophisticated international systems are almost non-existent, a serious weakness in the payment business. Without effective street side systems, banks face great difficulties to satisfy the transaction and payment needs of their customers in a globalised world.

In future, a potential *competitive situation* between the banks and their street side systems may exist or emerge. For any type of clients, but primarily for large multinational and institutional customers, it might be worth having direct access to street side systems, thus reducing or eliminating the intermediary role of the bank. In spite of this potential conflict of interest between the banks and their street side utilities the banking industry has a long-term self-interest in the development and operation of street side systems, because without these systems outsiders may develop competitive structures and give direct access to the customers.

For practical purposes we can discern *three different methods* to solve the street side problem of payments:[5]

- The traditional method of using *correspondent banks* for the transfer of funds was already well developed by the Italian money-changers in the fourteenth century. In theory, each bank maintains an account with each other, debiting and crediting the payments to these accounts. In practice, some banks in the various countries have specialised in such correspondent banking systems and serve as centralised nodes for other banks. This structure reduces the number of necessary accounts and connections throughout the systems, but it lengthens the process chain.
- *In clearing systems* banks present the payment documents at one central location, the clearinghouse. This procedure often includes a mechanism for the calculation of the participating banks' net positions, which are settled at a designated time. The clearinghouse with a multilateral netting mechanism was the traditional interbank infrastructure in domestic cheque-based payment systems. Such netting systems are still common in many national systems, especially for clearing low-value retail payments.
- In *real time gross settlement systems* (RTGS) the settlement of payments between banks takes place continuously at a central point without prior clearance, transaction by transaction. RTGSs are usually linked to the central bank and have been made feasible thanks to the advances in information and network technology. They enjoy the advantage of direct use of central bank money and have become the dominant method for the settlement of large value payments. In some countries the RTGS-mechanism is also used for the settlement of retail payments.

In *international payments* the dominant method to settle payments between banks is still the *correspondent banking* mechanism. Sophisticated S.W.I.F.T.[6] networks and standards support the system. However, this technical upgrading does not make the model an appropriate infrastructure for global payments in a global economy. Correspondent banking is an obsolete architecture for this type of transactions, and the system suffers additionally from a lack of international standardisation between the various national payment systems.

One of the most pressing problems in international payments, the counterparty risk in the settlement of foreign exchange transactions (named 'Herstatt risk' after a bank failed in 1974), will soon be solved. *The Continuous Linked Settlement Bank* (CLS) (Lambe 2000) should become operational by next year. CLS is a highly sophisticated central RTGS-system, whereby the two payment legs of a forex-transaction are settled simultaneously in a self-collateralising mechanism called 'payment versus payment' (PVP). The system is expected to be effective and efficient in eliminating the Herstatt risk and reducing cost and time between banks. The system will facilitate the global foreign exchange business and thus indirectly global trade. But it is not designed to be used for the settlement of other financial or commercial transactions, although the basic concepts of CLS[7] would also be suitable to rationalise other trans-border and trans-currency payments.

Outside the forex business there is a new initiative 'WATCH' (NACHA Cross Border Council 1999) for a *Global Automated Clearing House*, which should make B2B and B2C payments across borders as easy as domestic payments. The goal of the initiative is to build a low-cost system that provides certainty of payment delivery, ease of use, global reach, and multi-currency capabilities. These objectives should be reached with an electronic system for batch-based cross-border payments for commercial and private banking customers. WATCH is designed as an automated clearing system without netting functionality. In the terminology of the Bank for International Settlements it is a 'designated-time gross settlement system' (Bank for International Settlements 1997: 4–5). The project is presently in its initial phase with forty-eight international banks and banking organisations from fourteen different countries participating. It is scheduled to go ahead with 175 to 200 participating financial institutions in the year 2002.

Until the successful implementation of the WATCH-initiative (or a competing concept), global *credit card* systems are the only efficient infrastructure for trans-border retail payments. Accordingly credit cards are among the fastest growing segments of cash-less payment instruments.

Ever since the successful implementation of the Euro as a common currency in Europe, *Euroland* should be considered a domestic market for payments rather than an international one. Yet this has not been the case so far. The European Commission, the European Central Bank, and the customers are all complaining about the fact that the single market is not supported by any efficient system for cross-border payments within Euroland (European Central Bank 1999). Ideally a payment between a payer and a payee in two member states of Euroland should be as simple and efficient as a domestic transaction, since no currency borders hinder the easy flow of money. From the beginning of the currency union the TARGET-System has been available for trans-border euro-payments, but it was not designed as a system for commercial and retail payments. Fundamentally TARGET seems to be an unnecessary or only temporarily necessary system, because in the forthcoming single currency area there will be no justification for national clearing and settlement systems any more, so there will be no need to connect such national systems. Any one (or several) of the existing national RTGS of the Euroland countries could serve the whole euro currency area. For the intermediate phase there is an urgent need for more efficient 'cross-border' payments. Right now the Euro1–System of the European Banking Association (EBA) seems to be the most successful platform for commercial payments in Euroland, and the operators plan to develop it into an automated clearinghouse (Young 1999: 101). The fact is that in the foreseeable future payments within Euroland will remain much closer to the international types than to the domestic ones.

2.5 *Traditional strengths and weaknesses of banks in payment systems*

In order to assess the strategic opportunities and threats for banks in payment services it is mandatory to analyse their traditional strengths and weaknesses. Traditional *strengths of banks* in the field of payment services are:

•   Access to central bank money and final settlement.
•   Privileged access to central trading, clearing, and settlement institutions.
•   Access to proprietary interbank networks and standards, e.g. S.W.I.F.T.
•   Access to transaction-based information, which the banks can use in a variety of value-added retail and corporate services,[5] and which can also be valuable for monitoring credit risk.
•   Access to established networks of customers, agents, and products.
•   In general banks enjoy the advantage of trust, credit-worthiness, prudential supervision, monetary supervision, and money laundering supervision.

The *weaknesses of banks* in payment intermediation are:

•   The fundamental weakness of payment intermediation is that banks have so far not been able or willing to make it a global business. With a few exceptions payments do not easily cross borders of geographical distance, time, states, and currencies. The reliance on traditional correspondent banking and the incompatibility of most national payment systems result in high costs and prices, long time delays, high financial risks, poor service quality, and a general lack of transparency. It is interesting to note that the Financial Action Task Force on Money Laundering (FATF) in its recent study concluded that even alternative remittance systems, pre-dating modern banking of the nineteenth and twentieth centuries, are 'secure and less expensive than traditional banks' (Financial Action Task Force on Money Laundering 2000: 5). These inefficiencies are a serious obstacle for the further globalisation of economic activities; they could also turn into a serious threat to the role of banks in payment intermediation.
•   A new weakness arises in the emerging world of E-commerce: New transaction intermediaries, which often have their roots in software-, Internet- and telecom-services, are supporting the whole value chain of market transactions for the payee and also the payer, and not only the payment phase.[9] These new intermediaries create additional value for their customers and the economy, leading to a relative decline of status and value in the traditional payment franchise of banks.

3   Globalisation and payment intermediation

The basic relationships between globalisation and payment intermediation are straightforward. If there is no global trade, there is no need for global payments. If there are no efficient global payment services, global trade is impossible or at least severely hindered. This is a classical hen and egg situation. Until recently the banking industry was not willing to support the development of a new common international cross-border payment system, on the basis that today's volumes and obvious customer demand would not justify the necessary big investments. Customers do not and cannot develop the demand for international and even European trade, because no efficient payment mechanism is yet available.

By closely analysing globalisation and the six fundamental forces of change in banking (Figure 11.1), you realise that the shrinking of the boundaries of distance, time, legal frameworks, cultures, languages, and currencies (all related to globalisation) has far-reaching consequences for the payment function of banks. The relevance of some important changes shall now be analysed for the different categories of market transactions developed in Section 2.2.

1   Further globalisation of the world economy will lead to a *growing demand for trans-border payment* services in the B2B- and also B2C-business.

2   The high proportion of global trade taking place among *multinationals* requires special global payment and transaction *services* for these companies, otherwise the multinationals provide (or continue to provide) such services internally for themselves and for their suppliers and customers, or they outsource them to non-bank providers.[10]

3   The emergence of *E-commerce* B2C and B2B, which is by nature not limited by national borders, might shift the balance of power from payment intermediaries to transaction intermediaries. The very optimistic view expressed by American Vice-President Al Gore in a remarkable document he published together with President Clinton, could be interpreted as a signal of a future challenge for banks (Clinton and Gore Jr. 1998: 1): 'Soon electronic networks will allow people to transcend the barriers of time and distance and take advantage of global markets and business opportunities not even imaginable today, opening up a new world of economic possibilities and progress.' In the case of digital E-commerce, which is growing much faster than physical trade, this trend is even stronger and also much more urgent than for physical transactions.

4   The rapid development of information technologies favours *new competitors* for *commercial payment* services.

5   In the area of financial transactions, the *internationalisation of exchanges* calls for an internationalisation of clearing and settlement systems. It is possible that the clearing and settlement systems will be more important in the global race for dominance in the security trading world than the exchanges themselves. Today international clearing and settlement is vastly inefficient compared to leading domestic systems.[11]

Changes in the context of globalisation	Commercial Transactions				Financial Transactions		Street Side Transactions	
	B2B		B2C		B2B B2C	B2B	Inter bank B2B	
	phy	dig	phy	dig				
1. Globalisation of economy	+++	+	+	+	–	–	+	7
2. Global trade within multinationals	+++	+	–	–	–	–	+	5
3. Global E-commerce	+	+++	+	+++	+++	+++	+++	17
4. New competitors comm. payments	+	++	+	+++	–	–	–	7
5. Internationalisation of fin. exchanges	–	–	–	–	+++	+++	+++	9
6. New competitors financ. transactions	–	–	–	–	+++	+	+	5
7. Initiatives Herstatt risk	–	–	–	–	–	+++	+++	6
8. Emergence of Euroland	+++	+	+++	+	+++	+	+++	15
	11	8	6	8	12	11	15	

Impact on payment intermediation by banks
+++ strong ++ medium + weak – none

Figure 11.4 Impact of globalisation on payment intermediation.

6   *Information technologies* also favour *new competitors for financial trans-actions* and payment services. Examples of such new competitors are Alternative Trading Systems (ATM), in recent times often in the form of Electronic Communication Networks (ECN), offered by financial infor-mation providers such as Reuters or new technology driven competitors.[12] These new competitors challenge the dominant role of organised exchanges and financial intermediaries for dealing and issuing securities and other financial instruments.

7   The initiative of *central banks and bank supervisors* regarding the elimi-nation or mitigation of the Herstatt-risk and the improvement of financial stability will exert a continuous pressure on the traditional pay-ment intermediaries to reduce the financial risks in all payment systems.

8   The completion of the *European currency* union will transform today's largest market for international commercial payments into a local pay-ment market. The pressure by the European Union and the European Central Bank will add to the demand by the customers for rapid improve-ments in the European payment systems.

The author's personal and admittedly subjective assessment of these changes for the different categories of payment transactions leads to the fol-lowing conclusions (Figure 11.4):

1   The most relevant *external developments* for the next years are:
    • the emergence of global E-commerce;
    • the development of Euroland;
    • the internationalisation of many financial transactions.

2   The most urgent and important *needs for action* by the banking industry and the individual banks are:
    • the establishment of effective and efficient trans-border street side systems;
    • the adjustments in the payment systems for financial transactions, both for β2B/β2C and β2β;
    • the improvement of international payment services for B2B transac-tions, with a special urgency for trade within Euroland.

4 Hypotheses for the future of payment intermediation by banks

Beyond these urgent action tasks, the challenges for the banks in their role as payment intermediaries shall be summarised in the form of ten hypotheses:

1   *Technology* is a revolutionary force that will change both global trade and global payment in often unpredictable ways. One aspect is the fact that modern information technology can help to overcome some of the

important weaknesses of today's payment systems and services in a global context. This is certainly the case for the reduction of risks and costs, and for the improvement of services, especially the information quality for payee, payer, and intermediary. Another promising trend is the steady move from paper-based towards electronic payments.[13]

2 *Digital money* may have an important impact through its potential to relegate banks to their historic role in a pure cash society. The role of counterparty substitution in the payment process of commercial transactions could thus be lost. Several large banks have experimented with digital money, but so far with no commercial success. It looks as if digital money can only succeed in a global and multi-bank context. So far, little or no initiatives to set up a global clearing and settlement process have been observed.[14] Such a system would be necessary for the implementation of a new global payment product. The early experiments by individual banks as well as the lessons learnt from the history of credit card systems suggest that a single bank cannot successfully implement a proprietary digital money system.

3 *New competitors* for banks are arising in payment services, especially in the E-commerce area. The balance of power in the commercial payment business is shifting from pure payment providers towards commerce enablers (The Boston Consulting Group 1999: 1).

4 *Role of banks in their customers' E-commerce.* Banks striving to remain successful in payments, and also trying to become successful in payments for E-commerce, must reconsider their role in the whole business process of their customers. Opportunities for banks may arise in areas such as purchasing platforms, certification, trade services and finance, electronic bill presentment, consumer Internet payments, and payment aggregation services (The Boston Consulting Group 1999: 13–4).

5 Banks will have to *specialise* their payment services. Many banks will not be able to offer local and global, traditional and new payment services. Banks will have to decide whether (and if yes, how) they want to compete in the global payment arena or whether they will concentrate on the still dominant local business. There will probably be only a few highly specialised banks that will be fully equiped to offer comprehensive global payment services to multinational and other corporate customers with sophisticated needs.[15] The extent to which a larger number of banks will be able to offer such global services will depend on the future of common industry infrastructures.

6 *Common infrastructures or utilities of banks* play, and will continue to play, an important role for the future of banks in global payment intermediation. To succeed as an industry against the new competitors it is vital for banks to extend the reach of the traditionally national infrastructures internationally. They will probably have to give their customers direct access to their payment networks such as S.W.I.F.T., at least to the large corporate and institutional clients. In the E-commerce arena for

B2C business there might be an urgent need for banks to build up some common, global infrastructure that includes some type of clearing and settlement mechanisms for digital money. In general, the better the global common infrastructure, the better the chances of the banking industry as a whole and of the smaller banks in particular to play a role in global payments.

7 *Euroland is a special case,* transforming 'trans-border' issues into 'national' or 'domestic' ones.

8 *B2B is more important than B2C.* Total market transaction costs and qualities are more important for businesses than just the costs and qualities of payments. The restructuring of the global value chain is paramount for the corporate customers, whereas this aspect matters less with private persons.

9 *In financial* (i.e. β –) *transactions,* which are normally characterised by high amounts, risk aspects are often more serious than the operational costs. In commercial transactions the transaction costs, ease of use, integration into the business process of the commercial customers are the more important factors.

10 *Building on the traditional strengths* and enlarging them to the new challenges of globalisation and the new technologies should give the banking industry a fair chance to remain the key payment intermediary in our globalised world.

These are tentative statements, hypotheses which may raise more questions than they answer. The author hopes to motivate academics to research these issues in more detail. At the same time he wants to point out to practitioners that payment intermediation is a strategically highly relevant subject both for individual banks and for the industry as a whole.

Notes

1 For examples see Neue Zürcher Zeitung (1999): 23.
2 Delayed delivery and payment corresponds logically to a 'forward contract' with the related risks (see Perold 1995: 56). This is an area in which the banks have a special expertise reaching far beyond a pure technical payment transaction.
3 According to The Boston Consulting Group 1999: 1, the price per payment averaged $1.11 for domestic transactions, $13.52 for cross-border transactions (figures for 1997). Similarly, the costs for cross-border securities clearing/settlement are about ten times higher than domestic transactions. See Cathomen 2000: 27.
4 For the 'Herstatt risk' in foreign exchange settlement systems see Bank for International Settlements 1996: 6.
5 There are other models, but more of academic interest than practical relevance, for example, the use of derivatives in lieu of settlement for financial market transactions (see Perold 1995: 74).
6 S.W.I.F.T.: Society for Worldwide Interbank Financial Telecommunication.
7 These concepts are: Unity of accounts principle, whereby settlement banks have only to maintain a positive value over all currencies, and additional rules, such as several short position limits and a minimum haircut on the overall positive value.

8 For examples see The Boston Consulting Group 1999: 6.
9 For more details see The Boston Consulting Group 1999: 7–8.
10 For examples see Hitachi Research Institute 1993: 86–7.
11 For specific figures see Cathomen 2000: 27.
12 The most important alternative systems are Instinet and Island.
13 For an analysis of the state and movements in different countries see The Boston Consulting Group 1998: 8–9.
14 Such clearing systems are analysed by Janssen and Lüthi 1999: 9–10.
15 BCG estimates that three to five global providers will emerge as winners over a ten-year period. The Boston Consulting Group 1998: 13–4.

References

Bank for International Settlements (1996) *Settlement Risk in Foreign Exchange Transactions*, Basle.

Bank for International Settlements (1997) *Real-Time Gross Settlement Systems*, Basle.

Bank for International Settlements (1998) *Risk Management for Electronic Bank and Electronic Money Activities*, Basle.

Cathomen, I. (2000) 'Monopoly im europäischen Clearing-Geschäft', *Neue Zürcher Zeitung*, 8/9 January 2000, p. 27.

Clinton, W. J. and Gore Jr., A. (1998) *A Framework for Global Electronic Commerce*. Online. Available HTTP: http://www.iitf.nist.gov/eleccomm.htm (September 1998).

Crameri, M. (2000) *Effiziente Verrechnung von Kleinsttransaktionen im Internet Commerce*, Zürich: vdf Hochschulverlag.

Crane, D. B., et al. (1995) *The Global Financial System. A Functional Perspective*, Boston: Harvard Business School Press.

Europäische Zentralbank (1998) *Bericht über elektronisches Geld*, Frankfurt am Main.

European Central Bank (1999) *Improving Cross-Border Retail Payment Services. The Eurosystem's View*, Frankfurt am Main.

Financial Action Task Force on Money Laundering (2000) *Report on Money Laundering Typologies 1999–2000*, Paris: FATF Secretariat, OECD.

Geiger, H. (1999) *Electronic Commerce. Herausforderung für Wirtschaft und Banken*, Zürich: Zürcher Handelskammer.

Hitachi Research Institute (1993) *Payment Systems. Strategic Choices for the Future*, Tokyo: F.I.A. Financial Publishing Co.

Janssen, M. and Lüthi, U. (1999) 'Token-basierte Bezahlsysteme für das Internet: zentrale und dezentrale Clearingverfahren', *Informatik*, vol. 5, August, pp. 9–11.

Lambe, G. (2000) 'The Risks and Rewards of Continuous Linked Settlement, *Risk Professional*, vol. 1, pp. 22–24.

Llewellyn, D. T. (1999) *The New Economics of Banking*, Amsterdam: Société Universitaire Européenne de Recherches Financières.

Marx, K. and Engels, F. (1848) *Manifesto of the Communist Party*. Online. Available HTTP: http://www.anu.edu.au/polsci/marx/classics/manifesto.html (November 1999).

McAndrews, J. and Roberds, W. (1999) *Payment Intermediation and the Origins of Banking*, New York, Atlanta: Federal Reserve Banks of New York and Atlanta.

Merton, R. C. and Bodie, Z. (1995) 'A Conceptual Framework for Analyzing the Financial Environment', in Crane, D. B., et al. *The Global Financial System. A Functional Perspective*, Boston: Harvard Business School Press, pp. 3–32.

NACHA Cross-Border Council (1999) *Concept Paper for a Global Automated Clearing House*, Herndon: WATCH Worldwide Automated Transaction Clearing House. Online. Available HTTP: http://www.globalach.org (February 2000).

Neue Zürcher Zeitung (ed.) (1999) *NZZ Folio Globalisierung*, Zürich.

Perold, A. F. (1995) 'The Payment System and Derivative Instruments', in Crane, D. B., et al. *The Global Financial System. A Functional Perspective*, Boston: Harvard Business School Press, pp. 33–79.

Retail Banking Research Ltd (1994) *Study in the Area of Payment Systems into the Transparency of Conditions for Remote Cross-Border Payment Services and the Performance of Cross-Border Transfers. Report for the Commission of the European Communities*, London: Commission of the European Communities.

Schmid, B. and Lindemann, M. (1997) *Elemente eines Referenzmodells Elektronischer Märkte*, St. Gallen: Institut für Wirtschaftsinformatik.

Stulz, R. M. (1999) 'Globalization, Corporate Finance, and the Cost of Capital', *Journal of Applied Corporate Finance*, vol. 12, pp. 8–25.

The Boston Consulting Group (1998) *Global Payments*, London.

The Boston Consulting Group (1999) *Global Payments*, London.

Weber, R. H. (1999) *Elektronisches Geld. Erscheinungsformen und rechtlicher Problemaufriss*, Zürich: Schulthess Polygraphischer Verlag.

White, W. R. (1998) *The Coming Transformation of Continental European Banking?*, Basle: Bank for International Settlements.

World Bank (2000) *Entering the 21st Century. World Development Report 1999/2000*, Oxford: Oxford University Press.

Young, K. (1999) 'Across the borders', *The Banker*, vol. 149, pp. 100–101.

12 A theoretical model of consumer behaviour in the financial services industry*

Barry Howcroft

Introduction

Within the traditional structure and operation of the financial services industry, consumers had little choice in terms of selecting financial instruments and delivery channels. The rigid structure of the industry, combined with the operation of cartels, meant that consumers had to accept the form and price of both financial instruments and delivery channels. Switching between financial providers generated little, if any, long-term benefit and forced the consumer to incur disruption and financial cost. Consumers were, therefore, locked into buying patterns and had little incentive to change. However, deregulation and the emergence of technology has created highly competitive market conditions which have had a critical impact on consumer behaviour. Consumers are now more disposed to change their buying behaviour when purchasing financial products and as a consequence bank providers are less certain that their customers will continue to bank with them or that they will be able to rely upon the traditional banker–customer relationship to cross-sell high value, so-called ancillary products.

In an era of unprecedented change where customer retention and the ability to cross-sell products to existing customers is critical in determining profitability, it is important that banks respond strategically to these changes. Bank providers must, therefore, attempt to better understand their customers not only to anticipate, but also to influence and determine consumer buying behaviour. This paper, accordingly, develops a model which attempts to articulate and classify consumer behaviour in the purchasing of financial products and services. The insights provided by this model should assist bank providers in identifying appropriate strategies which are conducive to increased customer retention and profitability.

* Paper presented at 22nd SUERF Colloquium, Vienna, 27–29 April 2000.

Consumer buying behaviour

A common approach to understanding consumer buying behaviour is to generate complex models of consumer decision-making. This method of building complex consumer behaviour models can be described as the 'consumer behaviouralist' approach (Blackwell, Engel and Kollat, 1986). Despite its widespread use, this approach has attracted criticism on the basis that it tries to explain why consumers behave as they do, without knowing or understanding in any 'quantitative detail' just how they do behave (Ehrenberg, 1988). For example, the Howard and Sheth model (1969) seeks to explain buyer behaviour through the use of constructs such as attention, attitude, motive, interaction, etc., which are combined with marketing inputs such as price, quality, social variables and aspects of actual behaviour such as overt search, ultimately leading to purchase and satisfaction. No detailed evidence exists as to how these constructs actually relate to specific facets of consumer behaviour and these models do not provide an adequate explanation of why consumers repeat patterns of purchase behaviour or why purchase behaviour is suddenly altered (Ehrenberg 1988).

Ideal types

An alternative approach is provided by Max Weber's 'ideal types' construct. Rather than break phenomena down into small elements and build these into general theories, Weber sought to characterise phenomena into broad groups or ideal types. Once classified into groups, the constituent elements of the phenomena being observed can be analysed. The rationale for this approach is that complex social interactions rarely, if ever, operate to a set pattern like elements in the physical sciences. Rather than postulate general theories that describe behaviour in all contexts, ideal types describe forms of behaviour in certain contexts. The ideal type describes what Weber described as an 'objectively possible' course of actions within a relevant frame of reference (Parsons, 1951). Behaviour is, therefore, dependent on both the nature and the context in which it occurs. An ideal type will possess a number of distinguishing characteristics which are constructed by the researcher to describe the complexities of behaviour within a particular frame of reference.

Weber argued that the key to developing ideal types was to identify characteristics that shaped both the form of the ideal type and the frames of reference. It follows that in developing ideal types which characterise consumer buying, it is necessary to identify the underlying constructs which determine consumer behaviour within a particular environment or frame of reference. Ideal types, therefore, reflect certain underlying constructs or imperatives and individual buying behaviour is shaped to accommodate them. This is consistent with the work of Fishbein which links attitudes and outcomes, arguing that individuals' attitudes toward certain outcomes, motivate behaviour (Fishbein, 1967).

Two general factors can be identified from the academic literature, which affect all forms of buying behaviour:

* the ability of the individual to make decisions, termed 'rationality'; and
* the moral conduct that underlies the decision, i.e. so-called 'self-interest orientation'.

Rationality

The buyer–seller interchange is relatively straightforward where little uncertainty exists, but as uncertainty increases, the interchange becomes more difficult and more expensive. Costs increase because increased uncertainty reduces the transacting parties' knowledge of ex-post outcomes, thereby increasing the likelihood of making mistakes and purchasing either an inferior product or using an inappropriate delivery channel. Consumers, therefore, attempt to reduce uncertainty by limiting the range of possible future outcomes or creating systems through which unexpected outcomes are handled. However, the ability to handle uncertainty assumes that the individual acts rationally.

Rationality as an explanation of human decision-making appeared in the work of eighteenth-century philosophers, but it was not fully articulated until 1953 (Von Neumann and Morgenstern). Rational consumers are perceived as being able and motivated to get the best possible deal when making purchases. To facilitate this outcome, they are assumed to have perfect information, which enables them to behave in a perfectly rational manner. In this respect, the assumption of perfect information removes any uncertainty from the choice environment. However, the problem with rationality as an explanation of consumer behaviour lies in the assumption of perfect information. In the real world, it is not always appropriate to assume that decision makers possess perfect information, simply because various degrees of uncertainty are existent in all choice environments.

Lack of perfect information and the existence of uncertainty explain why Simon (1957) and Williamson (1975) rejected 'full rationality' as an effective explanation of human decision-making. It does, however, serve as an ideal type in the sense that consumers can be regarded as behaving in a manner which approximates to rationality, where they have high levels of information or are familiar with a particular product or service. Under these circumstances they are likely to adopt a rational approach to decision-making, but they are not fully rational but rather can be regarded as approximating rationality (Eztioni, 1988).

The literature reveals that consumer behaviour models have focused on the extensive role of information in shaping and directing rational choice. Nicosia (1966), for example, identifies the search and evaluation of information; Howard and Sheth (1969) link the amount of information held with the extent of learning and thus problem solving; Blackwell, Engel and Kollat

(1986) identify information input and processing as central elements in decision-making; Bettman (1979) recognises that individuals have limited capabilities for processing information and this limitation affects their decision-making activities. The common causal link in all of these approaches can be summarised as: information – attitude – purchase. As an explanation of behaviour this form of linkage is not only predominant in the social sciences, but can also be clearly identified in behavioural economics (Katona, 1960; Scitovsky, 1976). All of these models are based on information which is necessarily assumed to be freely and readily available. No reference is made to the context in which information is found and used and decision-making accordingly takes place within a vacuum.

An alternative to rationality as an explanation of decision-making emerges in the work of Simon (1957). Simon acknowledged that an individual's cognitive abilities are sequential and limited in nature and that the environment within which decisions are made is so uncertain and complex that it is impossible to specify all of the potential outcomes. He argues that individuals still desire to behave rationally, but there exists a tension between an individual's actual decision-making abilities and desired decision-making behaviour. This tension is reconciled through the use of simplified models of the real choice environment. This simplification of the decision environment Simon terms 'bounded rationality' – rationality still operates, but with certain limitations.

Within the concept of bounded rationality the environment is described by a series of 'givens', i.e. premises that are accepted by the individual as shorthand means of describing the decision environment. Simon termed these simplifications 'heuristics', whose purpose is to economise on the costs of information search and processing and thereby reduce decision-making costs. By limiting the range of possible outcomes, the individual can approximate rational decision-making within a limited subset of the total choice environment. In limiting the choice environment in this way, decision-making is unlikely to generate outcomes which maximise objectives. Satisfactory, rather than maximised outcomes are generated and Simon referred to this behaviour as 'satisficing'. Individuals know when outcomes are satisfactory because they can compare current results with past experience, or use some absolute measure of satisfaction. Past experience is important because it provides the individual with information about the quality or level of results they should expect from particular transactions. If satisfactory results are not achieved, they can alter the transaction, for example, by transacting with other parties or using alternative delivery channels. Conversely, if results are satisfactory or exceed expectations, future requirements from transactions are adjusted in the light of that experience.

In this study, the individual's decision-making behaviour is taken as being boundedly rational and a key focus of the research is to identify appropriate heuristics which guide consumer buying behaviour in financial services. Bounded rationality can be regarded as an ideal type of decision-making just like rationality. The use of brands to guide purchase is an example of bounded rational decision-making because the brand acts as a heuristic, simplifying the decision environment and thereby reducing uncertainty and transaction costs. It follows that as greater reliance is placed on heuristics to simplify the choice environment, the more the individual's behaviour approximates to bounded rationality.

In making decisions in an uncertain environment Williamson (1985) argued that, *ceteris paribus,* individuals will seek to reduce their costs of transacting and will adopt approaches to achieve this aim. In a known environment, rational behaviour allows an individual to minimise transaction costs, but in highly uncertain environments the lack of perfect information makes rational decision-making impossible. Bounded rationality and the use of heuristics reconciles an individual's need to behave rationally within an uncertain choice environment. By using heuristics and simplifying decision-making, transaction costs are reduced and the speed of decision-making is increased.

Self-interest orientation

Self-interest orientation explicitly recognises that a contributory element of uncertainty emanates from the behaviour of the transacting parties. These parties may, for example, act in their own interests and attempt to achieve an advantage over the other party. Diamond (1971) identified three levels of self-interest: opportunism, self-interest seeking and obedience. Obedience is effectively the null form of opportunism because it assumes that transacting parties are totally submissive and is probably most strongly associated with Communism and centrally planned economies. Self-interest seeking assumes that transacting parties would fully disclose their positions and stick to any bargains made. Such 'model citizens' would not lie, fail to pay or argue over terms of a contract and the future would hold no surprises for contracting parties.

The real world of transactions is, therefore, perhaps best depicted by opportunism which reflects the propensity of parties to lie, steal and cheat, mislead, disguise, obfuscate and otherwise distort the disclosure of information to achieve advantage (Williamson, 1975, 1985). As such, it is a source of 'behavioural uncertainty', an uncertainty that would vanish if individuals were open and honest in their efforts to realise individual advantage. The existence of bounded rationality and opportunism results in asymmetric information between contracting parties. Such asymmetries can increase as information is revealed and will confer greater advantage on to one of the contracting parties.

Asymmetric information represents a significant comparative advantage to a bank provider and is consequently at the very heart of the traditional banker–customer relationship. Banks effectively exploit their privileged positions regarding information about their customers, the array of financial products currently available in the market, the attributes of the various alternative delivery channels, etc.; and this is in stark contrast to the relative lack of information and, therefore, uncertainty of the average consumer of financial services.

Given these considerations, transacting parties such as a bank and its customers must have some form of 'system' which enables exchanges to take place within the parameters of uncertainty and opportunism and simultaneously reflect the decision-making abilities of the individual parties. Given that the methods of transacting and contracting must reflect the consumer's motivations and desires within the constraints of bounded rationality and opportunism, it is essential to examine the primary forces which motivate consumers in buyer–seller interactions.

Banker–customer interactions

In order to understand consumer behaviour and ideal types within the financial services market, it is important to discuss the nature of banker–customer interactions and the extent to which these are affected by the characteristics of specific products and services. The banker–customer relationship is not an homogeneous concept because it involves a variety of interactions that vary according to content, frequency, duration, etc. Interactions incorporate all instances where the consumer interacts with the bank-provider's employees, technology and physical resources. They may not necessarily involve the physical or intellectual involvement of the other party because a customer, for example, can interact with a bank by reading a brochure or conversely a bank may perform some sort of automatic transaction without the involvement of the customer.

Another important consideration in understanding banker–customer interactions is time. Time consists of two basic modes:

- the active mode during which the customer interacts with the bank in order to exchange value; and
- the inactive mode during which the customer is totally passive with regard to the bank.

The fundamental nature of most banker–customer relationship is such that these interactions are typically short and consequently the customer is in the passive mode for most of the time, but during these periods the customer may be in an active relationship with another bank.

Time is important in another respect because the very word 'relationship' suggests that there is more than one interaction between bank and customer. Accordingly, the frequency of interactions, i.e. the number of interactions in the overall relationship, is important. From the bank's perspective, high frequency or high demand products and services have to be delivered in a cost-effective manner with equal emphasis placed on efficiency and quality. These fundamental prerequisites of high frequency interactions are largely determined by the customer's need for speed, accuracy and reliability, etc., at relatively low prices.

In addition to frequency, the duration of the interaction is another important aspect of the banker–customer relationship. Speed of service may be important in high frequency interactions, but in certain types of financial products (so-called 'high-credence' products), the investment of customer time is an important part of the search and buy process. From the customer's perspective, duration is, therefore, determined by the fundamental characteristics of financial products and services (Bateson, 1977; Shostack, 1977; McKechnie, 1992; Betts, 1994), which can increase consumer uncertainty and thereby reduce consumer confidence when purchasing certain types of financial products.

Chant (1987), in attempting to explain how consumers reduce or, at least accommodate, uncertainty when purchasing financial services, identified two important considerations:

- the need to identify good from bad products; and
- the need to monitor and enforce the anticipated outcome from the purchase.

In order to distinguish between good and bad purchases, the consumer engages in a process of search prior to purchase in order to reduce uncertainty and generate favourable outcomes (Bettman, 1979; Howard and Sheth, 1969; Nicosia, 1966). Outcomes in financial products, however, are not always immediate and, therefore, the customer needs to monitor performance and ensure the eventual outcomes of any purchase contract. Monitoring costs continues throughout the lifetime of the financial product, but to do it effectively requires access to appropriate information and the ability to interpret and understand it. Effective monitoring of financial products by customers is, therefore, not always possible.

Enforcement costs arise out of the need to ensure that outcomes are those which the two parties (bank and customer) agreed in the initial purchase contract. From the consumer's perspective, the main problem is that the outcome can occur long after the initial purchase. An insurance company, for example, may refuse to make a payment or go into liquidation. Similarly, an investment or pension plan may pay out less than was anticipated.

Monitoring and enforcement attempt, therefore, to reduce *ex ante* uncertainty which varies in direct accordance with the uncertainty inherent in the decision-making environment. The decision-making environment is greatly determined by the type or complexity of the financial product being purchased and this partly explains why consumers adopt different types of contracting behaviour. In essence, where the inherent characteristics of financial products are complicated and *ex ante* uncertainty cannot by reduced by conventional search and buy methods, the duration of the interactions will be longer and the consumer may even pass on part of the responsibility for decision-making to an independent broker. Inherent in this interaction is the dependence of the consumer on either the bank or a third party in making the decision because conventional search and buy criteria, such as price and quality, are difficult to apply. Decision-making for more complicated financial products is, therefore, almost divorced from ownership and having a relationship with a bank (or an independent broker) based on considerations such as trust, reputation, image, etc., is very important.

During the interaction mode, the consumer participates in the value creation process. Eiglier and Langeard (1987), Lehtinen (1983) and Lovelock and Young (1979) view consumer participation as an opportunity for marketing, enhancing quality and improving production efficiency. Mills and Morris (1986) have stated that consumers in service organisations play important roles in creating services. This suggests that bank providers should introduce corporate strategies which increase the frequency or duration of interactions and change consumer behaviour by making customers more active in the choice environment. As such, banks should focus on defining customer roles and harness their skills and abilities especially in the provision of relatively more complicated financial products. This move towards greater customer participation or 'empowerment' is dependent upon the ability of bank providers to introduce new technology or adapt existing delivery channels to encourage greater participation. As the propensity for customers to participate in the choice environment will vary not only according to their age, income, social background, etc., but also to the complexity of the product being purchased, it is imperative that bank providers understand the banker–customer relationship. This will enable them to address a number of important strategic questions. For example, which customers are inclined or disinclined towards greater participation? What can the bank provider do to encourage customer participation? Which financial products are best suited to greater participation? Are certain delivery channels best suited to particular types of financial product? Finally, does greater customer participation, especially if it is driven by new technology and access to greater customer information, necessarily undermine the idea of having a long-term relationship with a bank?

An interaction typology

In a retail banking environment, there are many different types of interaction ranging from simple money transmission services to complicated discussions about pension plans, etc. In order to understand and gain an insight into the banker–customer relationship, it is important, therefore, to consider the configuration of these interactions. Creating a typology for interactions will facilitate an understanding of the heuristics which consumers use in different choice environments when purchasing different types of financial project. The typology will also help to explain how a bank provider can influence the consumer during and between the different types of interactions.

Each banker–customer interaction consists of two components: the content of the interaction and the interaction process. Content can be classified as economic exchange, information exchange and social exchange (Czepiel,

1990; Johansson and Mattsson, 1987). Although economic exchange, i.e. the exchange of money and services, predominates in retail banking, information exchange and social exchange are important too. Information exchange, which refers to giving and receiving information, reveals itself in the counselling and financial planning advice which banks provide to customers. Similarly, social exchange, i.e. contact between two (or more) people, has traditionally been important for banks and possibly explains why branch networks remain attractive to certain segments of the customer base despite not being as convenient or even as cost effective as alternative delivery channels.

The interaction process consists of a number of dimensions: frequency and duration of contact (Venkateson and Anderson, 1985), which have already been discussed. In addition to these two 'time-dimensions', the literature of the process of interactions can be divided into two schools: the involvement school, which is represented by the degree of contact between consumers and provider staff (Chase, 1978), the degree of control exercised by the consumer (Bateson and Hui, 1987; Bateson, 1989) and the degree of personalisation (Suprenant and Solomon, 1985). The second school of thought can be classified as the confidence school, which is represented by the degree of complexity and divergence in the interaction (Shostack, 1987) and the certainty of outcome reflected in the complexity of the financial product. Other writers such as Bowen and Larsson (1989), who emphasise the consumer's disposition to participate, and Lehtinen (1983), who focuses on the degree and modes of customer participation, combine elements of both schools.

An interaction typology in retail banking must incorporate a combination of these process dimensions, but also take into account the different needs of consumers from the content of the interaction. According to Normann and Haikola (1986), there are two basic consumer needs. The first is concerned with the need to balance consumption over a certain time period and is primarily concerned with 'deposit and lending' services. As such, they appear on the bank's balance sheet as either liabilities or assets, generate income in the form of interest spread and involve an element of risk for the bank (Channon, 1986). Banks attempt to reduce risk exposure by obtaining information, especially at the outset of a contract and by placing a certain amount of emphasis on the contact between staff and customers. Credit scoring techniques and telephone banking have changed and lessened the contact between staff and personal customers, but for commercial and corporate businesses there is still a significant emphasis placed on personal contact between bank and customer.

The second basic consumer need is concerned with the need to transfer money between different parties at a particular point in time. These interactions relate to the consumer's need for the bank's infrastructure role in order to transfer funds within the economy as a whole. The banks refer to these interactions as 'transactions' which are usually characterised by being fairly standardised and require a relatively small amount of information exchange.

As such, transactions can usually be totally automated, i.e. direct debits, standing orders, etc., or involve only a small intervention by bank staff or consumers.

A number of other consumer needs have to be discussed which do not impact on customer accounts, but which are nevertheless important. The first one can be classified as 'counselling', which involves a wide range of interactions in which the customer receives advice on financial products. The selling of financial products would normally come under this classification and, although the bank does not usually levy a tariff, counselling can be extremely important in the search and buy process. The second interaction can be classified as 'specialist services' (Gupta and Torkzadeh, 1988) which incorporates the provision of expert advice on financial or legal matters and usually involves a fee. The final interaction relates to the different types of investment services that banks offer to consumers, i.e. stocks and shares, mutual funds, pensions, insurances, etc. It usually requires appreciable competences on the side of the bank providers and the customer, but some of the more basic investment services can be selected by consumers on the conventional criterion of price. From this analysis it becomes clear that bank–customer interactions are extremely varied. Table 12.1 shows how the process dimensions are determined by the consumer's need for different products and services.

Table 12.1 A typology of interactions

	Transactions	*Deposit and lending*	*Counselling*	*Specialist services*	*Investment services*
Frequency	High	Low	Medium	Low	Medium
Duration	Short	Long/medium	Medium/long	Long	Medium
'Involvement'					
Customer control	Low	Low/medium	Medium	Low	Medium
Customer participation	Low	Medium/long	Medium	High	Medium
Level of contact	Low	High	Medium/high	High	Medium
'Confidence'					
Level of complexity*	Low	Medium	Medium	High	Medium
Certainty of outcome	High	Medium	Medium	Low	Medium

* The level of complexity is inversely related to confidence.

Consumer behaviour matrix

The discussion has identified two types of fundamental mode in the banker–customer interchange: an active mode during which the consumer interacts with the bank provider, and an inactive mode during which the consumer is essentially passive.

By placing the two principal factors that motivate and determine individual contracting choices, involvement and uncertainty, on to a simple continuum running from high to low, it is possible to construct a matrix of consumer behaviour (see Figure 12.1) which provides greater insight into the interaction modes. This matrix describes the purchasing/contracting alternatives available to consumers to structure their interactions when acquiring products and services. Each quadrant represents a different combination of involvement and uncertainty, referred to as confidence, and thus a different mode of interaction to accommodate consumer needs when purchasing different financial products and services.

From the literature review on the process of interactions and consumer need, it is postulated that 'involvement' in the buyer–seller interchange incorporates a number of subsets: customer control, customer participation and level of contact; and that 'confidence', which is largely determined by the characteristics of the product, is represented by complexity of the product being purchased and certainty of outcome associated with the product. In addition to these product-specific considerations, the model necessarily incorporates 'exogenous' factors or 'institutional' factors which influence the consumer's disposition to purchase financial products. These factors relate to the importance of trust and loyalty and to the degrees and modes of consumer participation which, within the context of this study, are defined as relating to alternative distribution channels.

The matrix is based on the work of Dwyer, Schurr and Oh (1987) and Thibaut and Kelly (1959). The limitation of previous models stems from the factors hypothesised to explain consumer motivation and behaviour, particularly in the creation and maintenance of relationships. Consumer decisions to create relationships are regarded as being largely motivated by the benefits and costs associated with a transaction. However, as the discussion of bounded rationality highlighted, consumers in financial services frequently cannot calculate benefits and costs and it is because of this inability that

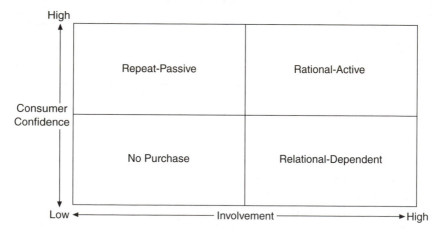

Figure 12.1 Consumer behaviour matrix.

they create relationships. Similarly, these earlier models ignored consumer involvement with the purchase and their ability or confidence when making purchase decisions (Morgan and Hunt, 1994).

The advantage of the consumer behaviour matrix, as an approach to understanding consumer buying and contracting behaviour, is that it draws on the economics, consumer behaviour and psychology literature (discussed earlier) and combines it into a single framework. The rich diversity of literature in these areas is brought together to create ideal types of behaviour which can be applied to actual buying and contracting in financial services. In this way, the consumer behaviour matrix places observed behaviour into an overall context. By identifying the underlying factors influencing buying and contracting behaviour and linking these very directly with consumer needs, the rationale for consumer interactions and relationship may become apparent.

Forms of consumer behaviour

Rational-active

In this quadrant it is postulated that the consumer's involvement in terms of the process dimensions of control, participation and contact is high and so too is their confidence in terms of product complexity and certainty of outcome. It is these active consumers that economic theory has viewed as the norm, possessing the ability and inclination to make carefully considered purchase decisions across all choice environments. In terms of ideal types these consumers are rational or rationally inclined.

Eztioni (1988) notes that rationality can be defined in a number of forms and argues that individuals make decisions in a more or less rational manner depending on the nature of the choice environment and item purchased. Examples of individuals approximating rationality would include purchases of commodity goods and services such as petrol, milk, orange juice, flour and so forth. Within these purchase environments the consumer can articulate requirements and use short-term contracts to structure the purchase. These contracts are described by MacNeil (1978, 1980) as 'discrete', they have a clear beginning, short duration and a definite end. No interactions are expected after the transaction, there is a clear division of benefits and costs, disputes are settled through reference back to the original contract and the switching costs between contracts are low. Discrete contracting is a reflection of the characteristics of the product or service transacted and the underlying rational behaviour of the decision maker.

Consumers will tend towards discrete, rational contracting to structure their buying behaviour, whenever possible, because it enables them to reduce transaction costs and to exert a high degree of control over the purchase decision (Eztioni, 1988). To purchase in an 'instrumentally rational' manner, the individual consumer is assumed to possess sufficient ability and information to enable them to make clear comparisons between competing products and thus make an informed choice. If the information is not available or the consumer lacks the ability to make choices, they have to move away from 'instrumental' rationality as discrete contracting is no longer an effective means of structuring the transactions.

Repeat-passive

In this quadrant consumers display low levels of involvement with the financial product as they are fully aware of the product's salient features. Given the low levels of involvement and the limited perception of uncertainty, these consumers can be described as 'passive' in the sense that they will make repeated interactions without actively seeking alternatives. This repeated pattern of purchase behaviour, which is described as 'behavioural loyalty' in the literature, has been extensively researched. Brown (1952) and Johnson (1973, 1982), for example, have identified markets and social factors which encourage or coerce individuals into repeated behaviour patterns. Their work indicates that considerations, such as the absence of a motivating event to encourage a search for alternatives, a lack of choice or a lack of incentive to alter purchasing patterns, encourage consumers to maintain existing purchasing patterns. In maintaining their existing patterns of purchase, these consumers are adopting a boundedly rational approach to their buying and contracting behaviour. Having selected a heuristic to guide their behaviour, such as a brand for example, this behaviour is repeated until a better alternative becomes available. Making repeated purchases from a single source or type also reduces the 'cost' of purchasing by limiting uncertainty, whereas a more rational approach may expose the consumer to uncertainties which could result in financial loss. This form of repeat purchase behaviour is common in fast-moving consumer good (FMCG) markets where consumers use brands and brand identities to determine purchasing behaviour.

No purchase

This quadrant describes consumers who, because they have no involvement with the financial product and do not possess the ability or the confidence to make transaction decisions, make no purchase. Individuals who leave significant sums of money on deposit rather than purchase financial services that could generate greater returns are an example of this behaviour. This is not strictly speaking an interaction mode and is hardly (if at all) discussed in the banker–customer relationship literature, but a significant amount of marketing activity is directed at individuals in this quadrant in an attempt to increase their awareness of alternative products and convince them of their relative merits.

Relational-dependent

In this quadrant consumers are highly involved, but are not in control due to the complexity of the product and uncertainty of eventual outcome and this reduces consumer confidence. In order to make choices, the consumer will seek advice and help from banks or third parties and can, therefore, be described as 'dependent consumers' who form relationships to reduce uncertainty and structure their pattern of purchases.

Relational contracting does not fit easily into the concept of either an active or a passive interaction, but it is clearly an important aspect of the banker–customer relationship. It emerged from the work of MacNeil (1978) and Williamson (1975, 1985), who recognised that in particular contexts rational-active and repeat-passive contracting were not effective in structuring exchange. It is used in highly uncertain environments where consumers lack the information to make rational decisions yet perceive that differences in quality exist between competing products/services. In this instance they will want to make informed choices and have to draw on the assistance of more informed third parties. The relationship then effectively replaces the information search and processing activities found in repeat-passive and rational-active contracting. Trust plays a critical role in this relationship and the role of professional associations is to protect consumers from third parties acting opportunistically.[1]

Conclusions

Each of the ideal types described in the consumer behaviour matrix has implications for strategy, in that they give rise to contingencies which demand a strategic response. For example, the strategic threat of rational-active consumer behaviour for banks is that consumers reappraise their repeat-passive behaviour and as a result change their existing patterns of buying behaviour. Encouraging consumers to change their behaviour requires the provision of a financial product or service that is typically cheaper and better than existing products. Consumer involvement in the financial product or service can also be increased and cause existing patterns of repeat-passive behaviour to be reconsidered. Direct banking and insurance is largely based on their success in switching consumers out of the repeat-passive quadrant into the rational-active quadrant by raising levels of involvement and offering a low priced improved service. Consequently, financial products and services associated with 'transactions' and certain types of 'deposit and lending' have revealed a propensity to migrate from repeat-passive into the rational-active quadrant. Similarly, certain types of 'basic investment services' have revealed a similar propensity to migrate into the rational-active quadrant from relational-dependent.

Consumers have traditionally used repeat-passive behaviour to structure their purchases of simple financial services, especially 'transactions' and, to some extent, 'deposits and lending'. Consumers' interest or involvement in these services has decayed, but they are still necessary. However, in order to limit cognition and search costs or simply out of consumer inertia, purchases are repeated. Strategically the challenge facing banks depends on whether they are new entrants or existing players. New entrants have to encourage consumers to move into the rational-active quadrant, but existing players need to retain consumers within the repeat-passive quadrant (at least in the short term) through improvements in product/service provision. In the financial services markets, it had been possible to retain large numbers of consumers within this quadrant simply because the benefits of switching were low and the costs high, thereby making changes in the pattern of buying behaviour prohibitively expensive. However, as the industry becomes more competitive, there is a distinct possibility that switching costs and inertia will be increasingly eroded and it may be increasingly difficult to retain consumers in the repeat-passive quadrant.

No current strategic contingencies flow from the no purchase quadrant, but the consumers within it represent an important source of potential new business. Banks need to adopt strategies which raise levels of involvement and increase consumer confidence so as to encourage purchases of financial instruments.

In strategic terms the relational-dependent quadrant offers a potential basis for the creation of differentiation. By forming a relationship with a bank or individual, the consumer prefers that relationship to alternatives. The relationship enables the banks (or an individual) to differentiate itself from competing alternatives. Companies frequently use brands as the basis for relationships between themselves and consumers. Brands embody a cluster of values and meanings which through consumption are transferred to the individual. A relationship exists between a brand and an individual where the individual consumer prefers a particular brand over all others and is prepared to pay a premium for that choice.

Creating such brand loyalty demands that the brand in some sense be unique, either in terms of its physical properties or through the values it communicates about those who consume the brand. Brands and brand loyalty are the basic building blocks of differentiation advantage and this advantage can only be created where consumers recognise and value the product features. If this is not the case, as is common for products where low levels of involvement exist, establishing brands and brand loyalty is difficult. This problem of a lack of differentiation in the market place affects banks and financial products and services generally and, therefore, makes it difficult to create consumer relationships. Direct providers of insurance and banking services have generated differentiation by changing the channel of distribution and this also may explain their success in entering the industry. However, over a longer period their success is likely to be imitated and their differentiation advantages eroded.

Given that the contractual nature of individual finance products is easily imitated, creating and sustaining meaningful differentiation on the basis of a 'good product' is likely to be extremely difficult. An alternative approach might be to to focus on the 'nature of the interactions' that occur between the consumer and the bank.

As consumers have a predisposition to create relationships and put emphasis on trust and loyalty when they find it difficult to make rational choices on the basis of available information, high credence 'investment and specialist services' fall naturally into this quadrant. Bank providers, however, need to focus on the dynamics of this quadrant in order to generate sustainable competitive advantage. This approach is termed relationship marketing (Berry, 1983; Crosby, Evans and Cowles, 1990; Dwyer, Schurr and Oh, 1987) and it is based on the premise that consumers create relationships with companies on the basis of loyalty and trust which encourages them to make multiple and cross-purchases, from a single source. Moreover, loyalty and trust create barriers to entry, thereby making it more difficult for new players entering the market.

Historically, this approach has not been widely explored or used in the financial service industry as choice was traditionally limited and consumers had little incentive to switch between bank providers. However, this situation no longer prevails as competitive forces enable and encourage consumers to adopt rational-active forms of buying behaviour. As these changes occur the retention of customers assumes greater importance as the costs of recruiting new customers are significant and because existing customers should provide cross-selling opportunities.

Acknowledgements

The author gratefully acknowledges the financial assistance provided by NCR's Knowledge Laboratory in conducting this research.

Note

1 The strength of the relationship between two parties can be judged by the extent to which the consumer will incur costs to consume within their preferred relationship, even where an alternative relationship exists. The greater the costs the consumer is willing to incur, the stronger the relationship and vice versa. Often firms mistake repeat-passive behaviour for the existence of a relationship, assuming that consumers making repeat purchases have a relationship with the firm. That error of judgement is revealed when the consumer is presented with an alternative providing only marginal benefits and yet still switches to the new alternative. The existence of marginal benefits encourages the consumer to switch into the rational-active ideal-type and to reassess and possibly alter their existing patterns of consumption. In this instance consumers are not prepared to incur costs and consume from their existing provider and in any real sense a relationship has not existed between the parties.

References

Bateson, J (1977) 'Do We Need Service Marketing?', *Marketing Consumer Services: New Insights Report*, pp 77–115, Boston: Marketing Science Institute.

Bateson, J E G (1989) *Managing Services Marketing – Text and Readings*, USA: Dryden Press.

Bateson, J E G and Hui, M K M (1987) 'Perceived Control as a Crucial Perceptual Dimension of the Service Experience', in Surprenant, C (Ed), *Add Value to Your Service*, pp 187–193, Chicago: American Marketing Association.

Berry, L L (1983) 'Relationship Marketing', in Berry, L L, Shostack, L G and Upah, G D (Eds), *Emerging Perspectives on Services Marketing*, pp 25–28, Chicago: American Marketing Association.

Bettman, J R (1979) 'An Information Processing Theory of Consumer Choice', MA Thesis, University of Reading, Addison-Wesley.

Betts, E (1994) 'Understanding the Financial Consumer', in McGoldrick, P J and Greenland, S (Eds), *Retailing of Financial Services*, pp 41–84, London: McGraw-Hill.

Blackwell, R D, Engel, J F and Kollat, D T (1986) *Consumer Behaviour*, New York: Holt, Rinehart and Winston.

Bowen, D E and Larsson, R (1989) 'Organisation and Customer: Managing Design and Co-ordination of Services. Customer Participation', *Academcy of Management Review*, April, Vol 14.2, pp 213–233.

Brown, G N (1952) 'Brand Loyalty: Fact or Fiction?', *Advertising Age,* Vol 23, pp 53–55.

Channon, D F (1986) *Bank Strategic Management and Marketing*, New York: John Wiley.

Chant, J (1987) 'Regulation of Financial Institutions – A Functional Analysis', No 45, Ottawa: Bank of Canada.

Chase, R B (1978) 'Where Does the Customer Fit in a Service Organization?', *Harvard Business Review*, Vol 56.6, pp 137–142.

Crosby, L A, Evans, K R and Cowles, D (1990) 'An Interpersonal Influence Perspective', *Journal of Marketing,* July, pp 68–81.

Czepiel, J A (1990) 'Service Encounters and Service Relationships: Implications for Research', *Journal of Business Research,* Vol 20, pp 13–21.

Diamond, P (1971) 'Political and Economic Evaluation of Social Effects and Externalities: Comment', in Intrilligator, M (Ed), *Frontiers of Quantitative Economics*, pp 30–32, Amsterdam: North-Holland Publishing Company.

Dwyer, F R, Schurr, P H and Oh, S (1987) 'Developing Buyer-Seller Relationships', *Journal of Marketing*, Vol 51, April, pp 11–27.

Ehrenberg, A S C (1988) *Repeat Buying: Facts, Theory and Applications*, London: Oxford University Press.

Eiglier, P and Langeard, E (1987) *Servuction – Le Marketing des Services*, Paris: McGraw-Hill.

Eztioni, A (1988) *The Moral Dimension: Towards a New Economy*, New York: Free Press.

Fishbein, M (1967) *Readings in Attitude Theory and Measurement*, New York: John Wiley.

Gupta, Y P and Torkzadeh, G (1988) 'Re-designing Bank Service Systems for Effective Marketing', *Long Range Planning*, Vol 21, pp 38–43.

Howard, J A and Sheth, J N (1969) *The Theory of Buyer Behavior*, New York: John Wiley.

Johansson, J and Mattsson, L-G (1987) 'Interorganizational Relations in Industrial Systems – A Network Approach Compared with the Transaction Cost Approach', Working Paper, University of Uppsala, Sweden.

Johnson, M P (1973) 'Commitment: A Conceptual Structure and Empirical Application', *The Sociological Quarterly*, Vol 14, Summer, pp 395–406.

Johnson, M P (1982) 'Social and Cognitive Features of the Dissolution of Commitment to Relationships', in Duck, S (Ed), *Dissolving Personal Relationships*, pp 51–73, New York: Academic Press.

Katona, G (1960) *The Powerful Consumer*, New York: McGraw-Hill.

Lehtinen, J R (1983) 'Customer Oriented Service System', Working Paper, Service Management Institute, Helsinki, Finland.

Lovelock, C H and Young, R F (1979) 'Look to Customers to Increase Productivity', *Harvard Business Review*, Vol 57.3, pp 168–178.

MacNeil, I R (1978) 'Contracts: Adjustments of Long-Term Economic Relations Under Classical, Neoclassical and Relational Contract Law', *Northwestern University Law Review*, Vol 72, pp 854–902.

MacNeil, I R (1980) *The New Social Contract, An Inquiry into Modern Contractual Relations*, New Haven, CT: Yale University Press.

McKechnie, S (1992) 'Consumer Buying Behaviour in Financial Services: An Overview', *International Journal of Bank Marketing*, Vol 19.5, pp 4–12.

Mills, P K and Morris, J H (1986) 'Clients as "Partial" Employees of Service Organizations: Role Development and Customer Participation', *Academy of Marketing Review*, Vol 11.4 October, pp 726–735.

Morgan, R M and Hunt, S D (1994) 'The Commitment-Trust Theory of Relationship Marketing', *Journal of Marketing*, Vol 58, pp 20–38.

Nicosia, F M (1966) *Consumer Decision Processes*, Englewood Cliffs, NJ: Prentice Hall.

Normann, R and Haikola, B (1986) *Winning Strategies in Financial Services. A Multiclient Study*, Helsinki: The Service Management Group Oy.

Parsons, T (1951) *The Social System*, Chicago: Free Press.

Scitovsky, T (1976) *The Joyless Economy*, Oxford: Oxford University Press.

Shostack, L G (1977) 'Breaking Free from Product Marketing', *Journal of Marketing*, Vol 41.2, pp 73–80.

Shostack, L G (1987) 'Service Positioning Through Structural Change', *Journal of Marketing*, January, Vol 51, pp 34–43.

Simon, H A (1957) *Models of Man*, New York: John Wiley.

Surprenant, C F and Soloman, M R (1985) 'Dimensions of Personalisation', in Bloch, Th M, Upah, G D and Zeithaml, V A (Eds), *Services Marketing in a Changing Environment*, pp 56–61, Chicago: American Marketing Association Proceedings Series.

Thibaut, J W and Kelly, H H (1959) *The Psychology of Groups,* New York: John Wiley.

Venkateson, M and Anderson, B B (1985) 'Time Budgets and Consumer Services', in Bloch, Th M, Upah, G D and Zeithaml, V A (Eds), *Services Marketing in a Changing Environment*, pp 52–55, Chicago: American Marketing Association Proceedings Series.

Von Neumann, J and Morgenstern, O (1953) *Theory of Games and Economic Behaviour*, New Jersey: Princeton University Press.

Williamson, O E (1975) *Markets and Hierarchies: Analysis and Anti-Trust Implications. A Study in the Economics of Internal Organisation,* New York: Free Press.

Williamson, O E (1985) *The Economic Institutions of Capitalism,* New York: Free Press.

13 Inflation, monetary transparency, and G3 exchange rate volatility*

Kenneth N. Kuttner and Adam S. Posen

Short-term volatility in G3 bilateral exchange rates has been a fact of life since the beginning of the post-Bretton Woods float. It has become established, surprisingly, that this volatility is not only disproportionately large relative to the variation in relative macroeconomic fundamentals of Germany, Japan, and the United States, but is in fact largely unrelated to them.[1] The apparent disconnect between fundamentals and dollar-yen and dollar-euro exchange rate fluctuations has led to perennial complaints about persistent exchange rate 'misalignments', and their real effects on the G3 (and other) economies, giving rise in turn to recurring proposals for government policies to limit this volatility.[2,3] The idea that volatility reflects nothing more than the (perhaps rational, certainly profit-seeking) behavior of foreign exchange traders seems to give justification for a policy response. Yet, the disjunction between macroeconomic expectations and the volatility seems to indicate as well that some deviation from domestic monetary policy goals would be necessary to intervene against exchange rate swings.[4]

In fact, as demonstrated to most observers' satisfaction in the instance of the ERM crises of 1992–1993, in a world of free movement of capital and domestic monetary policy autonomy (for the G3 at least), exchange rate commitments cannot be maintained without sacrifice of one or the other.[5] In other words, if there are no capital controls, when an exchange rate commitment comes under attack, monetary policy must move in the opposite direction from that usually mandated by domestic inflation and output concerns in order to support the peg.[6] This is because of a limited number of degrees of freedom for economic policymakers. Contrary to the expectations of Friedman (1953) and Johnson (1969) prior to the advent of floating rates, it appears that domestically responsible monetary policy may be destabilizing for exchange rates.

Yet, the movement towards greater transparency in monetary policymaking in recent years may partially reconcile Friedman's and Johnson's instincts that a more disciplined monetary policy should diminish exchange rate volatility with the apparent reality that macroeconomic fundamentals do not

* Paper presented at 22nd SUERF Colloquium, Vienna, 27–29 April 2000.

drive exchange rates in the short run. If transparency can be increased by central banks, either through institutional developments or through being more systematic in policymaking, without altering the fundamental monetary policy capabilities or decisions, this may give central banks an additional degree of freedom with which to work. Since it is at least arguable that transparency may enhance the flexiblity as well as the credibility of monetary policy by providing a better nominal anchor for inflation expectations, it is worth exploring whether use of this additional policy option (more a structure than an instrument) might have a meaningful effect on exchange rate volatility.[7]

Our paper assesses this possibility by posing two questions: first, to what extent do domestic inflation and interest rate surprises – fluctuations unexplained by past history and the systematic response of policy – contribute to short-run volatility in G3 exchange rates?[8] These are precisely the type of shocks which should diminish in frequency and effect as monetary transparency increases, if the hypothesized relationship between transparency and inflation expectations holds. Second, to what extent do variations over time in American, German, and Japanese monetary transparency actually match up with the timing of these shocks and the magnitude of their impact? Taken together, the empirical estimates in answer to these questions should give some sense of whether increased transparency in the G3 central banks would diminish exchange rate volatility.

The paper is structured as follows. In the first section, we set out a simple model of the implications of different monetary regimes (discretionary, anti-inflationary conservative, and transparent 'optimal state contingent rule' [OSCR] following) for the response of inflation, interest rates, and exchange rates to shocks.[9] In the second section, we develop an operational measure of central bank transparency, and apply it to the history of the Bank of Japan, the Bundesbank, and the Federal Reserve in the period 1975–1998, finding significant shifts in institutional transparency for the Federal Reserve and for the Bank of Japan in the late 1980s. In the third section, we estimate structural VAR (trivariate vector autoregression) models of relative interest rates, inflation rates, and exchange rates for the DM–yen and DM–\$, and conduct a number of analyses, including both comparing impulse response functions before and after the shifts in transparency, and interpreting historical decompositions for evidence of the exchange rate impact of smaller deviations from systematic monetary policy. The fourth section concludes with an assessment of the importance of domestic inflation and interest rate shocks to G3 exchange rate volatility, and the likelihood of increases in central bank transparency to diminish those shocks.

A simple model of inflation, exchange rates and monetary policy

In understanding the macroeconomic sources of exchange rate volatility, useful starting points are the familiar principles of purchasing power parity

(PPP) and uncovered interest rate parity (UIP). The latter is a difference equation linking the change in the exchange rate and the gap between foreign and domestic interest rates:

$$E_t \Delta e_{t+1} = i_t^* - i_t,$$

where e is the log of the exchange rate (defined as the foreign currency units per domestic currency unit), and i^* and i are the foreign and domestic interest rates. The UIP condition can be solved forward to yield:

$$e_t = E_t \Sigma_{j=0}^{\infty} (i_{t+j} - i_{t+j}^*) + \bar{e},$$

which expresses the exchange rate at time t as the sum of current and expected future interest rate differentials, plus the long-run equilibrium exchange rate, $\bar{e}$. Domestic interest rates in excess of the foreign are associated with a high – but falling – exchange rate.

While interest rate differentials govern short-run exchange rate dynamics, the (log) ratio of foreign to domestic price levels pins down the the long-run exchange rate, $\bar{e}$, via PPP:

$$\bar{e} = \lim_{j \to \infty} E_t (p_{t+j}^* - p_{t+j}),$$

where p^* and p are the logs of the foreign and domestic price levels. The condition can also be expressed in terms of the sum of expected future inflation rates:

$$\bar{e} = p_{t-j}^* - p_{t-1} + E_t \Sigma_{j=0}^{\infty} (\pi_{t+j}^* - \pi_{t+j}).$$

The PPP and UIP conditions by themselves obviously do not represent a complete macroeconomic model. But even without closing the model, the two conditions suggest a tradeoff between short-run and long-run exchange stabilization.

To see this, imagine an economy subject to supply shocks – events that presented the central bank with a tradeoff between output and inflation stabilization. A vigorous policy reaction will reduce the shocks' impact on the price level, mitigating their long-run effect on the exchange rate. But such a policy will create larger interest rate differentials, which, in the near term, will generate exchange rate volatility. A more accommodative policy response, on the other hand, reduces short-run interest rate induced volatility, but at the expense of destabilizing the long-run value of the exchange rate. Either way, inflation shocks generate exchange rate volatility; how much will depend, of course, on the specifics of the macro model.

One way to close the model is to append the PPP and UIP relations to the model of Svensson (1997), as extended by Kuttner and Posen (1999). This model is far too stylized to think about directly estimating. It nonetheless illustrates the theoretical reasoning behind a role for central bank transparency in minimizing the effects of inflation shocks on the exchange rate.

In Svensson's model, the policymaker chooses inflation to minimize the discounted sum of single-period loss functions of the form,

$$L_t = \pi_t^2 + \lambda \, (y_t - y^*)^2 \, ,$$

subject to an aggregate supply relation given by

$$y_t = \rho y_{t-1} + \alpha \, (\pi_t - \pi_t^e) + \varepsilon_t \, ,$$

where y is the output gap, π is inflation, and λ is the relative weight on output versus inflation stabilization. Persistence is introduced through the ρy_{t-1} term in the supply equation. Solving the minimization problem yields policy rules giving inflation as a function of expected inflation, the lagged output gap, and the supply shock, ε. An IS equation,

$$y_t = \delta \, (i_t - E_t \, \pi_{t+1} - r^*) \, ,$$

is then used to determine the corresponding path of interest rates.

Under discretion, the monetary authority accommodates supply shocks by allowing them to affect inflation: $\pi_t - E_{t-1} \, \pi_t = -b \, \varepsilon_t$. Not surprisingly, a higher weight on output stabilization implies a more accommodative policy, which in this context means a larger value of b. Expected inflation itself obeys $E_t \, \pi_{t+1} = a - cy_t$; if the central bank targets a nonzero output gap, inflation will contain a constant inflation bias, a; output gap fluctuations also create a state contingent inflation bias, $-cy_t$. The higher the weight on output stabilization, the larger are a and c.

Having derived the behavior of inflation, it is straightforward to use the IS equation, and the interest rate parity and purchasing power parity relationships to solve for the response of the exchange rate under discretion. The response of the nominal exchange rate at time $t+j$ to an ε equal to -1 at time t (i.e. a unit adverse supply shock) is given by:

$$e_{t+j} = - (\delta^{-1} - c) \, (1 - \alpha b) \, (1 - \rho)^{-1} \, \rho^j - [b + c(1 - \alpha b) \, (1 - \rho)^{-1}]$$

The first term, which comes from the interest rate differential, tends to increase the exchange rate, reflecting the increase in domestic interest rates used to combat inflation. The second term captures the shock's long-run effect on the price level. The net effect could go either way in a given period, depending on the strength of the initial policy response versus the long-run price-level implications. Over time, however, the interest rate effects die out, so in the long run, an adverse supply shock leads to a depreciation.

This exchange rate response is characterized by the tradeoff between short-run and long-run exchange rate stabilization alluded to earlier. As λ the weight on output stabilization falls (the central bank becomes more 'conservative'), b and c (the central bank's degree of accommodation) shrink. This reduces the supply shocks' effect on the long-run exchange rate, because the disinflation is greater and faster, but increases the short-run volatility through increasing the interest rate differential. In the limiting case of $\lambda=0$ (the 'inflation nutter'), there is no long-run effect, but the short-run effect is maximized.

If the central bank can commit to a constant rate of *expected* inflation, the inflation bias problems associated with discretion disappear. King (1997) refers to this as the 'optimal state-contingent rule', and argues that a properly implemented inflation targeting policy can move the monetary authority in this direction. The central bank is believed to anchor inflation expectations, and so is not punished for its deviations.

In this case, the monetary authority creates inflation *only* in the period of the shock: $\pi_t - E_{t-1} \pi_t = -b^* \varepsilon_t$.[10] The response of the nominal exchange rate to a unit adverse supply shock would then be:

$$e_{t+j} = -\delta^{-1}(1 - \alpha b^*)(1 - \rho)^{-1} \rho^j - b^*$$

The main difference between this exchange rate response and that under discretion is the lack of terms involving the coefficient describing the degree of state-contingent inflation bias, c. The lack of these terms means that the long-run effect of a supply shock on the price level and the PPP exchange rate is smaller. Furthermore, the absence of an inflation premium in the nominal interest rate implies smaller interest rate differentials, and attenuated short-run exchange rate volatility.

To summarize: When faced with supply shocks that entail a tradeoff between output and inflation stabilization, central banks can differ in their response to those shocks, and in the markets' response to them. Compared to the pure discretionary case, a 'conservative' monetary policy can stabilize inflation and the long-run nominal exchange rate, but at the expense of introducing greater short-term volatility into the nominal (and real) exchange rate. In the limiting 'inflation nutter' case (of no weight on output stabilization goals), inflation shocks have no long-run effect on inflation or even the nominal exchange rate, but maximum short-run effect on the volatility of the exchange rate. Following the OSCR through transparently anchoring inflation expectations, however, produces a more stable exchange rate in both the short- and long-run relative to a discretionary policy.

A functional measure of transparency in the G3 central banks

While the path to central bank conservatism is well known (and increasingly well trod), the means to the OSCR is less widely recognized. As asserted in King (1997), a transparent monetary policy – interpreted in practice as inflation targeting – grants the central bank the credibility and flexibility characterizing the OSCR. Transparency has become a central bank watchword in recent years, and it is not disingenuous to claim that most people know it when they see it practiced.[11] Designing a more objectively reproducible measure of monetary transparency, however, requires a bit more rigor in classification. Following the discussion in Posen (1999), it is possible to characterize the elements of monetary transparency as they relate to parts of the central bank's optimal control problem for monetary policy. In this view, a central bank has a preference (weighting losses over various macroeconomic goals), a model of the economy and of the effects of monetary policy (through an intermediate target) on that economy, a forecast of what will occur to the economy (with uncertain lags and shocks), and a record of what the monetary policy choice and the realization of shocks were last period. For the public and the markets, this means there are four potential areas of revelation for the central bank: its goal, its target, its forecast, and the outcome of its policies.

In theory, if the public and markets are given three or even two of these, and we assume markets have equivalent information to the central bank about the economy, and that the central bank engages in optimizing behavior, the remainder can be derived. In practice, however, such backwards induction is unlikely to be successfully undertaken, or fully trusted by those who undertake it. Thus, there is room for the central bank to disclose (make transparent) its views on each aspect of the control problem. For such transparency to work, the central bank has to not only announce these as numbers, but provide sufficient explanation to grant understanding of the numbers' significance.[12] So this gives us four potential disclosures with which, by whether or not they are provided, to evaluate central banks' transparency:

- a public numerical long-run goal for monetary policy;
- an *Inflation Report* or similar document describing the bank's model of the economy, estimate of the likely effect of monetary policy changes, and updates thereof;
- the central bank's forecast of the goal variable, including an explicit statement of the instrument setting underlying that forecast (e.g. unchanged interest rates);
- an *ex post* evaluation of what monetary policy moves were made in the past, what shocks were realized, and what outcome for the goal variable resulted.

These criteria make up what we will call *institutional transparency*. We do not create here an index of transparency, allowing for degrees of openness on each criterion and a means of aggregating them, like those indices for central bank independence.[13] Clearly, though, there is room for making some ordinal assessment on each criterion rather than just checking yes/no – a central bank can have a clear mandate for price stability, without a numerical target, and still be more transparent than a central bank with a mandate containing multiple competing goals;[14] a central bank can put greater or lesser emphasis on public explanation and consistency of presentation in its publications, rather than being limited to either simply printing backwards-looking numbers or giving a full *Inflation Report*-type of document.

Of course, in reality, even a fully transparent central bank with an explicit long-run goal is likely to have multiple policy goals in the short run. Responsible central banks will not follow a simple policy rule as in the idealized optimal control literature, especially when large shocks occur with some frequency. As argued in Kuttner and Posen (1999), the key issue for monetary transparency in a world of unexpected economic shocks is the ability to anchor expectations when policy deviates from its normal response to those shocks (e.g. where inflation is the long-run goal, for there to be limited pass-through to inflation expectations when the central bank accommodates an adverse supply shock).[15] In practical terms, when a central bank does something contrary to expectations, is that action acknowledged and explained to the public and to markets? We term the degree of commitment to this type of explanation *transparency in discretion*. To operationalize this measure, one can assess whether a central bank issues a public explanation when it deviates significantly from a reaction function (e.g. a 'Taylor rule') estimated on its past behavior, and whether it acknowledges that there was a conscious deviation from systematic policy.

It is likely that a central bank with high institutional transparency will have no choice but eventually to offer a great deal of transparency in discretion as well – otherwise, its forecast competence and/or its commitment to its goals would come into question. For central banks which do not have in place the full apparatus of institutional transparency, however, it is conceivable that they could still wish to maintain a reputation for systematically opposing certain outcomes (e.g. demand-driven increases in inflation), and so they might display transparency in discretion without much institutional transparency. Moreover, the fact that central banks would find it difficult to simultaneously be institutionally transparent and be opaque in discretion, that is, repeatedly deviate from systematic policy without explanation, does not imply that the resolution is immediate or in what manner the tension is likely to be resolved.[16] The relationship between accountability, independence, and transparency merits further research.[17] For purposes of this paper, we can and do distinguish between these two aspects of transparency in our empirical investigations, with changes in institutional transparency defining structural breaks in central bank behavior, and transparency in discretion relating to the market response to specific incidents in a central bank's timeline.

Applying these functional measurements of monetary transparency to the G3 central banks gives interesting results, though it should be noted that comparisons of institutional transparency 'levels' across countries are to a large degree judgmental on our ordinal scale (the sign of changes in institutional transparency within a country over time are easier to ascertain). Getting more than a broad sense of the degree of a central bank's transparency in discretion, however, is not possible without a baseline for that bank's systematic response function; initial estimates of those are given in our empirical work below.

The Bundesbank was extremely stable in institutional transparency over the period 1975–1998.[18] From the time of the first monetary target, the Bundesbank annually announced the inflation goal (usually, but importantly not always, 2 percent) which underlay its quantity equation derivation of the year's monetary targets. Moreover, on several occasions when meeting the monetary target would have come into conflict with meeting the inflation goal, the inflation goal was pursued first and was publicly acknowledged to have been. On the two occasions when inflation was deemed likely to diverge noticeably from the goal for an extended period – following the 1979 oil shock, and after German monetary unification in 1990 – the Bundesbank used its definition of 'price stability' to point to a public long-run target. In terms of reporting, the Bundesbank was consistent in producing a *Monthly Report* which amassed a great deal of information beyond simply tracking the monetary aggregates, along with explanatory articles about issues in the German economy. The *Report* gave general indications of the likely direction of monetary policy, as fiscal, external, and labor market developments unfolded, but did not ever give strict forecasts for inflation. The Bundesbank did, however, publish its model of the economy in complete but highly technical form. Finally, on the matter of *ex post* evaluation, the Bundesbank was scrupulously transparent, using the occasion of the annual setting of monetary growth targets to track not only how well it did in meeting those intermediate targets, but also in meeting the inflation goal, and explaining deviations from the targets in terms of specific shocks.

In terms of transparency in discretion, the Bundesbank's record is also consistent. To illustrate from the two major instances of potential inflationary pressures mentioned, in the episode of the second oil shock, the Bundesbank made clear that it would be more gradual than usual in disinflating, and even gave a path for the intended rate of deflation (moving its 'Unavoidable Rate of Inflation' up to 4 percent in 1980 and bringing it down slowly until declaring victory in 1986). In the instance of monetary unification, the Bundesbank made clear that it was primarily concerned with inflation pass-through, and had to essentially ignore initial money demand shocks, and (perhaps as a result) found that neither was as large as expected.

In the case of the Federal Reserve, measurement of institutional transparency shows an accelerating trend towards greater openness from 1975 through the present.[19] The Federal Reserve has never set a public numerical long-run goal for policy, but the recent trend has been towards greater clarity in objective setting. Moving away from its explicit pledge of loyalty to the potentially contradictory goals of its 1978 Humphrey-Hawkins mandate, the Fed signaled an increased emphasis on inflation by following money targets in the early 1980s. This emphasis was made more explicit in Chairman Greenspan's July 1988 Humphrey-Hawkins testimony (restated in February

1989), stating that the sole long-run goal of monetary policy should be price stability, and further clarified by the abandonment ('downgrading') of the M2 monetary aggregate in 1993 for the reason that it no longer tracked inflation. The point for institutional transparency is not the increasing emphasis on inflation *per se*, but the increasing clarity and consistency with which that emphasis was made, especially beginning in July 1988.

The Federal Reserve Board and the twelve Reserve Banks publish an abundance of materials, including research papers, the 'Beige Book' assessing regional economic developments, the 'Green Book' showing with a five-year lag the Board staff's national forecast, and the *Federal Reserve Bulletin*. Unlike an *Inflation Report*-type document, however, no publication exists to summarize the macroeconomic outlook guiding policy. The *Bulletin* consists mainly of retrospective numbers in great density; and the 'Green Book' forecasts cannot be interpreted either as policy goals, or as representing the consensus of the FOMC members – and in any case, the five-year publication lag renders the forecasts irrelevant for the evaluation of current policy. On this score, little has changed since the 1970s. Starting in February 1994, however, the FOMC began announcing changes in the Federal funds target, instead of requiring market participants to draw inferences from the Desk's open market operations. These announcements are also accompanied by a brief statement of the rationale for the move. While discount rate changes had always been announced with press releases, they too began to be accompanied by explanatory statements.

It is in terms of *ex post* evaluation of shocks and outcomes that the Federal Reserve remains least transparent. While the Chairman does report twice yearly to Congress ahead of the Humphrey-Hawkins hearings, and is in that sense formally accountable, policy's contribution to macroeconomic performance *vis à vis* that of exogenous shocks is not assessed. The lack of an explicit goal with which to benchmark performance makes such an assessment all the more difficult. Similarly, the Federal Reserve has often deviated from its 'normal' response to macroeconomic developments (specified, e.g., by a 'Taylor rule' or similar reaction function) without articulating the rationale for the deviation. In the aftermath of the October 1987 stock market crash, the Federal Reserve *did* make clear immediately what it would do and why; but other financial problems (e.g. the 'headwinds' of 1991–1993) were addressed without a clear statement of what was being tracked. The use of monetary targets from 1979–1985 has been widely recognized (both at the time, and even more clearly since) as a means of signaling a general commitment to disinflation, but the failure to follow them strictly (especially after the first three years or so) left the impression that considerable discretion remained.

The Bank of Japan pursued a 'money focused' monetary policy from 1975 to 1985 (see Cargill, Ito and Hutchison 1997, and Ueda 1997 for details). This meant pursuing a generally stable declining trend in broad money growth, with clear reference to this objective – although not to specific annual monetary targets, just quarterly 'forecasts' (starting in July 1978) – and explicit mention that the stability of the financial system was the other main pursuit of policy. During the period from the Plaza Accord in 1985 to the Louvre Accord in 1987, much the same approach was taken, except explicit target zones for the yen–dollar rate substituted for money growth. (Prior to that, it is difficult to discern a consistent major role for exchange rates in Japanese monetary policy, though there certainly were occasional interventions.) After April 1987, and the G-7 agreements at that time, monetary policy appears to have shifted between various goals, without a clearly articulated rationale for those shifts. For a time, the proximate and stated goals were domestic demand growth linked with a decline in the value of the dollar, but these were replaced by a focus on asset prices starting in June 1989, a shift which was confirmed by the incoming Bank of Japan (BoJ) Governor Mieno in December 1989. After the bubble burst, the BoJ gradually switched to a limited reflationary strategy, followed by direct efforts to keep the payment system afloat in 1996–1998.[20]

In terms of the second criterion for institutional transparency, the publication of a regularly updated description of the bank's model of the economy and estimates of the effect of monetary policy, the BoJ was similar to the Federal Reserve during the period examined. The BoJ did issue monthly reports of data on Japanese economic conditions, but stopped short of making specific forecasts. Changes in the monetary transmission mechanism were alluded to (e.g. that the collapse of the banking system in the 1990s undermined the effects of expansionary policy), but not quantified. There is no regular mechanism for reporting forecasts of macroeconomic variables such as inflation, and the goals and even their relative priority remain unspecified. *Ex post* evaluations were unstructured, and, unlike the Federal Reserve, there was no commitment to report to the Diet on its performance. This had some logic so long as the Ministry of Finance (MoF) officially controlled policy, but MoF representatives were not held publicly accountable on a regular basis for monetary performance either.

As indicated by the discussion of the shifting goals of Japanese monetary policy in the 1990s, transparency in discretion was somewhat lacking. Bernanke and Gertler (1999) and Jinushi, Kuroki, and Miyao (2000) both document several periods in which the BoJ diverged from the rather steady pattern of systematic policy established from 1975–1987. While the bank's activities in 1997 and 1998 to buy commercial paper, keep the discount rate low, and the like, were well and explicitly explained as responses to the financial crisis (as was the government's failure to respond until October 1998), other instances were less clear. In particular, the slow pace of easing policy from 1992–1995, and to a lesser degree the slow rise in interest rates in 1990–1991, were only clear in direction: the pace, intermediate target or path to the goal, and the assessment of the effects of shocks were left unspecified. This would lead one to expect increasing volatility in Japanese interest rate responses in the 1990s, which would in turn create additional exchange rate volatility.

Quantifying the macroeconomic sources of exchange rate volatility

It is worth beginning with an interesting stylized fact. The yen–dollar exchange rate has consistently shown significantly greater volatility than either of the other bilateral G3 exchange rates (see, e.g. Clarida 1999). On any standard explanation of exchange rate volatility, this is an anomaly. Macroeconomic differences between Japan and the United States, even if they were more unstable than those between Germany and the United States or Germany and Japan (which is by no means clear for the entire period), should not be the source of greater short-run volatility, given the literature's demonstrated unimportance of fundamentals. Both the United States and Japan had rising inflation in the 1970s, and declining inflation in the 1990s, relative to Germany's stable inflation rate, so the convergence on low inflation does not explain the pattern either. The market microstructures in terms of forex traders' incentives, information, liquidity, regulation, technology, and so on, which are usually considered the primary underlying cause of exchange rate volatility, are *identical* across the G3 bilateral rates; the same firms, if not precisely the same traders, are dealing in all three currencies simultaneously.

By taking monetary transparency into account, however, there seems to be a way of making sense of this pattern: as argued in the previous section, the Bundesbank consistently exhibited greater institutional transparency than either the Bank of Japan or the Federal Reserve since 1975. This would be consistent with there being smaller reactions of inflation expectations and interest rates to inflation surprises originating in the DM-zone. When one considers the additional fact that all three central banks pursued Tayloresque reaction functions over the 1975–1998 period (see Clarida, Galí and Gertler 2000), and that this relative ranking of bilateral average volatility even holds including German unification, the ERM crisis, and their aftermath, it is more striking that the one apparent difference in monetary practice – the expectation anchoring effects of transparency – is consistent with this pattern.[21]

This gives us two reasons for focusing our empirical investigations on the DM–yen and DM–dollar exchange rates (and not the yen–dollar): First, since the Bundesbank's institutional transparency is essentially invariant over the 1975–1998 time period, but both the Federal Reserve's and the BoJ's transparency shift markedly, this lets us track the effect of changes in transparency. Second, since it is the DM cross-rates which were the subject of less direct political pressure over the period, studying the DM rates makes it more difficult to ascribe the influence of changes in transparency to an additional (unmeasured in this paper) source of shocks.

Figure 13.1 displays two measures of exchange rate volatility since 1976 for the DM-bilateral rates. The solid line in each panel is the standard deviation (in percent) of monthly exchange rate changes, computed over a moving 24-month window. (The exchange rates are from the first business day of each month.) The dashed line is similar, but rather than weighting each observation equally within a fixed window, they decline geometrically and the sample expands: the weight on observation $t - i$ is 0.9^i, normalized so that the sum of the weights equals unity.

Both measures tell identical stories. The volatility of the DM–$ exchange rate has gradually declined by about one-quarter, from its peak of over 4 percent (standard deviation of monthly changes) to around 3 percent by 1994, where it has remained ever since. This is consistent with the measurement of increasing institutional transparency from Burns to Volcker to Greenspan, culminating in the additions to the Federal Reserve's institutional transparency in 1994. While the dollar has become more stable in recent years, the yen seems to have become quite a bit more volatile. From its peak near 5 percent in the late 1970s, the volatility of the DM–yen declined to a nadir of around 2 percent in 1989. It subsequently increased to 3 percent, and surged to over 5 percent in 1998 as the yen appreciated sharply. This is also consistent with the measurement of decreasing transparency by the BoJ since 1987, after the Louvre Accord, and the increasing uncertainty about the priorities of the bank in responding to the challenges of the 1990s.

Beyond the overall pattern, it is essential to ask to what extent these changes in exchange rate volatility have roots in domestic inflation and

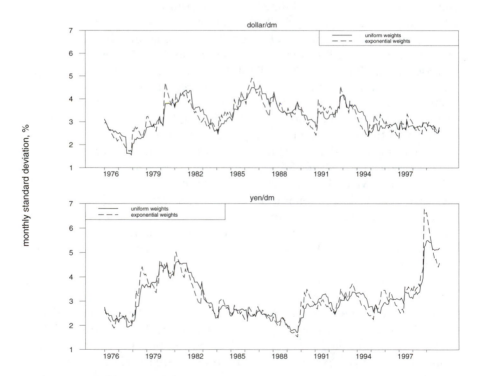

Figure 13.1 Exchange rate volatility.

interest rate surprises. These are the shocks whose prevalence and effects should relate to transparency, if transparency matters. If these shocks are important sources of volatility, the next question is whether the changes in the frequency and effect of these surprises sensibly track the trends in central bank transparency in detail, as they do in broad brush. Those are the questions we try to address in our econometric investigations of macroeconomic shocks and monetary policy as sources of exchange rate volatility.

Our main focus is on the effect of inflation shocks: how the exchange rate responds when inflation comes in higher than expected, taking systematic monetary policy response into account (and assuming that the markets and public do the same).[22] As discussed in the first section, for a more transparent central bank, the central bank's and the market's responses to an inflation shock should look more like the OSCR model, with lower inflation persistence, smaller inflation and exchange rate effects from a given inflation shock, and a smaller accompanying rise of interest rates. A second question is the extent to which fluctuations in relative interest rates unrelated to inflation differentials can account for exchange rate movements. The size of the interest rate response is a noisy measure of markets' trust in the central bank's long-run commitment to its goal (see Kuttner and Posen 1999). To answer both of these questions, it is useful to distinguish between inflation's long-run effect on the nominal exchange rate (via PPP), and its short-run effect from the interest rate differentials produced by the policy response to inflation.

The framework used for the analysis is a VAR involving the bilateral exchange rate (deutschemark versus dollar or yen), the inflation differential (US or Japanese CPI inflation relative to West German), and the interest rate differential (the Federal Reserve funds or Gensaki rates relative to the German repo rate). The exchange rate is entered as a log difference, and cointegration between the exchange rate and relative price levels is not imposed; consequently, the real exchange rate is not assumed to be stationary. To examine possible changes in the degree of monetary transparency and the hypothesized resulting changes in inflation dynamics, the model is estimated separately over two roughly equal periods, with the breakpoints in April 1987 for Japan and in July 1988 for the United States, as suggested by the institutional transparency changes discussed above.[23] For both pairs of countries, nine lags of monthly data from 1976 through 1998 are used in the estimation.[24]

Identifying the model and extracting well-defined inflation and interest rate 'shocks' requires three assumptions. One corresponds to a version of the PPP condition: inflation shocks are assumed to have no long-run effect on the real exchange rate, that is, that inflation shocks have the same effect on the price level differential and on the nominal exchange rate in the long run. The second restriction is that shocks to the interest rate differential also have no long-run effect on the real exchange rate. The third identifying assumption is simply that shocks to the interest rate differential have no contemporaneous (within the month) effect on the inflation differential.

Having specified the statistical model, there are two ways to draw out its implications for the behavior of the exchange rate. One is to invert the autoregression and compute the impulse response functions from the moving average representation in the usual way. This can be used to look for changes in the response of monetary policy and exchange rates to inflation shocks before and after break points in institutional transparency. By matching up the patterns of these shifts in impulse response functions with the predictions of our model in the first section, this is the first of our investigations.

This procedure, however, does not take advantage of the fact that the VAR can also be used to generate a forecast of future inflation and interest rate differentials which, according to purchasing power and uncovered interest rate parity, determine the exchange rate. The second procedure, then, is essentially to plug those forecasts into the solved-forward UIP relationship to determine the response of the exchange rate, constrained to satisfy the interest rate parity condition (and the homogeneity implied by PPP).[25] As a complement to these historical decompositions, we also estimate policy reaction functions to look for shifts in central bank preferences, and identify deviations from the central bank's systematic response to macroeconomic conditions. We report the results from both methods for each country, first for the United States, then for Japan, below.

United States

Figure 13.2 displays the basic data on the DM–$ bilateral rate, and the other components of the VAR. Looking at the bottom panel, the trend in the two countries' relative price levels matches up well with the general downward trend in the value of the dollar since 1972, indicating that our long-run restrictions are plausible. Figure 13.3 shows the estimated response of United States inflation, interest rates, and exchange rates to an inflation shock of 1 percent. As suggested by the discussion above, a plausible breakpoint for the analysis is July 1988, when Alan Greenspan's testimony signaled a heightened clarity of focus on price stability. The top left panel of Figure 13.3 shows that before 1988, the effects of shocks to the US/German inflation differential died out very gradually. These effects, cumulated over a period of years, had large implications for relative price levels. As shown in the next panel down, the interest rate differential did not, however, rise as much as inflation, resulting in a fall in the *real* rate in the United States, relative to Germany, after an inflation shock in the United States relative to Germany.

This apparently accommodative monetary policy response in the United States prior to July 1988, similar to that of the discretionary case in our model, is reflected in the behavior of the exchange rate, shown in the bottom left panel of Figure 13.3. The dotted line shows the nominal exchange rate movement corresponding to the inflation shock's long-run effect on relative prices, which in this case is roughly 0.4 percent lower. The dashed line shows the path of the exchange rate constrained to satisfy UIP; after falling sharply

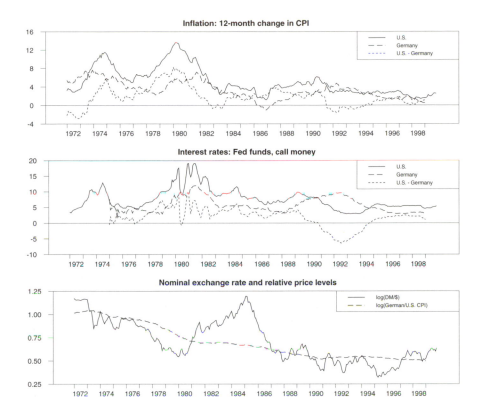

Figure 13.2 US and German data.

in the in the month of the shock, it declines gradually towards the level implied by PPP. The unconstrained response, given by the dashed line, falls by a comparable amount on impact, but it subsequently overshoots by about 0.3 percent before converging (by assumption) to its PPP level.

Things look very different after July 1988. As shown in the top right-hand panel, United States inflation shocks now die out immediately, and have virtually no implications for future inflation. The response of the interest rate differential is mild, showing only a very small increase in the real rate. And, as expected given the small response of relative price levels and interest rates, inflation shocks' effect on the exchange rate is minimal (and there is much less overshooting as well). This pattern of less pass-through of inflation shocks and lower persistence is consistent in terms of our model with a move by the Federal Reserve towards the OSCR through increasing transparency.

The top panel of Figure 13.4 shows how inflation shocks have contributed historically to fluctuations in the nominal DM–$ exchange rate. The July 1988 breakpoint is indicated by a vertical line. In the pre-1988 period, inflation shocks' contribution is large: in the unconstrained series shown as the

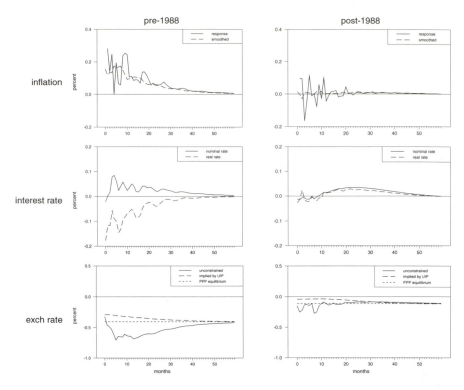

Figure 13.3 Response of interest rate and exchange rate to a 1 percent inflation shock, the US.

dashed line, a large share of the 1976–1980 depreciation and the 1980–1985 appreciation are attributable to inflation disturbances.[26] (As always, much of the 1980–1985 appreciation is *not* explained, however.) The dotted line shows the path of the exchange rate implied by inflation shocks' effect on expected future inflation and interest rate differentials, constrained to satisfy the UIP condition.[27] This shows the same qualitative pattern as the unconstrained series, albeit with a smaller magnitude. After 1988, neither method attributes any significant exchange rate variation to inflation shocks. This pattern is confirmed by the variance decompositions displayed in the top panel of Table 13.1. In the early part of the sample, interest rate shocks account for as much as 20 percent of the nominal exchange rate variance; after 1988, they contribute a trivial 3 percent of the variance. ('Own' shocks to the exchange rate account for nearly all of the exchange rate variation.)

The bottom panel of Figure 13.4 traces out the effects of fluctuations in the interest rate differential unrelated to inflation or exchange rate movements. These may represent either the normal policy response to macroeconomic factors not present in the VAR, or unsystematic deviations of policy from 'normal' behavior. The unconstrained decomposition, again shown as a dashed

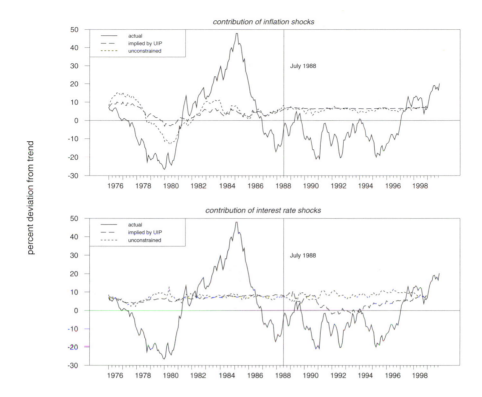

Figure 13.4 Contribution of inflation and interest rate shocks to nominal exchange
rate fluctuations, US.

line, attributes very little of the variation in the exchange rate to interest rate differentials, and this is confirmed by the variance decompositions in the top
panel of Table 13.1. The decomposition based on UIP, on the other hand,
associates a certain amount of the dollar's weakness to (predictably) lower
interest rates in the United States *vis-à-vis* Germany in the early 1990s.

To understand whether differences in these responses can be traced to the
behavior of monetary policy, it is useful to examine monetary policy reaction
functions, like those studied by Clarida, Galí and Gertler (2000). The top
panel of Table 13.2 presents forward- and backward-looking versions of a
reaction function for the United States, allowing for a change in the coefficients on inflation and output after July 1988. What is striking in these results
is the lack of any significant difference in terms of the relative weight on
output and inflation goals between the two periods. The inflation coefficient
(which is significant only in the forward-looking specification) is nearly
unchanged, and the coefficient on real output (detrended log industrial production) increases slightly.[28] Notice, however, that the standard error drops
markedly, perhaps indicating more systematic policy in the second period. In

Table 13.1 Decomposition of nominal exchange rate variance

United States

	Percent of nominal exchange rate variance attributed to					
	Pre-1988			Post-1988		
Horizon, months	*Inflation shocks*	*Interest rate shocks*	*Own shocks*	*Inflation shocks*	*Interest rate shocks*	*Own shocks*
1	14	6	79	2	0	98
6	20	1	79	3	3	96
12	17	1	82	2	2	96
120	8	0	92	1	2	97

Japan

	Percent of nominal exchange rate variance attributed to					
	Pre-1987			Post-1987		
Horizon, months	*Inflation shocks*	*Interest rate shocks*	*Own shocks*	*Inflation shocks*	*Interest rate shocks*	*Own shocks*
1	18	16	66	0	4	96
6	14	12	74	5	4	91
12	9	6	85	3	10	88
120	4	3	93	0	2	98

Note: Variance decompositions are calculated from the trivariate vector autoregression described in the text, unconstrained by the UIP condition.

any case, there is no evidence to suggest that the more subdued response of inflation and the nominal exchange rate to inflation shocks was obtained by an increase in conservatism. A decline in inflation persistence (an increase in the anchoring of inflation expectations) without a change in monetary policy goals is likely attributable to an increase in transparency – this is the potential additional degree of freedom for policymakers hypothesized about in our introduction.

Japan

As with the United States, Figure 13.5 displays the basic data used in the VAR. Unlike in the case of the dollar, the yen's appreciation against the deutschemark since 1980 appears largely unrelated to changes in the two countries' relative price levels. Figure 13.6 shows the response of inflation, interest rates, and the exchange rate to shocks to the Japanese–German inflation differential. The upper left-hand panel shows that prior to April

Table 13.2 Estimated monetary policy reaction functions

United States

Specification	r_{t-1}	Pre-1988		Post-1988		Change		Standard error	
		Inflation	IP	Inflation	IP	Inflation	IP	Pre-88	Post-88
Backward	0.94 (0.02)	0.03 (0.03)	3.95 (1.56)	0.07 (0.07)	2.34 (1.57)	0.04 (0.06)	-1.61 (2.35)	0.94	0.18
Forward	0.95 (0.02)	0.08 (0.02)	0.45 (1.55)	0.08 (0.05)	2.29 (0.96)	0.01 (0.12)	1.84 (1.06)	0.96	0.18

Japan

Specification	r_{t-1}	Pre-1988		Post-1988		Change		Standard error	
		Inflation	IP	Inflation	IP	Inflation	IP	Pre-88	Post-88
Backward	0.96 (0.01)	-0.03 (0.01)	5.84 (1.08)	0.08 (0.04)	0.35 (0.86)	0.11 (0.04)	-5.49 (1.36)	0.50	0.17
Forward	0.93 (0.03)	-0.02 (0.01)	5.50 (2.83)	0.20 (1.10)	-1.35 (1.02)	0.22 (0.10)	-6.85 (3.40)	0.47	0.19

Notes: Numbers in parentheses are standard errors connected for 11th-order serial correlation. The break date for the US is July 1988, and for Japan it is April 1987. Data are monthly. The dependent variable for Japan is the 3-month Gensaki rate, for Germany it is the overnight call money rate. IP is detrended log industrial production; for Japan, the trend is allowed to change in January 1990. The inflation regressor in the 'backward' specification is the lagged twelve-month inflation rate; in the 'forward' specification, which is estimated via 2SLS, the regressor is the inflation rate over the coming twelve months. The instruments for the 2SLS regression consist of lagged inflation, IP, and the interest rate, and the same variables interacted with the post-breakpoint dummy.

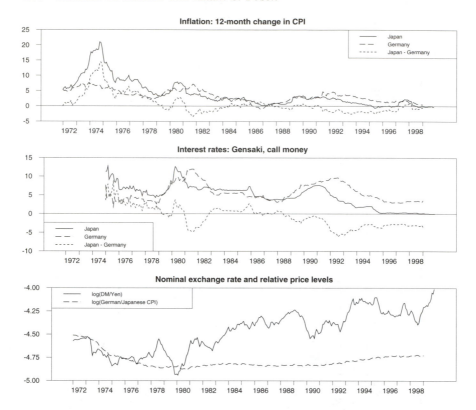

Figure 13.5 Japanese and German data.

1987, shocks to the inflation differential displayed a fair amount of persistence (albeit not as much as the persistence of shocks to the United States–German differential). Nominal interest rates responded relatively gradually (center-left panel), leading to a near-term decline in the real rate, followed by an increase after about six months. The unconstrained response of the nominal exchange rate (bottom-left panel) overshoots its PPP level somewhat, before appreciating; the path constrained by UIP shows an immediate decline followed by a further depreciation towards the PPP level.

As in the United States, there is much less persistence in the Japanese inflation differential after the breakpoint in the late-1980s; in fact, there is some tendency in the latter period for shocks to reverse themselves (top-right panel). In line with our model in the first section, this could be the result of either increased conservatism or transparency (movement towards the OSCR). Despite the more muted behavior of inflation, the response of nominal rates is broadly similar across the two periods: somewhat smaller in magnitude in the latter period, but more prolonged (center-right panel). The result is a more pronounced increase in the real rate post-April 1987, consistent with the movement towards conservatism in our model. The exchange

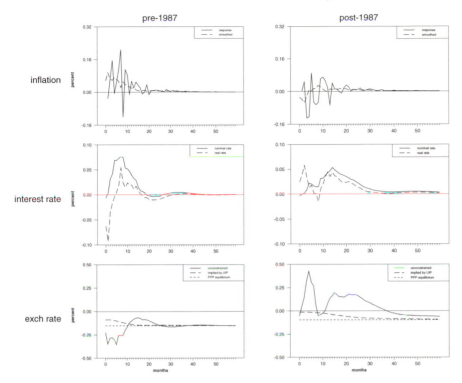

Figure 13.6 Response of interest rate and exchange rate to a 1 percent inflation shock, Japan.

rate path (lower-right panel) is just what one would expect in light of the more aggressive response to inflation: in the unconstrained estimate, the nominal exchange rate actually *appreciates* initially in the face of an inflation shock, before declining to the level implied by PPP. The path constrained by UIP does not show an appreciation, but the increase in interest rates staves off the depreciation for a period of several months. This is the sort of volatility tradeoff of short-term exchange rate volatility versus long-term inflation volatility predicted for an increase in conservatism by our model.

Turning to the historical decompositions, the top panel of Figure 13.7 displays the contribution of inflation shocks to nominal DM–yen exchange rate fluctuations. Only in the mid- to late-1970s do inflation shocks contribute tangibly to the yen's fluctuations, accounting for some of the yen's gradual downward trend prior to 1980. Except for this episode, Japanese and German inflation rates remained close to one another, so it is no surprise that shocks to the inflation differential should have played a small role. Nonetheless, as shown in the bottom panel of Table 13.1, overall inflation shocks did account for as much as 18 percent of the nominal exchange rate variance in the pre-April 1987 portion of the sample.

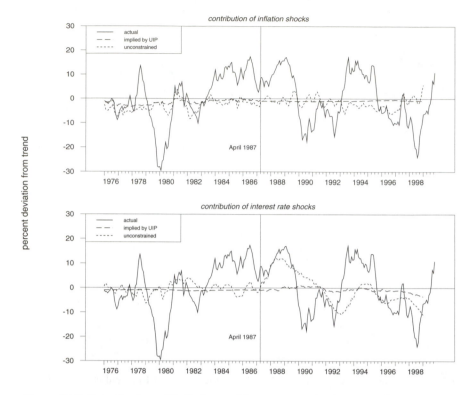

Figure 13.7 Contribution of inflation and interest rate shocks to nominal exchange rate fluctuations, Japan.

There is somewhat more variation in the interest rate differential, and shocks to it account for a surprising amount of the movements in the DM–yen exchange rate post-1987. In the unconstrained estimate, rising rates in the late 1980s are associated with a rising yen, and falling rates in the early 1990s with the yen's subsequent decline. As shown in Table 13.1, shocks to the interest rate differential account for 10 percent of the nominal exchange rate variance at a 12-month horizon.[29] In this latter portion of the sample, the exchange rate appears to be unusually sensitive to interest rate shocks: a 1 percent shock to the differential generates a peak response of over 6.5 percent – far in excess of the 1.3 percent or so that would be consistent with uncovered interest rate parity, given the shock's impact on future interest rate differentials. This sizable magnitude might be attributable to the decline in discretionary transparency, as BoJ monetary policy became less systematic in the face of the challenges of the 1990s; given the limited room for maneuver of the Japanese near-zero instrument interest rate, every monetary policy move was scrutinized for its uncertain implications for exchange rate levels.

Finally, to better understand the factors affecting Japanese interest rates, we examine an estimated reaction function for the Bank of Japan, displayed in the bottom panel of Table 13.2. The results confirm a distinct shift in the conduct of monetary policy in the late 1980s. Prior to 1987, the BOJ's emphasis seems to have been on real activity: the coefficient on detrended output is large and significant, while even in the forward-looking specification, the coefficient on inflation is small, and has the wrong sign. After 1987, the inflation coefficient is large (implying a two- or three-to-one response of the interest rate), and the coefficient on IP is insignificant.[30] Both coefficients' changes are statistically significant at the 5 percent level. In short, counter-inflationary conservatism markedly increased in Japanese monetary policy in the 1990s, and this added to short-run exchange rate volatility.

Would increased transparency meaningfully diminish G3 exchange volatility?

The premise of this paper's investigations was that differences in transparency of monetary policy within the G3 could explain part of the variation over time in short-run exchange rate volatility. As set out in the model in the first section, a central bank which increases its transparency of monetary policy making can be thought of as moving from discretion towards the OSCR, thereby better anchoring inflation expectations, and decreasing its need to be aggressive in response to inflation surprises. Working from a standard model of central bank goals under time-inconsistency, following Svensson (1997) and Kuttner and Posen (1999), but adding a short-run UIP condition, and long-run PPP, it becomes clear that movements from discretion towards the OSCR will diminish exchange rate volatility, while increases in conservatism (i.e. the relative weight on inflation goals) without compensating increases in transparency will increase that short-run volatility.

Using a measure of institutional transparency for central banks developed in the second section, it was established that the Bundesbank was consistently, and noticeably though not fully, transparent for the duration of its post-Bretton Woods lifetime (1975–1998). The Federal Reserve significantly increased transparency with a clarification of its goals in 1988, and showed a trend towards greater openness from that date forward, including the explicit abandonment of monetary targets in 1993 and the addition of explanations to interest rate announcements in 1994. The Bank of Japan moved in the opposite direction, cycling between multiple goals starting in 1987, with diminishing clarity over time.[31] These trends, and the stability of the Bundesbank's framework, allowed us to examine the behavior of DM–yen and DM–$ nominal exchange rates for evidence of transparencies impact in line with the predictions of the model.

Both in the broad and the specific, our investigations support the belief that monetary transparency matters for exchange rate volatility. Broadly speaking, this characterization of the G3 central banks' transparency provides a means of explaining the previously anomalous pattern that yen–$ exchange rate volatility was consistently higher than either of the deutschemark bilateral rates in the G3, despite one unified market for all three currencies. More specifically linking to the predictions of our model, the DM–$ exchange rate showed diminishing volatility over time in line with the increase in the Federal Reserve's transparency. Most tellingly, United States inflation persistence declined significantly after 1988, despite stability before and after 1988 in the relative weights on inflation and output goals in an estimated Federal Reserve response function. This is consistent with a view of the Federal Reserve as a central bank moving from discretion towards the OSCR through increasing transparency. Marked changes in the impulse response functions of inflation, interest rates, and exchange rates after 1988 in the United States also fit the picture of what should happen for a central bank moving towards the OSCR without an increase in conservatism.[32]

In the case of Japan, there is ample evidence of an increase in counter-inflationary conservatism – while inflation persistence declines after 1987, the weight on inflation goals in an estimated Taylor rule significantly increased, and the impulse response functions for interest rates, et al., look like those of a central bank moving towards being an 'inflation nutter' (in the sense of King 1997). Also, the volatility of the DM–yen exchange rate steadily rises from 1987 onwards, consistent with a more aggressive pursuit of price stability at the expense of short-run exchange rate volatility. The role of inflation shocks in explaining movements in the variation of exchange rates falls for both the BoJ and the Federal Reserve after their respective late-1980s breakpoint, but only in Japan is this accompanied by an increase in the explanatory power of interest rate shocks (their explanatory power declines for the DM–$ post 1988), again consistent with the interpretation of the Federal Reserve moving towards the OSCR while the BoJ moved toward greater conservatism.

So, in practice as well as in prospect, increasing monetary transparency does offer an additional degree of freedom with which the G3 central banks can address short-run exchange rate volatility. As exemplified by the shift in the Federal Reserve transparency after 1988, without an increase in conservatism – and the Federal Reserve and the markets' response to inflation surprises after that – it is not necessary to change a central bank's macroeconomic priorities in order to better anchor expectations, and thereby diminish exchange rate volatility. In fact, for reasonable parameter values, transparency enhancement is more likely to be win-win than increasing conservatism, decreasing both inflation persistence and forex volatility. As illustrated by the experience of the Bank of Japan after 1987, increasing conservatism is more likely to trade a drop in inflation persistence for an increase in exchange rate volatility. Transparency is independent of the 'impossible trinity' tradeoff usually cited as a reason for the inability or unwillingness of major central banks to respond to volatility, as well as of the 'fundamentals' which do not determine exchange rates (except to the extent that increased transparency improves inflation performance).

The magnitude of the impact of increased monetary transparency on G3 exchange rate volatility, however, remains open to question. There is no quantitative, cardinal, metric for transparency, and so no way of knowing how much stability is bought for a given increase. In the case of the United States, while there is certainly room for additional clarity, given the marked increases in the Federal Reserve's institutional transparency in 1988 and 1993–1994, it is not evident how much the additional efforts will 'buy' in terms of exchange rate stability. If the entire decline in DM–$ volatility after 1988 were to be attributed to the Fed's increase in transparency – a binding but not outrageous upper-bound – over 1 percent of the initial 4 percent monthly standard deviation of would have been taken away by the efforts. A similar attribution for the rise in DM–yen volatility gives an upper bound of over 2 percent, but given the Japanese economic crisis, it is much less credible that the only major shift in policy or forex environment was the shift in BoJ transparency and preferences. Taking only half that amount as the effect of transparency, however, puts us back at the same estimate as that for the DM–$. The average amount by which the yen–$ volatility exceeds either of the deutschemark bilateral rates – which could be interpreted largely as the Bundesbank's relative transparency bonus, since there are no significant differences from the other two central banks in central bank independence or in monetary response functions for much of the period, let alone in structure of the foreign exchange markets – is also of a similar order of magnitude.

If these ballpark but consistent estimates of the benefits of transparency were correct, that would still leave more than two-thirds of the present monthly volatility, which would still swamp (and be unrelated to) the movement in underlying macroeconomic fundamentals. The problem of G3 exchange rate volatility would not go away, nor should it so long as financial markets' microstructure is the source of it (see Rogoff 1999). Yet, assuming that part of the dislike for exchange rate volatility is generated by its extreme magnitudes, removing 20–30 percent of it would be significant for emerging markets and international businesses – especially since the means for so doing, increasing monetary transparency, increases political legitimacy without economic cost, and adds potentially significant economic benefits (such as diminished inflation persistence and pass-through).

Meanwhile, were all three of the G3 central banks to maximize their institutional transparency, say by moving to explicit inflation targeting frameworks in today's believed best practice for openness, there is likely to be even greater demand for transparency in discretion. The major central banks' explanations of deviations from systematic policy would no longer be compared against just their own published goals, forecasts, and explanations, but also those of their peers. While this framework thankfully would not constitute a fixed rule, such an institutionalization of transparency would seem to bode well for more disciplined, better understood, monetary policy. This disciplining of discretion might in turn imply still further decreases in exchange rate volatility beyond those to be expected from each of the G3 central banks becoming more transparent on their own.

Acknowledgements

This paper is reprinted with permission of the Institute for International Economics, USA. Copyright 2000.

Notes

1 This result began to be established with the seminal paper of Meese and Rogoff (1983); later work extending and confirming this result includes Baxter and Stockman (1989), Flood and Rose (1995), and Flood and Rose (1999). Note that this characterization applies to *short-term* volatility between the G3 currencies – evidence exists that medium-to-long-term trends in these exchange rates, and even the short-run volatility of exchange rates for high-inflation countries, do correspond to a significant degree to macroeconomic fundamentals.
2 'Misalignments' might be characterized as resulting from exchange rate movements not warranted by changes in the underlying macroeconomic fundamentals. The analysis in this paper does not emphasize this distinction, however, but focuses on exchange rate volatility broadly defined.
3 Volcker (1998) and Williamson (1998) are two recent well-argued examples.
4 Of course, a policy intervention could also be targeted at the micro-level, in terms of regulating exchange market behavior, but few of these proposals tend to go in that direction. Moreover, the number of viable proposals for governments to effectively and beneficially regulate exchange rate trading appears for the moment to be limited.
5 See Krugman (1998) or Clarida (1999) for a review of the 'impossible trinity' assessment.
6 There is no reason for an exchange rate commitment to come under attack when the move required to support the peg is in the same direction as intended monetary policy, e.g. when inflation is rising and the currency is under stress, an interest rate rise is credible. It is when the economy is slowing and the currency is going to the weak edge of the zone (e.g. UK or Sweden in fall 1992) that the peg comes under attack, and the attack itself generally worsens the conflict between goals.
7 See King (1997), Laubach and Posen (1997), Bernanke, et al. (1999), and Kuttner and Posen (1999) for a combination of theoretical, historical, and econometric arguments to this effect.
8 Clarida and Galí (1994) and Eichenbaum and Evans (1995), among others, also assess various shocks' contributions to exchange rate fluctuations. Their focus, however, is on the contribution of unsystematic monetary policy shocks, while ours is on inflation shocks, and the effects of policy's systematic response to those shocks.
9 This model modifies Kuttner and Posen's (1999) application of Svensson (1997) by replacing the long-term interest rate and bond market with long-run PPP and an uncovered interest-rate parity (UIP) condition.
10 For the same set of parameters, b^*, the OSCR-following central bank's response to the shock, will be less than the b under discretion, an effect referred to as 'stabilization bias'. See Svensson (1997).

11 Arguments for the benefits of transparency, in terms of movement towards the OSCR and therefore to a better outcome of the central bank's time-inconsistency dilemma on average and in response to supply shocks, are given in the preceding section and in Kuttner and Posen (1999). For broader discussions of the merits of transparency, in terms of democratic legitimacy, reduced market uncertainty, and improved central bank behavior, see *inter alia* King (1997), Blinder (1998), and Bernanke et al. (1999).

12 As Friedman (1997) states, 'Central bank purchases and sales of securities, the resulting changes in bank reserves, and fluctuations in the relevant short-term interest rate are all known data not long after the fact. But few central banks make clear – genuinely clear – just why they have chosen the actions they have taken.' Similarly, Bomfim and Reinhart (2000) distinguish between announcements of monetary policy decisions in general and those which explain as well why the move was made.

13 We are currently at work on creating such an index for the major OECD central banks in recent decades, and exploring its explanatory power for different countries' proclivities to inflation scares (*à la* Goodfriend (1983)) and to overreact to monetary accommodation of shocks.

14 See Svensson's (2000) discussion of the mandate and goal of the European Central Bank as an example of just this kind of assessment.

15 Our working assumption is that transparency enhances flexibility, in the sense that a central bank which explains its deviations from its pattern is better able to get away with exercising discretion, and Kuttner and Posen (1999) provide some evidence to this effect. Faust and Svensson (1998) address much the same issue and definition of transparency from a theoretical perspective – 'Increased transparency (smaller unobserved noise) improves the precision of private sector inference about central bank goals, and makes the bank's reputation and the private sector's inflation expectations more consistent' – and come to the opposite conclusion. We intend to employ our (in progress) index of transparency to test this empirically.

16 As we will argue later, this is relevant for the Bank of Japan in the 1990s, which increased its institutional transparency with the passage of the new Bank of Japan Law in 1998, but repeatedly deviated from systematic policy without explanation in the face of shocks.

17 One paper which begins to tackle these issues is Briault, Haldane and King (1997). In that paper, the authors create an index of central bank accountability, and establish a negative relationship between that index and goal independence for central banks. Their index combines measures of legal accountability and transparency, only one of which is in common with our criteria (publication of an inflation report). We prefer to focus solely on transparency as the direct means of accountability to the public and markets; see also Kohn's (1997) and Koenig's (1997) discussions of that index.

18 Laubach and Posen (1997) go through the Bundesbank's institutional framework in detail. Neumann (1997) comes to many of the same conclusions in more summary form.

19 This paragraph draws on Blinder (1998), Friedman (1997), Bomfim and Reinhart (2000), and the authors' own reading of Federal Reserve Chairman's testimony before Congress.

20 See Bernanke and Gertler (1999) and Jinushi, Kuroki and Miyao (2000) for detailed assessments of the changes in, and unsystematic behavior of, Bank of Japan monetary policy in the 1990s. Starting in January 1998, essentially beyond the end of our data set for this paper's analyses, the Bank of Japan did increase its institutional transparency in line with its impending independence. Despite a

clarification of mandate – to price stability in the long run, with concern for financial stability as required – and new efforts to release minutes and other information, a lack of transparency in discretion has beset Japanese monetary policy since mid-1998. See Mikitani and Posen, eds, (2000) for details.

21 Laubach and Posen (1997) discuss the ability of the Bundesbank to anchor expectations even during reunification and the German monetary unification which followed.

22 Which means that the emphasis here is on the systematic component of monetary policy, rather than on monetary policy 'shocks' as in Eichenbaum and Evans (1995) or Faust and Rogers (2000).

23 It is possible to argue for breaks in transparency for the BoJ in June 1989 (when interest rates began to rise to prick the bubble), and for the Federal Reserve in February 1989 (when Greenspan reiterated his definition of the price-stability goal in congressional hearings, and this was picked up by the major press), rather than these dates. As one would expect, this makes little difference to the results, especially for the US, and the break points used in our investigations are statistically significant as they are.

24 Estimation ends in 1998 to avoid any possible break associated with Germany's adoption of the euro in 1999.

25 The restrictions implied by UIP are testable, although we do not perform those tests here. In Clarida and Galí (1994), the restrictions are rejected.

26 This is just the standard historical decomposition of the nominal exchange rate in terms of past inflation shocks; see Doan (1992): 14–116.

27 This series is related to a multivariate Beveridge–Nelson decomposition.

28 The results in Clarida et al.'s own investigations suggest that the inflation coefficient would probably be smaller in the 1976–79 portion of the sample, however.

29 The share peaks at 14 percent at the 24-month horizon. Shocks to the interest rate differential actually contribute slightly more to the nominal exchange rate variance pre-1987 at the shorter 1–6 month horizon, presumably due to the high-frequency volatility of short-term interest rates.

30 Jinushi, Kuroki, and Miyao (2000) find a similarly timed break in the BoJ's response function in 1987, and a similar move towards more strict pursuit of inflation goals.

31 The new Bank of Japan Act of 1998, and the BoJ's preparations for operational independence, did increase institutional dependency on two of our four criteria, but this takes place at the very end of our sample period (and arguably was accompanied by a decrease in transparency in discretion).

32 Future work using Monte Carlo methods will give us standard error bands on the impulse response functions, allowing us to assess whether these changes are statistically significant.

References

Baxter, Marianne and Alan Stockman. 1989. Business Cycles and the Exchange-Rate System, *Journal of Monetary Economics*, 23, 377–400.

Bernanke, Ben. 2000. Japanese Monetary Policy: A Case of Self-Induced Paralysis?, in Mikitani and Posen, eds., *The Japanese Financial Crisis and its Parallels with US Experience*. Washington, DC: Institute for International Economics.

Bernanke, Ben et al. 1999. *Inflation Targeting: Lessons from the International Experience*. Princeton, NJ: Princeton University Press.

Bernanke, Ben and Mark Gertler. 1999. Monetary Policy and Asset Price Volatility. In

New Challenges for Monetary Policy. Kansas City, MO: Federal Reserve Bank of Kansas City.

Blinder, Alan. 1998. *Central Banking in Theory and Practice*, Cambridge: MIT Press.

Bomfim, Antulio and Vincent Reinhart. 2000. Making News: Financial Market Effects of Federal Reserve Disclosure Practices, mimeo, Federal Reserve Board.

Briault, Clive, Andrew Haldane and Mervyn King. 1997. Independence and Accountability,' in Kuroda, ed., *Towards More Effective Monetary Policy*. New York: St. Martin's Press.

Cargill, Thomas, Takatoshi Ito and Michael Hutchison. 1997. *The Political Economy of Japanese Monetary Policy*, Cambridge: MIT Press.

Clarida, Richard. 1999. *G3 Exchange Rate Relationships: A Recap of the Record and a Review of Proposals for Change*. NBER Working Paper 7434, December.

Clarida, Richard and Jordi Galí. 1994. Sources of real exchange-rate fluctuations: How important are nominal shocks? *Carnegie-Rochester Conference Volume on Public Policy* 41, 1–56.

Clarida, Richard, Jordi Galí and Mark Gertler. 2000. Monetary Policy Rules and Macroeconomic Stability: Evidence and Some Theory, *Quarterly Journal of Economics* 115 (1), 147–180.

Doan, Thomas. 1992. *Rats User's Manual version 4*, Evanston: Estima.

Eichenbaum, Martin and Charles Evans. 1995. Some Empirical Evidence on the Effects of Shocks to monetary Policy on Exchange Rates, *Quarterly Journal of Economics* 110, 975–1010.

Faust, Jon and John Rogers. 2000. Monetary Policy's Role in Exchange Rate Behavior, mimeo, Board of Governors of the Federal Reserve System.

Flood, Robert and Andrew Rose. 1995. Fixing Exchange Rates: A Virtual Quest for Fundamentals, *Journal of Monetary Economics*, 36, 3–37.

Flood, Robert and Andrew Rose. 1999. Understanding Exchange Rate Volatility Without the Contrivance of Macroeconomics, *Economic Journal*, 109, F660–72.

Frankel, Jeffrey and Andrew Rose. 1995. Empricial Research on Nominal Exchange Rates, *Handbook of International Economics*, Volume 3, Amsterdam: Elsevier.

Friedman, Benjamin. 1997. 'The Rise and Fall of Monetary Targets for US Monetary Policy, in Kuroda, ed., *Towards More Effective Monetary Policy*. New York: St. Martin's Press.

Friedman, Milton. 1953. The Case for Flexible Exchange Rates, *Essays in Positive Economics*. Chicago: University of Chicago Press.

Goodfriend, Marvin, 1983. Interest Policy and the Inflation Scare Problem: 1979–1992. *Federal Reserve Bank of Richmond Economic Quarterly* 79, 1–24.

Jinushi, Toshiki, Yoshihiro Kuroki and Ryuzo Miyao. 2000. Monetary Policy in Japan Since the Late 1980s: Delayed Policy Actions and Some Explanations, in Mikitani and Posen, eds, *The Japanese Financial Crisis and its Parallels With U.S. Experience*. Washington, DC: Institute for International Economics.

Johnson, Harry, 1973. The Case for Flexible Exchange Rates, 1969, *Further Essays in Monetary Economics*. Cambridge: Harvard University Press.

King, Mervyn. 1997. Changes in UK Monetary Policy: Rules and Discretion in Practice, *Journal of Monetary Economics* 39, 81–87.

Kohn, Donald. 1997. Comment on Briault et al., in Iwao Kuroda, ed., *Towards More Effective Monetary Policy*. New York: St. Martin's Press.

Koenig, Reiner. 1997. Comment on Briault et al., in Iwao Kuroda, ed., *Towards More Effective Monetary Policy*. New York: St. Martin's Press.

Krugman, Paul. 1998. The Eternal Triangle, mimeo, MIT.

Kuroda, Iwao, ed. 1997. *Towards More Effective Monetary Policy*, New York: St. Martin's Press.

Kuttner, Kenneth N. and Adam S. Posen. 1999. *Does Talk Matter After All? Inflation Targeting and Central Bank Behavior*. Federal Reserve Bank of New York Staff Report 88.

Laubach, Thomas and Adam Posen. 1997. 'Disciplined Discretion: Monetary Targeting in Germany and Switzerland,' *Princeton Essays in International Finance*, December.

Meese, Richard and Kenneth Rogoff. 1983. Empirical Exchange Rate Models of the Seventies: Do They Fit Out of Sample?, *Journal of International Economics*, 14, 3–24.

Mikitani, Ryoichi and Adam Posen, eds. 2000. *The Japanese Financial Crisis and Its Parallels With U.S. Experience*, Washington, DC: Institute for International Economics.

Neumann, Manfred J. M. 1997. Monetary Targeting in Germany. In Kuroda, ed., *Towards More Effective Monetary Policy*. New York: St. Martin's Press.

Obstfeld, Maurice and Kenneth Rogoff. 1995. The Mirage of Fixed Exchange Rates, *Journal of Economic Perspectives*, 9, 33–96.

Posen, Adam. 1999. No Monetary Masquerades for the ECB. In *The European Central Bank: How Accountable? How Decentralized?*, ed. Ellen Meade. American Institute for Contemporary German Studies.

Rogoff, Kenneth. 1999. Monetary Models of Dollar/Yen/Euro Nominal Exchange Rates: Dead or Undead? *Economic Journal*, 109, 655–59.

Svensson, Lars. 1997. Optimal Inflation Contracts, 'Conservative' Central Banks, and Linear Inflation Contracts, *American Economic Review* 87, 98–114.

Ueda, Kazuo. 1997. Japanese Monetary Policy, Rules or Discretion? A Reconsideration. In Kuroda, ed. *Towards More Effective Monetary Policy*. New York: St. Martin's Press.

Volcker, Paul. 1995. The Quest for Exchange Rate Stability, mimeo, Washington DC, Institute for International Economics.

Williamson, John. 1998. Crawling Bands or Monitoring Bands, *International Finance*, 1, 59–79.

14 Challenges to the structure of financial supervision in the EU*[1]

Karel Lannoo

Introduction

A debate on the most appropriate structure for financial supervision has been initiated in Europe. The reasons are manifold and relate not only to the transfer of monetary policy-making powers to the ECB and the role this institution will play in financial supervision, which is a national responsibility at present anyway. In several member states, financial conglomerates have become the dominant players, posing a challenge to supervisors of all disciplines in the exercise of effective control. At the same time, financial products have become increasingly complex, combining features of different disciplines, whose supervision requires new and enhanced skills. Against this background, the traditional functional division of financial sector supervision looks increasingly outdated.

Other problems are emerging as a result of increased market integration, which has been stimulated by EMU and the establishment of the single market. European financial market liberalisation is based on the principle of home country prudential control. Strictly speaking, the increasing size and scope of large cross-border financial groups should not affect this rule, but it is debatable how far this principle can continue to be applicable. The demand will also grow for further rationalisation and standardisation of the methods of supervision, to simplify pan-European operations and to reduce their costs. European groups that are active in different member states today face multiple reporting requirements, supervisory techniques and hence costs. If cross-border financial sector consolidation is to be encouraged in Europe, this issue will need to be tackled as well.

Efforts to introduce reforms at national level have, to varying extents, led to more horizontal or cross-sectoral approaches in financial supervision. At the extreme end, some states have merged the different areas of financial sector supervision within a single authority, thereby introducing a radical supervisory redesign based on the objectives of supervision, while others have

* Paper presented at 22nd SUERF Colloquium, Vienna, 27–29 April 2000.

provided for structures of cross-sectoral supervisory cooperation of varying degrees of formality.

The purpose of this paper is to extend this discussion to the European level and to examine what changes are required to bring about an integrated financial market. There is clearly an awareness that things need to be adapted at European level, as reflected in the European Commission's Financial Services Action Plan as well as in statements by various regulators and by members of the ECB. But the debate has only begun.

We start in Section I with an analysis of the changes that have taken place in the European financial system. The second section examines the institutional structure of financial supervision at the national level. Section III discusses the European angle of this design, the current provisions, the role of the ECB, and the required changes in the institutional structure to accommodate growing market integration.

I The European financial system in evolution

Europe's financial system remains firmly based on banking institutions. Banks play a much more dominant role in Europe than they do in the US, where bond and equity markets are more developed. The asymmetry between the two systems results largely from different regulatory preferences: Europe adopted universal banking as its model, whereas the US financial system was defined by the 1933 Glass-Steagall Act, which separated commercial from investment banking. The US regime stimulated tough competition between intermediaries and provided the environment in which capital market financing, specialisation and innovation flourished. Under the EU's single market rules, banks are allowed to combine their commercial and investment banking activities under a single roof, which further stimulates bank financing.

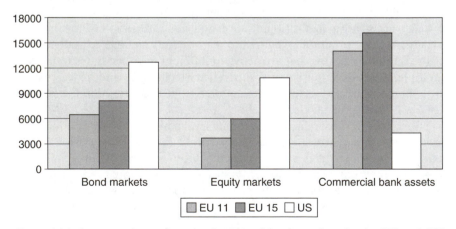

Figure 14.1 A comparison of equity, bond and bank markets in the US and EU. Total assets in euro bn (1998, except for bank assets 1997).

European financial market liberalisation and the creation of the single market started a process of restructuring and scale enlargement in European banking, which is being further advanced by EMU. The number of banks is falling and concentration is increasing. The total assets of EU-based banks continue to grow. They went up from 177% of GDP in 1985 to reach 215% of GDP in 1997 (OECD, 1999). Total assets of US commercial banks remained stable and stood at 57% of GDP in 1997. During the same period, securitisation increased dramatically in the US, but only very moderately in Europe (BIS, *Quarterly Review,* June 1999).

At the same time, a tendency towards conglomeration started in European finance. In contrast to the US, where the 1965 Bank Holding Company Act restricted links between banks and non-bank financial corporations, no such limitations are in place in Europe. Although bank and insurance companies need to be separately incorporated, nothing prohibits their falling under the control of a single holding company. Data on mergers and acquisitions in financial services in the US and Europe document this process (see Table 14.1). In Europe, close to one-third of all deals (29.7%, and 7% bank-insurance) in the financial services sector in the period 1985–99 were cross-sector, whereas this was 17% in the US (and 7.0% for bank-insurance). The US figure is heavily influenced by the Citicorp-Travellers merger, as suggested by the fact that it was 15.4% for the period 1985–97 (and only 0.2% for bank-insurance). Mergers and acquisitions among banks in the same period represent close to half of all financial sector deals in the US, compared to 36.2% in Europe.

There are, however, important cross-country variations. In smaller European countries, such as the Benelux, conglomerates have become the dominant financial services providers, whereas in France and Germany, specialisation has prevailed. The latter was probably also due to limited foreign entry in both countries' markets.

The strong contrast between the EU and the US financial systems may diminish in the years ahead. In the EU, the start of EMU signalled a shift towards more direct capital market financing, with a strong growth of the corporate and other non-government bond markets. The corporate bond market has grown by a factor of 2.5 in the first year of EMU. Several countries enacted legislation to allow a mortgage bond market to emerge. In the US, the segmentation of the financial sector may become definitively repealed. The Gramm-Leach-Bliley Act (1999) lifts restrictions on US-based financial institutions to work as financial conglomerates if they are licensed as a Financial Holding Company (FHC). Some 117 institutions have applied for FHC status in the US at the time of writing.

At product level, financial institutions have responded to growing competition through the introduction of new products and services and diversification of the product range. Combined bank-securities, bank-insurance, insurance-securities and even bank-securities-insurance products are offered on the market by a single firm. The sector-specific characteristics

Table 14.1 Mergers and acquisitions in the financial services sector, 1985–99 (total value, billions of $)

Domestic

M&As	US				Europe			
	Bank	Securities	Insurance	Total	Bank	Securities	Insurance	Total
Bank	475	24	0.3	499.3	229	15	22	266
Securities	6	111	32	149	55	40	41	136
Insurance	73	16	153	242	14	10	74	98
Total	554	151	185.3	**890.3**	298	65	137	**500**
Cross-sector as % of total				*17.0*				*31.4*
Bank-insurance as % of total				*8.2*				*7.2*

Cross-border M&As

	US–non-US				Intra-Europe				Europe–non-Europe			
	Bank	Securities	Insurance	Total	Bank	Securities	Insurance	Total	Bank	Securities	Insurance	Total
Bank	32.1	7.4	0.2	39.7	37.6	6.7	0.4	44.7	39	6.8	1	46.8
Securities	5.7	25.2	6	36.9	8.8	17	1.9	27.7	19.6	19.6	22.2	61.4
Insurance	0.6	4.1	62.6	67.3	20.2	1.5	79.4	101.1	1.1	3.8	57.9	62.8
Total	38.4	36.7	68.8	**143.9**	66.6	25.2	81.7	**173.5**	59.7	30.2	81.1	**171**
Cross-sector as % of total				*16.7*				*22.8*				*31.9*
Bank-insurance as % of total				*0.6*				*11.9*				*1.2*

Table 14.1 cont.

Total M&As in financial services

	Total US acquirers				Total Europe acquirers			
	Bank	Securities	Insurance	Total	Bank	Securities	Insurance	Total
Bank	507.1	31.4	0.5	539	305.6	28.5	23.4	357.5
Securities	11.7	136.2	38	185.9	83.4	76.6	65.1	225.1
Insurance	73.6	20.1	215.6	309.3	35.3	15.3	211.3	261.9
Total	592.4	187.7	254.1	**1034.2**	424.3	120.4	299.8	**844.5**
Cross-sector as % of total				17.0				29.7
Bank-insurance as % of total				7.2				7.0
Bank-bank as % of total				49.0				36.2
Insurance-insurance as % of total				20.8				25.0

Note: The figures reported are the sum of equity values of the target institutions.

Source: Data kindly provided by Ingo Walter, Director of New York University Salomon Center, based on figures compiled by Thomson Financial Securities Data Company.

of such products are irrelevant for consumers; they only wish to see that the same level of consumer protection and similar conduct-of-business rules are applied to each product. This development has rendered the job of financial supervisors more difficult.

Although one could initially find no support in the economies of scope and scale literature for this process of financial sector consolidation, recent research has found a higher degree of cost efficiency in universal banks and conglomerates as compared to more specialised banks. De-specialisation may lead to more efficient financial systems (Vander Vennet, 1998). Also technological progress has affected efficient bank size, by allowing management to keep growing business under control. Recent research also showed that the overall cost savings of IT investments increased with the size of the bank (Molyneux, 1997). Others have demonstrated that the overall profitability of large banks is higher than that of small banks, with about twice as many small banks (weighted average) being non-profit-making as compared to large banks. This difference is even larger in the US (Inzerillo et al., 2000). Financial sector consolidation can thus be expected to continue.

Financial market liberalisation has hardened competitive conditions for European banking. On an aggregate basis, the performance of European banking did not change up to 1997 (the last year for which comparative figures are available), and it was low compared to that of US commercial banks. In certain countries, probably those that previously had the most protected markets, performance levels actually declined. Return on assets of all European banks, measured as profit before taxes as a percentage of total assets, stood at about 0.50% annually for the period 1995–97, as compared to 1.83% for the US commercial banks (OECD, 1999). Banks in some countries have consistently performed much better than the EU average, such as those based in the UK, but for others, such as French and Italian banks, the situation has been well below average, with a return on assets of 0.31% in 1997.

EMU should lead to a greater degree of financial market inter-penetration, which has been limited so far. The disappearance of the constraints of currency-matching rules and the prominence of European-wide bond and equity indexes should stimulate European banks and institutional investors to start to spread assets at a euro-wide level. Also cross-border banking penetration should grow. In 1997, the market share of foreign branches and subsidiaries exceeded 10% in only five EU countries: in declining order of proportion, if not absolute size, Luxembourg, Ireland, the UK, Belgium and Greece (ECB, 1999). By the end of December 1999, only 8.7% of the total loans of financial institutions in the eurozone were cross-border (ECB, 2000).

In sum, monetary union involves the continuation of a process of financial market liberalisation in Europe that is starting to acquire more European-wide dimensions. Three issues are important for supervisors in redesigning the supervisory framework at European level:

1 The Europeanisation of financial markets and the emergence of Europe as a whole as the home market.
2 The changes that EMU is bringing about in the largely bank-based European financial system.
3 The trend towards conglomeration.

Europeanisation of financial markets may reduce the grip that supervisors have had in a national context on institutions under their supervision and may increase the possibility for regulatory arbitrage. While regulatory competition is in itself not a problem, as long as the minimum standards are sufficiently high, the question emerges whether the structure of supervisory cooperation is sufficiently developed to cope with stronger cross-border market integration, or whether supervisors will continue to seek to favour the national public interest.

The trend towards more market-based finance may ease the job of supervisors, since it should strengthen market discipline in European finance. Other elements of the regulatory set-up and the attitude of market actors will need to move in parallel, however, in order to increase the transparency of the financial system. This relates to accounting standards, reporting systems and corporate governance mechanisms.

The trend towards conglomeration is an additional challenge for supervisors. While conglomeration may increase cost efficiency and diversifies the risk for financial groups, the task of supervision does not become easier. With entities separately authorised and controlled, supervisory authorities risk being unaware of the overall risk profile of the group. The risks at group level are not necessarily the same as the sum of the risks of the different entities of the group: the group might have large exposures that are not readily apparent at the single entity level. Risks in the different parts of the business are simply aggregated and less transparent, which may also reduce market discipline. The danger of double-gearing of capital or uncontrolled intra-group transactions to cover losses in one entity with gains from another also arises. Finally, a loss of confidence in one part of the group can affect the whole business, and thus increase volatility (Danthine et al., 1999). In the following section, we discuss how some countries have tackled this problem by adapting the institutional structure of financial supervision. We first look at the changes taking place at national level, and then move to the European dimension.

II The structure of financial supervision

The single financial market programme was a process of financial reregulation in the EU. National regulation was redrafted on the basis of European benchmarks, set forward in directives. This did not, at least directly, affect the structure of financial supervision at local level. Nothing in EU financial services law currently prescribes how financial supervision should be organised.

Member states are simply required to ensure that the sectors covered are adequately supervised and that basic minimum requirements (own funds, large exposures) are observed.

Traditionally, the structure of financial supervision was based on the functional divisions in the financial services sector and the perceived differences in risk profiles. Supervision in banking has typically had a higher profile than that in insurance, because of the systemic element and hence the close involvement of the central bank. Securities market supervision was until recently largely based on sectoral self-regulation, but internationalisation of markets and European harmonisation of securities regulation have forced many member states to create securities supervisory bodies.

The move of monetary policy powers to the ECB has stimulated a debate in some countries whether banking supervision needs to remain under the same roof as the central bank, at least in the countries where this is still the case. The tendency towards conglomeration in the financial services industry is an argument in favour of a single supervisory authority, although conglomeration may also strengthen the arguments for more supervision by the functions of regulation. The pros and cons of these different constellations are analysed below.

A Central bank versus separate banking supervision

Monetary policy and banking supervisory functions are separated in half of the EU countries and combined in the other half (see Table 14.2). Generally speaking, the arguments in favour of combining both functions revolve around the fact that it is the central bank's role to ensure the stability of the financial system and prevent contagious systemic crises (Goodhart et al., 1997). The supervision and regulation of banking institutions contribute to better control of overall financial stability, regardless of who performs these functions. The issue is whether they can be done better in a central bank. Through its role as lender-of-last-resort (LOLR), the central bank should, it is argued, be involved in supervision as well. At the same time, however, the possibility that a conflict of interest may arise (even when a central bank only has one vote in overall euro monetary policy) argues against combining both functions. The central bank's participation in bank rescues may endanger price stability and increase moral hazard. It may create competitive distortions if central bank money is allocated at preferential rates to a bank in trouble as compared to other banks. Finally, it may raise the expectation in the private sector that a central bank supervisor would be unduly influenced because of the reputational risk by considerations of financial system stability, for example, when determining monetary policy. This could seriously undermine the central bank's credibility.

The fact that both regimes are equally represented in the EU suggests that there are no conclusive arguments for or against either model. According to Goodhart and Schoenmaker (1995), the question of the appropriate design has to be approached in the context of the particular financial or banking structure of each country rather than in the abstract. Their analysis of bank failures over the last two decades shows a much higher frequency of failures in countries with a separated regime than in those with a combined one. This does not, however, lead immediately to the conclusion that the latter regime is better. Many other factors come into play, such as the degree of financial deregulation, the quality of regulation, the willingness of the government to let a bank fail, or the existence of oligopolies in banking. Goodhart and Schoenmaker also found a stronger likelihood of commercial banks being involved in rescues in a combined regime, through the authority of the central bank, but they see this as a receding possibility.

Table 14.2 Supervisors of banking, securities and insurance in Europe, Japan and the US

	Banking	*Securities*	*Insurance*
B	BS	BS	I
DK	M	M	M
DE	B	S	I
EL	CB	S	I
E	CB	S	I
F	B/CB	S	I
I	CB	S	I
IRL	CB	CB	G
L	BS	BS	I
NL	CB	S	I
AU	G	G	G
P	CB	S	I
SF	BS	BS	I
SW	M	M	M
UK	M	M	M
CH	BS	BS	I
CZ	CB	SI	SI
H	B	S	I
N	M	M	M
PL	CB	S	I
SLOE	CB	S	G
USA	B/CB	S	I
J	M	M	M

Note: CB = Central Bank, BS = banking and securities supervisor, M = single financial supervisory authority, B = specialised banking supervisor, S = specialised securities supervisor, I = specialised insurance supervisor, SI = specialised securities and insurance supervisor, G = government department.

In recent years, the trend towards more integrated supervision has led to moving bank supervisory functions away from the central bank. The arguments for keeping banking supervision under the roof of the central bank have become less authoritative in comparison to the need to respond effectively to the increasing complexity of finance (see Briault, 1999). This was most clearly exemplified by the announcement in May 1997 of the proposed establishment in the UK of the Financial Services Authority (FSA), an integrated financial supervisor, involving the transfer of the banking supervisory function from the Bank of England.[2] An additional reason for this development is the acceptance that only the government, and not the central bank, can take responsibility for ultimate financial support of banks in trouble. The ability of central banks to organise and coordinate bank rescues has been slipping, and bank rescues have become more expensive, going beyond the sums which the central bank can provide from its own resources. This was demonstrated earlier this decade in Finland, Norway and Sweden, but also more recently in Italy and France. There has consequently been no alternative but to rely on taxpayer funding, leading to more demand for political control of supervisory functions. Close cooperation between the supervisory and the monetary policy authorities remains crucial, however. Only the monetary policy authorities can provide immediate liquidity to the market in case of trouble. But price stability cannot be achieved if financial stability is not in place. This distinction is operational in the eurozone, where, under the Maastricht Treaty, the European System of Central Banks (ESCB) is responsible for monetary policy, and the national authorities for financial stability.

B Integrated financial supervisor versus specialist supervisors

A second issue to be addressed is whether financial supervision should be assigned to one entity or whether it should be determined by the function of the business of the institutions under supervision or by the type of supervision (prudential or conduct of business). The conglomeration trend in the financial sector and the creation of the FSA in the UK has stimulated a discussion elsewhere in Europe on integrated financial supervisory authorities. An integrated authority is seen to generate economies of scale (and probably economies of scope) in supervision, as well as some practical and political advantages (see Table 14.3). It offers one-stop shopping for authorisations of conglomerate financial groups and eliminates any confusion over who exercises lead supervision and final control. Expertise is pooled and cooperation between the different functional supervisors is guaranteed. Unnecessary overlaps are avoided and support services such as personnel, administration and documentation can be merged. An integrated authority should thus over time lead to lower supervisory fees, at least in these countries where the financial sector contributes directly to the cost of supervision, and to a lower cost of supervision in general.

An integrated supervisor will however only be effective if it is more than a combination of divisions, and if synergies can be exploited. It has been argued that the crucial thing is not whether all the functional supervisors are under a single roof, but whether they communicate with one another. If an integrated supervisor is no more than a combination of banking, insurance

Table 14.3 Comparative advantages of the dominant model in financial supervision

Integrated financial supervisor	Specialist supervisor
• One-stop shopping for authorisations • Pooling of expertise and economies of scale (certain units could be merged, e.g. authorisations, support services) • Lower supervisory fees • Adapted to evolution in financial sector towards more complex financial products and financial conglomerates • Cooperation between types of financial business guaranteed; one lead supervisor or a single supervisory team for conglomerates • Can reduce regulatory arbitrage and deliver regulatory neutrality • More transparent to consumers • Single rulebook (a possibility)	• Lower profile • Clearly defined mandate • Easier to manage • Better adapted to the differences in risk profiles and nature of the respective financial business (e.g. retail versus wholesale), clear focus on objectives and rationale of regulation • Closer to the business (but not necessarily) • Better knowledge of the business, more specialisation • Stimulates inter-agency competition

and investment business divisions, the full benefits of a single regulatory authority will not be achieved.

A possible argument against an integrated supervisor is its potentially higher profile. It might be argued that the perception could somehow be created that the whole financial sector is secure, which may reduce the incentives for providers to prudently manage their business, and for users to carefully choose their financial services provider. It could also be argued that the failure of one institution could have more widespread effects in a combined regime because the supervisor was active in a number of different sectors. This risk has to be offset by educating users of financial services in the risks as well as the benefits of financial products.

The advantages of a specialist supervisor are a lower profile and a clearer focus on the sector under supervision. It could allow for a greater proximity to smaller firms on which a single regulator may be less inclined to focus, more specialisation and better awareness of the problems of the sector. Two arguments stand out: a growing need for specialisation in supervision and inter-agency competition. Very distinct skills are required from supervisors, ranging from monitoring potentially dangerous exposures in increasingly globalised financial markets and validating statistical models in a bank's value-at-risk models to supervising complex financial groups or tracking market behaviour of investment funds, as well as a large degree of financial specialisation. It is an open question whether a single regulator can find it easier to recruit and retain specialists. It could be easier where there are specialisations such as market risk, credit risk and most forms of legal and operational risk, which apply across a range of different firms, and not just to firms in a particular sector (Briault, 1999).

The second argument, the advantage of inter-agency competition, is relevant, although perhaps difficult to advance in this context. Where several agencies work side by side, institutional competition can work and create incentives for each agency to work efficiently, while reducing capture (Fender and von Hagen, 1998). An example is the US structure of banking supervision, where banks can be chartered at either the state or national level. In the EU, regulatory competition between states forms an integral part of the single market programme. Many will argue, however, that inter-agency competition does not make sense. Competition between regulatory regimes runs the risk of reducing rather than improving quality, and it may better serve the interest of the supervised than that of the public.

An overview of financial sector supervision in the EU and the rest of Europe demonstrates that three EU countries (Denmark, Sweden and the UK) as well as Norway have an integrated financial services authority. In some of these countries (as also recently in Japan and South Korea), the integration of supervision resulted from serious trouble in their financial sectors or grave oversights in surveillance. In the other countries, a broad mixture of systems exists, ranging from separate supervisors with banking supervisors usually in association with the central bank and sometimes split between two agencies in the same supervisory discipline, to combined banking-and-securities or combined securities-and-insurance supervisors (see Table 14.2). In Austria, Belgium, Germany and Ireland, the creation of an integrated authority has been raised or is on the political agenda.

C Supervision by objective

Another outcome of the conglomeration trend is that supervision will become more objective-driven, since the functional divisions of the business will be increasingly blurred. One possible model calls for one agency to carry out surveillance separately for systemic stability reasons, a second for prudential supervision and a third for conduct-of-business. Conduct-of-business supervision looks after transparency, disclosure, fair and honest practices, and equality of market participants. The 'stability' agency should concentrate on macro-prudential problems, which affect the conduct of monetary policy or overall financial stability, while the prudential agency controls the solvency and soundness of individual financial institutions and enforces depositor and investor protection.

Such a horizontal supervisory structure was instituted in Australia, further to the Wallis Committee of Inquiry in 1997. The Australian Prudential Regulatory Authority (APRA) supervises financial institutions on prudential grounds; the Reserve Bank of Australia looks after systemic stability and provides liquidity assistance; and the Australian Securities and Investment Commission (ASIC) controls market integrity and conduct-of-business rules. APRA and ASIC report to the Treasury. Several EU countries have elements of an objective-driven system of supervision, mainly as far as the relationship between the banking and the securities supervisor is concerned. In Italy, for example, banks and securities houses are controlled by the Banca d'Italia on financial stability and prudential grounds and by CONSOB for conduct-of-business rules for the banking and securities industry. The UK had a broadly similar structure before all supervisory functions were merged in the FSA. However, one of the reasons for bringing together prudential and conduct of business supervision in the UK was the increasing overlap in their activities with the growing tendency of both types of supervisor to pay heightened attention in the same firms to senior management capabilities, high level systems and controls and other common issues (Briault, 1999).

A compromise solution was recently adopted by the Netherlands, which has the highest market share for financial conglomerates in the EU. To avoid institutional reorganisation and all the related political problems, but to allow for adaptation to market developments and a clear focus on the objectives of supervision, a Council of Financial Supervisors was established in August 1999. The Council is not a separate institution, but is an organ for regular consultation between the three sectoral supervisors (the banking supervisor in the central bank, and the separate insurance and securities supervisors) for cross-sectoral problems in prudential and non-securities related conduct-of-business control. The Dutch central bank remains solely in charge of systemic control, and the securities supervisor becomes responsible for all securities-related conduct-of-business control. According to the Ministry of Finance (1999) in the Netherlands, the Council will force supervisors to agree on effective control of cross-sectoral issues, but the final responsibility remains with the individual supervisors. It remains to be seen how effectively these arrangements work.

The Dutch experiment points to interesting routes for other countries and for the European structure. It may only be a partial solution towards a more streamlined structure of financial supervision in the longer run, but it could also indicate that the optimal solution needs to combine sectoral and cross-sectoral supervision. Three relevant implications for the European debate are the need for regular cross-sectoral consultation, the decision to leave the central bank in charge of systemic issues, while keeping securities market supervision separate.

III The European angle

European financial market regulations allowed markets to integrate under the control of the home country. Home country supervisors are in charge of licensing branches across the EU and exercising consolidated supervision. To that end, a framework for regular exchange of information and cooperation at bilateral and European level is in place. A variety of committees have been established to carry out a variety of functions, ranging from advising the Commission on improvements to the legal and regulatory framework at European level, to exchanging views about supervisory policy and practice, and, in some cases, discussing specific cases. The host country remains in charge of dealing with problems related to the stability of the financial system. With the start of EMU, macro-prudential oversight is coordinated by the ECB.

The developments outlined in Section I raise the question whether this framework is still appropriate. While it is not the role of the EC institutions to prescribe the supervisory structure at national level, adaptations may be required to face growing market interpenetration, conglomeration and Europeanisation of financial institutions.

A On the home country principle

The principle of home country control was successful in opening up markets in the EU, at least in banking. The harmonisation of the essential elements of authorisation and supervision of banks in the Second Banking Coordination Directive (2BCD) allowed the single licence for cross-border provision of services and branching to work. Host country controls for prudential purposes were virtually abolished, administrative burdens reduced and capital requirements for branches (where they applied) eliminated. Moreover, the introduction of European legislation provided a major incentive for national legislators to streamline their applicable laws. Some problems remained relating to the application of the notification procedure for host country operations and the application of the general good clause. These were tentatively clarified in an interpretative Communication of the European Commission (1997a), which was not, however, wholeheartedly supported. Another issue, the liquidity control of branches by host country authorities for monetary policy reasons (Art. 14, 2BCD), has become irrelevant in EMU. The article is under review by the authorities.

The home country is in charge of exercising consolidated supervision of a bank throughout the EU. To avoid opaque structures, it is required that the home country is the place of the head office of the bank in the EU (in the so-called 'post-BCCI directive'). From an international perspective, home country control is also the basic method for the supervision of cross-border banking in the Core Principles on Banking Supervision of the Basel Committee. The general intention is that the home supervisor has to act as the lead supervisor for branches, joint ventures and subsidiaries all over the world and needs to exercise consolidated supervision. Host country supervisors are expected to communicate all necessary information to the home country authorities.

In the area of investment services and retail insurance, the home country control principle has only been partially put into effect. The harmonisation in the investment services directive has gone less far than in banking, and more powers reside with the host country for the control of the respect of local conduct of business rules, which have not been harmonised, although they work on the basis of harmonised principles. The European Commission is committed to further harmonisation, as was indicated in the Financial Services Action Plan. In insurance, differences in contract law and taxation have limited the reach of the single licence for small risks, and thus of the home country control principle. For large risks, however, markets have become integrated.

Harmonisation of conduct-of-business rules in financial services has proven more challenging, because it revolves around differing views on what constitutes appropriate protection for consumers in historically very different marketplaces. It also tends to require more on-site examination, which is more demanding on a cross-border basis. It is notable that new EU legislation involving conduct of business regulation goes for maximum harmonisation, as seen, for example, most recently in the draft directive on distance-selling of financial services.

Two fundamental questions can be raised with regard to the working of the home country control principle: (1) How well has the principle functioned in an EU context so far? (2) Will it continue to be relevant in a more integrated European financial market? The home country control principle is part of the limited harmonisation approach of the single market as set out in the Cassis de Dijon ruling (1978) of the European Court of Justice. Only essential requirements are harmonised to allow markets to integrate. Additional rules should adjust in a competitive process between jurisdictions. This raises the issue of regulatory competition, and the degree of competition that is permissible in an EU context.

The home country control principle was probably well adapted to an environment of limited competition. As long as cross-border business is limited, as was generally the case until the start of EMU (see Section I), regulatory competition probably had some effect in aligning the most striking differences between regimes, while the overall impact remains limited, because markets have not been very integrated. In a more integrated market, a process of further harmonisation can be expected as a result of pressures from the market and the authorities at national and European level. This will be required to reduce remaining powers of the host country in each of the disciplines (e.g. the notification procedure and the general good principle) or to expand harmonisation where it was limited (e.g. in banking, the deposit guarantee directive prohibited the 'export' of higher levels of depositor protection in the EU).

The second question is whether the home country *per se* will continue to be relevant in an EU context. The big players in the European market will increasingly have a range of home markets, so could the EU as a whole become the home market? It has been suggested in the past (Gros, quoted in Schoenmaker, 1995) that the single financial market could follow the two-tier US system of state and federally chartered banks. Large European banks could than choose to be federally chartered and be allowed to regard Europe as a whole as their 'home' country. This does, however, raise several fundamental problems:

1   Financial services legislation is not sufficiently harmonised today to allow this to happen.
2   It would require an EU Treaty change to create such a body (as would be required for a European SEC, single banking regulator,[3] or a euro-FSA).
3   Financial supervision implies accountability and tax powers for eventual bail-outs. While the former could perhaps be created to exist at European level, the latter would be much more difficult, and would entail explicit agreement between member states for burden-sharing of bail-outs.
4   There is no appropriate European framework of courts to impose sanctions for violations of law or to challenge the use made of powers.
5   Smaller banks (and member states) may see a dual framework as a competitive distortion.
6   There would be major company law ramifications to be considered.

B   European supervisory cooperation

Growing cross-border banking, home country control and the operation of host state regulation all raise the issue of bilateral and European cooperation between supervisory authorities. Memoranda of Understanding provide the underpinning for cooperation at the bilateral level. At European level, several committees are in place to ensure collaboration between supervisors.

1   Cooperation at bilateral level

A Memorandum of Understanding (MoU) is a form of agreement between supervisors, which has no legal force, but sets out the respective tasks and obligations of both parties. In principle, the EU directives make formal agreements between supervisory authorities of the member states superfluous, since they make cooperation a legal obligation. In practice, supervisors have continued to conclude MoUs to clarify what is involved in the supervision of financial institutions and markets, such as information exchange and mutual assistance, establishment procedures and on-site examinations. In banking, some 78 bilateral MoUs had been signed between EEA banking supervisors by the end of 1997 (Padoa-Schioppa, 1999), while there is a multilateral Protocol to the Insurance Directives which serves as an MoU and the EEA securities commissions have also signed a multilateral MoU in relation to exchange of information for market surveillance purposes.

Little more is available in the public domain about the scope of MoUs that have been negotiated on the supervision of banks. Perhaps this can be justified from a moral hazard and liability point of view, but it does raise the question whether the authorities should consider a higher degree of transparency. This could signal to the markets that supervisors have kept pace with growing market integration. More information is available on MoUs between securities commissions and regulated markets. In the latter case, the arguments against transparency do not apply, and regulatory tasks are often shared, and on a different basis across countries, between the securities commission and the stock exchange.

Cooperation through MoUs raises the question of effective coordination of supervision. Although not formalised, the supervisor who exercises consolidated supervision is generally seen as the coordinator. This does however raise a problem for the insurance sector, where consolidation is not commonly accepted as a principle. According to a recent report by the Economic and Financial Committee (European Commission, 2000b), there is a lack of clarity on the coordinated supervision of insurance groups. This applies even more for conglomerates with a predominantly insurance focus. It has been reported that some conglomerates recently restructured as principally insurance groups to escape consolidated supervision.

MoUs raise the question of supervisory methods and the content of information exchange. According to Mayes (1999), MoUs do not provide for regular transfer of routine information among supervisors, but only in the case where possible supervisory problems arise, including suspected misconduct. This is perhaps natural, but when information is transferred, the question arises what precise information is transferred and whether supervisory methods have been sufficiently harmonised for information transfer to be effective. Limited evidence suggests that much may remain to be done in this domain. According to Prati and Schinasi (1998), supervisory practices differ considerably in the EU. The Vice-Governor of the Austrian National Bank was recently quoted as saying that the differences in banking and supervisory systems in the EU are so big that they will only be overcome in the very long term, if at all.[4]

As a way around this problem, it has been proposed that enhanced market disclosure about the bank's capital structure and its risk profile would help in providing the necessary information to supervisors (Mayes, 1999). Since information exchange between supervisors may not be sufficiently developed in certain areas, strengthening market discipline would probably be a more efficient and faster way to facilitate the work of supervisors in a European context. This point is also stressed in the proposed 'pillar three' of the Basel Capital Accord Review.

2 Cooperation at European level

At European level, several committees exist to promote cooperation between supervisory authorities. Their principal tasks are to:

1   Provide a forum for the exchange of views and to act as a sounding board for the Commission on any proposals for supplements or amendments to legislation.
2   Discuss and adopt technical adaptations to the directives within the perimeters foreseen in the directives (the 'comitology' procedure).
3   Discuss and compare issues of supervisory technique and to facilitate the

exchange of information and cooperation with respect to problems with individual institutions.

This is, however, a general characterisation, which varies between the sectors of financial services. The committees are most developed in banking. The highest number of committees exists for securities markets, but with the least powers. An umbrella, cross-discipline EU committee of financial supervisors does not exist.

In banking, three committees are in place (see listing in the Annex). The Banking Advisory Committee (BAC) principally advises the European Commission with regard to policy issues in the formulation and implementation of EC legislation for the banking sector. It can also, if foreseen by the directives, agree on technical adaptations to the directives (the 'comitology' procedure). In order to do this, it brings together senior supervisory and finance ministry officials. The Groupe de Contact, which consists only of banking supervisors of the European Economic Area (EEA), has dealt for nearly 30 years with issues of banking supervision policy and practice including the carrying out of comparative studies, arranging the exchange of information and handling cooperation with respect to issues arising from individual institutions. The Banking Supervisory Committee of the ECB brings together the authorities responsible for monetary policy and payment systems oversight in the European System of Central Banks with EU banking supervisors to discuss macro-prudential matters and financial stability issues. It also assists the ECB in the preparation of the ECB's advice on draft EU and national banking legislation (within euro area countries) as laid down in Art. 105(4) of the EU Treaty and Art. 25(1) of the ESCB/ECB Statute. Each of these three committees cooperates closely with one another, making papers available as appropriate.

In insurance, the BAC is broadly paralleled by the Insurance Committee and the Groupe de Contact by the Conference of Insurance Supervisors.

In the securities field, strictly speaking, there is no parallel structure to the legislative committees existing in the banking and insurance field. This means that any technical adaptation of the core directives (the investment services directive and the capital adequacy directive) needs to take the form of a formal amendment, with the problems and delays this can imply. This situation should now be remedied, following the agreement in the European Parliament on the structure of legislative committees. It should be noted, however, that a High Level Securities Supervisors Committee, which brings together representatives of member states' securities supervisory authorities and finance ministries, has been in place since 1992. It assists the Commission on policy issues relating to securities markets and the development of the relevant European legislation. Two Contact Committees, one for the listing and prospectus rules and one for unit trusts (UCITS), exist to facilitate harmonised implementation of directives through regular consultations between the member states and to advise the Commission on any supplements or amendments. These committees have no 'comitology' powers, which partially explains why they never acquired any particular influence.

The unresolved conflict between the European Commission, Council and Parliament on the implementing powers of a formal securities committee led in December 1997 to the creation of the Forum of European Securities Commissions (FESCO). FESCO brings together the statutory securities commissions of the European Economic Area (EEA). FESCO's work concentrates on developing common regulatory standards and enhancing cooperation between members on enforcement and market surveillance issues.

C The role of the ECB

According to the EU Treaty, the ECB is in charge of monetary policy and the smooth operation of payment systems, whereas financial supervision and stability remain the competence of the member states. This division of roles has been the subject of wide debate over the last months that focused principally on the potentially unrestrained lender-of-last-resort (LOLR) facilities of the separate national central banks in EMU, which may potentially conflict with the monetary policy role of the ECB. It has therefore been argued that the ECB should be giving an explicit LOLR function.

In essence, the reason for giving the ECB an explicit lender-of-last resort role is the possible conflict between the ECB's responsibility for determining liquidity in the Eurosystem and the financial stability competences at local level. Local responsibility for LOLR operations can conflict with euro monetary policy and possibly stimulate excessive risk-taking. This was related to the fear, which has now receded, that the national central banks would dominate the Eurosystem, and that the ECB would not be sufficiently powerful to impose common rules. It has now been agreed that the ECB's Governing Council should be consulted on LOLR operations that have EMU-wide implications.[5] This also implies, however, that the ECB will coordinate LOLR operations in relation to banks with widespread operations across Europe. As soon as a bank operates in more than two EU countries on a major scale, and is of systemic importance at European level, it is more likely that the ECB will take a leading role in rescue operations as *primus inter pares* and as a politically neutral body. The ECB's Banking Supervisory Committee should be instrumental in ensuring regular consultation on these matters between national central bank officials and supervisors, and ensuring that the ECB is sufficiently informed.

Unlike the national central banks, however, the ECB has limited financial means and is not backed by a ministry of finance for an eventual bank rescue involving injections of capital. The ECB can only lend against good collateral. Even if the ECB assumes the coordinating role for the monetary policy aspects of LOLR operations relating to European financial groups, a solution will need to be found for this issue as well. A bail-out of such groups will only be possible under a burden-sharing arrangement between the different home countries. However, the risk is not imaginary that national ministries of finance and parliaments will be unwilling to pick up problems which have, in their eyes, originated in other parts of the EU (Goodhart, 1999).[6] This discussion also raises problems related to European competition policy, as approaches to banks in trouble differ across countries and affect the level playing field. The latter issue is discussed in more detail below.

The recent debate on the LOLR role of the ECB also revealed that the issue had been confused with a generalised liquidity problem in the Eurosystem. This is closely related to the monetary policy function of the central bank, on which there is no disagreement on the responsibility of the ECB to act. The ECB should be well informed about one of the reasons for such liquidity shortages, a gridlock in the payment system, through its task in promoting the smooth operation of payment systems. The ESCB's large value payment system, TARGET, had a market share of 70% in large value payments in the first year of EMU.

Another element of the current consensus is the agreement that the procedure to confer specific tasks concerning policies relating to prudential supervision of banks and other financial institutions to the ECB, as foreseen under Art. 105.6 of the EU Treaty, should not be activated. It could give rise to conflicts of interest with the ECB's monetary policy functions, which should at this stage be avoided. It would also require a complete redesign of the structure of financial supervision in the EU, which is based on the principle of member state home country control. The provision is currently seen as an ultimate fallback option, if the relationship between the ECB and the national supervisory authorities did not work or in case irresponsible behaviour by authorities at national level would have spillover effects in the whole eurozone.

D How to respond to growing market integration

The deeper challenges in financial supervision are related to the characteristics of the European financial system and the increased competition and market integration that is stimulated by EMU. It will require agreement on the part of policy-makers and supervisors to act rapidly on the completion of the regulatory framework and the adaptation of the structure of financial supervision to market developments. Elements of the provisions worked out in the Netherlands provide at least some indication of the issues to be addressed at a European level – but because the tasks are different at a national and a European level, it is unlikely that any national structure will offer a model suitable at the European level. It comprises three elements: the surveillance of systemic issues, involving regulators, central banks and finance ministries; the need for closer cooperation between supervisors in a European board of financial supervisors to discuss cross-sectoral matters and to handle issues related to conglomerate groups; and the option to handle market supervision separately. If supervision is to remain at a national level, then a further levelling of the playing field for financial institutions in the EU also needs to be considered urgently.

1 Systemic issues

National central banks and supervisory authorities should step up their efforts to monitor market developments at European level and alert national and European authorities to exposures with a potentially systemic impact. Monetary union has connected eleven previously separate markets into a single currency zone. That this has effectively happened is clear from the interbank market, which has developed a deep euro-denominated money market. Banks have integrated their euro-denominated treasury operations and manage their euro-denominated collateral on a single basis. The parallel to this development is also that systemic effects will immediately have much wider dimensions, whereas previously they tended to be largely limited to within national boundaries. Interbank deposits represent about 19% of bank assets in euroland.

It is therefore essential that the eurozone is watched as one market. The ECB has its Banking Supervisory Committee, but the question has been raised whether this group will be sufficiently comprehensive in its approach to European financial markets, and whether the ECB will have sufficient access to research to effectively monitor markets. A case has therefore been made for a European Observatory of Systemic Risk (Aglietta and de Boissieu, 1998). The aim would be to have one body in place to monitor market developments across Europe and alert national and European authorities to exposures with a potentially systemic impact. In practice, such an entity could most efficiently operate in a cooperative structure within the ESCB.[7] Such work is already undertaken within the existing structure of the ECB's Banking Supervision Committee. However, some think it could be useful to create a clearly distinct structure for this, and to signal this to the markets to provide reassurance that adequate account is being taken of the new environment created by the euro. Secondly, it will be important to take account of developments in securities markets and of non-bank intermediaries.

2 A future structure for European regulatory and supervisory cooperation

Three layers can be distinguished in the European structure of regulatory and supervisory cooperation, for each of which one coordinating body should be appointed:

1 *Coordination of regulatory policy.* The Financial Services Policy Group (FSPG), instituted in 1999, should continue to discuss priorities in financial regulation at European level. After the adoption of the Financial Services Action Plan, it was announced that the FSPG would continue

'to provide strategic advice, to discuss cross-sectoral developments and to monitor progress under the Action Plan' (Ecofin Council, 25 May 1999). A higher profile and a clear hierarchy in the decision process may, however, be needed, and more transparency and openness in its deliberations.

2   *Coordination of supervisory matters.* No satisfactory, high-level structure is in place to deal with cross-sectoral supervisory issues at the moment. A European Forum of Financial Supervisors should therefore be urgently considered. This Forum should have two major tasks:

- *Ensure effective supervisory coordination for large European financial conglomerates.* The Forum will have to monitor whether the different bilateral Memoranda of Understanding (MoUs), on a sectoral and cross-sectoral basis, provide a sufficient overall picture of the exposures of a group. A multi-sectoral MoU or protocol could be worked out for the exchange of information between supervisors on a cross-sectoral and cross-border basis to ensure that financial groups with operations in a range of different countries are properly supervised, with clear arrangements for the appointment of a lead supervisor.

- *Coordination of supervisory practices.* The Forum should set as an objective to make consistent supervisory practices in the EU, whether through legislative or non-legislative means. The exchange of information on supervisory techniques should allow the Forum to make arrangements for the establishment of standards of best practice in financial supervision, which should over time lead to more convergence in supervisory practices in the EU and hence to a more efficient and integrated single market.

The Forum could be composed of the chairmen of the different sectoral supervisory committees, with the European Commission acting as secretariat. Individual supervisors would need to be invited on an *ad-hoc* basis.

3   *Coordination in financial stability matters.* Monitoring of financial stability should happen through the mechanism of something like the Observatory for Systemic Risk, discussed above. Effective emergency intervention should be coordinated by an *ad-hoc* committee of the Economic and Financial Committee (EFC), the body for regular consultation between the finance ministries, the ECB and the European Commission. Such an *ad-hoc* committee should be composed of the competent representatives of the member states' finance ministries, central banks and supervisory authorities, with the Chairman of the European Forum of Financial Supervisors, a representative of the European Central Bank and the European Commission.

Expressed schematically, the structure might look as shown in Figure 14.2. Committees between square brackets do not yet exist; committees in italics relate to proposals made in this report.

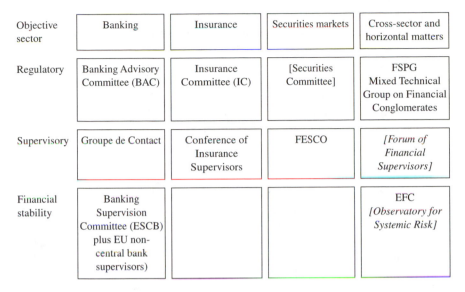

Figure 14.2 The structure of European supervisory and regulatory cooperation.

The creation of a European Forum of Financial Supervisors could also be a useful way to stimulate cooperation where necessary between sectoral supervisors at the national level. Banking and insurance supervisors have gone their own ways in, for example, negotiating directives, and it is only with the growth of conglomerates that the resulting inconsistencies are beginning to be recognised and require resolution. Such a Forum would encourage them to agree on joint approaches to integrated groups or common views on cross-sectoral matters.

3 Supervision of securities markets

Securities market supervision involves both the supervision of markets and exchanges, narrowly defined, and of the firms that trade in them. It is essentially focused on devising, implementing and enforcing conduct-of-business rules: the control of integrity and transparency of markets, the behaviour of individual participants and the protection of investors. It is a different task from supervising the financial soundness of institutions, and it can be argued that the two tasks should be kept separate.

The development of a harmonised regulatory framework for EU securities markets and for investment business generally is less advanced than in the area of banking. Harmonisation has not gone as far here and more reliance is placed on mutual recognition, as for example in conduct-of-business rules, which has hampered market integration. At member state level, the creation of separate supervisory authorities is of recent, and in some cases, very recent origin. Far-reaching differences remain in the institutional structure of supervision, the division between regulation and self-regulation, or between the powers of the national securities market regulator and the various market authorities.

The rapid integration of capital markets in EMU and the lack of a regulatory framework for the integration of stock markets in the EU have led some to argue for a European SEC to help overcome these barriers. Although it is not always clear just what the proponents mean, and whether they are focused simply on markets and exchanges or also on firms, we believe that it would at present be a step too far. Not only is there a prior need for more regulatory harmonisation, which the European Commission is committed to achieving, but also the arguments for a more integrated supervisory authority are less compelling for securities markets than for financial institutions. Risks related to inadequate respect of conduct-of-business rules are overall less disturbing than those related to insufficient institutional supervision. It follows that some degree of competition between systems may do little harm and could indeed be desirable. This is implicit in the principles governing the single market, as long as it does not hamper market integration. It also fits with the current structure of supervision of EU securities markets, where the dividing line between regulation and self-regulation differs significantly from country to country (Lannoo, 1999).

In order to achieve further harmonisation of securities market regulation, the next step should be an acceleration of the decision procedure towards the creation of an EU Securities Committee, to parallel the other two EC regulatory committees, to review not only to the ISD and CAD, but also the other securities directives. Moreover, clarity should be achieved to establish its relationship with the other existing securities committees that are in place, and a division of labour agreed with FESCO, the Forum of European Securities Commissions.

FESCO was created in December 1997, to enhance the exchange of information between the national securities commissions, to provide the broadest possible mutual assistance to strengthen market surveillance and effective enforcement against abuse, to ensure uniform implementation of EU directives and to develop common regulatory standards in areas that are not harmonised by European directives. Each FESCO member is committed to implementing these standards in its home jurisdiction. Despite its recent creation, FESCO has rapidly gained wide recognition and support for its work.

4 A further levelling of the playing field at EU level

A more integrated financial market will highlight the shortcomings in the EU regulatory framework. Three areas are at the core of the policy debate, and are closely related to the level playing field: (1) common approaches to banks in trouble; (2) the strict application of EU competition policy rules to state aids in banking; and (3) greater transparency in the rules applicable to banking mergers.

Several European banks have been bailed out over the last decade at great public expense. The governments in question were motivated by a variety of fears, including the belief that the bank was 'too big to fail' and would cause too much economic damage to both depositors and borrowers, that a failure might be contagious and spread through interbank settlement systems (as in the so-called Herstatt risk), or lead to a general loss of confidence in the banking system and trigger damaging bank runs. As a result, a moral hazard problem remains.

Designing a safety net in the banking sector is a difficult exercise. The problem is how to respond to the phenomenon of systemic risk without creating adverse incentives for bank managers. So far, governments have kept LOLR procedures deliberately vague. To reduce moral hazard, procedural and practical details of emergency actions are secret. The design of LOLR support in EMU is also seen as part of this 'constructive ambiguity' (Prati and Schinasi, 1998). Others have argued that this approach should no longer be applicable. Maintaining a high degree of ambiguity may itself have led to excessive risk-taking by financial institutions and too much forbearance by the authorities in the face of banking problems. Such a policy can only be modified in a climate of greater transparency concerning the support that will be offered to banks in trouble, and under what circumstances (Enoch et al., 1997).

Within a European context, the choice of responses is limited, since several policies have been applied in the member states. Some states have selectively let certain banks fail, whereas others have used large amounts of taxpayers' money to rescue a bank and/or gone to considerable efforts to arrange rescues through mergers. Such policies may have reduced market discipline in European banking and stimulated overcapacity. A more common policy for bank exit policies can thus only be implemented with clear indications from governments.

A combination of preventive (*ex-ante*) and remedial (*ex-post*) measures is needed. As part of the *ex-ante* policies, preventive corrective action (PCA) should be implemented across the EU. With PCA, supervisors undertake a gradualist response to banks in trouble. They typically set pre-specified minimum capital ratios, which initiate a progressive series of restrictions on the problem bank's activities. This reduces the potential for regulators to apply forbearance and allow problems to become magnified, and reduces the danger that responses will be inconsistent with competitive neutrality (ESFRC, 1998).

The need for preventive corrective action is now formally proposed by the Basel Committee in its capital review, as part of the so-called 'pillar two', the supervisory review process. It sets out that early intervention by the authorities may be needed where a bank's capital is falling relative to its risk. The focus of Basel is primarily on moral suasion to improve risk management and internal controls, whereas higher minimum capital ratios for supervisory intervention, so-called 'trigger ratios', are the exception: 'In a few regimes, capital ratios represent triggers for supervisory action' (Basel consultative paper, 1999, p. 58). This position was supported in the recent Commission paper on the review of the regulatory capital requirements (European Commission, 1999b). The question could however be raised whether the Commission is not overemphasising the appropriateness of differences in supervisory approaches, now that they should converge more.[8]

As regards pillar three of the supervisory review, disclosure, it is unclear at this stage how far it should go. The Basel Committee came out in favour of extensive disclosure of actual regulatory capital ratios, the capital structure and risk exposure, without clarifying whether the capital requirement imposed by supervisors should be disclosed. The Commission, however, while generally being supportive of disclosure, affirmed that the capital requirement imposed by supervisors upon a bank (as distinct from its holding of regulatory capital) should not be made public. Publication of supervisors' assessments could blunt the incentive for depositors and investors to make their own credit assessment, according to the European Commission, and changes in ratios could be incorrectly interpreted by analysts and/or lead to overreaction such as deposit runs. The latter could in its turn constrain action by supervisors (European Commission, 1999b, p. 79). It could on the other hand also be argued that non-disclosure may maintain the old thinking on constructive ambiguity, and perhaps not provide the right incentives to supervisors on how to deal with institutions in trouble.

Harmonised remedial policies are probably less of a policy priority at the moment. With PCA procedures in place, the likelihood of the supervisors actually needing to liquidate banks should be reduced. However, harmonised bank and insurance winding-up procedures have become more urgent given the increasing scale of cross-border business. Proposals were blocked for many years because of differences in views on the feasibility of a European approach to bankruptcy procedures. The Commission's Financial Services Action Plan reiterated the need for urgent adoption of these measures, which seems now finally to have been given effect. Both measures were recently adopted by the EU Council.[9]

In the event that a bank is bailed out, the process is in principle subject to the EU rules on state aid, as set out in Art. 92 of the EU Treaty. These rules have been detailed, as far as their application to the banking sector is concerned, in the Crédit Lyonnais case.[10] While acknowledging the special nature of the banking sector, the Commission says that Community law, especially the solvency ratio directive, has clearly set a criterion of 'equal competitive conditions'. Thus, if state financial support is provided to banks, the Commission must establish whether the Treaty rules are being respected. Exceptions can be made, however, if a serious disturbance threatens the economy (Art. 92.3.b).

It has been argued that the banking sector should be exempted from the application of Art. 92 of the Treaty because of its special character and its role in financial stability (Grande, 1999). Banking supervisors should have independence in their assessment of the means of dealing with problem banks. Since banking supervision is kept at the local level in the EU, state aid should also be taken out of EU hands and decentralised. This would, however, open the door to dangerous precedents, and clear the way for all other forms of hidden state aids, such as state-guaranteed loans. It would also be inconsistent with giving the ECB some a priori involvement in LOLR procedures at local level, as discussed above. What could be argued for is some form of accelerated procedure for handling state aid issues in relation to state support for banks.

If state aid control were somehow to be decentralised, there would also be no way to equalise competition in Community-wide bank take-overs. As indicated earlier, restructuring of financial markets in the EU has hitherto mainly taken place at national level, which has led to high levels of concentration in certain national markets. More European cross-border consolidation will increase competition and reduce the danger of oligopolies at national level. Emphasising the arguments for the special character of the banking sector would make it easier for local authorities to intervene in foreign hostile bank take-overs and further stimulate purely national consolidation. It should be clear that cross-border transactions involving the control of banks, or indeed other financial institutions, should not be prevented or burdened for reasons other than antitrust or safety and soundness concerns.

Take-over legislation, however, is not harmonised at EU level. Securities laws differ importantly from one country to another in the Community, with large differences in the rights attached to shares, in the powers of boards of directors and shareholders and in company law generally. Also the role of the supervisory authorities for take-overs differs importantly, and in some countries rules do not even yet exist (Lannoo, 1999). In the domain of banking, the national central bank, banking supervisor and ministry of finance are, to different degrees across countries, entitled to scrutinise bank take-overs, on the grounds that they are responsible for financial stability and prudential supervision. These authorities often have extensive discretionary powers, as was exemplified recently in France, Italy and Portugal. EU authorities should make sure that the general EU Treaty rules are respected, and the supervisory aspects of bank take-overs are based on the prudential rules of the EU's second banking and solvency ratio directives, so as to ensure that eventual refusals have a clear basis. In the case of the Portuguese objections to the BSCH/Champalimaud merger, the European Commission referred the case to the European Court for non-compliance with the merger control regulation. This case was withdrawn in March 2000, after Portugal lifted its opposition to the concentration.

Some of the securities law aspects of take-overs are dealt with in the draft EU take-over bids directive, on which a common position was reached in June 2000. This directive may, however, not change so much, since many matters are left to the national implementing law. Moreover, the directive has 2004 as its implementation deadline.

A summary of the required changes in light of EMU and growing market integration is given in Table 14.5.

Table 14.4 Objectives of financial supervision and changes in the perspective of growing European market integration

Objective of supervision	Current structure	Required changes
Systemic risk (financial stability)	National supervisory authorities and/or NCBs	Role for ESCB/ECB and national supervisors in monitoring systemic exposures in European financial markets
		Create European Observatory of Systemic Risk
		Give role to Economic and Financial Committee (EFC) to coordinate emergency intervention
Prudential control (solvency control/ protection of depositors/investors/ policy-holders	National supervisory authorities (home country)	Strengthen supervisory coordination through creation of Forum of Financial Supervisors
	Bilateral Memoranda of Understanding	
	Different attitudes to banks in trouble	Preventive corrective action policies EU-wide
	Excessive forbearance	Harmonise supervisory practices
		Harmonise winding-up arrangements
		Align bank exit policies
Conduct of business (protection of consumers and investors)	Host country (country where service is provided) for retail and wholesale business	Home country rules for wholesale business
		Common interpretation of rules (FESCO)
	No level playing field for bank take-overs	Application of EU Treaty rules for bank take-overs

IV Conclusions

Financial supervision in a European context needs to evolve progressively with growing market integration, but a more centralised approach in financial supervision can only be justified where national or local approaches are no longer adequate for performing the task. A coordinated approach is now necessary to handle systemic issues that will no longer be limited to national borders, but also, and increasingly, for monitoring financial institutions with operations in a range of European countries. There is a vital need to identify a lead supervisor for each financial group and to reach agreement on precisely what the responsibilities of a lead supervisor would be. On the other hand, the externalities are lower in the case of limited coordination of control of conduct-of-business rules in retail financial services or in dealing in securities markets.

In addressing the structure of financial supervision at European level, a more horizontal approach, based on the objectives of supervision, is required. It is adapted to the conglomeration trend in the financial sector and makes it easier to detect and handle lacunae in the present supervisory structure. For systemic issues, there is no suggestion of leaving the central banks solely in charge of these matters, but the role of the ESCB could still benefit from more public clarification, and some joint body with the supervisors created to monitor aggregate risks. In addition, central banks, supervisors and finance ministries will need to cooperate to draft principles governing bail-outs of European-wide groups, which currently implicitly fall to the country of control and consolidated supervision. Since the LOLR role presumes the back-up of a finance ministry, which may not be prepared to bail out creditors in other member states, burden-sharing between European countries is for the time being the only way forward.

On the supervisory side, more coordination is needed between the different sectoral supervisory committees at senior level. This is not in place for the time being, but is probably what is most needed in view of the continuing restructuring in European finance. A kind of European Forum of Financial Supervisors should therefore be urgently created. This forum should primarily discuss problems in the adequate supervision of large European financial groups, and if necessary, draft a multilateral and multi-sectoral MoU. Such a body should also set a work programme to align supervisory practices in the EU to ease pan-European operations.

What the institutional framework for financial supervision will look like in a decade is still an open question at this point. From what is already happening in the markets, a more uniform system of supervision will at some stage be required, and the strict sectoral division of financial supervision will be increasingly out of date. A reconfiguration of the structures of financial supervision, based on a clear setting out of the objectives of financial supervision, would be useful.

A further institutionalisation of supervisory functions at European level is, as circumstances currently stand, legally and practically impossible and in any case unlikely to be politically acceptable. Whether in due course there will be unified European institutions rather than networks of national authorities will depend a lot both on the ways in which markets develop and authorities react. Efficiency of operation will be a major issue, as will consistency with underlying national differences, not least in many detailed aspects of market structure. Whether EU and national authorities will see any merit in transcending their individual perspectives when reacting to developments set into motion by EMU and the internal market, and contemplate the establishment of transnational supervisors remains a very open question.

ANNEX: EU AND EEA FORA FOR COOPERATION IN FINANCIAL SUPERVISION

Banking

1 Banking Advisory Committee (BAC)[11]
   - Established in 1977 by the First Banking Coordination Directive.
   - Threefold role: (1) assists the European Commission in drawing up new proposals for banking legislation; (2) helps to ensure adequate implementation; and (3) serves as the 'regulatory committee' under the so-called 'comitology' procedures for technical amendments to EC banking legislation. The latter are changes that can be made outside the normal legislative procedure.
   - Consists of high-level officials from finance ministries, central banks and supervisory authorities of the member states and from the Commission, with a maximum of three representatives per national delegation; officials from other EEA countries and the ECB participate as observers; the chairman of the Groupe de Contact also attends.
   - Chairman is chosen for a three-year period from representatives of member states; secretarial services are provided by the European Commission.
   - Meets three to four times a year.
   - Discussions are confidential, but a tri-annual report is published by the chairman.
   - When committee acts as 'regulatory committee', it is chaired by the European Commission.
   - Does not consider specific problems related to individual credit institutions.
2 Groupe de Contact (established 1972)
   - Set up by banking supervisors of EEA member states on a cooperative basis.
   - Deals with micro-prudential cooperation, including information-sharing both in general and in particular cases, and carries out comparative studies on policies and techniques of supervision. It also assembles, as required under the banking directives, various EEA-wide statistical services including on solvency, profitability and liquidity.
   - Consists of one official from each banking supervisory authority in the EEA; an official from the Commission also attends as adviser on legal issues but does not attend discussions dealing either with individual firms or sensitive supervisory assessments.
3 Banking Supervision Committee of the ECB (established 1998)
   - Succeeded Subcommittee on Banking Supervision of the European Monetary Institute, which had originally been created in 1990 as the

Banking Supervisory Subcommittee of the Committee of Governors of the EC Central Banks.

- Assists the ESCB with regard to policy issues in the area of macro-prudential supervision, that is, the stability of financial institutions and markets, and in preparing ECB opinions on legislation as provided for under the Treaty.
- Consists of high-level officials from all central banks and non-central bank supervisory authorities in member states plus ECB officials; Commission officials participate as observers.

Duplication of work is avoided through regular informal coordination meetings between chairmen of each of the three committees dealing with banking supervisory matters.

Securities markets

4 Contact Committee (established 1979)
- Advisory committee, without comitology role (except for one issue, which was never touched).
- Facilitates harmonised implementation and advises the Commission on any supplements or amendments to the 1979 stock exchange admission, 1980 listing particulars, 1989 prospectus, 1989 insider dealing, 1988 major holdings and forthcoming take-over bids directives.
- Allows regular consultation between the member states on these matters.

5 UCITS Contact Committee (established 1985)
- Advisory committee, without comitology role.
- Facilitates harmonised implementation and advises the Commission on any amendments to the 1985 UCITS directive (unit trusts directive).

6 High-Level Committee of Securities Market Supervisors (established 1985)
- Strategic committee, meets two to three times a year at the initiative of the European Commission.
- No formal legal basis, functions as Commission working group until Securities Committee is formally established by an EU directive.
- Advises the European Commission on regulatory and supervisory matters.

7 FESCO (Forum of European Securities Commissions, established December 1997)
- Originates from Informal Group of Chairmen of EU Securities Commissions.
- Brings together securities commissions of the European Economic Area (the EU, Iceland and Norway).

- Aims to enhance the exchange of information between national securities commissions, to provide the broadest possible mutual assistance to enhance market surveillance and effective enforcement, to enhance uniform implementation of EU directives and to develop common regulatory standards in areas that are not harmonised by European directives.

8 Securities Committee (proposed)
- High-level committee with implementing powers for the investment services and capital adequacy directives.
- Rejected twice because of procedural problems and sensitivity of European Parliament to 'comitology'.
- Relaunched in the Commission's financial services action plan (May 1999), proposed in Lamfalussy report (February 2001).

Insurance

9 Insurance Committee (established 1992)
- Assists the European Commission with regard to policy issues in the formulation and implementation of EC legislation for the insurance sector, consultative role for new Commission proposals.
- Consists of high-level officials from finance ministries and supervisory authorities of the member states plus Commission officials; officials from other EEA countries participate as observers.
- Serves as 'regulatory committee' under the so-called 'comitology' procedures for technical amendments to EC insurance legislation (life and non-life insurance).
- Does not consider specific problems related to individual insurance undertakings

10 Conference of Insurance Supervisory Authorities of the EU (established 1958)
- Forum for debate among EU supervisors on micro-prudential issues relating to individual insurance undertakings.
- Agreed on 'protocols', a form of multilateral memorandum of understanding between insurance supervisors, to deal with supervisory problems.
- Composed of fifteen EU states and three EEA countries, with European Commission as observer (no formal link with EU).
- Meets twice a year.

Cross-sector fora

11 Commission Mixed Technical Group on Financial Conglomerates
- Established in 1999, involving representatives of the sectoral regulatory committees.

- Considers information sharing between supervisors and co-ordination of prudential supervision on a cross-sectoral and cross-border basis, capital adequacy at group level and intra-group transactions.

Notes

1 This report was written in the context of a CEPS Working Party on Financial Supervision in EMU, chaired by David Green, Head of International Policy Coordination and EU Affairs of the UK Financial Services Authority. It was published earlier as CEPS working party report. On CEPS, see www.ceps.be.
2 The FSA has rule-making powers and is accountable to the government and Parliament. The Bank of England remains responsible for ensuring the overall stability of the financial system. The Bank would be the vehicle for lender-of-last-resort operations, if any, informing the Chancellor of the Exchequer, with the possibility then of an override by the Treasury. A Memorandum of Understanding between the Treasury, the Bank of England and the FSA sets out the respective responsibilities of the different bodies.
3 It has been suggested that the ECB might assume such a role but it should be noted that Art. 105.6 of the Treaty, which reads: 'The Council may . . . confer upon the ECB specific tasks concerning policies relating to the prudential supervision of credit institutions and other financial institutions with the exception of insurance undertakings', only refers to 'specific tasks concerning policies', not to day-to-day supervision, in which case a Treaty change would also be required.
4 'Die Unterschiedde in den Banken- und Aufsichtssytemen sind so gross, dass sie sich, wenn uberhaupt, nur auf sehr lange Sicht überwinden lassen', Gertrude Tumpel-Gugerell, Vice-Governor of the National Bank of Austria at the Alpbach Forum, quoted in *Handelsblatt*, 3 September 1999.
5 As stated by Tommaso Padoa-Schioppa, member of the ECB Executive Board, at the CFS Conference on 'Systemic risk and lender of last resort facilities', in Frankfurt, 11 June 1999. An agreement on this subject is said to have been reached in the ECB's Governing Council at the end of July 1999.
6 Some ministries of finance are currently thought to be pushing for a debate on this subject, but others potentially involved are said to be unwilling to address such issues in the abstract.
7 One function that could be performed by the Observatory is that it could act as a European risk-monitoring centre (see Meister, 2000).
8 'Beyond basic enabling powers, each competent authority operates in a different legal, accounting and cultural context, and it is appropriate that supervisory approaches differ. The Instruments chosen to implement the new principles should allow supervisors to adopt different supervisory approaches', European Commission (1999b, p. 70).
9 The EU Council reached a political agreement on the winding-up procedures for banks on 8 May 2000 and on those for insurance companies on 25 May.
10 Commission decision of 26 July 1995 giving conditional approval to the aid granted by France to Crédit Lyonnais, OJ L 308 of 21.12.1995.
11 This survey is largely based upon the Banking Advisory Committee's most recent report of the chairman (1994–97).

References

Aglietta, Michel and Christian de Boissieu (1998), 'Problèmes prudentiels', in *Co-ordination européenne des politiques économiques*, Conseil d'analyse économique, Paris.

Basel Committee on Banking Supervision (1999), 'A New Capital Adequacy Framework', Consultative Paper, June.

BIS, *Quarterly Review*, 'International banking and financial market developments', various issues.

Briault, Clive (1999), *The rationale for a single national financial services regulator*, FSA Occasional Paper.

Chance, Clifford (1998), *The draft financial services and markets bill: A framework for the future*, September.

Dale, Richard and Simon Wolfe (1998), 'The structure of financial regulation', *Journal of financial regulation and compliance*, Vol. 6, No. 4, pp. 326–350.

Danthine, Jean-Pierre, Francesco Giavazzi, Xavier Vives, Ernst-Ludwig von Thadden (1999), *The Future of European Banking*, Monitoring European Integration, CEPR.

Davies, Howard (1999), 'Euro-Regulation', Lecture for the European Financial Forum, Brussels, 8 April.

Deutsche Bank Research (1999), *M&A rules in Europe's banking industry: A need for reform?*, August 20.

Dewatripont, Mathias and Jean Tirole (1994), *The prudential regulation of banks*, Cambridge, MA: MIT Press.

Di Giorgio, Giorgio, Carmine Di Noia and Laura Piatti (2000), *Financial Market Regulation: The case for Italy and a proposal for the euro area*, Wharton Financial Institutions Center, Working Paper Series 00–24.

Enoch, Charles, Peter Stella and May Khamis (1997), *Transparency and Ambiguity in Central Bank Safety Net Operations*, IMF Working Paper 97/138, October.

European Central Bank (1999), *Effects of EMU on the EU banking system in the medium to long term*, February.

European Central Bank (2000), EMU and Banking Supervision, *Monthly Bulletin*, April.

European Commission, Banking Advisory Committee, Report of the Chairman, various issues.

European Commission (2000a), *Institutional Arrangements for the Regulation and Supervision of the Financial Sector*, January.

European Commission (2000b), *Report on Financial Stability*, Prepared by the ad-hoc working group of the Economic and Financial Committee, Economic Papers, No. 143, May.

European Commission (1999a), *Financial Services Action Plan*.

European Commission (1999b), *A review of regulatory capital requirements for EU credit institutions and investment firms*, Consultation document, November.

European Commission (1998), 'Financial services: Building a framework for action', Communication to the Council and the European Parliament, 28 October.

European Commission (1997a), Commission Interpretative Communication, 'Freedom to provide services and the interest of the general good in the second banking directive', OJ C 209 of 10.7.1997.

European Commission (1997b), Report to the Insurance Committee on the Need for Further Harmonisation of the Solvency Margin, COM(97)398, 24.07.97.

European Investment Bank (1999), *European banking after EMU*, EIB Papers, Vol. 4, No. 1.

European Shadow Financial Regulatory Committee (ESFRC) (1998), 'Dealing with problem banks in Europe', Statement No.1, 22 June.

European Shadow Financial Regulatory Committee (1998), 'EMU, the ECB and financial supervision', Statement No. 2, 19 October.

Favero, Carlo, Xavier Freixas, Torsten Persson and Charles Wyplosz (2000), *One Money, Many Countries,* Monitoring the European Central Bank 2, CEPR.

Fender, Ingo and Jürgen von Hagen (1998), Central bank policy in a more perfect financial system, ZEI policy paper B98–03.

Goodhart, Charles (1999), 'Myths about the Lender of Last Resort', mimeo.

Goodhart, Charles, Philipp Hartmann, David T. Llewellyn, Liliana Rojas-Suarez and Steven R. Weisbrod (1997), *Financial regulation: Why, how and where now?*, London: Routledge.

Goodhart, Charles and Dirk Schoenmaker (1995), 'Should the functions of monetary policy and banking supervision be separated?', *Oxford Economic Papers*, Vol. 47, pp. 539–560.

Grande, Mauro (1999), 'Possible decentralisation of state aid control in the banking sector', Paper presented at the EU Competition Workshops on State Aid, EUI, June.

Green, David (2000), 'Enhanced co-operation among regulators and the role of national regulators in a global market', *Journal of International Financial Markets*, Vol. 2, Issue 1, pp. 7–12.

Gros, Daniel (1998), *European Financial Markets and Global Financial Turmoil: Any Danger of a Credit Crunch?*, CEPS Working Document No. 127, Centre for European Policy Studies, Brussels.

Inzerillo Ugo, P. Morelli and Giovanni Pittaluga (2000), 'Deregulation and changes in the European banking industry', in Giampaolo Galli and Jacques Pelkmans (eds), *Regulatory Reform and Competitiveness in Europe*, Vol. 2, Cheltenham, UK: Edward Elgar, 2000.

Kaufman, George G. (1995), 'Comment on systemic risk', *Research in Financial Services Private and Public Policy*, Vol. 7, pp. 47–52.

Kaufman, George G. (1996), 'Bank failures, systemic risk and regulation', *Cato Journal*, Vol. 16, No. 1, pp. 17–45.

Lannoo, Karel and Valentina Stadler (2000), *The EU Repo Markets*, CEPS Working Document.

Lannoo, Karel (1999), *Does Europe Need an SEC?*, European Capital Markets Institute (ECMI), Occasional Paper No. 1, November.

Lannoo, Karel and Daniel Gros (1998), *Capital Markets and EMU*, Report of a CEPS Working Party, CEPS, Brussels.

Lannoo, Karel (1995), 'The Single Market in Banking – A First Assessment', *Butterworths Journal of Banking and Financial Law*, November, London.

Mayes, David (1999), 'On the problems of the home country', mimeo.

Meister, Edgar (2000), 'Die Hüter eines stabilen Finanzsystems', *Frankfurter Allgemeine*, 8 April.

Ministry of Finance, The Netherlands (1999), *Institutionele vormgeving van het toezicht op de financiële marktsector*, April.

Molyneux, Philip (1997), 'Internet and the Global Challenges for Financial Services in Europe', Paper presented at a CEPS seminar, October.

OECD (1999), *Bank Profitability Statistics*.

Padoa-Schioppa, Tommaso (1999), 'EMU and Banking Supervision', *International Finance*, Vol. 2, No. 2, pp. 295–308.

Prati, Alessandro and Garry Schinasi (1998), 'Will the ECB be the lender of last resort in EMU?', Paper presented at the SUERF Conference, Frankfurt, October 1998.

Schoenmaker, Dirk (1995), *Banking Supervision in Stage Three of EMU*, in Lannoo, Karel, Dirk Schoenmaker and Stéphane Van Tilborg, The Single Market in Banking: From 1992 to EMU, CEPS research report No.17.

Shadow Financial Regulatory Committees of Europe, Japan, and the US (1999), 'Improving the Basle Committee's New Capital Adequacy Framework', Joint Statement of a Sub-group, June.

Vander Vennet, Rudi (1998), 'Cost and profit dynamics in financial conglomerates and universal banks', Paper presented at the Suerf Conference, October.

White, William R. (1998*), The Coming Transformation of Continental European Banking*, BIS Working Papers No. 54, June.

15 Impact of globalization on efficiency in the European banking industry

What can we learn from the cost to income ratio?*

Peter Van Dijcke[1]

Abstract

Increased competition, ongoing consolidation, continuing pressure for the reduction of existing excess capacity and shrinking profitability in the European banking industry have put efficiency high on the agenda of most banks as they monitor their performance over time and against competitors. The research literature provides little consensus on the efficiency topic as no broad pattern can be detected for scale-, scope- and X-efficiency. However, it is generally documented that X-inefficiencies tend to be much larger than scale- and scope-inefficiencies. The rationale of looking at the cost to income ratio and its dispersion is the growing use of it as a proxy for bank (in)efficiency. Possible dispersion is often interpreted as an indication of (in)efficiency. This paper gives a brief overview of the cost to income ratio within the European banking industry as the recent consolidation wave is reflected in only an overall small reduction of the ratio. Linear benchmarking of the cost to income ratio may be misleading as the interpretation is often not unambiguous. Based on a regression model for a sample of European banks, the residual-analysis could be used as a simple indication of possible (in)efficiency. The results reveal that both for commercial banks and savings banks the ratio is initially quite high and robust. Changing the composition of the bank income (all other elements remaining equal) through increasing the share of interest income and trading income should result in a lower ratio, while shifting towards fee business has an upward pressure on the ratio. As expected, lowering the share of personnel costs in the total overhead tends to move the cost to income ratio downwards. The regression model tends to signal that changing the composition of the bank income and overhead has on average a small impact. The findings therefore seem to confirm that changing scale and scope has a limited impact on the cost to income ratio. By using the available inputs efficiently in order to generate a given (or higher) output level the direct impact on the ratio itself is much larger.

* Paper presented at 22nd SUERF Colloquium, Vienna, 27–29 April 2000.

Nevertheless, when looking at the residuals (and the ratio itself), it is necessary to compare 'similar' bank types in order to minimize the differences in output mix (and thus the differences in cost of production). Under these conditions, the residuals may give a simple indication of efficiency (or inefficiency).

1 Introduction: A short story on bank strategies, consolidation and the cost to income ratio in Europe

EMU, increased competition, continuing pressure on profitability and, more recently, technology have provoked in general three main strategic directions in *banks' strategies* (ECB, 1999): (1) quality and efficiency in services and procedures (staff, IT, risk management, control systems, cost-efficiency); (2) shift in product ranges (search for alternative income sources, from traditional revenue to new income sources, re-allocation of product ranges); and (3) M&A, strategic alliances and co-operation agreements, thereby focusing on cost controlling, efficiency improvements, geographic expansion and, more recently, entering the domain of e-banking. The data show that most transformation of the banking industry is done via M&A (compared with the other alternatives such as co-operation agreements, partnership and alliances, restructuring and internal growth) given the immediate impact on the growth pace and the rapid implementation of strategies. It is generally accepted that on the European playing field, size and European coverage will be an important factor on certain banking segments ('big is not beautiful but necessary').

Between 1985 and 1998, the domestic (or in-market) *consolidation* of both the European banking industry and the European insurance industry was quite pronounced (see Figure 15.1). However, insurance companies were also

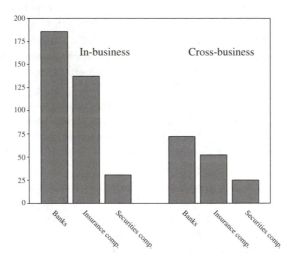

Figure 15.1 European *domestic* M&A, 1985–1998 (billions of US$*).
Source: Walter, 1999.
* Sum of the equity values of the target institutions.

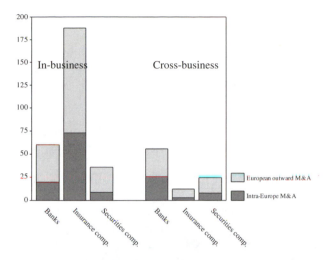

Figure 15.2 European *cross-border* M&A, 1985–1998 (billions of US$*).

Source: Walter, 1999.

* Sum of the equity values of the target institutions.

quite active cross-border (or cross-market) both intra-Europe as outside Europe (see Figure 15.2). Both figures show clearly the defensive European consolidation trend in banking over the considered period. This domestic consolidation was (and still is) based on the conviction of the necessity of a strong home market (before moving abroad) and the fear of the control of banks by foreigners (Boot, 1999). It also shows that the single market programme has initially triggered a strong domestic consolidation process. Forced by EMU and the euro, it is clear that this first wave of domestic banking consolidation is gradually fading out and showing signs of maturing. General expectations are that the domestic consolidation is actually being replaced by cross-border merger and acquisition activity and cross-border coverage through electronic distribution channels. However, since 1998 Germany, Spain, France and Italy have continued their domestic consolidation as they were somewhat behind the other EU countries in their 'national' consolidation process. In the field of bancassurance, the data show that banks took more initiatives to acquire insurance companies. Nevertheless, the large step forward of insurance companies in in-business and cross-border merger and acquisition, points out that they will take a prominent position in the further development of bancassurance. There is some irony in the fact that both for banks and insurance companies the European outward M&A was larger than the intra-European M&A. Both banks and insurance companies seemed to prefer to take first initial positioning in the US, Latin America (led by Spanish banks) and Eastern Europe before looking their European counterparts in the eye.

Are there specific driving forces behind an M&A trend? In general, M&A

tend to develop and accelerate on four broad conditions (Smith and Walter, 1998; White, 1998):

- changing government regulatory or economic policies;
- a strong economic or technological rationale for restructuring;
- an undervaluation of companies relative to their replacement value;
- the existence of a strong bull market.

All four factors seem applicable actually to the European banking industry and thus supporting the generally accepted view on the expected future wave of cross-border consolidation.

But how is the recent surge in M&A being justified? The important factors are (Smith and Walter, 1998; Groeneveld, 1998): (1) accessing information and proprietary technologies; (2) increasing market power; (3) reduce unit costs; (4) economies of scale; (5) economies of scope; (6) diversification; (7) geographical coverage; (8) tax benefits; (9) satisfaction of management goals;(10) increased pressure for shareholders' value; and last but not least (11) herding behaviour.

Undoubtedly, the most cited motivation in the past was the improvement of performance by cost cutting or searching economies of scale as the domestic consolidation was mainly driven by the cost-cutting factor (Dermine, 1999). This traditional argument for domestic M&A will be less present or valid when going cross-border.

What are the remaining cross-border restructuring barriers in Europe? Most elements are not new (Hurst, 1999):

- the remaining high level of public ownership of banks;
- non-economic motives ('national flagships');
- still a large number of co-operative savings banks;
- the present labour rigidities and the problem of staff reduction.

Striking is that until recently, the domestic consolidation was not leading to a significant reduction in the branch network (Abraham, 1998). Walter (1999) is quite clear on this subject and states that 'the potential for change (in Europe) is set against the state of substantial overcapacity and inefficiency in broad segments of the euro-zone ...'.

EMU and the euro will certainly continue to intensify competition, remove remaining 'national' barriers and change the macro-economic context. Furthermore, it is quite difficult to estimate the full impact of technology on banking activity. However, surplus capacity, branch networks and the predominance of traditional banking in Europe remain actually a burden for the European banking industry and require a reorientation of strategy as 'new entrants' (although actually still lacking market share) are entering the market via alternative distribution channels and thus low-cost margins (telephone, internet, mail, supermarkets, automotive, . . .).

Intense global competition and the direct and indirect effects of EMU have strongly accelerated the need among banks to increase efficiency and reduce costs. As the banking industry also becomes less labour-intensive, thereby increasing the pressure to reduce the number of branches and employees, benchmarks emerge to measure this effort in relation to profitability. The cost to income ratio[2] appears to become one of these cost-efficiency benchmarks (regularly the term 'cost to income ratio' is cited as 'efficiency ratio' in the financial press). The general idea remains that the banking industry is still characterized by a considerable surplus capacity resulting in a higher cost to income ratio. In the urge to lower their cost to income ratio, banks may have ignored a number of important factors which put the interpretation and comparison of the cost to income ratio between banks in a different perspective. According to the ECB (1999), efforts to increase efficiency (recorded by the evolution of the cost to income ratio) in the EU banking industry are taking place at a slow pace on aggregate, but at a significantly different pace across EU countries.

Aware of the existing criticism on cost ratio studies, compared with the extensive cost function research on efficiency, it is the central point of view in this paper. The rationale of looking at the cost to income ratio and its dispersion, is the recent use of the ratio as a key measure of bank efficiency. Possible dispersion of the European average is often interpreted as inefficiency and/or excess capacity. The purpose of this paper is to go more in-depth into this ratio and to benchmark EU countries and bank types against each other.

2 The research literature on efficiency

Summarizing very briefly, three types of efficiencies have been studied in the literature:

1 Scale efficiency: defined as the effect on aggregate costs by choosing the right amount of outputs (size-efficiency).

2 Scope-efficiency: defined as the effect on aggregate costs by choosing an optimal or efficient combination of outputs (product-mix efficiency).

3 X-efficiency: defined as the effect on aggregate costs by using the available inputs efficiently in order to produce a given level of output, also called operational-efficiency or allocative (optimal input mix) and technological (non-excess use of inputs) efficiency. It is also often defined as the difference in costs between a particular bank and a bank producing exactly the same outputs but operating at the industry's best practice.[3]

Despite the extensive research, efficiency in banking remains a somewhat contested and controversial subject (see Table 15.1 for a brief overview of the

Table 15.1 Some recent research and conclusions on bank efficiency of European data, mixed data and US data

	The data	Scale-inefficiencies[1]	Scope-inefficiencies[2]	X-inefficiencies	Other remarks/conclusions
European Data[3]					
Bourgeois, Fortésa & Leroyer (2000)	86 European banks (1994–1997)			On average only a small improved efficiency of 0.8% is noted between 94 and 97.	Costs are unnecessarily high in more than 80% of the cases.
Wagenvoort & Schure (1999 a,b,c)	1,974 European banks (1993–1997)	Rapidly exhausted economies of scale, indicating no major gains from scale economies (disappear at a balance sheet total of 600m EUR).		On average an estimated X-inefficiency of 16% in 1997 (but large differences between EU-countries). X-inefficiency: large banks (14%), small banks (20%), commercial banks (13%), savings banks (9%). Significant drop in costs between 96 and 97 for efficient savings banks of 9%. No significant change in cost improvement for commercial banks.	
Bikker (1999)	3,085 European banks (1989–1997)			Average X-inefficiency is estimated to be probably higher than the 20% found in literature. Average European X-efficiency ranges from 51% to 38%.	Cost to income ratio proven to be totally inappropriate as a proxy of efficiency. Existence of large differences in average cost level and X-efficiency between EU countries.

Table 15.1 cont.

	The data	Scale-inefficiencies[1]	Scope-inefficiencies	X-inefficiencies[2]	Other remarks/conclusions
Carbo, Gardener & Williams (1998)	852 European Savings banks (1989–1996)	Scale economies are widespread across different countries and increase with bank size. Overall scale economies are estimated at 7–10%.		X-inefficiencies estimated on average at 22%.	Larger savings banks realize greater scale economies and benefit more from technical progress (highlighted as an important factor promoting consolidation in the European savings bank indusry). Largest cost savings by focusing on reduction of X-inefficiencies than on scale-inefficiency.
Casu & Molyneux (1999)	530 European banks (1993–1997)			On average large inefficiency levels are noted (35%).	Efficiency differences across European banking markets appear to be mainly determined by country-specific factors. Since EU's SMP only small improvement in bank efficiency level are recorded. Widening of efficiency gap over the considered period.
Maudos, Pastor, Pérez & Quesada (1999)	879 European banks (1993–1996)			On average cost would reduce by 8–9% by eliminating X-inefficiencies.	Product-mix is important for the proper measurement of efficiency.

Table 15.1 cont.

	The data	Scale-inefficiencies[1]	Scope-inefficiencies	X-inefficiencies[2]	Other remarks/conclusions
Vander Vennet (1996)	2,375 European banks (1995–1996)	Large unexploited scale economies for small banks (esp. specialized banks); for the large size banks there are neither scale benefits nor disadvantages.	Unexploited scope economies only for the smallest size categories.	Overall average cost inefficiency of approximately 20%.	Financial conglomerates are more revenue efficient than more specialized competitors. Degree of both cost and profit efficiency higher in universal banks than in non-universal banks. Further despecialization may lead to a more efficient banking system.
Dietsch & Weill (1998)	661 European banks (1991–1996)	Scale efficiency decreased between 92 and 96.		High levels of inefficiency in Europe. Increase of cost efficiency of +4.4% between 92 and 96. Allocative efficiency increased firmly between 92 and 96 (change in mix of inputs).	No large increase of efficiency during 1992–1996. Low positive effect on banking efficiency due to European integration.
Altunbas & Chakravarty (1998)	2,412 European banks (1988–1995)			Average X-inefficiency of 25%. Commercial banks (27%), savings banks (20%).	Country differences in X-inefficiency observed between countries could arise due to the differences in the structure of banking.

Table 15.1 cont.

	The data	Scale-inefficiencies[1]	Scope-inefficiencies	X-inefficiencies[2]	Other remarks/conclusions
Pastor et al. (1997)	400 European banks (1992)			Large differences of technical efficiency across countries.	
Lang & Weizel (1996)	German universal banks	Economies of scale among German universal banks up to a size of 5 billion DM.	Absence of scope economies, changing product mix has only a minor impact on average costs.		
Goldberg & Rai (1993)	79 European banks (1998–1991)	Scale-inefficiency estimated to range from 3% to 8%.		X-inefficiency estimated to range from 18% to 36%.	No positive relationship between concentration and profitability.
Vander Vennet (1994)	1,436 banks (1991–1992)	Scale economies present for medium to large banks (optimal scale of 3–10 billion US$ asset).	Scope economies recorded for the largest banks.		Efficiency does not have a statistical effect on profitability.

Table 15.1 cont.

	The data	Scale-inefficiencies[1]	Scope-inefficiencies	X-inefficiencies[2]	Other remarks/conclusions
Mixed Data					
Berger et al. (1999)	Overview of 250 studies on the consolidation of the financial services industry	1980 & early 1990 data: average cost curve has a relatively flat U-shape with medium-sized banks being slightly more efficient than either large or small banks (location of scale efficient point between $100 million and $10 billion in assets). No significant scale efficiencies to be gained from M&A involving large banks. Increased cost scale efficiency in the 1990s (probably due to technological progress).	Very few cost savings from consolidating the outputs of different banks.	Great potential for X-efficiency from M&A, averaging 20%. Little or no cost X-efficiency improvement on average from M&A in the 1980s. At best only modest gains from M&A in most cases in the 1990s.	
Berger & Humphrey (1997)	Survey of 130 studies on efficiency in 21 countries.			On average X-inefficiencies range from 20% to 25%.	Cost efficiency is found to be more important than market concentration in explaining profitability. M&A may improve profit efficiency (due to altering output mix toward more profitable products) rather than cost efficiency.

Table 15.1 cont.

	The data	Scale-inefficiencies[1]	Scope-inefficiencies	X-inefficiencies[2]	Other remarks/conclusions
Allen & Rai (1996)	194 banks in 15 countries (1988–1992)			Average cost inefficiency of 21% (large banks 27%, small banks 16%). Large banks in separated banking countries are less efficient than other bank groups.	
Berg et al. (1996)	945 banks in 4 Nordic countries (1990)				Large banks are more efficient.
Ruthenberg & Elias (1996)	75 banks in 15 countries (1989–1990)			Cost efficiencies ranging from 6% to 81% for different size classes.	
Saunders & Walter (1994)	World 200 largest banks	Economies of scale up to 25 billion US$ in loans.	Diseconomies of scope between loans and fee-earning business.		
Fecher & Pestiau (1993)	OECD-countries (1971–1986)				Low gains of productivity due to technical inefficiency.
Some results on US data (non-exhaustive)					
Rhoades (1998)	9 mergers of relatively large banks.				Cost cutting objectives were achieved fairly quickly. 4 out of 9 were successful in improving efficiency while 7 improved profitability.

Table 15.1 cont.

	The data	Scale-inefficiencies[1]	Scope-inefficiencies	X-inefficiencies[2]	Other remarks/conclusions
Various Berger et al., various research papers (1999, 1997, 1993, 1987, . . .)	US banks	Shifting of the optimal scale in banking and substantial unexploited scale economies for medium-sized and large banks in the 1990s. Scale and scope inefficiency account in general for less than 5% of costs.	Economies of scope exhausted at very low output levels.	Decrease of the cost-inefficiency noted from 20% in the 1980s to 13% in the 1990s. Average unit costs in the banking industry lie some 20% above best practice.	On average bank mergers increase profit efficiency relative to other banks, but have little effect on cost efficiency: efficiency gains are more pronounced when merging banks are inefficient ('wake up' sign), while efficiency tends to decline after mergers for banks that were relatively efficient ex ante.
Clark (1996) & Clark (1988)	US banks	No scale economies or diseconomies above 2 billion US$ of total assets. Exhausted at relatively small output levels.		Economic cost inefficiency estimated to be small (3%). Production cost inefficiency is found to be larger (9%).	

1 Doubling the level of all outputs would not lead to twice as much costs (i.e. costs would increase with 100% minus the scale-inefficiency %).
2 The same level of output could be produced with less current inputs if banks were operating on the efficient frontier (i.e. a reduction of the inputs with the X-inefficiency %).
3 Most surveys provide also an insight into individual EU-countries' efficiency.

most recent articles and conclusions on efficiency based on European data, mixed data and US data). The available studies have not found (or failed to find) general applicable and consistent economies of scale, scope or X-efficiencies within the banking industry. However a number of broad guidelines can be drawn across the available empirical studies.

Economies of scale seem to be exhausted at relatively small output levels, signalling a relatively flat U-shaped average cost curve with some evidence of scale-inefficiencies for both the smallest and largest banks. However, recent research indicates that regulatory and technological changes may have shifted the optimal scale in banking.

For the *economies of scope*, little consensus can be found in the literature. Scope economies in banking, if at all present, may vary largely but also seem to be exhausted at very low levels of output. Both the result for economies of scale and economies of scope remain mixed and estimates may vary largely across countries and studies. Furthermore, few indications are actually available on the full impact of the recent technological changes and the introduction of the euro on the optimal scale and scope as defined in the literature.

The most important factor found in the literature on efficiency gains is a reduction in *X-inefficiency*. Some authors put it quite clearly and state that 'the way banks are run is more important than the business that they pursue' (Smith and Walter, 1998; Walter, 1999). But X-inefficiencies seem to vary largely when calculated across countries, bank types, output levels and over time (see Figure 15.3). X-inefficiencies are on average estimated to be around 20% and gradually decreasing since the beginning of the 1990s.

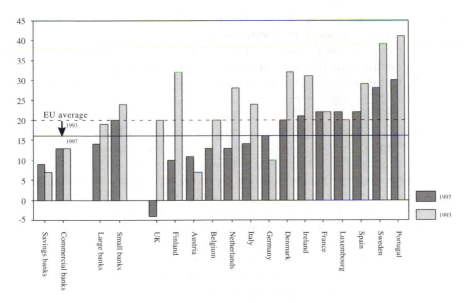

Figure 15.3 Estimated X-inefficiencies in the EU, 1993–1997 (in %).

Source: Wagenvoort and Schure, 1999.

Overlooking the efficiency literature, it is generally documented that X-inefficiencies are in general much larger than scale-inefficiencies and scope-inefficiencies (Berger, 1999; Molyneux, 1999; and others). This means that banks can improve their overall cost efficiency to a greater extent if they emulate the banking industry's best practice, thereby increasing their managerial and technological efficiency (reducing X-inefficiencies), rather than by increasing their size (scale economies) or diversifying (scope economies). According to Milbourn, Boot and Thakor (1999) banks are still expanding their size and their scope for two reasons: (1) the reputation enhancement of the management (which could lead to herd behaviour despite a dissipation of shareholders' wealth); (2) the higher shareholders' wealth from increasing the size and expanding scope (through the announcement effect and post-merger performance of the bank).

Several authors have indicated why the efficiency gains, given the strong consolidation process, are on average not explicitly present or even not observable. A number of conceptual difficulties may explain the differences in the empirical findings or the failure of finding evidence: existence of a unique optimum output level, optimizing behaviour of banks, form of the cost function, conformity of data, data distorting effect of M&A (unpredictable noise in the integration process), difficulties of measuring changes in the product mix, changes in input prices, difficulties of measuring additional services or higher service quality, time period insufficiently long (see Hurst, Perée and Fischbachs 1999; Smith and Walter, 1998; Berger, 1999; Bikker, 1999; Piloff and Santomero, 1998). Calomiris (1999) adds four additional methodological problems when considering the effect of consolidation on efficiency:

• poor measures of market perception on the efficiency of mergers (e.g. when including stock price variables);
• the lack of counterfactual benchmarks of comparison (what if-analysis);
• the question whether inefficient transactions are permanent;
• the fact that bank performance may not be a sufficient measure of economic efficiency (e.g. consumer gains).

When looking at *cost ratios* (in comparison with cost function research), the problem of disentangling changes in market power from changes in efficiency arises. Simple cost ratios do not control for input prices or a reduction in cost per unit of income may, for example, reflect either lower interest expenses due to increased market power or greater efficiency in input usage. Using cost ratios also does not account for the fact that some product mixes cost more to produce than others. Banks may produce different output mixes that have different cost of production. Most studies under review in Table 15.1 used X-efficiency methods that employ cost functions to control for input prices, outputs and other factors, to measure the efficiency effects of countries, bank type, size groups or M&A. Despite the differences in approach between the X-efficiency studies and the cost ratio studies, both come essentially to the same conclusion (Berger, 1999).

3 Empirical analysis: What can we learn from the cost to income ratio?

3.1 Bank selection

Our main data source is the FitchIBCA Bankscope CD-Rom. For the country analysis a selection was made for the EU banks (unconsolidated annual accounts) on a number of criteria. Starting from this large dataset and for the individual data analysis, outlying banks or banks that did not report all relevant items were excluded (see Table 15.5 for a country distribution of the sample). The following banks are also excluded: non-banking credit institutions, holding companies and central banks. It is important to notice that for each graphical comparison, the data are calculated on a *weighted basis*.

3.2 Country analysis of the cost to income ratio

As already mentioned in the introduction, the cost to income ratio and its standard deviation may give an indication of potential inefficiency. The following illustrations and analysis are based on this assumption.

- **Cost to income ratio across EU member states**
  The cost to income ratio varies largely between EU countries (Figure 15.4): from 75 (Netherlands) to 42 (Luxembourg). The *reference line* in each graph represents the average for the EU. On an aggregated basis, the

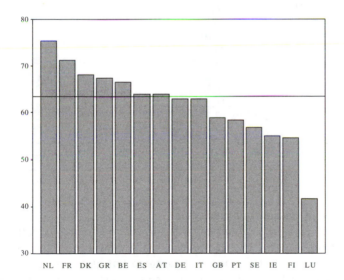

Figure 15.4 Cost to income ratio, 1998.

Source:Bankscope, own calculations.

Note: Reference line = EU average.

Netherlands, France, Denmark, Greece and Belgium are clearly above the EU average. The large dispersion of the *standard deviation* indicates that the results should be interpreted with caution (Table 15.2). The high standard deviations for Belgium and France show that a large number of Belgian and French banks have a cost to income ratio that differs from the country mean and suggest a large dispersion in cost structure and/or income structure. For the Netherlands and Denmark, two countries at the upper end of Figure 15.4, the dispersion is far less pronounced. In these two countries banks tend to have 'similar' cost to income structure, but are according to their cost to income ratio marked as rather inefficient (under the assumption that the cost to income ratio is a proxy for efficiency). Later in this paper, it is demonstrated that a bank's focus on a specific income structure may justify a higher cost level (additional services or higher service quality may raise costs but also revenues – by more than the cost – resulting in the measurement of worsened cost productivity, but an improved profit productivity, Berger, 1999).

Table 15.2 The standard deviation of the country cost to income ratio, 1998

Std Deviation	
FR	51.2
GB	40.9
SE	38.0
BE	36.3
DE	30.8
ES	26.4
LU	25.7
IT	25.0
GR	23.5
PT	21.7
FI	19.8
IE	19.7
NL	18.7
DK	17.3
AT	14.0
EU	*32.3*

Source: Bankscope, own calculations.

- **Evolution of the cost to income ratio**
  A general tendency is noted towards a lower cost to income ratio (shift to the left on Figure 15.5). However, as noted by the ECB, this trend is taking place at a slow pace on aggregate but at significantly different speeds across EU countries. The average EU cost to income ratio reduced from 65.6 to 63.4 over the considered period. Three countries showed an increase in the cost to income ratio: Netherlands, Sweden and Denmark.

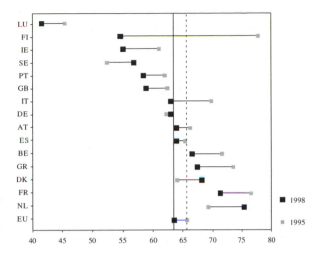

Figure 15.5 Evolution of the cost to income ratio, 1995–1998.

Source: Bankscope, own calculations.

- **Income per unit of personnel expenses**

    The figures below show a (reversed) decomposition of the cost to income ratio and could be interpreted as an indication of productivity (bank income per unit of personnel cost). Not surprisingly, the same countries can be found as in Figure 15.4 at the lower end in Figure 15.6. The results are more interesting when we decompose total operating income in its three components:

    - net interest revenue: still the same countries at the lower end (Figure 15.7);
    - trading income: Belgium and France show up at the higher end of the figure, indicating their strong focus on trading income (Figure 15.8);
    - commission income: indicating the very poor performance of Belgium (Figure 15.9). Recent data indicate that Belgian banks are catching up quite rapidly on commission income.

Note that the Netherlands remains in each figure below the EU average. This indication of inefficiency in the Netherlands partly coincided with the strong surge in consolidation in the Netherlands during this period (see also Figures 15.14 to 15.17).

Figures 15.6 to 15.9 are presented in tabular form in Table 15.3. For one unit of personnel cost, Belgian banks generate on average 2.86 units of total operating income. This is composed of 1.77 units of net interest income, 0.61 units of trading income and 0.40 units of commission income.

Table 15.3 Bank income per unit of personnel expenses (PE) – 1998

	Total operating income/PE	Net interest income/PE	Trading income/PE	Commission income/PE
LU	5.18	2.26	0.43	1.53
FI	4.15	2.48	0.47	0.87
SE	3.84	2.66	0.27	0.77
GB	3.41	2.11	0.16	0.90
PT	3.30	1.92	0.56	0.55
IE	3.23	2.09	0.10	0.78
DK	3.00	1.99	0.08	0.60
DE	2.98	2.13	n.a.	0.53
AT	2.95	1.82	0.19	0.57
BE	2.86	1.77	0.61	0.40
IT	2.78	1.67	0.23	0.68
ES	2.59	1.88	0.14	0.55
FR	2.42	1.26	0.51	0.60
NL	2.42	1.50	0.18	0.65
GR	2.33	1.33	0.33	0.56
EU	2.92	1.85	0.27	0.66

Source: Bankscope, own calculations.

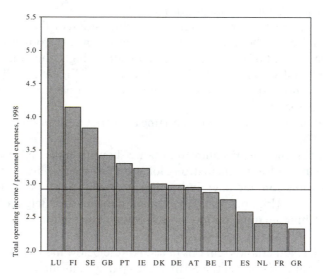

Figure 15.6 Total operating income per unit of personnel cost, 1998.

Source: Bankscope, own calculations.

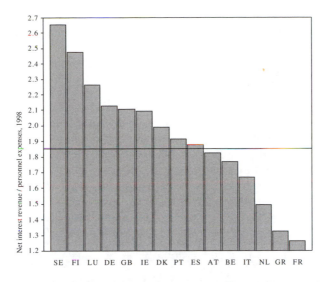

Figure 15.7 Net interest revenue per unit of personnel cost, 1998.
Source: Bankscope, own calculations.

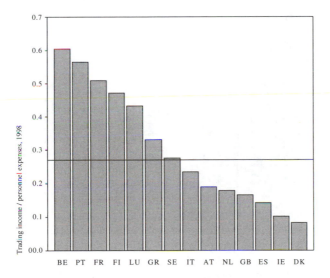

Figure 15.8 Net trading income per unit of personnel cost, 1998.
Source: Bankscope, own calculations.

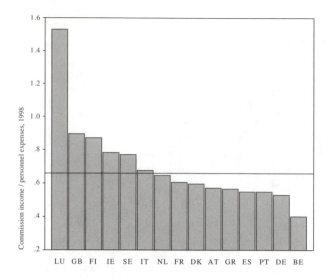

Figure 15.9 Net commission income per unit of personnel cost, 1998.
Source: Bankscope, own calculations.

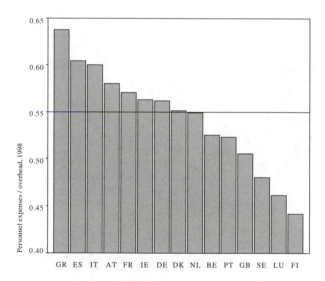

Figure 15.10 Share of personnel cost in total overhead, 1998.
Source: Bankscope, own calculations.

- **Personnel expenses as a percentage of overhead**
  Apparently Belgian banks have a significantly lower share of personnel
  expenses in their overhead (Figure 15.10). This gives no indication on the
  personnel cost per employee. Unfortunately no significant European

comparison is possible on the number of employees, as very few banks report their employment level within Bankscope.

- **Cost to income and profitability**

  If the cost to income ratio could be used as a proxy for efficiency, this should be reflected in a negative and high correlation between the cost to income ratio and profitability (although the loan loss provision may disturb this correlation). Apparently no such correlation exists in general between size, ROE and cost to income ratio (Table 15.4). As could be expected, this correlation does somewhat emerge when looking at approximately similar bank types. This raises an important point on the cost to income ratio, namely that it could be used as a proxy for efficiency when used and benchmarked against 'similar' competitors.

Table 15.4 Correlation between size, ROE and cost to income ratio

	Asset–ROE	*Asset–CTI*	*ROE–CTI*
Top 100	0.12	0.14	−0.07
Top 500	0.13	−0.04	−0.25
Top 2000	0.09	−0.08	−0.23
Savings banks & Cooperative banks	0.14	−0.02	−0.32
Commercial banks	0.05	0.01	−0.14
Investment banks	−0.09	0.14	−0.14
High net interest income*	0.24	−0.41	−0.46
High commission income and personnel expenses**	0.37	−0.34	−0.57

* Net interest revenue > 90% of total operating income.
** Commission income > 70% of total operating income and personnel expenses > 50% of overhead.

Source: Bankscope, own calculations.

Nevertheless the relationship between the cost to income ratio and profitability on a country basis provides an interesting insight in the evolution of a country's bank environment over time (Figures 15.11 to 15.13). Local competition and regulation will to a large extent determine whether a country will be situated at the upper line of Figure 15.12 or the lower line (given an equal cost to income ratio). When looking at the evolution from 1995 to 1998, it is noted that mainly the countries situated at the lower end and the higher end of the cost to income ratio have lifted their ROE. In Figure 15.12, it is interesting to see how Belgium and Spain are located at the upper line and this compared with Italy and Austria which are situated at the lower line. The four countries have approximately the same cost to income ratio and a similar (and rather low) productivity score (see Figure 15.6). However, due to the low loan loss provision (Belgium and Spain) and a high leverage (Belgium), a country can shift to the upper line.

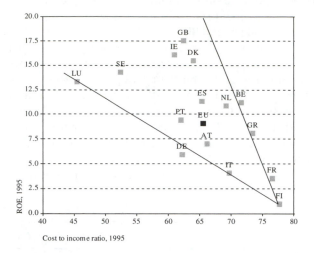

Figure 15.11 Cost to income and profitability, 1995.

Source: Bankscope, own calculations.

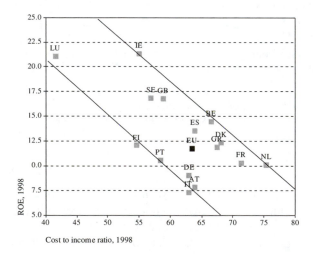

Figure 15.12 Cost to income and profitability, 1998.

Source: Bankscope, own calculations.

- **Impact of consolidation** (expressed as the increase in total assets and in total operating income) on the cost to income ratio
  The medium group (see Figure 15.14, asset increase between 30% and 50% over the considered period) has in general succeeded in lowering the cost to income ratio since 1995. Lower size-growth tends to deliver a more mixed result, while for the Netherlands, the strong growth in total

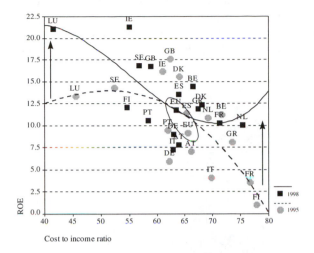

Figure 15.13 Cost to income and profitability, 1995–1998.

Source: Bankscope, own calculations.

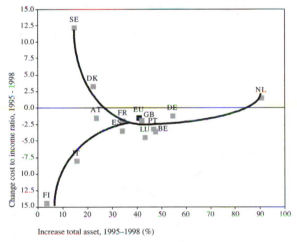

IE, GR not included. Only banks with data available in both years
(analysis based on the unconsolidated annual accounts)

Figure 15.14 Average impact of growth in total asset on the country cost to income
ratio, 1995–1998.

Source: Bankscope, own calculations.

asset has resulted in a higher cost to income ratio. When looking at the growth of total operational income, the result is broadly the same (Figure 15.16). Figures 15.15 and 15.17 show the consolidation volume in each country (rebased, namely Belgium = 100). Consolidation was considerably

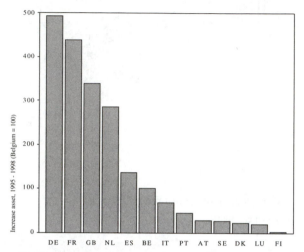

IE, GR not included. Only banks with data available in both years
(analysis based on the unconsolidated annual accounts)

Figure 15.15 Increase of total asset compared, 1995–1998 (Belgium = 100).
Source: Bankscope, own calculations.

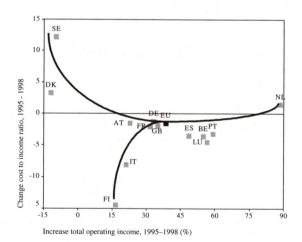

IE, GR not included. Only banks with data available in both years
(analysis based on the unconsolidated annual accounts)

Figure 15.16 Average impact of the growth in total operating income on the country cost to income ratio, 1995–1998.
Source: Bankscope, own calculations.

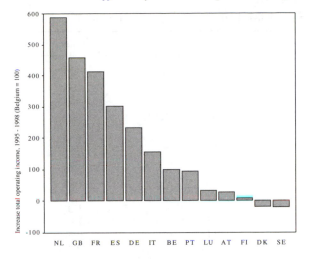

IE, GR not included. Only banks with data available in both years
(analysis based on the unconsolidated annual accounts)

Figure 15.17 Increase of total operating income, 1995–1998 (Belgium = 100).

Source: Bankscope, own calculations.

higher in Germany, France, UK and the Netherlands, with German banks strongly focusing on asset increase and to a lesser extent on the growth of operating income. For the Netherlands this has been the reverse.

3.3 Individual data analysis of the cost to income ratio

Starting from a broad database, outliers and banks that did not report relevant items concerning the cost to income ratio were removed from the country database (Section 3.2.). For the individual benchmarking this resulted in a sample of 1,305 banks (Table 15.5):

- **Bank type and the cost to income ratio**
  Table 15.6 shows clearly that savings banks and co-operative banks tend to have a higher cost to income ratio, while the standard deviation indicates that the dispersion is considerably lower than for the other bank types (indicating a consistent or similar income and cost structure among savings banks). Commercial banks compose the largest banks group with on average a lower cost to income ratio (compared to savings banks), but with a relatively large standard deviation (indicating large differences in income and cost structure among commercial banks).

- **Bank size and cost to income ratio**
  Very small banks and large banks tend to have a smaller cost to income ratio (Table 15.7). The high standard deviation indicates that the table should be interpreted with caution.

Table 15.5 Country distribution of the analysed financial institutions

Country	Frequency	Percent
DE	413	31.6
FR	250	19.2
ES	143	11.0
LU	103	7.9
IT	79	6.1
GB	70	5.4
BE	61	4.7
AT	51	3.9
DK	38	2.9
NL	25	1.9
PT	23	1.8
IE	17	1.3
GR	13	1.0
SE	11	0.8
FI	8	0.6
EU	1305	100

Source: Bankscope, own calculations.

Table 15.6 Cost to income ratio per bank type (EU banks)

	Cost to income ratio, 1998		Frequency	Percentage
	Mean	Std Deviation		
Savings banks & Cooperative banks	66.3	13.0	484	37
Commercial banks	59.6	21.5	646	50
Real estate & Mortgage banks	52.5	22.5	74	6
Other*	51.7	23.0	46	4
Investment banks	51.3	23.6	55	4
Total	61.1	19.5	1305	100

* Medium- and long-term credit banks, specialized government banks.
Source: Bankscope, own calculations.

Table 15.7 Cost to income ratio per bank size (EU banks)

Total asset in mio euro	Mean	Std deviation	Count	Count %
< 100	58.6	21.2	91	7
100–300	63.1	19.9	220	17
300–600	63.8	18.1	201	15
600–1,000	60.9	19.6	152	12
1,000–2,500	61.9	18.7	224	17
2,500–10,000	62.0	19.1	262	20
10,000–100,000	52.7	20.4	140	11
> 100,000	59.5	16.2	15	1
Group total	61.1	19.5	1,305	100

Source: Bankscope, own calculations.

- **Regression results**
  Separate regressions are performed for the full bank sample, for commercial banks and for the sample of savings banks. Due to data limitations, no separate regressions were performed for the other bank types.

How to 'read' Table 15.8
- The three regressions have a very large explaining value (R^2) for the cost to income ratio. (R^2 is a goodness-of-fit measure of a linear model. It is the proportion of variation in the dependent variable explained by the regression model. It ranges in value from 0 to 1. Values close to 1 indicate that the model fits the data well.)
- The constant terms (the terms which represents the average response) for commercial banks and savings banks are almost equal and suggest a similar 'average' cost to income ratio.
- More interesting are of course the unstandardized and standardized coefficients of the commercial banks and savings banks regression model.
  For both bank types, the importance of the ratio's personnel expenses/total operating income and personnel expenses/overhead is quite clear (high unstandardized coefficient).
  What are the differences between commercial banks and savings banks?
  - Apparently, savings banks cannot change their cost to income ratio significantly by replacing net interest revenue by commission income or trading income if their cost structure remains unchanged.
  - For commercial banks, commission income has the lowest unstandardized coefficient compared to trading income and net interest revenue. This implies that focusing on commission income generally results in a higher cost to income ratio compared to banks which focus on trading income (cf. the Netherlands). For Belgian banks (which tend to have a high trading income compared to their commission income) this means that shifting from trading income towards commission income generally would result in a higher cost to income ratio (under the assumption that the cost structure remains unchanged). Simulations show that if this shift is accompanied with a higher cost structure, the cost to income ratio will increase rapidly.

Table 15.8 Regression results (dependent variable = cost to income ratio)

	All banks			Commercial banks			Savings banks		
	Unstandardized	t-value	Standardized	Unstandardized	t-value	Standardized	Unstandardized	t-value	Standardized
Constant	8.077•	3.64		64.559*	32.24		63.132*	63.83	
Net interest revenue/TOI	-4.95*	-2.42	-0.09	-11.111*	-6.84	-0.18	-1.055*	-2.32	-0.02
Commission income/TOI	-2.948*	-1.71	-0.04	-2.537*	-2.26	-0.04	-1.917*	-2.17	-0.02
Trading income/TOI	-7.123*	-3.13	-0.10	-12.053*	-6.02	-0.15			
Personnel expenses/TOI	95.549*	33.68	0.62	172.469*	59.55	1.12	186.613*	106.88	1.17
Other expenses/TOI	90.365*	26.86	0.49						
Personnel expenses/overhead	-0.0654*	-2.47	-0.04	-94.938*	-33.97	-0.60	-117.985*	-67.40	-0.64
Equity/total asset	0.003464*	2.01	0.03	-0.159*	-7.18	-0.11	0.152*	12.12	0.10
Interbank ratio	0.00	0.97	0.02						
Net loans/Customer & ST funding				0.01	1.94	0.03	0.01	1.90	0.02
ROE				-0.0452*	-2.00	0.03	-0.04	-1.75	-0.02
R^2	0.904			0.914			0.972		

* Significant coefficient at the 95% confidence level are marked with an asterisk.
TOI = Total operating income.

Source: Bankscope, own calculations.

• **Residual analysis**

Based on the regression models above, the bank sample has been tested to what extent they vary from the predicted cost to income value. It is important to take into account that Figures 15.18 and 15.19 only give an indication to what extent an individual bank disperses from the regression model of a European banking peer group. This dispersion may have in general three causes: (1) the residual (i.e. defined as the difference between the reported cost to income ratio and the predicted cost to income ratio) may be the result of the specific structure of the individual bank, that is, different type of cost and income structure resulting from its product area or market focus; (2) potential inefficiencies; and (3) differences in reporting method of costs and/or income.

(For the Netherlands and the UK, a large number of banks are not included in the regression model as they do not report all requested variables. Therefore the interpretation of the country analysis should be taken with the necessary caution. In the commercial banks regression model, German banks are not included since no data are available on the trading income.)

The country residuals for savings banks show that on average the UK, Luxembourg and the Netherlands (!) have a cost to income ratio which is lower than their predicted cost to income ratio according to the savings banks regression model (i.e. a negative residual). On the other side, German banks show on average a positive residual. To a large extent the ranking is the same for the commercial bank regression model but with a larger dispersion

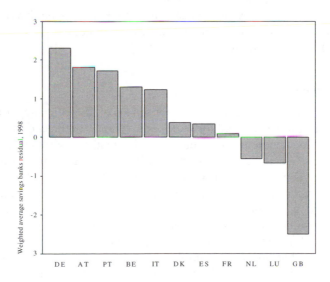

Figure 15.18 Savings banks regression model: country residuals, 1998.

Source: Bankscope, own calculations.

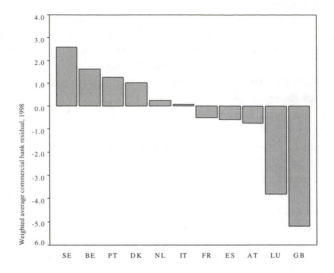

Figure 15.19 Commercial banks regression model: country residuals, 1998.

Source: Bankscope, own calculations.

between the residuals. The country results should again be interpreted with caution, but individual bank residual analysis may give a simple indication on possible bank (in)efficiency. When looking at the country and individual results, one should be aware of the drawbacks of the analysis (different consolidation stages, country differences, including various bank types in the sample, differences in output mix and cost of production, comparison on a European level, static analysis).

4 Conclusions

The research literature provides little consensus on the efficiency topic as no broad pattern can be detected for scale-, scope- and X-efficiency. However, it is generally documented that X-inefficiencies tend to be much larger than scale- and scope-inefficiencies. The rationale of looking at the cost to income ratio and its dispersion is the growing use of it as a proxy for efficiency. Despite the recent consolidation, on average only a small reduction of the ratio is recorded. The problem with cost ratios is that they do not account for the fact that some product mixes cost more to produce than others. Banks may produce different output mixes that have a different cost of production. This indicates that linear and simple benchmarking of the cost to income ratio may be misleading as the interpretation is often not unambiguous. Nevertheless, useful and valuable benchmark information is available when the cost to income ratio is set against the bank's main competitors and similar banks. A residual-analysis may give a simple indication of possible efficiency or inefficiency. The empirical results show that increasing scale or changing scope has a limited impact on the cost to income ratio. Banks can substantially lower their cost to income ratio by using the available inputs efficiently in order to generate a given (or higher) output level. When looking at efficiency, it seems more appropriate to benchmark the cost to income residuals of a sample of banks (based on a fitted regression model) then to compare linear cost to income ratios. Overall, the analysis shows that the reduction of the cost to income ratio is taking place at a rather slow pace mainly due to the consolidation process. However, the residual analysis shows that changes in efficiency are taking place at a different pace across individual banks and across EU countries.

ANNEX: THE BELGIAN BANKING SECTOR COMPARED

Overall, the net interest margin in the EU continues to decline, while it remains much lower in Belgium than in most other EU countries. Large interbank operations, lower development level of the capital market (compared to the US), focus on high quality corporate borrowers and high public sector lending may explain the low net interest margin.

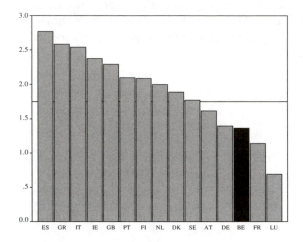

Figure 15.A1 Net interest margin, 1998.

Source: Bankscope, own calculations.

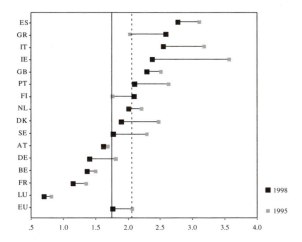

Figure 15.A2 Net interest margin, 1995–1998.

Source: Bankscope, own calculations.

Non-interest income has grown for nearly all EU countries over the period 1995–1998, and represents on average some 35% of gross income. One of the main reasons of this surge in non-interest income is the downward trend in interest rates over the considered period, thereby boosting capital gains and trading and underwriting activities. Belgium has recorded a strong growth in non-interest income but this is partly due to the continued growth in trading income.

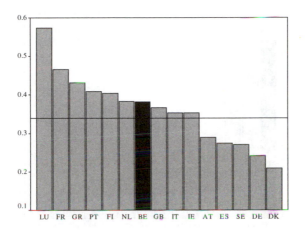

Figure 15.A3 Ratio non-interest income/total operating income, 1998.
Source: Bankscope, own calculations.

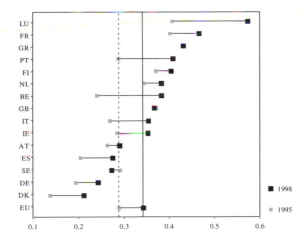

Figure 15.A4 Ratio non-interest income/total operating income, 1995–1998.
Source: Bankscope, own calculations.

Trading income in Belgium continues to outweigh commission income, reflecting a somewhat unbalanced (and thus rather vulnerable) income structure for Belgian credit institutions.

The cost to income ratio decreased in most EU countries over the considered period but also showed the rather slow pace of cost reduction in the production and distribution of financial services. Given the shrinking net interest margin in recent years and the slow pace of cost reduction, profitability will remain in

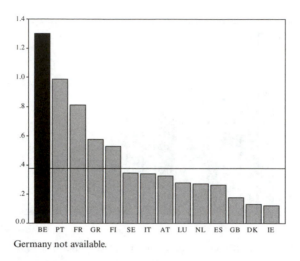

Germany not available.

Figure 15.A5 Ratio trading income/commission income, 1998.
Source: Bankscope, own calculations.

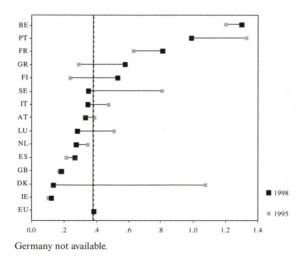

Germany not available.

Figure 15.A6 Ratio trading income/commission income, 1995–1998.
Source: Bankscope, own calculations.

general under pressure. Only three countries recorded an increase in the cost to income ratio: the Netherlands, Denmark and Sweden. Belgium remains in a rather unfavourable position in relation to the other countries. The improved positioning of Belgium since 1995 could to a large extent be explained by the strong progress in non-interest income. As this effect is partly based on trading income, a large portion of the improved positioning may only be temporary if no substantial changes in the cost structure are recorded. Preliminary (but still incomplete) data for 1999 confirmed that the cost to income ratio for Belgium has increased substantially compared to 1998.

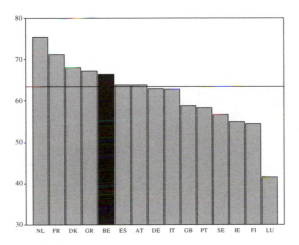

Figure 15.A7 Cost to income ratio, 1998.

Source: Bankscope, own calculations.

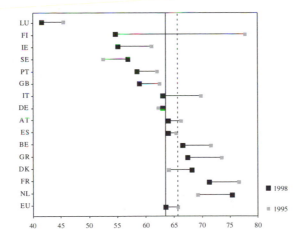

Figure 15.A8 Cost to income ratio, 1995–1998.

Source: Bankscope, own calculations.

Loan loss provision is substantially lower in Belgium than in most other EU countries as traditional risks (in particular credit risk) are generally well controlled, resulting in a fairly solid asset structure. These limited risks, combined with a low net interest margin, result in a relatively low profitability (ROA). This handicap is in Belgium partially offset by a higher leverage and thus an EU comparable ROE.

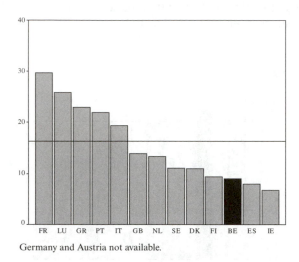

Germany and Austria not available.

Figure 15.A9 Loan loss provisions/net interest revenue (in %), 1998.

Source: Bankscope, own calculations.

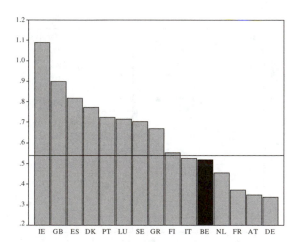

Figure 15.A10 ROA, 1998.

Source: Bankscope, own calculations.

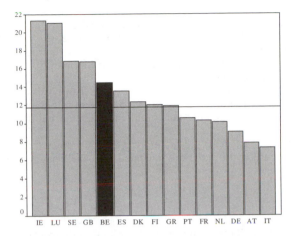

Figure 15.A11 ROE, 1998.

Source: Bankscope, own calculations.

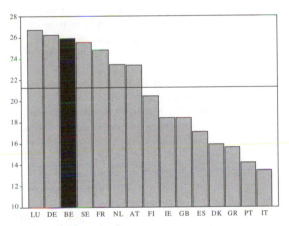

Leverage = total asset/equity.

Figure 15.A12 Leverage, 1998.

Source: Bankscope, own calculations.

Notes

1 Needless to say the author is solely responsible for the views and conclusions presented in this article. The views expressed are those of the author and not necessarily those of Artesia Banking Corporation. The author wishes to thank Jean-Paul Abraham, Stefan Hulpiau and Frank Lierman for their helpful comments on a former version of this article.
2 The cost to income ratio is calculated as a ratio of overheads (sum of personnel expenses and other non-interest expenses) to the sum of net interest revenue and other operating income (sum of net commission income, net trading income and other income).
3 The optimal (most efficient) production is called the efficient frontier and deviations from this efficient frontier are indicated as X-inefficiency.

References

Abraham, J.P. (1998). 'Bank strategies in Euroland with special reference to the Benelux area'. Paper presented at the *European Association of University Teachers in Banking and Finance*, Paris-Dauphine, September 3–4.

Ahmid, Y. and Miller, G. (1998). 'Introduction on bank mergers and acquisitions'. *Bank Mergers and Acquisitions (Kluwer Academic Publishers)*, pp. vii–xiii.

Allen, L. and Rai, A. (1991). 'Operational efficiency in banking: An international comparison'. *Journal of Banking and Finance*, 20, pp. 655–72.

Altunbas, Y. and Chakravarty, S.P. (1998). 'Efficiency measures and the banking structure in Europe'. *Economic Letters*, 60, pp. 205–208.

Artesia BC (2000). 'De uitdagingen voor de Belgische financiële sector'. *Artesia BC Economische Berichten*, Nr. 204, februari.

Association Belge des Banques (1998). Vade-mecum statistique du secteur bancaire.

Berger, A.N. (1999). 'The efficiency effects of bank mergers and acquisitions: A preliminary look at the 1999s data'. *Bank Mergers and Acquisitions (Kluwer Academic Publishers)*, pp. 79–111.

Berger, A.N. and Humphrey, D.B. (1997). 'Efficiency of financial institutions: International survey and directions for future research'. *European Journal of Operational Research*, 98, pp. 175–212.

Berger, A.N. and Mester, L.J. (1998). 'Inside the black box: What explains differences in the efficiencies of financial institutions'. *Journal of Banking and Finance*, 21, pp. 895–947.

Berger, A.N. and Mester, L.J. (1999). *'What Explains the Dramatic Changes in Cost and Profit Performance of the U.S. Banking Industry'*, Finance and Economics Discussion Series, 13, 1999.

Berger, A.N., Demsetz, R.S. and Strahan, P. (1999). 'The consolidation of the financial services industry: clauses, consequences and implications for the future'. Forthcoming *Journal of Banking and Finance*, Vol. 23.

Bikker, J.A. and Groeneveld, H.J. (1998). 'Competition and concentration in the EU banking industry'. *DNB Staff Reports*, October.

Bikker, J.A. (1999). 'Efficiency in the European banking industry: An exploratory analysis to rank countries'. *DNB Staff Reports*, No. 42, October.

BIS (1999). 'Restructuring in the global banking industry'. *BIS Quarterly Review*, August.

Boot, A.W.A. (1999). 'European lessons on consolidation in banking'. *Journal of Banking and Finance*, 23, pp. 609–613.

Bourgeois, P., Fortésa, M. and Leroyer, I. (2000). 'Productivité: les banques françaises sur la bonne voie'. *Banque Stratégie*. No. 167, janvier, pp. 36–40.

Calomiris, C.W. (1999). 'Guaging the efficiency of bank consolidation during a merger wave'. *Journal of Banking and Finance*, 23, pp. 615–621.

Carbo, S., Gardener, E.P.M. and Williams, J. (1998). 'Efficiency and technical change in the European savings bank sector'. *SUERF Conference Paper*, October.

Casu, B. and Molyneux, Ph. (1999). 'A comparative study of efficiency in European banking'. *European Association of University Teachers of Banking and Finance*, Lisbon, September.

Clark, J.A. (1996). 'Economic cost, scale efficiency, and competitive viability in banking'. *Journal of Money, Credit, and Banking*, Vol. 28, No. 3, August, Part 1.

Cornett, M.M. and Tehranian, H. (1992). 'Changes in corporate performance associated with bank acquisitions'. *Journal of Financial Economics*, 31, 1992, pp. 211–234.

Datamonitor (1999). *'The future of E-Banking in Europe: 1999–2004'*.

Davis, E.P. and Salo, S. (1998). 'Indicators of potential excess capacity in EU and US banking sectors'. *SUERF Conference Paper*, October.

De Bandt, O. and Davis, E.P. (1999). 'A cross-country comparison of market structures in European banking'. *ECB Working Paper Series*, Working Paper No. 7, September.

Degryse, H. and Bouckaert, J. (2000). 'Implications of EMU for Banking: an Industrial Organization Perspective'. *24th VWEC (Vereniging voor Economie)*, pp. 507–534.

Dermine, J. (1999). 'The case for a European-wide strategy'. *EIB Papers*, Vol. 4, No. 1, pp. 137–143.

DeYoung, R. (1999). 'Mergers and the changing landscape of commercial banking (Part I)'. *Chicago Fed Letter*, September, No. 145.

Deitsch, M. and Weill, L. (1998). 'Banking efficiency and European integration: productivity, cost and profit approaches'. *SUERF Conference Paper*, October.

European Central Bank (1999). 'Possible effects of EMU on the EU banking systems in the medium to long term', February.

European Central Bank (1999). 'Banking in the euro area: structural features and trends'. *ECB Monthly Bulletin*, April, pp. 41–53.

Fecher, F. and Pestieau, P. (1993). 'Efficiency and competition in O.E.C.D. financial services'. In *The measurement of productive efficiency: Techniques and applications*, edited by Harold O. Fried, C.A. Knox Lovell and Shelton S. Schmidt, Oxford University Press, pp. 374–385.

Federal Reserve Bulletin (1999). 'International activities of US banks and in US banking markets'. September.

Gascon, F. and Arrondo, R. (1999). 'Economic efficiency and value maximization in banking firms'. Paper presented at the *European Association of University Teachers of Banking and Finance*, Lisbon, September.

Generale Bank (1999). 'De Europese banksector: recente evolutie'. *Bulletin*, 404, April.

Girardone, C., Molyneux, Ph. and Gardener, E.P.M. (1999). 'An analysis of the determinants of Italian banks' efficiency'. Paper presented at the *European Association of University Teachers of Banking and Finance*, Lisbon, September.

Goldberg, L.G. and Rai, A. (1993). 'The structure-performance relationship for European banking'. *Journal of Banking and Finance*, 20, pp. 745–771.

Groeneveld, J.M. (1998). 'Fusies in het Europese bankwezen: achtergronden en implicaties'. *Maandschrift Economie*, Jrg. 62, pp. 293–308.

Heonig, T.M. (1999). 'Financial industry megamergers and policy challenges'. *Economic Review*, Federal Reserve Bank of Kansas, Third quarter, pp. 7–13.

Houpt, J.V. (1999). 'International activities of U.S. banks and in U.S. banking markets'. *Federal Reserve Bulletin*, September, pp. 599–615.

Hurst, C., Perée, E. and Fischbach, M. (1999). 'On the road to wonderland? Banking restructuring after EMU'. *EIB-Papers*, Vol. 4, No. 1, pp. 83–103.

KBC Economisch Financiële Berichten. *Fusies en overnames. Is de praktijk zo goed als de goede theorie?* Jaargang 54, nr. 6, maart 2000.

Kluis, C.E. (1999). 'Britse banken: winst is een keuze!'. *Bank- en Effectenbedrijf*, December, pp. 22–25.

Lang, G. and Welzel, P. (1998). 'Technology and cost efficiency in universal banking: A tick frontier approach'. *Journal of Productivity Analysis*, 10, pp. 63–84.

Maudos, J., Pastor, J., Péres, F. and Quesada, J. (1999). 'The single European market and bank efficiency: The importance of specialisation'. Paper presented at the *European Association of University Teachers of Banking and Finance*, Lisbon, September.

Milbourn, T.T., Boot, A.W.A. and Thakor, A.V. (1999). 'Megamergers and expanded scope: Theories of bank size and activity diversity'. *Journal of Banking and Finance*, 23, pp. 195–214.

Molyneux, Ph. (1999). 'Increasing concentration and competition in European banking: The end of the anti-trust?'. *EIB Papers*, Vol. 4, No. 1, pp. 127–136.

Pastor, J.M., Francisco Perez and Javier Quesada (1997) 'Efficiency analysis in banking firms: An international comparison'. *European Journal of Operational Research*, 98, pp. 396–408.

Piloff, S.J. and Santomero, A.M. (1998). 'The value effects of bank mergers and acquisitions'. *Bank Mergers and Acquisitions (Kluwer Academic Publishers)*, pp. 59–78.

Resti, A. (1997). 'Linear programming and econometric methods for bank efficiency evaluation: an empirical comparison based on a panel of Italian Banks'. Research paper – *Institute of European Finance*.

Rhoades, S.A. (1998). 'The efficiency of bank mergers: An overview of case studies on nine mergers. *Journal of Banking and Finance*, 22, pp. 273.

Ruthenberg, D. and Elias, R. (1996). 'Cost economies and interest rate margins in a unified European banking market', *Journal of Economics and Business*, 48, pp. 231–49.

Saunders, A. and Walter, I. (1994). *Universal banking in the United States: What could we gain? What could we lose?*, Oxford University Press.

Smith, C. and Walter, I. (1998). 'Global patterns of mergers and acquisitions activity in the financial service industry'. *Bank Mergers and Acquisitions (Kluwer Academic Publishers)*, pp. 21–36.

Srinivasan, A. (1992). 'Are there cost savings from bank mergers?'. *Economic Review*, Federal Reserve Bank of Atlanta, March/April, pp. 17–28.

Timmermans, T. and Delhez, Ph. (1999). 'Restructuring of the Belgian banking sector and financial stability'. *BIS Conference Papers*, Vol. 7, pp. 55–69, March.

Udell, G.F. (1998). 'The consolidation of the banking industry and small business lending'. *Bank Mergers and Acquisitions (Kluwer Academic Publishers)*, pp. 221–235.

Vander Vennet, R. (1996). 'The effect of mergers and acquistions on the efficiency and profitability of EC credit institutions'. *Journal of Banking and Finance*, 20, pp. 1531–1558.

Vander Vennet, R. (2000). 'Cost and profit efficiency of financial conglomerates and universal banks in Europe'. *Universiteit Gent Working Paper*, 2000/81, January.

Wagenvoort, R. and Schure, P. (1999a). 'Who are Europe's efficient bankers?'. *EIB Papers*, Vol. 4, No. 1, pp. 105–126.

Wagenvoort, R. and Schure, P. (1999b). 'The recursive and thick frontier approach to estimating efficiency'. *EIB Economic and Financial Reports*. Report 99/02.

Wagenvoort, R. and Schure, P. (1999c). 'Economies of scale and efficiency in European banking: New evidence'. *EIB Economic and Financial Reports*. Report 99/01.

Walter, I. (1999). 'Financial services strategies in the euro-zone'. *EIB Papers*, Vol. 4, No. 1, pp. 145–168.

Welch, P. (1999). 'New tools of the trade'. *The Banker*, May, pp. 48–49.

White, W.R. (1998). 'The coming transformation of continental European banking?'. *BIS Working Papers*, No. 54, June.

Index

The letter n *after a number indicates an entry in the notes. A number appearing in italic indicates an entry in a figure or table.*